Life as Politics

Life as Politics

HOW ORDINARY PEOPLE CHANGE THE MIDDLE EAST

Asef Bayat

Stanford University Press
Stanford, California

Stanford University Press
Stanford, California

Printed in the United States of America on acid-free, archival-quality paper

Library of Congress Cataloging-in-Publication Data

Bayat, Asef.
    Life as politics : how ordinary people change the Middle East / Asef Bayat.
        p. cm.
    Includes bibliographical references and index.
    ISBN 978-0-8047-6923-5 (alk. paper) — ISBN 978-0-8047-6924-2 (pbk. : alk. paper)
1. Social movements—Middle East.   2. Social change—Middle East.   3. Political participation—Middle East.   4. Middle East—Foreign relations—1979-   I. Title.
    HN656.A8B378 2010
    303.48'40956—dc22   2009021941

Typeset by Westchester Book Group in 10/14 Minion

To: Eric Hobsbawm, historian par excellence.

CONTENTS

PART 3   PROSPECTS

PREFACE

THE ESSAYS compiled in this volume are about agency and change in the Muslim Middle East, the societies in which religion seems to occupy a prominent position. More specifically, they focus on the configuration of sociopolitical transformation brought about by internal social forces, by collectives and individuals. Here I focus on the diverse ways in which the ordinary people, the subaltern—the urban dispossessed, Muslim women, the globalizing youth, and other urban grass roots—strive to affect the contours of change in their societies, by refusing to exit from the social and political stage controlled by authoritarian states, moral authority, and neoliberal economies, discovering and generating new spaces within which they can voice their dissent and assert their presence in pursuit of bettering their lives. The vehicles through which ordinary people change their societies are not simply audible mass protests or revolutions, even though they represent an aspect of popular mobilization; rather, people resort more widely to what I will elaborate as "nonmovements"—the collective endeavors of millions of noncollective actors, carried out in the main squares, back streets, courthouses, or communities. This book, then, is about the "art of presence," the story of agency in times of constraints. The essays constitute the core of my reflections for the past decade or so on the social movements and nonmovements that are seen through the prism of historical specificity of the Muslim Middle East, yet ones that insist on both critical and constructive engagement with the prevailing social theory. By so doing my hope has been not only to produce rigorous empirical knowledge about social change in this complex region, but in the meantime to engage with and contribute to social theory in general. My wish is that this book might offer a Middle Eastern contribution, however modest, to scholarly debates on social movements and social change.

ACKNOWLEDGMENTS

A VOLUME that has taken about a decade of research and reflections must have been written with the assistance and support, whether intellectual or practical, of many people—scholars, students, and colleagues, in the Middle East, the United States, and Europe. Understandably, it is difficult to pinpoint them in order to record my sincere appreciation. But I do wish to register my deepest gratitude to them all. Most of the pieces in this volume were produced or finalized during my work as the Academic Director of the Dutch-based International Institute for the Study of Islam in the Modern World (ISIM), a unique scholarly enterprise that combined rigorous scholarship with constructive social engagement. I am grateful to the colleagues at ISIM, especially staff members and the internationally diverse fellows who enriched the institute by their enthusiasm and their valuable and varied experiences. Some of the ideas in this book developed out of my short contributions to the *ISIM Review*, and some others from preparing numerous lectures, which I delivered in different parts of the world in the course of these years. I am grateful for the individuals and organizations who welcomed cooperation. As always, my greatest debt is to my family, Linda, Shiva, and Tara, without whose unfailing love and support none of these endeavors would have materialized in the way they have.

Life as Politics

1 INTRODUCTION

The Art of Presence

THERE IS NO SHORTAGE of views, whether regional or international, suggesting that the Middle East has fallen into disarray. We continue to read how the personal income of Arabs is among the lowest in the world, despite their massive oil revenues. With declining productivity, poor scientific research, decreasing school enrollment, and high illiteracy, and with health conditions lagging behind comparable nations, Arab countries seem to be "richer than they are developed."[1] The unfortunate state of social development in the region is coupled with poor political governance. Authoritarian regimes ranging from Iran, Syria, Egypt, Jordan, and Morocco to the sheikhdoms of the Persian Gulf, and chiefly Saudi Arabia (incidentally, most with close ties to the West), continue to frustrate demands for democracy and the rule of law, prompting (religious) opposition movements that espouse equally undemocratic, exclusive, and often violent measures. Not surprisingly, the current conditions have caused much fear in the West about the international destabilizing ramifications of this seeming social and political stagnation.

Thus, never before has the region witnessed such a cry for change. The idea that "everywhere the world has changed except for the Middle East" has assumed a renewed prominence, with different domestic and international constituencies expressing different expectations as to how to instigate change in this region. Some circles hope for a revolutionary transformation through a sudden upsurge of popular energy to overturn the unjust structures of power and usher in development and democracy. If the Iranian Revolution, not so long ago, could sweep aside a long-standing monarchy in less than two years, why couldn't such movement be forged in the region today? This is a difficult position to sustain. It is doubtful that revolutions can ever be planned.[2] Even though revolutionaries do engage in plotting and preparing, revolutions do not necessarily result from prior schemes. Rather, they often follow their own intriguing logic, subject to a highly complex mix of structural, international, coincidental, and psychological factors. We often analyze revolutions in retrospect, rarely engaging in ones that are expected or desired, for revolutions are never predictable.[3] On the other hand, most people do not particularly wish to be involved in violent revolutionary movements. People often express doubt about engaging in revolution, whose outcome they cannot foresee. They often prefer to remain "free riders," wanting others to carry out revolutions on their behalf. Furthermore, are revolutions necessarily desirable? Those who have experienced them usually identify violent revolutions with massive disruption, destruction, and uncertainty. After all, nothing guarantees that a just social order will result from a revolutionary change. Finally, even assuming that revolutions are desirable and can be planned, what are people under authoritarian rule to do in the meantime?

Given these constraints, an alternative view postulates that instead of waiting for an uncertain revolution, change should be instigated by committing states to undertaking sustained social and political reforms. Such a nonviolent strategy of reform requires powerful social forces—social movements (of workers, the poor, women, youth, students, and broader democracy movements) or genuine political parties—to challenge political authorities and hegemonize their claims. Indeed, many activists and NGOs in the Middle East are already engaged in forging movements to alter the current state of affairs. However, while this may serve as a genuinely endogenous strategy for change, effective movements need political opportunities to grow and operate. How are social and political movements to keep up when authoritarian regimes exhibit a great intolerance toward organized activism, when the repression of civil-society organizations has been a hallmark of most Middle Eastern states?

It should not, therefore, come as a surprise that growing segments of people, frustrated by the political stalemate, lament that although most people in the Middle East suffer under the status quo, they remain repressed, atomized, and passive. Popular activism, if any, goes little beyond occasional, albeit angry, protests, with most of them directed by Islamists against the West and Israel, and less against their own repressive states to commit to a democratic order. Since there is slight or no agency to challenge the ossified status quo, the argument goes, change should come from outside, by way of economic, political, and even military pressure. Even the *Arab Human Development Report*, arguably the most significant manifesto for change in the Arab Middle East, is inclined to seek a "realistic solution" of a "western-supported project of gradual and moderate reform aiming at liberalization."[4] Still, the perception that the Middle East remains "unchangeable" has far greater resonance outside the region, notably in the West and among policy circles, the mainstream media, and many think tanks. Indeed, a strong "exceptionalist" outlook informs the whole edifice of the "democracy promotion industry" in the West, which pushes for instigating change through outside powers, one which does not exclude the use of force.[5]

The idea of Middle Eastern exceptionalism is not new. Indeed, for a long time now, change in Middle Eastern societies has been approached with a largely western Orientalist outlook whose history goes back to the eighteenth century, if not earlier.[6] Mainstream Orientalism tends to depict the Muslim Middle East as a monolithic, fundamentally static, and thus "peculiar" entity. By focusing on a narrow notion of (a rather static) culture—one that is virtually equated with the religion of Islam—Middle Eastern societies are characterized more in terms of historical continuity than in terms of change. In this perspective, change, albeit uncommon, may indeed occur, but primarily via individual elites, military men, or wars and external powers. The George W. Bush administration's doctrine of "regime change," exemplified in, for instance, the occupation of Iraq and the inclination to wage a war against Iran, represents how, in such a perspective, "reform" is to be realized in the region. Consequently, internal sources of political transformation, such as group interests, social movements, and political economies, are largely overlooked.

But in fact the Middle East has been home to many insurrectionary episodes, nationwide revolutions, and social movements (such as Islamism), and great strides for change. Beyond these, certain distinct and unconventional forms of agency and activism have emerged in the region that do not get adequate attention, because they do not fit into our prevailing categories and conceptual imaginations. By elaborating on and highlighting these latter forms, or what I call "social nonmovements," I wish also to raise a number of theoretical and methodological questions as to how to look at the notions of agency and change in the Muslim Middle East today. Indeed, conditioned by the exceptionalist outlook, many observers tend to exclude the study of the Middle East from the prevailing social science perspectives. For instance, many narratives of Islamism treat it simply in terms of religious revivalism, or as an expression of primordial loyalties, or irrational group actions, or something peculiar and unique, a phenomenon that cannot be analyzed by the conventional social science categories. In fact, Islamism had been largely excluded from the mode of inquiry developed by social movement theorists in the West until recently, when a handful of scholars have attempted to bring Islamic activism into the realm of "social movement theory."[7] This is certainly a welcome development. However, these scholars tend largely to "borrow" from, rather than critically and productively engage with and thus contribute to, social movement theories. Indeed, it remains a question how far the prevailing social movement theory is able to account for the complexities of socioreligious movements in contemporary Muslim societies, in particular when these perspectives are rooted in particular genealogies, in the highly differentiated and politically open Western societies, where social movements often develop into highly structured and largely homogeneous entities—possibilities that are limited in the non-Western world. Charles Tilly is correct in alerting us to be mindful of the historical specificity of "social movements"—political performances that emerged in Western Europe and North America after 1750. In this historical experience, what came to be known as "social movements" combined three elements: an organized and sustained claim making on target authorities; a repertoire of performances, including associations, public meetings, media statements, and street marches; and finally, "public representations of the cause's worthiness, unity, numbers, and commitment."[8] Deployed separately, these elements would not make "social movements," but some different political actions. Given that the dominant social movement theories draw on western experience, to what extent can they help us understand the process of solidarity building or the collectivities of disjointed yet parallel practices of noncollective actors in the non-western politically closed and technologically limited settings?[9]

In contrast to the "exceptionalist" tendency, there are those often "local" scholars in the Middle East who tend uncritically to deploy conventional models and concepts to the social realities of their societies, without acknowledging sufficiently that these models hold different historical genealogies, and may thus offer little help to explain the intricate texture and dynamics of change and resistance in this part of the world. For instance, considering "slums" in light of the conventional perspectives of urban sociology, the informal communities in the Middle East (i.e., *ashwaiyyat*) are erroneously taken to be the breeding ground for violence, crime, anomie, extremism, and, consequently, radical Islam. There is little in such narratives that sees these communities as a significant locus of struggle for (urban) citizenship and transformation in urban configuration. Scant attention is given to how the urban disenfranchised, through their quiet and unassuming daily struggles, refigure new life and communities for themselves and different urban realities on the ground in Middle Eastern cities. The prevailing scholarship ignores the fact that these urban subaltern redefine the meaning of urban management and de facto participate in determining its destiny; and they do so not through formal institutional channels, from which they are largely excluded, but through direct actions in the very zones of exclusion. To give a different example, in early 2000 Iranian analysts looking uncritically at Muslim women's activism through the prism of social movement theory—developed primarily in the United States—concluded that there was no such a thing as a women's movement in Iran, because certain features of Iranian women's activities did not resemble the principal "model." It is perhaps in this spirit that Olivier Roy warns against the kind of comparison that takes "one of the elements of comparison as norm" while never questioning the "original configuration."[10] A fruitful approach would demand an analytical innovation that not only rejects both Middle Eastern "exceptionalism" and uncritical application of conventional social science concepts but also thinks and introduces fresh perspectives to observe, a novel vocabulary to speak, and new analytical tools to make sense of specific regional realities. It is in this frame of mind that I examine both contentious politics and social "nonmovements" as key vehicles to produce meaningful change in the Middle East.

CONTENTIOUS POLITICS AND SOCIAL CHANGE

A number of remarkable social and political transformations in the region have resulted from organized contentious endeavors of various forms, ranging from endemic protest actions, to durable social movements, to major revolutionary mobilizations. The constitutional revolution of 1905–6 heralded the end of Qajar despotism and the beginning of the era of constitutionalism in Iran. The Egyptian Revolution of 1952, led by free officers, and the Iraqi Revolution of 1958 terminated long-standing monarchies and British colonial rule, augmenting republicanism and socialistic economies. In a major social and political upheaval, the Algerians overthrew French colonial rule in 1962 and established a republic.

The Islamic Revolution of 1979 galvanized millions of Iranians in a movement that toppled the monarchy and ushered in a new era, not only in Iran, but in many nations of the Muslim world. Some twenty-five years earlier, a nationalist and secular democratic movement led by Prime Minister Muhammad Mossadegh had established constitutionalism, until it was crushed by a coup engineered by the CIA and the British secret service in 1953, which reinstated the dictatorship of the Shah. In 1985 in Sudan, a nonviolent uprising by a coalition of students, workers, and professional unions (National Alliance for National Salvation) forced President Jaafar Numeiri's authoritarian populist regime (born of a military coup) to step down in favor of a national transitional government, paving the way for free elections and democratic governance. The first Palestinian intifada (1987–93) was one of the most grassroots-based mobilizations in the Middle East of the past century. Triggered by a fatal accident caused by an Israeli truck driver, and against the backdrop of years of occupation, the uprising included almost the entire Palestinian population, in particular women and children, who resorted to nonviolent methods of resistance to the occupation, such as civil disobedience, strikes, demonstrations, withholding taxes, and product boycotts. Led mainly by the local (versus exiled) leaders, the movement built on popular committees (e.g., women's, voluntary work, and medical relief) to sustain itself, while serving as an embryonic institution of a future independent Palestinian state.[11] More recently, the "Cedar Revolution," a grassroots movement of some 1.5 million Lebanese from all walks of life demanding meaningful sovereignty, democracy, and an end to foreign meddling, resulted in the withdrawal of Syrian forces from Lebanon in 2005. This movement came to symbolize a model of peaceful mobilization from below that could cause momentous change in the region. At almost the same time, a nascent democracy movement in Egypt, with Kifaya at its core, mobilized thousands of middle-class professionals, students, teachers, judges, and journalists who called for a release of political prisoners and an end to emergency law, torture, and Husni Mubarak's presidency. In a fresh perspective, this movement chose to work with "popular forces," rather than with traditional opposition parties, bringing the campaign into the streets instead of broadcasting it from headquarters, and focused on domestic issues rather than international demands. As a postnational and postideological movement, Kifaya embraced activists from diverse ideological orientations and gender, religious, and social groups. This novel mobilization managed, after years of Islamist hegemony, nationalism, and authoritarian rule, to break the taboo of unlawful street marches, and to augment a new postnationalist, secular, and nonsectarian (democratic) politics in Egypt. It galvanized international support and compelled the Egyptian government to amend the constitution to allow for competitive presidential elections. More spectacularly, the nonviolent Green Wave mobilized millions of Iranians against the Ahmadinejad's hardline government (accused of fraud in the presidential elections of June 12, 2009) pushing for democratic reform.

Movements like Green Wave, Kifaya, and the Cedar Revolution emerged against the background of, and indeed as alternatives to, the more formidable Islamist trends in the Muslim Middle East, which have grown on the ruins of secular Arab socialism—a mix of Pan-Arabism and (non-Marxist) socialism, which wielded notable impact on political ideas and social developmental arenas in the 1950s and 1960s but declined after the Arab defeat in the Six Day War with Israel. Islamist movements have posed perhaps the most serious challenge to secular authoritarian regimes in the region, even though their vision of political order remained largely exclusivist and authoritarian. They expressed the voice of the mainly middle-class high achievers—products of Arab socialist programs—who in the 1980s felt marginalized by the dominant economic and political processes in their societies, and who saw no recourse in the fading socialist project and growing neoliberal modernity, thus charting their dream of justice and power in religious politics. The influence of Middle Eastern Islamism has gone beyond the home countries; by forging transnational networks, it has impacted global politics on an unprecedented scale. Yet the failure of Islamism to herald a democratic and inclusive order has given rise to far-reaching nascent movements, what I have called "post-Islamism," that can reshape the political map of the region if they succeed. Neither anti-Islamic nor secular, but spearheaded by pious Muslims, post-Islamism attempts to undo Islamism as a political project by fusing faith and freedom, a secular democratic state and a religious society. It wants to marry Islam with individual choice and liberties, with democracy and modernity, to generate what some have called an "alternative modernity." Emerging first in the Islamist Iran of the late 1990s (and expressed in Mohammad Khatami's reform government of 1997–2004), post-Islamism has gained expression in a number of political movements and parties in the Muslim world, including Egypt's Al-Wasat, the current Lebanese Hizbullah, the Moroccan Justice and Development Party, and the ruling Turkish Justice and Development Party (AK Party). This trend is likely to continue to grow as an alternative to undemocratic Islamist movements.

Parallel to the current post-Islamist turn, Islam continues to serve as a crucial mobilizing ideology and social movement frame. But as this book demonstrates, Islam is not only a subject of political contention, but also its object.

In other words, while religious militants continue to deploy Islam as an ideological frame to push for exclusive moral and sociopolitical order, secular Muslims, human rights activists, and, especially, middle-class women have campaigned against a reading of Islam that underwrites patriarchy and justifies their subjugation. Indeed, the history of women's struggle in the Middle East has been intimately tied to a battle against conservative readings of Islam. Throughout the twentieth century, segments of Middle Eastern women were mobilized against conservative moral and political authorities, to push for gender equality in marriage, family, and the economy, and to assert their social role and ability to act as public players.[12] While the earlier forms of women's activism, in the late nineteenth and early twentieth centuries, focused primarily on charity work, the 1940s saw women collectively engaged in anticolonial struggles, while protesting against polygamy and advocating female education. Women's campaigns were galvanized in associational activism, which in this period flourished in Egypt, Tunis, Morocco, Lebanon, Sudan, and Iraq.[13] In the meantime, the nationalist and leftist political parties and movements wished to strengthen women's rights; yet issues relating to gender equality took a backseat to political priorities, in particular the broader objective of national liberation. It was largely in the postcolonial era, when women's presence in education, public life, politics, and the economy had been considerably enhanced, that women's organizations dedicated their attention primarily to gender rights. Yet the tide of conservative Islamism and Salafi trends since the 1980s has posed a new challenge to efforts to decrease the gender gap in Middle Eastern societies.[14] Many women are now in the throes of a battle that aims to retain what the earlier generations had gained over years of struggle. The desire to play an active part in society and the economy and to assert a degree of individuality remains a significant women's claim.

If historically women used charity associations to assert their public role and other gender claims, currently the professional middle classes (teachers, lawyers, pharmacists, engineers, and doctors) deploy their fairly independent syndicates both to defend their professional claims and to carry out political work, since traditional party politics remain in general corrupt and ineffective. Thus, it is not uncommon to find professional syndicates to serve nationalist or Islamist politics—a phenomenon quite distinct from labor unions. Unlike the professional syndicates, the conventional trade unions remain engaged chiefly with economic and social concerns. Despite corporatism and governmental pressures, trade unions in the Middle East have spearheaded defending workers' rights and their traditional social contract. While Jordan, Lebanon, Morocco, and Turkey have enjoyed more or less pluralist and relatively independent unions, in the ex-populist countries of the region, such as Algeria, Egypt, Iraq, Libya, and Syria, unions remain in the grip of corporatism. But even such corporatist unions have been used by the public-sector workers to fight against redundancies, price increases, and traditional benefits. Clearly, unionism covers only a small percentage of working people, organized in the formal and public sectors. Where trade unions have failed to serve the interests of the majority of working poor, workers have often resorted to illegal strikes or mass street protests.[15] Thus, the Economic Reform and Structural Adjustment Program (ERSAP) has, since the 1980s, coincided with a number of cost-of-living protests in many cities of the region, protests with little or no religious coloring. Indeed, the 2006, 2007, and March–April 2008 spate of mass workers' strikes in Egypt's public and private sectors, in particular among the textile workers of Mahalla al-Kubra, was described as the most effective organized activism in the nation's history since World War II, with almost no Islamist influence.[16]

It is clear that contentious collective action has played a key role in the political trajectories of the Middle Eastern nations. These collectives represent fairly organized, self-conscious, and relatively sustained mobilizations with identifiable leadership and often a particular (nationalist or socialist) ideology or discourse. However, this type of organized activism does not develop just anywhere and anytime. It requires a political opportunity—when the political authorities and the mechanisms of control are undermined by, for instance, a political or an economic crisis, international pressure, or infighting within the ruling elites. For example, the Cedar Revolution in Lebanon resulted from the slaying of Prime Minister Hariri, which offered a political and psychological opportunity to forge a broad anti-Syrian movement. Alternatively, an opportunity may arise when a sympathetic government or a faction within the government comes to power (e.g., as a result of an election), which then diminishes risk of repression and facilitates collective and organized mobilization; this was the case during the reform government under President Khatami in Iran (1997–2004). Otherwise, in ordinary conditions, the authoritarian regimes in the region have expressed little tolerance toward sustained collective dissent. The Freedom House reported in 2003 that while only five states in the Middle East and North Africa region allowed some limited political rights and civil liberties, the remaining twelve states allowed none.[17] In Iran in 2007 alone, thousands of activists—journalists, teachers, students, women, and members of labor, civil, and cultural organizations—were arrested and faced court charges or were dismissed from their positions.[18] Dozens of dailies and weeklies, and hundreds of NGOs, were shut down. An Amnesty International report on Egypt cites police violence against peaceful protestors calling for political reform, the arrest of hundreds of Muslim Brothers members, and the detention, without trial, of thousands of others suspected of supporting banned Islamic groups. Torture and ill-treatment in detention continued to be systematic.[19] Restriction of political expression has been, by far, worse in Saudi Arabia and Tunis. The following report about a group of young Egyptians launching a peaceful campaign gives a taste of the severe restrictions against collective actions:

> **July 23, 2008.** Under the scorching sun on a beach in Alexandria, Egypt, a few dozen political activists snap digital pictures and chatter nervously. Many of them wear matching white T-shirts emblazoned with the image of a fist raised in solidarity and the words "April 6 Youth" splashed across the back. A few of them get to work constructing a giant kite out of bamboo poles and a sheet of plastic painted to look like the Egyptian flag. Most are in their twenties, some younger; one teenage girl wears a teddy bear backpack. Before the group can get the kite aloft, and well before they have a chance to distribute their pro-democracy leaflets, state security agents swarm across the sand. The cops shout threats to break up what is, by Western standards, a tiny demonstration. The activists disperse from the beach, feeling hot and frustrated; they didn't even get a chance to fly their kite. Joining up with other friends, they walk together toward the neighborhood of Loran, singing patriotic songs. Then, as they turn down another street, a group of security agents jump out of nowhere. It's a coordinated assault that explodes into a frenzy of punches and shoves. There are screams and grunts as about a dozen kids fall or are knocked to the ground. The other 30 or so scatter, sprinting for blocks in all directions before slowing enough to send each other hurried text messages: *Where are you? What happened?* Those who didn't get away are hustled into a van and two cars. The security men are shouting at them: "Where is [the leader] Ahmed Maher?"[20]

In the absence of free activities, the political class is forced either to exit the political scene at least temporarily, or to go underground. All of the region's guerilla movements, whether the Marxist Fedaian of prerevolutionary Iran, the nationalist Algerian resistance against the French colonialism, or the more recent Islamist al-Gama'a al-Islamiyya of Egypt and the Islamic Salvation Front (FIS) of Algeria, resorted to subversive revolutionism largely because open and legal political work was limited. The sad truth is that the dissident movements of this sort are likely to spearhead undemocratic practices. Surveillance and secrecy disrupt free communication and open debate within a movement, leading either to fragmentation of aims and expectations—a recipe for discord and sedition—or to outright authoritarian tendencies and a cult of leadership. Still, while only a handful of revolutionary activists would venture into such perilous subversive operations, others would find recourse in street politics, expressing grievance in public space and engaging in civic campaigns, or resort to the type of "social nonmovements" that interlock activism with the practice of everyday life.

STREET POLITICS AND POLITICAL STREET

The contentious politics I have outlined so far are produced and expressed primarily in urban settings. Indeed, urban public space continues to serve as the key theater of contentions. When people are deprived of the electoral power to change things, they are likely to resort to their own institutional clout (as students or workers going on strike) to bring collective pressure to bear on authorities to undertake change. But for those urban subjects (such as the unemployed, housewives, and the "informal people") who structurally lack intuitional power of disruption (such as going on strike), the "street" becomes the ultimate arena to communicate discontent. This kind of *street politics* describes a set of conflicts, and the attendant implications, between an individual or a collective populace and the authorities, which are shaped and expressed in the physical and social space of the streets, from the back alleyways to the more visible streets and squares.[21] Here conflict originates from the *active use* of public space by subjects who, in the modern states, are allowed to use it only *passively*—through walking, driving, watching—or in other ways that the state dictates. Any *active* or *participative* use infuriates officials, who see themselves as the sole authority to establish and control public order. Thus, the street vendors who proactively spread their businesses in the main alleyways; squatters who take over public parks, lands, or sidewalks; youth who control the street-corner spaces, street children who establish street communities; poor housewives who extend their daily household activities into the alleyways; or protestors who march in the streets, all challenge the state prerogatives and thus may encounter reprisal.

Street politics assumes more relevance, particularly in the neoliberal cities, those shaped by the logic of the market. Strolling through the streets of Cairo, Tehran, Dakar, or Jakarta in the midst of a working day, one is astonished by the presence of so many people operating in the streets—working, running around, standing, sitting, negotiating, driving, or riding on buses and trams. These represent the relatively new subaltern of the neoliberal city. For the neoliberal city is the "city inside-out," where a massive number of inhabitants become compelled by the poverty and dispossession to operate, subsist, socialize, and simply live a life in the public spaces. Here the outdoor spaces (back alleys, public parks, squares, and the main streets) serve as indispensible assets in the economic livelihood and social/cultural reproduction of a vast segment of the urban population, and, consequently, as fertile ground for the expression of street politics.[22]

But "street politics" has another dimension, in that it is more than just about conflict between authorities and deinstitutionalized or informal groups over the control of public space and order. Streets, as spaces of flow and movement, are not only where people express grievances, but also where they forge identities, enlarge solidarities, and *extend* their protest beyond their immediate circles to include the unknown, the strangers. Here streets serve as a medium through which strangers or casual passersby are able to establish latent communication with one another by recognizing their mutual interests and shared sentiments. This is how a small demonstration may grow into a massive exhibition of solidarity; and that is why almost every contentious politics, major revolution, and protest movement finds expression in the urban streets. It is this epidemic potential of street politics that provokes authorities' severe surveillance and widespread repression. While a state may be able to shut down colleges or to abolish political parties, it cannot easily stop the normal flow of life in streets, unless it resorts to normalizing violence, erecting walls and checkpoints, as a strategic element of everyday life.

Thus, not only does city space serve as the center stage of sociopolitical contentions, it at the same time conditions the dynamics and shapes the patterns of conflicts and their resolution. Cities inescapably leave their spatial imprints on the nature of social struggles and agency; they provoke particular kinds of politics, of both micro and macro nature. For instance, revolutions in the sense of "insurrections" not only result from certain historical trajectories, but are also shaped by certain geographies and are facilitated by certain spatial influences. Thus, beyond asking why and when a given revolution occurred, we should also be asking *where* it was unleashed and why it happened where it did. As sites of the concentration of wealth, power, and privilege, cities are as much the source of epidemic conflicts, social struggles, and mass insurgencies as the source of cooperation, sharing, and what I like to call "everyday cosmopolitanism"—a place where various members of ethnic, racial, and religious groupings are conditioned to mix, mingle, undertake everyday encounters, and experience trust with one another. Cosmopolitan experiences in cities, in turn, may act as a spatial catalyst to ward off and contain sectarian strife and violence. In this book, I examine how, for instance, Muslims and Coptic Christians in Cairo experience an intertwined culture, shared lives, and inseparable histories—a social intercourse that subverts the language of clash, one that has dominated the current "interreligious" relations around the globe. And yet, along with providing the possibility for mixing and mingling of diverse ethnic and religious members, modern cities—due to density, advanced media, high literacy, and communication technologies—can also facilitate swift and extensive forging of sectarian, albeit "distanciated," communities along ethnic or religious lines. Such collective feelings, grievances, and belonging have no better place for expression than urban streets. In other words, urban streets not only serve as a physical space where conflicts are shaped and expressed, where collectives are formed, solidarities are extended, and "street politics" are displayed. They also signify a crucial symbolic utterance, one that goes beyond the physicality of streets to convey collective sentiments of a nation or a community. This I call *political street*, as exemplified in such terms as "Arab street" or "Muslim street." *Political street*, then, denotes the collective sentiments, shared feelings, and public opinions of ordinary people in their day-to-day utterances and practices that are expressed broadly in public spaces—in taxis, buses, and shops, on street sidewalks, or in mass street demonstrations.

The types of struggles that characterize the societies of the Middle East are neither unique to this region nor novel in their emergence. Similar processes are well under way in other parts of the world. The integration of the Middle East into the global economic system has created socio-political structures and processes in this region that find resemblance in other societies of the global South. Yet the continuing authoritarian rule, the region's strategic location (in relation to oil and Israel), and the predominance of Islam give the politics of dissent in the Muslim Middle East particular characteristics. Notwithstanding its characterization as "passive and dead" or "rowdy and dangerous," the "Arab street" exhibited a fundamental vitality and vigor in the aftermath of 9/11 events and the occupation of Iraq, despite the Middle East's regimes' continuous surveillance of political dissent. However, much mobilizational energy is spent on nationalistic and anti-imperialist concerns at the expense of the struggle for democracy at home. Even though street politics in the Arab world has assumed some innovations in strategy, methods, and constituencies, it remains overwhelmed by the surge of religio-nationalist politics. Yet it is naive to conclude a priori that the future belongs to Islamist politics. The fact is that Islamism itself is undergoing a dramatic shift in its underlying ideals and strategies. Thus, while Islam continues to play a major mobilizational role, the conditions for the emergence of Iranian-type Islamic revolutions seem to have been exhausted. I suggest that the evolving domestic and global conditions, namely, the tendency toward legalism and reformist politics, individualization of piety, and transnationalization (both the objectives and the actors) among radical trends, tend to favor not Islamic revolutions, but some of kind of "post-Islamist refolutions"—a type of indigenous political reform marked by a blend of democratic ideals and, possibly, religious sensibilities. Given the continuous authoritarian rule that curbs organized and legal opposition movements, the social *nonmovements* of fragmented and inaudible collectives may play a crucial role in instigating such a transformation.

SOCIAL NONMOVEMENTS

What are the "social nonmovements"? In general, *nonmovements* refers to the collective actions of noncollective actors; they embody shared practices of large numbers of ordinary people whose fragmented but similar activities trigger much social change, even though these practices are rarely guided by an ideology or recognizable leaderships and organizations. The term *movement* implies that social nonmovements enjoy significant, consequential elements of social movements; yet they constitute distinct entities.

In the Middle East, the nonmovements have come to represent the mobilization of millions of the subaltern, chiefly the urban poor, Muslim women, and youth. The nonmovement of the urban dispossessed, which I have termed the "quiet encroachment of the ordinary," encapsulates the discreet and prolonged ways in which the poor struggle to survive and to better their lives by quietly impinging on the propertied and powerful, and on society at large. It embodies the protracted mobilization of millions of detached and dispersed individuals and families who strive to enhance their lives in a lifelong collective effort that bears few elements of pivotal leadership, ideology, or structured organization. More specifically, I am referring to the mass movement of rural migrants who, in a quest for a better life-chance, embark on a steady and strenuous campaign that involves unlawful acquisition of lands and shelters, followed by such urban amenities as electricity, running water, phone lines, paved roads, and the like. To secure paid work, these migrants take over street sidewalks and other desirable public spaces to spread their vending businesses, infringing on and appropriating popular labels to promote their merchandise. Scores of people subsist on turning the public streets into parking spaces for private gains, or use sidewalks as sites for outdoor workshops and other businesses. These masses of largely atomized individuals, by such parallel practices of everyday encroachments, have virtually transformed the large cities of the Middle East and by extension many developing countries, generating a substantial outdoor economy, new communities, and arenas of self-development in the urban landscapes; they inscribe their active presence in the configuration and governance of urban life, asserting their "right to city."

This kind of spread-out and encroachment reflects in some way the non-movements of the international illegal migrants. There exist now a massive border check, barriers, fences, walls, and police patrol. And yet they keep flooding—through the air, sea, road, hidden in back of trucks, trains, or simply on foot. They spread, expand, and grow in the cities of the global North; they settle, find jobs, acquire homes, form families, and struggle to get legal protection. They build communities, church or mosque groups, cultural collectives, and visibly flood the public spaces. As they feel safe and secure, they assert their physical, social and cultural presence in the host societies. Indeed, the anxiety that these both national and international migrants have caused among the elites are remarkably similar. Cairo elite lament about the 'invasion of fallahin' (peasants) from the dispersed Upper Egyptian countryside, and Istanbul elite warn of the encroachment of the 'black Turks,' meaning poor rural migrants from Anatolia, who, they say, have altogether ruralized and transformed the social configuration of "our modern cities." In a strikingly similar tone, white European elites express profound anxiety about the 'invasion of foreigners'—Africans, Asians, and in particular Muslims—who they see as having overwhelmed Europe's social habitat, distorting the European way of life by their physical presence and cultural modes—their hijab, mosques and minarets. Truth is, rhetoric notwithstanding, the encroachment is real and is likely to continue. The struggles of such migrant poor in the Middle East or those of the international migrants constitute neither an organized and self-conscious social movement nor a coping mechanism, since people's survival is not at the cost of themselves but of other groups or classes. These practices also move beyond simple acts of everyday resistance, for they engage in surreptitious and incremental encroachments to further their claims. Rather, they exemplify a poor people's nonmovement.

It is often claimed that radical Islamism in the Middle East voices the interests of the poor as the victim of the urban ecology of overcrowded slums, where poverty, anomie, and lawlessness nurture extremism and violence, of which militant Islamism is a variant. But this view finds less plausibility when it is tested against the general reluctance of the urban poor to lend ideological support to this or that political movement. A pragmatic politics of the poor, one that ensures tackling concrete and immediate concerns, means that political Islam plays little part in the habitus of the urban disenfranchised. The underlying politics of the poor is expressed not in political Islam, but in a poor people's "nonmovement"—the type of fluid, flexible, and self-producing strategy that is adopted not only by the urban poor, but also by other subaltern groups, including middle-class women.

Under the authoritarian patriarchal states, whether secular or religious, women's activism for gender equality is likely to take on the form of nonmovement. Authoritarian regimes and conservative men impose severe restrictions on women making gender claims in a sustained fashion—establishing independent organizations and publications, lobbying, managing public protests, mobilizing ordinary women, acquiring funding and resources, or establishing links with international solidarity groups. In the Iran of early 2007, for instance, women activists who initiated a "million-signature campaign"—to involve ordinary women nationally against misogynous laws—encountered constant harassment, repression, and detention. Many young activists were beaten up, not only by morals police, but in some cases by their own male guardians. Recognizing such constraints on organized campaigns, women have tended to pursue a different strategy, one that involves intimately the mundane practices of everyday life, such as pursuing education, sports, arts, music, or working outside the home. These women did not refrain from performing the usually male work of civil servants, professionals, and public actors, from carrying out chores such as banking, taking cars to mechanics, or negotiating with builders. They did not stop jugging in public parks, climbing Mount Everest, or contesting (and winning) in male-dominated car racing, despite unsuitable dress codes. So, women established themselves as public actors, subverting the conventional public–private gender divide. Those who did not wish to wear veils defied the forced hijab (headscarf) in public for more than two decades in a "war of attrition" with the public morals police until they virtually normalized what the authorities had lamented as "*bad-hijabi*"—showing a few inches of hair beneath the headscarves. In their legal battles, women challenged courthouses and judges' decisions on child custody, ending marriages, and other personal status provisions.

These mundane doings had perhaps little resemblance to extraordinary acts of defiance, but rather were closely tied to the ordinary practices of everyday life. Yet they were bound to lead to significant social, ideological, and legal imperatives. Not only did such practices challenge the prevailing assumptions about women's roles, but they were followed by far-reaching structural legal imperatives. Every claim they made became a stepping-stone for a further claim, generating a cycle of opportunities for demands to enhance gender rights. Thus, women's quest for literacy and a college education enabled them to live alone, away from the control of their guardians, or led to a career that might demand traveling alone, supervising men, or defying male dominance. The intended or unintended consequences of these disparate but widespread individual practices were bound to question the fundamentals of legal and moral codes, facilitating claims for gender equality. They at times subverted the effective governmentality of the state machinery and ideology, pushing it towards pragmatism, compromise, and discord. Women activists (as well as the authorities) were keenly aware of the incremental consequences of such structural encroachment and tried to take full advantage of the possibilities it offered both to practical struggles and to conceptual/discursive articulations.

What about the nonmovement of youth? Indeed, similar processes characterize Muslim youth activism. Very often "youth movements" are erroneously conflated with and mistaken for "student movements" or "youth chapters" of this or that political party or political movement, so that, for instance, the youth chapter of the Ba'th party is described as the "youth movement" in the Iraq of Saddam Hussein. I suggest that these categories should conceptually be kept separate, for they speak to different realities. Broadly speaking, a youth movement is about reclaiming youthfulness. It embodies a collective challenge whose central goal consists of defending and extending youth habitus—defending and extending the conditions that allow the young to assert their individuality, creativity, and lightness and free them from anxiety over the prospect of their future. Curbing and controlling youthfulness is likely to trigger youth dissent. But the different ways in which youth dissent is expressed and claims are made determine whether the young are engaged in a fully fledged youth movement or a nonmovement.

A cursory look at the Muslim Middle East would reveal that the claims of youthfulness remain at the core of youth discontent. But the intensity of youths' activism depends, first, on the degree of social control imposed on them by the moral and political authorities and, second, on the degree of social cohesion among the young. Thus, in postrevolutionary Iran the young people forged a remarkable nonmovement to reclaim their youth habitus—in being treated as full citizens, in what to wear, what to listen to, and how to appear in public, and in the general choice of their lifestyle and pursuit of youthful fun. Indeed, the globalizing youth more than others have been the target of, and thus have battled against, puritanical regimes and moral sensibilities that tend to stifle the ethics of fun and joy that lie at the core of the expression of youthfulness. "Fun"—a metaphor for the expression of individuality, spontaneity, and lightness—therefore became a site of a protracted political contestation between the doctrinal regimes and the Muslim youth, and a fundamental element in youth dissent, especially in the Islamic Republic of Iran. This remarkable dissent emanated partly from the contradictory positionality of youth. On one side, the young were highly valorized for their role in the revolution and the war (with Iraq), and, on the other, they remained under a strong social control and moral discipline by the Islamic regime. This occurred in a time and place in which the young people enjoyed an enormous constituency, with two-thirds of the total population being under thirty years of age. But this dissent was not a structured movement with extensive networks of communication, organization, and collective protest actions. As in many parts of the Middle East, the young in general remained dispersed, atomized, and divided, with their organized activism limited to a number of youth NGOs and publications. Youths instead forged collective identities in schools, colleges, urban public spaces, parks, cafés, and sports centers; or they connected with one another through the virtual world of various media. Thus, theirs was not a deliberate network of solidarity where they could meet, interact, articulate their concerns, or express collective dissent. Rather, they linked to one another passively and spontaneously—through "passive networks"—by sensing their commonalities through such methods as recognizing similar hairstyles, blue jeans, hang-out places, food, fashions, and the pursuit of public fun. In sum, just as with women and the poor, theirs was not a politics of protest, but of practice, a politics of redress through direct action.

While the battle over "fun" brings the globalizing urban youth to the center stage of political struggle against fundamentalist movements and regimes, youth nonmovements as such—those whose major preoccupation revolves around reclaiming youth habitus—should not necessarily be seen as the harbinger of democratic transformation, as it is often hoped. Youth may become agents of democratic change only when they act and think politically; otherwise, their preoccupation with their own narrow youthful claims may bear little impetus for engaging in broader societal concerns. In other words, the transforming or, in particular, democratizing effects of youth nonmovements depend partly on the capacity of adversarial regimes or states to accommodate youthful claims. Youth nonmovements, just like women's nonmovements, follow a strong democratizing effect primarily when they challenge the narrow doctrinal foundations of the exclusivist fundamentalist regimes.

LOGIC OF PRACTICE IN NONMOVEMENTS

How do we explain the logic of practice in nonmovements? Social movements, especially those operating in the politically open and technologically advanced western societies, are defined as the "organized, sustained, self-conscious challenge to existing authorities."[23] Very often, they are embedded in particular organizations and guided by certain ideologies; they pursue certain frames, follow specific leaderships, and adopt particular repertoires or means and methods of claim making.[24] What, then, differentiates the type of nonmovements that I have discussed here so far? What are the distinct features of nonmovements in general?

First, nonmovements, or the collective actions of noncollective actors, tend to be action-oriented, rather than ideologically driven; they are overwhelmingly quiet, rather than audible, since the claims are made largely individually rather than by united groups. Second, whereas in social movements leaders usually mobilize the constituencies to put pressure on authorities to meet their demands, in nonmovements actors directly practice what they claim, despite government sanctions. Thus, theirs is not a politics of protest, but of practice, of redress through direct and disparate actions. Third, unlike social movements, where actors are involved usually in *extraordinary* deeds of mobilization and protestation that go beyond the routine of daily life (e.g., attending meetings, petitioning, lobbying, demonstrating, and so on), the nonmovements are made up of practices that are merged into, indeed are part and parcel of, the *ordinary* practices of everyday life. Thus, the poor people building homes, getting piped water or phone lines, or spreading their merchandise out in the urban sidewalks; the international migrants crossing borders to find new livelihoods; the women striving to go to college, playing sports, working in public, conducting "men's work," or choosing their own marriage partners; and the young appearing how they like, listening to what they wish, and hanging out where they prefer—all represent some core practices of nonmovements in the Middle East and similar world areas. The critical and fourth point is that these practices are not carried out by small groups of people acting on the political margins; rather, they are *common* practices of *everyday life* carried out by *millions* of people who albeit remain *fragmented*. In other words, the power of nonmovements does not lie in the unity of actors, which may then threaten disruption, uncertainty, and pressure on the adversaries. The power of nonmovements rests on the *power of big numbers*, that is, the consequential effect on norms and rules in society of many people simultaneously doing similar, though contentious, things.

What effect do "big numbers" have? To begin with, a large number of people acting in common has the effect of normalizing and legitimizing those acts that are otherwise deemed illegitimate. The practices of big numbers are likely to capture and appropriate spaces of power in society within which the subaltern can cultivate, consolidate, and reproduce their counterpower. Thus, the larger the number of women who assert their presence in the public space, the more patriarchal bastions they undermine. And the greater the number of the poor consolidating their self-made urban communities, the more limited the elite control of urban governance becomes. Second, even though these subjects act individually and separately, the effects of their actions do not of necessity fade away in seclusion. They can join up, generating a more powerful dynamic than their individual sum total. Whereas each act, like single drops of rain, singularly makes only *individual* impact, such acts produce larger spaces of alternative practices and norms when they transpire in big numbers—just as the individual wetting effects of billions of raindrops

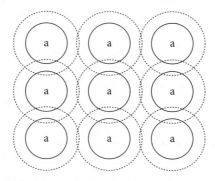

Figure 1.1. Power of big numbers: Exponential outcome of merging individual acts.

join up to generate creeks, rivers, and even floods and waves (Figure 1.1). Thus, what ultimately defines the power of nonmovements relates to the (intended and unintended) *consequences* of the similar practices that a "big number" of subjects simultaneously perform.

By thinking about nonmovements in this fashion, are we not in a sense conjuring up Hardt and Negri's concept of *multitude,* which they define as "singularities of social subjects that act in common"? At first glance, the enormous magnitude as well as the fragmentation of social subjects associated with *multitude* reminds one of nonmovements and the "power of big numbers." But the resemblance stops there. Unlike the categories of *working class, people,* or *mass,* which are marked by sameness and shared identities, *multitude* is made up of "singularities," or dissimilar or nonidentical social subjects, a mix of different social groups, gender clusters, or sexual orientations that are ontologically different (Figure 1.2). Their apparent similarity, in Hardt and Negri's view, lies in their producing "immaterial labor" and standing opposed to the "empire."[25] Thus, whereas *multitude* is assumed to bring together singular and ontologically different social subjects (men, women, black, white, various ethnicities, etc.), nonmovements galvanize members of the same, even though internally fragmented, groups (e.g., globalizing youth, Muslim women, illegal migrants, or urban poor), who act in common, albeit often individually. While in nonmovements, collective action is a function of shared interests and identities within a single group, especially when confronted by a common threat, in a multitude, it is not clear precisely how the singular components are to come and act together, and how these different groups (e.g., men and women, native working class and migrant workers, or dominant and subordinate ethnicities) avoid conflicts of interests between them, let alone act in common.

If, unlike in a multitude, common identities are essential for agents of non-movements to act collectively, how are these identities forged among fragmented and atomized subjects in the first place? And why do they act in common if they are not deliberately mobilized by organizations or leaders? Collective identities are built not simply in open and legal institutions or solidarity networks, of which they are in general deprived due to surveillance. Solidarities are forged primarily in public spaces—in neighborhoods, on street corners, in mosques, in workplaces, at bus stops, or in rationing lines, or in detention centers, migrant camps, public parks, colleges, and athletic stadiums—through what I have called "passive networks." The passive networks represent a key feature in the formation of nonmovements. They refer to instantaneous communications between atomized individuals, which are established by tacit recognition of their commonalities directly in public spaces or indirectly through mass media.[26] Thus, the poor street vendors would recognize their common predicaments by noticing one another on street corners on a daily basis, even though they may never know or speak to one another. Female strangers neglecting dress codes in public spaces would internalize their shared identities in the streets by simply observing one another; those confronting men and judges in courthouses would readily feel their commonly held inferior status. On street corners, at shopping malls, or in colleges, the young identify their collective position by spontaneously recognizing similar fashions, hairstyles, and social tastes. For these groups, space clearly provides the possibility of mutual recognition (Figure 1.5)—a factor that distinguishes them from such fragmented groups as illegal immigrants, who may lack the medium of space to facilitate solidarity formation unless they come together in the same workplaces, detention centers, or residential compounds. These latter groups rely often on mass media, rumors, or distanciated networks—that is, knowing someone who knows someone who knows someone in a similar position—a process that facilitates building "imagined solidarities" (Figure 1.3).[27]

The new information technology, in particular the current social networking sites such as Facebook, can bypass the medium of physical space by connecting atomized individuals in the world of the Web, and in so doing create a tremendous opportunity for building both passive and active networks. The Egyptian April 7 Youth Movement built on such media to connect some

Figure 1.2. No network: Atomized individuals without a common position. Source: Asef Bayat, *Street Politics: Poor People's Movements in Iran*. New York: Columbia University Press, 1997, p. 18.

Figure 1.3. No network: Atomized individuals with a common position. Source: Asef Bayat, *Street Politics: Poor People's Movements in Iran*. New York: Columbia University Press, 1997, p. 18.

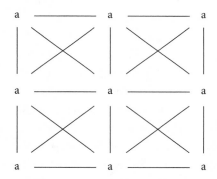

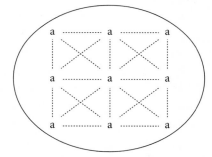

Figure 1.4. Active network: Individuals with similar positions brought together deliberately—association with an active network. Source: Asef Bayat, *Street Politics: Poor People's Movements in Iran*. New York: Columbia University Press, 1997, p. 18.

Figure 1.5. Passive network: Atomized individuals with similar positions brought together through space. Source: Asef Bayat, *Street Politics: Poor People's Movements in Iran*. New York: Columbia University Press, 1997, p. 18.

70,000 people, most of them young, who then called for the support of textile workers' strikes in April 2008 and protested against the Israeli aggression in Gaza in 2008–9.[28] But this venue is limited largely to young, literate, and well-to-do groups, whose mobilization of this kind can descend into a sort of "chic politics" of ad hoc and short-lived interventions. More importantly, this channel is too exposed and contained, and thus vulnerable to police surveillance, when compared to the fluidity and resiliency of "passive networks." In the war of un-equals, the weak will certainly loose if it follows the same rules of the game as those of the powerful. To win an unequal battle, the underdog has no choice but to creatively play different, more flexible and constantly changing games.

At any rate, what mediates between passive networks and possible collective action is a common threat. In other words, while making gains in non-movements takes place individually through direct practices, the defense of gains often takes place collectively, when a common threat turns the subjects' passive network into active communication and organized resistance. Thus, women who individually defy authorities by disregarding dress codes are likely to come together when they encounter morals police in the streets. The urban poor who usually carry on building illegal homes quietly and individually often resist a government's demolition efforts collectively. The massive public demonstration of illegal migrants in Los Angeles on March 26, 2006 to demand a legislation to protect them represents perhaps a more striking potential of episodic collection protest of the otherwise atomized agents of non-movements. Of course it is always possible that the subjects may, instead of engaging in immediate confrontation, rationally choose to resort to the "war of attrition"—a temporary compliance in times of constraint while carrying on with encroachments when the right time arrives. Unlike women, the young, or the poor, illegal immigrants cannot resist state action unless they begin to deliberately organize themselves, since the markers through which they can readily recognize their shared predicaments in public are limited (see Figure 1.4). But people with limited visible markers may still connect through shared sound (e.g. chants of "Allah Akbar" on rooftops or youngsters setting off firecrackers at night time) and symbols (like identical colors, handbands, or t-shirts).

These dynamics already point to the questions of how and when non-movements may turn into contentious politics and social movements. Indeed, actual (even though quiet and individualized) defiance by a large number of people implies that a massive societal mobilization is already under way. This may develop into contentious politics when opportunity for organized, sustained, and institutional activism becomes available—for instance, when states/regimes gripped in infighting, crisis, international pressure, or wars become weaker; or when a more tolerant government ascends to power. But the transformative effect of nonmovements should not be judged merely by their eventual elevation into organized social movements. Nonmovements, on their own, can have significant transformative impact if they continue to operate in society. They can diminish or impair a state's governmentality. For states rule not as external to society through mere surveillance but weave their logic into the fabric of society, into norms, rules, institutions, and relations of power. The operation of nonmovements challenges that logic of power. The states may conceivably attempt to offset nonmovements' subversive practices by, for instance, submerging them into their logic of power. But this may not be so easy, for the incremental disposition of claim making in nonmovements is likely to diminish states' ability to neutralize their effects. Should a state ultimately accommodate the claims of nonmovements, it would in effect be a notable reform of the state itself.[29]

Why are nonmovements the prevalent form of activism in particular social and political settings, such as in the Muslim Middle East? The first factor relates to the fact that authoritarian states do not tolerate any independent and organized dissent. So, they tend either to fragment the subaltern, especially the political class, or to subsume them under their own populist institutions. But the fact is that subaltern classes themselves are also experiencing new dispositions. The growing fragmentation of labor, informalization, the shrinking of public sectors, and "NGOization"—all associated with the neoliberal restructuring—further curtail the popular capacity for organized activism in the form of, say, traditional trade union organizations. Yet such a subaltern is confronted by states that are remarkably incapable of or unwilling to fulfill their social and material needs and expectations—ones that are swelled up by the escalating urbanization, educational growth, media expansion, and citizen awareness—thus pushing the populace to take matters into their own hands. When the states cannot provide adequate housing or jobs for the poor (and when the possible conventional legal channels, like lobbying, to achieve these goals are not trusted or get frustrated by state bureaucracy), the poor resort to direct squatting on land or shelters, or illegally spreading their street businesses. When the authorities fail to recognize gender rights or youth demands, women and youths may defy the official authority by directly executing their claims in the areas or institutions with least surveillance or otherwise appropriating and overturning those that enjoy official sanction. Such encroachments become possible—and this is the third point—because the authoritarian regimes, despite their omnipresent image, preside over the states—"soft states"—that lack the capacity, consistency, and machinery to impose full control, even though they may wish to. Consequently, there exist many escapes, spaces, and uncontrolled holes—zones of relative freedom—that can be filled and appropriated by ordinary actors. The genius of subaltern subjects—nonmovements—lies precisely in discovering or generating such escapes. In other words, I am speaking of the agency and perseverance of millions of women, young people, and the dispossessed who, notwithstanding their differences, understand the constraints yet recognize and discover opportunities, and take advantage of the spaces that are available to enhance their life-chances. The case of a physically small Iranian woman driver—her determination to take part, and to win, in male-dominated car racing—is only one example of how women find spaces where they can decisively subvert the dominant ideology that regards them as second-class citizens. This example illustrates what I have called the "art of presence"—the courage and creativity to assert collective will in spite of all odds, to circumvent constraints, utilizing what is available and discovering new spaces within which to make oneself heard, seen, felt, and realized. The art of presence is the fundamental moment in the life of nonmovements, in life as politics.

The story of nonmovements is the story of agency in the times of constraints. The concept is both descriptive and prescriptive. On the one hand, by bypassing the rigid dichotomies of 'active'/'passive,' 'individual'/'collective,' or 'civil'/ 'political' resistance which have limited our conceptual horizons, it opens up wholly new possibilities to explore unnoticed social practices that may in fact be harbinger of significant social changes. It helps uncover the logic of practice among dispersed and distant collectives under the conditions of authoritarian rule when free association and active communication are suppressed. It tells us how people manage, resist, and subvert domination through widespread collective (if fragmented) practices. On the other hand, the concept is prescriptive, in that it challenges the ideas and excuses that justify exit and inaction under conditions of surveillance. It help us to recognize, indeed gives us hope, that despite authoritarian rule, there are always ways in which people resist, express agency, and instigate change, rather than waiting for a savior or resorting to violence.

2 TRANSFORMING THE ARAB MIDDLE EAST
Dissecting a Manifesto

IN THE FIRST DECADE of the new millennium, the Middle East seems to have plunged into a deadlock, the way out of which few would say they know for sure. Despite its massive oil revenue, personal income of Arabs was among the lowest in the world. Productivity declined, scientific research was in a poor state, school enrollment decreased, and illiteracy remained considerable despite high spending. Arab countries had a lower information/media-to-population ratio than the world average—less than 53 newspapers per 1,000 citizens, compared to 285 per 1,000 people in the industrialized world. Translation of books remained negligible—only 4.4 translated books per million were published every year (compared to 519 in Hungary and 920 in Spain). The Arab world's developmental indexes in health and education lagged far behind comparable nations in the World Bank's income tables. In short "Arab countries [were] richer than they [were] developed."[1] At the same time, the region's authoritarian regimes, ranging from Egypt, Jordan, and Morocco to the sheikhdoms of the Persian Gulf (chiefly Saudi Arabia), and all with close ties to the West, have continued to defy persistent calls for democratization and accountability. Precisely such a historical trajectory has engendered opposition movements, which have been overwhelmingly articulated by religious (Islamist) political groups, and which have espoused equally undemocratic, exclusive, and often violent measures.

Adapted from Asef Bayat, "Transforming the Arab World: The *Arab Human Development Report* and the Politics of Change," *Development and Change* 36, no. 6, 2005, 1225–37.

The combination of such social and political conditions has more than ever reinforced, in the mainstream media and academic circles in the West, the already prevalent idea of "Middle Eastern exceptionalism"—that reifying kernel of the Orientalist paradigm. Thus, in comparison with its counterparts in the developing world, the Middle East—in particular the Arab world—has often been viewed as something very different, a "unique" cultural entity that does not fit into conventional frames of analysis. Policy personnel in the West, notably the United States, called for an urgent change in the region and yet believed that change would not come from within, but from without, and by force. This juncture encouraged the neoconservative ideologues in the George W. Bush administration to put into practice their Leo Straussian philosophy of force, illiberal elitism in politics, and the idea of uniting political order by means of creating external threat. Muslim countries in the region have been told to alter textbooks, abolish religious schools, and instruct religious preachers to refrain from anti-U.S. sermons. The United States toppled the Taliban regime in Afghanistan and dismantled Saddam Hussein's regime by occupation of Iraq, while threatening Iran in a quest to generate a "greater Middle East," to cultivate "democracy and development."

Few Arabs and Muslims in the region consider "change by force" as a viable and dignified strategy, not least because it is essentially immoral, inflicts widespread violence and destruction, and impinges on people's dignity. Having lived and worked in the Middle East for close to two decades, I feel that a call for political change from within has continued ceaselessly even though the "external" conflicts, notably Israel's continuing occupation of Palestinian lands and the aggressive U.S. foreign policy in the region, have seriously distorted internal struggles for social and political transformation. The stubborn resiliency of the authoritarian states against change, coupled with the threat of imperialist domination from outside, have brought the region to a depressing impasse. Perhaps never before has the quest for an endogenous vision for change in the Arab world been so urgent as today.

The significance of the *Arab Human Development Report* lay precisely in its publication at this debilitating regional and global juncture, notably after the crucial post-9/11 turning point. But even more than this, the *Report*, totaling four volumes—*Creating Opportunities for Future Generations* (2002), *Building a Knowledge Society* (2003), *Towards Freedom in the Arab World* (2004), and *Towards the Rise of Women in the Arab World* (2005)—came to represent the most significant "manifesto of change" "produced by the Arabs for the

Arab world." It aimed to show a way out of this profound malaise by calling for a "radical transformation" of the region.

To serve the strategic objective of "radical transformation," the authors adopt a broad understanding of development, in terms of a "process of expanding people's choices." Perceived as a mixture of Dudley Seers's notion of development as a process that allows the realization of human potential and Amartya Sen's "freedom as development," the *Report* views human development as a process in which people enlarge their choices, influence the processes that shape their lives, and enjoy full human rights.[2] Such a conceptualization clearly transcends the traditional perceptions of "development" in terms of the mere growth of GNP, rise of personal income, industrialization, technological advance, and social modernization, even though the latter may contribute to "development as freedom." Thus, in a comprehensive survey of development status ranging from education, health, and knowledge to culture and politics, the *Report* identifies three major "deficits"—in knowledge, in freedom/democracy, and in women's empowerment—which are at the core of Arab developmental decline. It describes how some sixty-five million adult Arabs, two-thirds of them women, have remained illiterate. The quality of education is in decline, and mechanisms for intellectual-capital development are lacking. College graduates do not find jobs in suitable occupations; the use of information communications technology (ICT) is remarkably limited, and, consequently, highly educated people are in short supply.

Disparity in the distribution of knowledge manifests only one aspect of gender inequality in the Arab countries. It is true that women's education and literacy have certainly improved, but the prevailing social attitudes and norms continue to focus on women's reproductive role and their unpaid tasks. Consequently, 50 percent of women remain illiterate, while their mortality rate is double that of Latin America.[3] In addition, women are treated unfairly before the law, and in pay, personal status, structures of opportunity, and occupational hierarchy. With the continuing discrimination against women, society undermines a major segment of its productive capacity.

As feminist theory has taught us, gender inequality reflects a deficit in democratic theory and practice in general. And in the Arab region in particular, this deficit is far more profound. According to the *Report*, the region in these respects lags far behind Latin America, Asia, and Eastern Europe. While the Arab states in general "talk the talk" of democracy, they have in practice exhibited highly authoritarian tendencies. Dominated by powerful executives and lifelong presidencies, the states curtail freedom of expression and association, while human rights have fallen victim to secretive and coercive institutions, unaccountable to anyone. Suppression of freedoms and human rights is the enemy of human development, the *Report* concludes. To remedy these debilitating conditions and to achieve meaningful development, the *Arab Human Development Report* calls for empowering women, building a knowledge society, and achieving freedom and good governance.

How plausible are these advocacies, and to what extent can such a manifesto of change bring the Middle East, its subaltern, out of its current deadlock? A careful appraisal of the *Report*, of what it calls for, the very mode of its production, and the politics surrounding it, tells us a great deal about the contradictions and complexities of political processes in the Middle East and its relationship to the Western world. It reveals how the fundamental ideals and expectations—freedom, development, democracy, women's emancipation—on the one hand reflect the genuine desire for autonomy and emancipation, and at the same time serve as discursive tools for imperialistic domination. The *Report,* which reflects the contradictions of the very region it wants to liberate, falls in the end to an elitist neoliberal vision in which the "emancipatory outcries" get sidelined.

POLITICS SURROUNDING THE DOCUMENT

No comparable Arab document in recent memory has been as much debated, commended, and contested as the *Arab Human Development Report*. Prepared by a team of over a hundred Arab intellectuals and professionals at a cost of some U.S. $700,000 as of 2005,[4] the *Report* has provoked unprecedented discussion in the West as well as in the Arab world about the predicament of the region—aired on television talk shows, in parliaments, and in print media. The first two volumes of the *Report* were received with great jubilation and enthusiasm in the West. The editorials of the major U.S. and European dailies praised the authors for their professionalism and honesty in disclosing the sad truths of their nations. "With uncommon candor and a battery of statistics," the *Middle East Quarterly* reacted, "the *Report* tells a sorry story of two decades of failed planning and developmental decline."[5] More than one million copies of the first issue of the *Report* were downloaded within the first year of its publication, while the website of the *Report* received some two million hits.[6] The U.S. State Department described the 2002 *Report* as "a groundbreaking document,"[7] and *Time* magazine deemed it the most important publication of 2002. The prestigious Dutch Prince Claus Award in 2003 went to this publication; and the G8 in 2004 endorsed the U.S. plan for a "greater Middle East" on the basis of the recommendations of this remarkable document. The deplorable state of development in the Arab world, it was thought, lay at the heart of the rising terrorism in the Middle East, which the G8 considered as jeopardizing these nations' interests.

The western overenthusiasm for the *Report* had largely to do with the perceived acknowledgment by the Arab elites of their own deficiencies in practicing freedom, democracy, and development—and this through a document that had been sanctioned by the credible United Nations Development Program. It reflected a confirmation of the western "expert" anxieties, claims, and strategies, raised particularly in the crucial conjuncture of post-9/11 about the Arab Middle East. The expert community would hear through the pages of the *Report* how the Arab world, now considered as the nest of global terrorism, acknowledged its own indictment, while proclaiming its desire to launch a political and economic reform.

Largely for the very same reasons (and the fact) that western officials and commentators exalted the *Report*, many Arab intellectuals slammed the publication at home. They lashed out at the *Report* for vilifying and degrading, as they saw it, the Arab peoples before Israel and the United States at a time when the Arabs were being besieged globally. They feared that the *Report* could be used to justify the American expansionist policy and Israeli domination in the region. They charged the *Report*'s exclusive emphasis on internal sources of decline as one-sided, totally ignoring the role of colonialism and "imperialist intervention" in causing the developmental malaise of the Arab peoples.[8] For them, the *Report* signified the defensiveness and dependence of its authors and their deference before western sensibilities. The fact that the document was originally written in English and only then translated into Arabic was seen as a further confirmation of the intended (western) audience of the publication. In addition, the Arab critics slammed the *Report* for adopting a concept of "human development" that drew on the Alternative Human Development Index (AHDI), which emphasizes individual freedom and gender— the major focus of western policymakers. What should be prioritized, they argued, should include tackling the problems of poverty, education, health, and equity, rather than simply democratization, not least because there is no necessary relationship between democracy and development (understood as income and Human Development Index indicators), in particular when the

Report adopts an American formula of democracy, "underlying free market with little attention paid to human entitlements and social services."[9]

Neither the overenthusiasm of the western commentators nor the disparaging tone of Arab counterparts does justice to the *Report*. Both tend to politicize the document, praising and blaming it for largely the wrong reasons. The Arab intelligentsia's suspicion of western enthusiasm about the *Report* is justified, given the destructive and debilitating effects of the western, especially the U.S. foreign policy over the region's development and democracy. In the name of fighting against communism, to maintain their geopolitical dominance and secure the flow of cheap oil, many western governments have invariably helped the region's authoritarian states to crush nationalist, socialist, and popular struggles (as in Iran, Oman, etc.). The U.S. support for Israel's continuing occupation of Palestinian lands, undermining resistance movements against the occupation, and its own illegal occupation of Iraq represent enough reasons for the Arab population to suspect western intents to "democratize" the region.

The Arab critics of the *Report* are correct when they suggest that the cause of the deplorable condition of knowledge is not just internal despotism, but also foreign interventions. The Israeli army's looting of the Palestinian universities, research centers, and archives in early 2000 surely did not further the growth of a knowledge society in Palestine. Indeed, volumes 2 and 3 of the *Report*, notwithstanding its UN official status, do take issue, even though briefly, with the destructive consequences for Arab human development of Israeli occupation and the Anglo-American invasion of Iraq. The killing by the Israeli army of 768 and the injuring of over 4,000 Palestinians between May 2003 and June 2004; the demolition of some 12,000 homes within only three years, not to mention the even more destructive Israeli bombardments of Lebanon in 2006 and Gaza in early 2009; and parcelizing the West Bank, with attendant economic and psychological damages, have led to devastating developmental consequences. In a similar vein, the occupation of Iraq, with its massive loss of lives, destruction of infrastructure, dismantling of the state institutions, and human rights violations, without doubt have impeded the development of the region.[10]

Yet speaking of foreign dominance as the cause of underdevelopment is nothing new among Arab intellectuals. The widespread view in the Middle East has long been infused by a strong nationalist discourse, often at the cost of externalizing internal problems and losing a balanced sense of self. By exclusive attention to the evils of colonialism and external intrigues, the prevailing dependency paradigm in the Arab region has for decades contributed to a debilitating nationalist and populist politics in which a critique of self, of patriarchy, and of authoritarian polity, as well as reaching out to the world, have been lost to defensiveness, political self-indulgence, and conspiracy theory. This outlook, still prevalent among the political classes in the Arab world, has distorted class politics, deviated from the struggle for democracy, curtailed transnational solidarity (with movements located in the West, for instance), and largely played into the hands of the authoritarian Arab regimes, which also play nationalist/nativist cards.

The *Report*'s major breakthrough lies precisely in its attempt and outlook to transcend such nationalist discourse, by highlighting the internal sources of developmental problems. Comprehensive, full of crucial data and insights, it covers major areas of developmental interests, including growth, distribution, poverty, education, health, demography, and infant mortality, as well as gender, knowledge, governance, culture, and politics. The *Report* self-consciously displays a major postnational and postdependency narrative of the Arab world. Significantly, it wants to show a way out of the malaise, hoping to establish a process within which Arab people can enhance their choices.

Yet this remarkable document displays a rather peculiar text, a schizophrenic transcript, wherein incongruity in language, format, audience, visions, and strategies perplexes the critical reader. On the one hand, the *Report* is a statement of fundamental importance, a "vision of an Arab renaissance," a guide to social and political transformation of the Arab world; and yet it is couched and squeezed in the administrative and soulless language of the World Bank. At times, radical tones are merged into neoliberal imagery of economy, polity, elites, and change. The reader is bewildered as to what to interpret the text as: a treatise on political transformation or a conventional UN report with its "executive summary" and countless sections and subsections, often embracing diverse views and perspectives so that logical consistency gets lost amid some kind of "representation of all of views." For instance, no possible explanation is left off the list of probable reasons for the undemocratic disposition of Arab states (authoritarian family, clannishness, a social structure antithetical to freedom, "oriental despotism," colonial domination, repressive legal structure, and rentier character of the Arab states), even though they may contradict one another. Several pages are devoted to the social, political, and cultural environment as "un-hospitable to freedom," and yet we read elsewhere how popular culture is replete with "longing for freedom" or how the

Arab bedouin culture is imbued with free-spirited legacies.[11] It is as if there has been an urge to practice a "democracy of explanations" among these many solicited authors of the *Report*, even though at the cost of incongruity and analytical inconsistency. But these analytical anomalies should not deter us from paying attention to the *Report* chiefly as a document of strategy, and it is here that its strengths as well as its major drawbacks lie.

STRATEGY OF CHANGE

Given the major deficits in knowledge, freedom/democracy, and woman empowerment in the region, the *Report* regards as the ultimate strategic objectives to build a "knowledge society," to establish freedom and democracy, and to empower women. These represent crucial strategic goals. But the challenge is to explore how the Arab nations are to fulfill such aspirations, and what social forces are to be deployed for their realization. Let us begin with the "knowledge society." The idea of a knowledge society, one that has lingered since the 1970s, is rooted in Daniel Bell's *The Coming of Post-Industrial Society* as a distinct stage in the development of capitalism. Since then this notion has submerged and resurfaced once again in the works of such social theorists as Alvin Gouldner, Jean-François Lyotard, Francis Fukuyama, and more recently Manuel Castells.[12] The World Bank followed suit and began to advocate the idea. In sociological and political-economy literature, "knowledge society" signifies a tendency in the "postindustrial" and post-Fordist phase of late capitalism, where science and technology are to play an increasingly important role in societies' governance and economic production; it presupposes an economy in which knowledge and skill become more significant for the accumulation of capital, or investment and profitability, than income or physical capital. This is due to the highly mobile and flexible disposition of knowledge, which is well in tune with the highly dynamic movement of capital in the age of globalization. Some observers view the "knowledge society" as representing a phase in late modernity in which knowledge seems to play the same role as labor in the classical economy.[13]

Whatever its dynamics—and some have expressed doubt about its usefulness[14]—knowledge society is an outcome not of planning but of highly developed market forces in postindustrial economies. The first question, then, is how realistic it is to envision and extend such a scenario to the socioeconomic reality of the Middle East, which still holds an inadequate industrial basis, and where property and income still play a far more important role in individuals' life-chances than does knowledge. Although higher education has contributed considerably, especially during the 1960s and 1970s, to upward mobility of many lower-class individuals, the growing "intellectual unemployment" in the region points to the fact that knowledge by itself does not necessarily bring material well-being for many people. What it certainly does is generate expectations, change status, and, in the absence of real purchase, cause a deep-rooted political resentment. Indeed, the rise of political Islam in the Arab world has partly to do with the failure of knowledge (university education) to secure reasonable life-chances, which the impoverished educated middle classes expected it to do. As some Arab economists suggest, the *Report*, following the current World Bank trend, tends to exaggerate the "potential role of information and communication in Arab development," simply because the Arab region still lacks a strong economic and technical infrastructure.[15] Perhaps one should search for those types of knowledge that are of urgent relevance to these political economies. Alternatively, perhaps we should imagine a different understanding of "knowledge society" than what is currently perceived.

Regardless of the relevance of the idea of "knowledge society" with respect to the future of the Arab region, the question of how to realize this aim of a knowledge society remains paramount. The *Report* proposes five preconditions necessary to build a knowledge society. They include developing a high-quality education for all, integrating science and information technology in all societal activities, shifting toward knowledge-based economic production, and reestablishing an Arab knowledge model based on rationality, the strength of the Arabic language, and cultural diversity. However, the most important element is considered to be achieving freedoms of opinion, expression, and assembly. I will not delve into the relationship between individual freedom/democracy and attaining knowledge; some have argued that there are few necessary relationships between the two. For instance, as Galal Amin suggests, Arabs could expand their knowledge during the despotic Abbasid Khilafat of Harun al-Rashid, when art, music, and science prospered; and Oxford and Cambridge certainly did not flourish in England's democratic era;[16] and the authoritarian regimes in such countries as Iran or Tunisia have not prevented a notable expansion of both general literacy and higher education. Nonetheless, a democratic society and polity clearly allow for wider opportunity for knowledge acquisition, even though unequal distribution of knowledge and information feature the intrinsic characteristics of capitalist democracies (for instance, given the unequal access to the mainstream media in the United States, it is difficult to develop an alternative narrative to the official version of the events of 9/11). Thus, my concern relates not to the relationship between knowledge acquisition and freedom, but rather to the modalities of bringing those freedoms (of expression and assembly) to fruition. And this is a point closely tied to the *Report*'s second major requirement to realizing Arab human development in general, that is, establishing freedom.

But what is "freedom"? The concept embraces "democracy" but is not limited to it. In fact, democracy, we are told, "can be used to legislate restrictions on freedom."[17] Freedom is defined as "liberation of the individual from all factors that are inconsistent with human dignity, such as hunger, disease, ignorance, poverty and fear."[18] Embedded in the concept are also civil and political rights. It is a credit to the authors of the *Report* to envisage such a comprehensive vision of freedom for the Arab peoples. However, a number of questions are raised. First, when "freedom" is perceived in such an all-inclusive fashion, then what is the need to bring in and discuss two more prerequisites for human development (i.e., knowledge and women's empowerment)? Because in this broad sense "freedom *is* synonymous with human development."[19] In addition, while the link between knowledge and development or democracy and development is fairly well discussed, there is no serious justification as to why women's empowerment is particularly crucial for human development. Certainly, empowering women accounts for an end in itself, to which the *Report*, to its credit, offers prominent attention. There is no doubt that women in the Arab world (as elsewhere, though in various degrees) suffer from gender discrimination, and this needs to be addressed. But discrimination targets also children, the elderly, the handicapped, and immigrants or refugees. What makes women in particular, as an analytical category, important for human development? Failing to delve into this question is likely to give credence to those critics who, even unjustifiably, may suggest that the "trendy" notion of "women's empowerment" serves primarily to satisfy the sensibilities of a "western audience."

Third, implicit in the *Report*'s understanding of freedom is also "economic freedom," the free market. Does this not clash with the objective of equity—a concern to which the *Report* makes only a passing reference? In the spirit of neoliberal orthodoxy, the *Report* implicitly celebrates the advent of the free market in the Middle East, because of its potential to free the economy from the domination of corrupt and inefficient states. It is true that state bureaucracy and corruption do hinder economic performance and discourage investment; and a measured deregulation is undoubtedly necessary. However, an unfettered economic freedom, as Sylvia Chan and others have shown, not only can undercut equity and civil and political freedoms,[20] but may also stand against the very spirit of "human development." Evidence suggests that the implementation of Economic Reform and Structural Adjustment, spread throughout the Middle East, has caused a significant shift in social policies, with adverse impacts on the very foundation of human development, in the areas of health, education, housing, and the supply of adequate food.[21] Market forces have drastically undermined the principle of equity, that is, equal access to life-chances. The result has been the development of a two-tier system of social provisions where high-quality private but expensive social services (in schooling, hospitals, food supply, air quality, entertainment, living environment) stand against the deteriorating state provisions. The expanded NGO sector in the region partially fills the vacuum of the shrunken involvement of the state in offering social services to the needy. Yet not only do NGOs fragment their beneficiaries, they may also reinforce communal cleavages. For unlike the state, which dispenses welfare provisions to all citizens irrespective of their communal affiliations, NGOs can function on ethnic lines, extending services to a particular community while excluding others (see Chapter 4).

Finally and most importantly, attaining "fundamental freedoms," in the sense of "civil and political rights," "good governance," and democracy, clearly represents an end in itself, no matter what other purposes it may serve. And these are objectives with which the political classes in the Middle East have continuously been preoccupied, but which have thus far failed to materialize. The key question, however, is how to bring about a "society of freedom and good governance." What kinds of human agency, social forces, are apt to carry out such a historic transformation? Can it be achieved by offering good advice to the incumbent governments, by rational dialogue between the states and opposition groups? Does the solution lie in "democracy by conquest," as in Afghanistan and Iraq, or is there a need to launch social and political movements to push for democratization from within?

It is possible to imagine, as the authors do, that the current status quo might lead to despair, violence, or even unpredictable revolutions. This, we are told, is not a solution. The ideal scenario would be to "pursue an historic, peaceful and deep process of negotiated political alteration" from above.[22] But because the elites (intellectuals and national political actors), as the agents of this strategy, are not as yet ready to face the challenge, then the whole strategy of political transformation, in the end, collapses into the "realistic solution" of a "western-supported project of gradual and moderate reform aiming at liberalization in Arab countries."[23] How far this strategy differs from the U.S.-driven idea of a "greater Middle East" remains unclear.

It would be naive to underestimate the enormous challenge facing those who wish to transform the region, and the authors of the *Report* seem to understand this. Yet Arabs are likely to question the wisdom behind this "realistic solution." Why should they expect the West to step in democratizing their region, other than for pursuing its own selfish interests? Why should the United States pursue changing the authoritarian Arab regimes (e.g., Saudi Arabia) if that would further escalate opposition to its vital economic and strategic interests in the region? Would such a "foreign-driven" initiative not be dismissed by the Arab states on the grounds that it interferes in their internal affairs? Of course, this is not to dismiss, a priori, any possible international solidarity and support (whether from foreign states or civil society organizations) for a project of political change. The point, rather, is to explore how to manage foreign support. Foreign support may be legitimately utilized if it is initiated in association with endogenous democracy movements in the Arab countries. Even a negotiated political change "from above" is not far-fetched if there exist social movements that would compel the power elites to negotiate toward what is currently termed "democratization by pact," as in Mexico, Chile, and elsewhere.[24] The fact that President Mubarak of Egypt accepted in February 2005 to allow rival candidates to run against him in the presidential elections had less to do with western pressure than with a nascent but vocal Kifaya ("enough is enough") movement, which instigated international momentum to bear on the Egyptian regime. Likewise, the Syrian withdrawal from Lebanon in 2005 resulted not directly from the western push, but primarily from a Lebanese popular movement, which in turn galvanized foreign support and pressure.

Yet despite their crucial role, the *Report* shows little interest in the ideas of social movements or grassroots mobilization for political transformation. For instance, to raise the status of Arab women, the *Report* not only advocates a series of legislative, institutional, religious/discursive, and economic (poverty reduction) reforms, but also envisages a "societal movement" at the national and regional levels, taking health care and education for girls as its prime focus, and establishing partnership with the governments, NGOs, the UN, and other international organizations. But this notion of "societal movement" consisting, presumably, of collective efforts and networks remains exceedingly broad and unmistakably depoliticized, rendering it distinct from a "social movement" as we understand it in political sociology. It appears, then, that speaking of popular movements or mobilization—and this displays one further instance of the schizophrenia of the *Report*—may imply radicalism and disorder, thus dismaying Arab officialdom or standing contrary to the "neutral" discursive package of the UN or the World Bank. Politics from below, therefore, has to be avoided.

This "elitist" approach in the *Report* not only derives from a distrust of "politics from below"; it has also related to the authors' liberal imagination of the "state" as the neutral apparatus representing the public interests, a notion deeply embedded in the conceptual paradigms that inform the general visions of the UNDP and World Bank. Here, the authoritarianism of the Arab states becomes simply a pathological matter—the states are either "benign but irrational" or "rational but ignorant" entities, which in either case can be put on the right path by proper counsel, sound legislation, or pressure from outside. This understanding, in particular the authors' overemphasis on legalities, clearly overlooks the *vested interests* behind those who cling to the status quo. Even a few women driving in the streets of Riyadh cause havoc within the Saudi regime, let alone acceptance of democracy, which can lead to the end of the monarchy. I do not wish to preclude the possibility of enhancing social development, democratic governance, rule of law, and fundamental freedoms in the region. On the contrary, I wish to stress that achieving these objectives is highly complex, closely tied to the structures of power, vested interests, and, above all, social struggles—themes that we will explore in the following chapters.[25]

SOCIAL NONMOVEMENTS

Part 1

3 THE QUIET ENCROACHMENT OF THE ORDINARY

NOTWITHSTANDING some overestimated claims of the globalization thesis (such as the waning role of nation-states, the breakdown of borders, the homogeneity of lifestyles, cultures, political systems, and so on),[1] it is generally agreed that the economics of globalization, comprised of a global market "discipline," flexible accumulation, and "financial deepening," has had a profound impact on postcolonial societies.[2] One major consequence of the new global restructuring in the developing countries has been a double process of, on the one hand, integration and, on the other, social exclusion and informalization.

The historic shift in the periphery from socialist and populist regimes into liberal economic policies, through the Economic Reform and Structural Adjustment Program, has led to the erosion of much of the social contract, collective responsibility, and welfare state structures. Thus, millions of people in the global South who depended on state provisions must now rely on themselves to survive. Deregulation of prices on housing, rent, and utilities jeopardizes many poor people's security of tenure, subjecting them to the risk of homelessness. Reduction of spending on social programs means shrinking access to decent education, health care, urban development, and government housing. Gradual removals of subsidies on bread, bus fares, and petrol have affected radically the living standard of millions of vulnerable groups. In the meantime, in a drive for privatization, public sectors have either been sold out or "reformed," which in either case has caused massive layoffs without a clear

Adapted from "From 'Dangerous Classes' to 'Quiet Rebels': Politics of the Urban Subaltern in the Global South," *International Sociology* 15, no. 3 (2000), pp. 533–57.

prospect of boosting the economy and creating viable jobs. According to the World Bank, in the early 1990s, during the transition to market economies in postsocialist, adjusting Latin American and Middle Eastern countries, formal employment fell by 5 percent to 15 percent.[3] In Africa the number of unemployed grew by 10 percent each year throughout the 1980s, while labor absorption in the formal wage sector kept declining.[4] By the late 1990s, a staggering one billion workers representing one-third of the world's labor force, most of them in the South, were either unemployed or underemployed.[5] A large number of once educated, well-to-do middle classes (professionals, government employees, and students) and public-sector workers, as well as segments of the peasantry, have been pushed into the ranks of the urban poor in labor and housing markets.

Thus, accompanied by the development of highly affluent groups, the new structuring has given rise to the growth of a marginalized and deinstitutionalized subaltern in Third World cities. There is now an increasing number of unemployed, partially employed, and casual labor, street-subsistence workers, street children, and members of the underworld—groups that have been interchangeably referred to as "urban marginals," "urban disenfranchised," and "urban poor." Such socially excluded and informal groups are by no means new historical phenomena. However, the recent global restructuring seems to have intensified and extended their operation. In the 1998 financial crisis at least two million people lost their jobs in South Korea, as did three million in Thailand, and a staggering ten million in Indonesia.[6] What is novel about this era is the marginalization of a large segment of middle classes. Slum dwelling, casual work, under-the-table payment, and street hawking are no longer just the characteristics of the traditional poor but also are spread among the educated young people with higher status, aspirations, and social skills—government employees, teachers, and professionals.

How does this growing urban grass roots in the Third World respond to the larger social and economic processes that affect their lives, if and when it does? Those who promote globalization suggest that the trickle-down of an eventual national economic growth will in the long run compensate for the inevitable sacrifices that the poor make in the transitional phase. In the meantime, social funds, NGOs and emergency aid are encouraged to create jobs and assist in social programs to alleviate the hardships and avert possible social unrest. Indeed, some view the upsurge of the NGOs in the South since the 1980s as a manifestation of organized activism and grassroots institutions for social development. However, granting that the development NGOs vary considerably, their potential for independent and democratic organization of development for the poor has generally been overestimated. As Neil Webster, reporting on India, has noted, advocates simply tend to expect too much from the development NGOs,[7] and by doing so underestimate their structural constraints (e.g., organizational rationale, unaccountability, and professional middle-class leadership) for a meaningful development strategy. My own work on Middle Eastern development NGOs supports this conclusion. The professionalization of the NGOs tends to diminish the mobilizational feature of grassroots activism while it establishes new form of clientelism (see Chapter 4).

Many on the Left point to a number of "reactive movements" (identity politics) that, they say, challenge globalization by appropriating technologies that it offers. While Alberto Melluci's "new social movements" focuses exclusively on the "highly differentiated" western societies, others who, like Manuel Castells and Ankie Hoogvelt, take a southern perspective suggest religious, ethnic, and feminist movements as well as the Latin American postdevelopment ideas as the backbone of antiglobalization forces. Identity movements do take up some of the challenges of globalization in postcolonial societies. However, they reflect more the sentiments of the middle-class intellectuals than the actual everyday practices of the ordinary people. What do the grass roots think or do? What form of politics, if any, do the urban marginalized groups espouse?

Critically navigating through the prevailing models, including culture of poverty, survival strategy, urban social movements, and everyday resistance, I would suggest that the new global restructuring is reproducing subjectivities (marginalized and deinstitutionalized groups such as the impoverished middle classes, the unemployed, casual labor, street-subsistence workers and street children), social space, and thus terrain of political struggles that current theoretical perspectives cannot on their own account for. I propose an alternative outlook—"quiet encroachment"—that I think might be more pertinent to examining the activism of the marginalized groups in the cities of the postcolonial societies. *Quiet encroachment* refers to noncollective but prolonged direct actions of dispersed individuals and families to acquire the basic necessities of their lives (land for shelter, urban collective consumption or urban services, informal work, business opportunities, and public space) in a quiet and unassuming illegal fashion. This perspective has emerged out of my observation of urban processes in the Muslim Middle East with its specific social and political structures; nevertheless, it might have relevance to other Third World cities.

PREVAILING PERSPECTIVES

The sociological examination of urban "marginality" dates back to nineteenth-century Europe. Problems associated with urbanization (crime, inner-city conditions, unemployment, migration, cultural duality, and so on) acquired scientific treatment from the social science community. Georg Simmel's "the stranger" dealt with sociopsychological traits of new urban settlers, and Durkheim was particularly keen on their "anomie." Such a conceptualization later informed the work of the Chicago School of Sociology and Urban Study in the United States during the 1920s and 1930s, when Chicago served as the laboratory for examining the social behavior of its many ethnic immigrants. For Everett Stonequist and Robert Park, many immigrants were "marginals"—a trait that was embedded in their social structure. Marginal personality was a manifestation of cultural hybridity, living on the margins of two cultures without being a full member of either.

Unlike the Chicago School functionalists, the mainstream Marxists, however, did not take the issue seriously. Relative to the centrality of the working class as the agent of the social transformation, Marxist theory either ignored the urban poor or described them as "lumpenproletariat," the "non-proletarian" urban groups, a term used by Marx himself; but, as Hal Draper notes, it gave rise to "endless misunderstanding and mistranslation."[8] For Marx, the lumpenproletariat was a political economy category. It referred to propertyless people who did not produce—"non-working proletariat," obsolete social elements such as beggars, thieves, thugs, and criminals who were in general poor but lived on the labor of other working people. Due to their economic existence, they were said to follow a politics of noncommitment, which in the end may work against the interests of the producing classes.[9] It is this uncertain politics that renders the lumpenproletariat, for both Marx and Engels, the "social scum," "refuse of all classes," the "dangerous classes." Although Marx theorized them later in terms of the "reserve army of labor," and thus a segment of the working class, controversy nevertheless continued as to the relevance of this concept in the current capitalist structuring, as it does not leave much chance for these people to be reemployed. Some suggested that far from being on "reserve," the urban disenfranchised were integrated into the capitalist relations.[10] Even with Frantz Fanon's passionate defense of lumpenproletariat as the revolutionary force in the colonies,[11] the Communist parties in the Third World did not go beyond looking at the urban marginals as the "toiling masses" who might have the potential for alliance with the working class.

However, the continuous prominence of the "informals" (which in many developing economies clearly outweighed the industrial working class) and their assumed threat to political stability in the developing countries returned them to academic analysis. Against the descriptive term of "informals" and the derogatory one of "lumpenproletariat," T. G. McGee and Robin Cohen opted for the notion of "proto-proletariat," and Peter Worsley "urban poor"—concepts that recognized some degree of agency.

More serious studies of the social conditions and the politics of the urban subaltern in the Third World emerged among U.S. social scientists during the 1960s. Modernization and urban migration in the developing countries had caused a dramatic expansion of impoverished urban settlements, and the growing urban "underclass" was thought to provide a breeding ground for the spread of radical guerrilla movements, which, in the midst of the cold war, were perceived to jeopardize the political interests of the United States and those of local elites. Political observers took the Chinese Revolution of 1949, the Cuban Revolution of 1959, and the growing guerrilla movements in parts of the Third World as convincing evidence. Latin America, however, acted as a laboratory for much-debated theories about the social and political behaviors of the urban underclass. Studies by Samuel Huntington and Joan Nelson, among others, reflected the concerns of the time.[12] Here, prevailing scholarship focused on the poor's "political threat" to the existing order. Scholars, mostly political scientists, were preoccupied with the question of whether the migrant poor constituted a destabilizing force. Joan Nelson argued that there was "no evidence that the new migrants are either radical or violence-prone."[13] Such preoccupations overlooked the dynamics of the poor's everyday life. Many viewed the politics of the poor in the binary terms of a revolutionary/passive dichotomy, consequently limiting how to look at the matter. Essentialism informed both sides of the controversy. The ensuing debates were galvanized in four identifiable perspectives: the "passive poor," "survival strategy," "urban territorial movement," and "everyday resistance" models.

The Passive Poor

While some observers working in the functionalist paradigm still viewed the urban poor as essentially disruptive and imbued with the sentiments of anomie, many considered the poor as a politically passive group struggling simply to make ends meet. Oscar Lewis's theory of a "culture of poverty," based upon ethnographies among the urban poor in Puerto Rico and Mexico, offered scientific legitimacy to such notion.[14] Highlighting certain cultural/psychological essentials as components of a culture of poverty—fatalism, traditionalism, rootlessness, unadaptability, criminality, lack of ambition, hopelessness, and so on—Lewis unintentionally extended the notion of the "passive poor." With an underlying emphasis on identifying the "marginal man" as cultural type, the "culture of poverty" remained a dominant perspective for many years, informing much of antipoverty discourse and policies in the United States as well as the Third World elites' perception of the poor.

The conceptual weaknesses of "culture of poverty," despite Lewis's empathy for the poor, became clear before long. Simply, Lewis essentialized the culture of the poor, since his "culture of poverty" was only one type of culture among many.[15] Lewis's generalization disregarded the varying ways in which the poor in different cultures handle poverty. Critiques such as Worsley's charged that Lewis was a middle-class scholar who blamed the poor for their poverty and passivity.[16] Interestingly, Lewis's conceptualization shared many traits with those of the Chicago School urban sociologists such as Stonequist and Robert Park and even the thinkers of an earlier generation like Simmel. Janice Perlman's powerful critique of the "myth of marginality" in 1976, together with Manuel Castells's critical contributions, undermined this outlook in academia, if not in officialdom. They demonstrated that the myth of marginality was an instrument of social control of the poor, and that the marginalized poor were a product of capitalist social structure.[17]

The Surviving Poor

As such, the "survival strategy" does not directly deal with the politics of the poor, but a relevant, implicit conceptual assumption underlies this perspective. The survival strategy model goes one step toward implying that although the poor are powerless, they do not sit around waiting for fate to determine their lives. Rather, they are active in their own way to ensure their survival. Thus, to counter unemployment or price increases, they often resort to theft, begging, prostitution, or the reorientation of their consumption pattern; to respond to famine and war, they choose to leave their homes even if emigration is discouraged by the authorities. In this thinking, the poor are seen to survive;

however, their survival is at the cost of themselves or their fellow humans.[18] While resorting to coping mechanisms in real life seems quite widespread among the poor in many cultures, an overemphasis on the language of survival strategy, as Escobar notes, may contribute to maintaining the image of the poor as victims, denying them any agency.[19] The fact is that poor people may also resist and make advances in their lives when the opportunity arises. Beyond that, evidence in many parts of the world does indicate that many of them also create opportunities for advancement—they organize and get involved in contentious politics. John Friedmann's notion of "empowerment" is indicative of just such an opportunity-creating tendency of the poor. It describes poor people's self-organization for collective survival through the institution of the household as the central element for the production of livelihood, the principle of moral economy (trust, reciprocity, voluntarism), and the utilization of their "social power" (free time, social skills, networking, associations, and instruments of production).[20]

The Political Poor

Critiques of "passive poor" and "culture of poverty" models opened the way for the development of an outlook in which the urban subaltern emerged as political actors—the "urban territorial movement" standpoint. Perlman, Castells, and some other scholars of Latin America insisted that the poor were not marginal, but integrated into the urban society. Rather, they argued, the poor were "marginalized"—economically exploited, politically repressed, socially stigmatized, and culturally excluded from a closed social system.[21] Not only did the poor participate in party politics, elections, and mainstream economic activities, more importantly, they establish their own territorial social movements. Thus, community associations, barrios, consumer organizations, soup kitchens, squatter support groups, church activities, and the like were understood as manifesting organized and territorially based movements of the poor who strive for "social transformation" (according to Castells), "emancipation" (according to Schuurmann and van Naerssen), or an alternative to the tyranny of modernity, in the words of John Friedmann.[22] In their immediate day-to-day activities, the poor struggle for a share in urban services, or "collective consumption."

The territorial character of these movements results from the mode of existence of the agents—the urban grass roots. Although quite differentiated (in terms of income, status, occupation, and production relations), the urban grass roots nevertheless are thought to share a common place of residence, community. Shared space and the needs associated with common property, then, offer these people the possibility of "spatial solidarity."[23] The attempts to highlight contentious politics as well as noncontentious cooperation among the urban poor undercut drastically both the "culture of poverty" and "survivalist" arguments, granting a significant agency to the urban subaltern. However, the "urban movement perspective" appears largely a Latin American model rooted in the sociopolitical conditions of this region. Not surprisingly, it is a perspective that has been offered primarily by scholars working in Latin America.[24] Local soup kitchens, neighborhood associations, church groups, or street trade unionism are hardly common phenomena in, say, the Middle East, Asia, or Africa (with the exception of countries like India and South Africa). In the Middle East, for instance, the prevalence of authoritarian states (of despotic, populist, or dictatorial kinds), which are wary of civil associations, together with the strength of family and kinship relations, render primary solidarities more pertinent than secondary associations and social movements. While collective entities such as the charity organizations and mosque associations do exist, they rarely lead to political mobilization of the popular classes. Although associations based upon neighborly relations, common origin and ethnic affiliation, or traditional credit systems are quite common, social networks that extend beyond kinship and ethnicity remain largely casual, unstructured, and paternalistic (see Chapter 4).

Some scholars tend to present the Islamist movements in the region as the Middle Eastern model of urban social movements. A few functional resemblances notwithstanding, the fact remains that the identity of Islamism does not derive from its particular concern for the urban disenfranchised. Islamism in general has broader aims and objectives. Unlike the Catholic Church, in particular the liberation theology movement, the Islamist movements tend often to mobilize not the poor, but largely the educated middle classes, which they view as the main agents of political change.[25] So it is mainly in exceptional circumstances (e.g., crises and revolutionary situations) that some degree of mobilization and contentious politics is encouraged, as in revolutionary Iran and the crisis-stricken Algeria. It is true that the Islamist Rifah Party in Turkey mobilized slum dwellers; this was so primarily because Turkey's free electoral system had granted the urban grass roots voting power, and thus a bargaining leverage that the Islamists as a legitimate political party could utilize.

Still, one must realize that the prevalence of urban movements in Latin America varies considerably. As Leeds and Leeds have shown, due to the multiplicity of competing interest groups (government, private interests, and others) the grass roots have had more opportunity for collective action in Peru than in Brazil, where the extremity of constraints forced the poor to "seek their betterment through the paternalistic, individualistic channels of favors and exchange of interests."[26] In Chile, in episodes of political openness and radical groupings, the poor have been organized more extensively.

The Resisting Poor

The dearth of conventional collective action—in particular, contentious protests among the subaltern groups (the poor, peasants, and women) in the developing countries, together with a disillusionment with dominant socialist parties, pushed many radical observers to "discover" and highlight different types of activism, however small-scale, local, or even individualistic. Such a quest, meanwhile, both contributed to and benefited from the upsurge of theoretical perspectives, during the 1980s, associated with poststructuralism that made micropolitics and "everyday resistance" a popular idea. James Scott's departure, during the 1980s, from a structuralist position in studying the behavior of the peasantry in Asia to a more ethnographic method of focusing on individual reactions of peasants contributed considerably to this paradigm shift.[27] In the meantime, Foucault's "decentered" notion of power, together with a revival of neo-Gramscian politics of culture (hegemony), served as a key theoretical backing for micropolitics, and thus the "resistance" perspective.

The notion of "resistance" came to stress that power and counterpower were not in binary opposition, but in a decoupled, complex, ambivalent, and perpetual "dance of control."[28] It based itself on the Foucauldian idea that "wherever there is power there is resistance," although the latter consisted largely of small-scale, everyday, tiny activities that the agents could afford to articulate given their political constraints. Such a perception of resistance penetrated not only peasant studies, but a variety of fields, including labor studies, identity politics, ethnicity, women's studies, education, and studies of the urban subaltern. Thus, multiple researchers discussed how relating stories about miracles "gives voice to popular resistance"[29]; how disenfranchised women resisted patriarchy by relating folktales and songs or by pretending to be possessed or crazy;[30] how reviving extended family among the urban popular classes represented an "avenue of political participation."[31] The relationships between the Filipino bar girls and western men were discussed not simply in terms of total domination, but in a complex and contingent fashion;[32] and the veiling of the Muslim working woman has been represented not in simple terms of submission, but in ambivalent terms of protest and co-optation— hence, an "accommodating protest."[33] Indeed, on occasions, both veiling and unveiling were simultaneously considered as a symbol of resistance.

Undoubtedly, such an attempt to grant agency to the subjects that until then were depicted as "passive poor," "submissive women," "apolitical peasant," and "oppressed worker" was a positive development. The resistance paradigm helps to uncover the complexity of power relations in society in general, and the politics of the subaltern in particular. It tells us that we may not expect a universalized form of struggle; that totalizing pictures often distort variations in people's perceptions about change; that local should be recognized as a significant site of struggle as well as a unit of analysis; that organized collective action may not be possible everywhere, and thus alternative forms of struggles must be discovered and acknowledged; that organized protest as such may not necessarily be privileged in the situations where suppression rules. The value of a more flexible, small-scale, and unbureaucratic activism should, therefore, be acknowledged.[34] These are some of the issues that critiques of poststructuralist advocates of "resistance" ignore.[35]

Yet a number of conceptual and political problems also emerge from this paradigm. The immediate trouble is how to conceptualize resistance, and its relation to power, domination, and submission. James Scott seems to be clear about what he means by the term:

> Class resistance includes *any* act(s) by member(s) of a subordinate class that is or are *intended* either to mitigate or deny claims (for example, rents, taxes, prestige) made on that class by superordinate classes (for example, landlords, large farmers, the state) or to advance its own claims (for example, work, land, charity, respect) vis-à-vis these superordinate classes.[36] [emphasis added]

However, the phrase "any act" blocks delineating between qualitatively diverse forms of activities that Scott lists. Are we not to distinguish between large-scale collective action and individual acts, say, of tax dodging? Do reciting poetry in private, however subversive-sounding, and engaging in armed struggle have identical value? Should we not expect unequal affectivity and implications from such different acts? Scott was aware of this, and so agreed with those who had made distinctions between different types of resistance—for example, "real resistance" refers to "organized, systematic, pre-planned or selfless practices with revolutionary consequences," and "token resistance" points to unorganized incidental acts without any revolutionary consequences, and which are accommodated in the power structure.[37] Yet he insisted that the "token resistance" is no less real than the "real resistance." Scott's followers, however, continued to make further distinctions. Nathan Brown, in studying peasant politics in Egypt, for instance, identifies three forms of politics: atomistic (politics of individuals and small groups with obscure content), communal (a group effort to disrupt the system, by slowing down production and the like), and revolt (just short of revolution to negate the system).[38]

Beyond this, many resistance writers tend to confuse an *awareness* about oppression with *acts* of resistance against it. The fact that poor women sing songs about their plight or ridicule men in their private gatherings indicates their understanding of gender dynamics. This does not mean, however, that they are involved in acts of resistance; neither are the miracle stories of the poor urbanites who imagine the saints to come and punish the strong. Such an understanding of "resistance" fails to capture the extremely complex interplay of conflict and consent, and ideas and action, operating within systems of power. Indeed, the link between consciousness and action remains a major sociological dilemma.[39]

Scott makes it clear that resistance is an intentional act. In Weberian tradition, he takes the meaning of action as a crucial element. This intentionality, while significant in itself, obviously leaves out many types of individual and collective practices whose intended and unintended consequences do not correspond. In Cairo or Tehran, for example, many poor families illegally tap into electricity and running water from the municipality despite their awareness of their behavior's illegality. Yet they do not steal urban services in order to express their defiance vis-à-vis the authorities. Rather, they do it because they feel the necessity of those services for a decent life, because they find no other way to acquire them. But these very mundane acts when continued lead to significant changes in the urban structure, in social policy, and in the actors' own lives. Hence, the significance of the unintended consequences of agents' daily activities. In fact, many authors in the resistance paradigm have simply abandoned intent and meaning, focusing instead eclectically on both intended and unintended practices as manifestations of "resistance."

There is still a further question. Does resistance mean *defending* an already achieved gain (in Scott's terms, denying claims made by dominant groups over the subordinate ones) or making fresh demands (to *"advance* its own claims"), what I like to call "encroachment"? In much of the resistance literature, this distinction is missing. Although one might imagine moments of overlap, the two strategies, however, lead to different political consequences; this is so in particular when we view them in relation to the strategies of dominant power. The issue was so crucial that Lenin devoted his entire *What Is to Be Done?* to discussing the implications of these two strategies, albeit in different terms of "economism/trade unionism" vs. "social democratic/party politics."

Whatever one may think about a Leninist/vanguardist paradigm, it was one that corresponded to a particular theory of the state and power (a capitalist state to be seized by a mass movement led by the working-class party); in addition, it was clear where this strategy wanted to take the working class (to establish a socialist state). Now, what is the perception of the state in the "resistance" paradigm? What is the strategic aim in this perspective? Where does the resistance paradigm want to take its agents/subjects, beyond "prevent[ing] the worst and promis[ing] something better"?[40]

Much of the literature of resistance is based upon a notion of power that Foucault has articulated, that power is everywhere, that it "circulates" and is never "localized here and there, never in anybody's hands."[41] Such a formulation is surely instructive in transcending the myth of the powerlessness of the ordinary and in recognizing their agency. Yet this "decentered" notion of power, shared by many poststructuralist "resistance" writers, underestimates state power, notably its class dimension, since it fails to see that although power circulates, it does so unevenly—in some places it is far weightier, more concentrated, and "thicker," so to speak, than in others. In other words, like it or not, the state does matter, and one needs to take that into account when discussing the potential of urban subaltern activism. Although Foucault insists that resistance is real when it occurs outside of and independent of the systems of power, the perception of power that informs the "resistance" literature leaves little room for an analysis of the state as a system of power. It is, therefore, not accidental that a theory of the state and, therefore, an analysis of the possibility of co-optation, are absent in almost all accounts of "resistance." Consequently, the cherished acts of resistance float around aimlessly in an unknown, uncertain, and ambivalent universe of power relations, with the end result an unsettled, tense accommodation with the existing power arrangement.

Lack of a clear concept of resistance, moreover, often leads writers in this genre to overestimate and read too much into the acts of the agents. The result is that almost any act of the subjects potentially becomes one of "resistance." Determined to discover the "inevitable" acts of resistance, many poststructuralist writers often come to "replace their subject."[42] While they attempt to challenge the essentialism of such perspectives as "passive poor," "submissive Muslim women," and "inactive masses," they tend, however, to fall into the trap of essentialism in reverse—by reading too much into ordinary behaviors, interpreting them as necessarily conscious or contentious acts of defiance. This is so because they overlook the crucial fact that these practices occur mostly within the prevailing systems of power.

For example, some of the lower class's activities in the Middle East that some authors read as "resistance," "intimate politics" of defiance, or "avenues of participation" may actually contribute to the stability and legitimacy of the state.[43] The fact that people are able to help themselves and extend their networks surely shows their daily activism and struggles. However, by doing so the actors may hardly win any space from the state (or other sources of power, like capital and patriarchy)—they are not necessarily challenging domination. In fact, governments often encourage self-help and local initiatives so long as they do not turn oppositional. They do so in order to shift some of their burdens of social welfare provision and responsibilities onto the individual citizens. The proliferation of many NGOs in the global South is a good indicator of this. In short, much of the resistance literature confuses what one might consider coping strategies (when the survival of the agents is secured at the cost of themselves or that of fellow humans) and effective participation or subversion of domination.

There is a last question. If the poor are always able to resist in many ways (by discourse or actions, individual or collective, overt or covert) the systems of domination, then what is the need to assist them? If they are already politically able citizens, why should we expect the state or any other agency to empower them? Misreading the behavior of the poor may, in fact, frustrate our moral responsibility toward the vulnerable. As Michael Brown rightly notes, when you "elevate the small injuries of childhood to the same moral status as suffering of truly oppressed," you are committing "a savage leveling that diminishes rather than intensifies our sensitivities to injustice."[44]

THE QUIET ENCROACHMENT OF THE ORDINARY

Given the shortcomings of the prevailing perspectives—that is, the essential-ism of the "passive poor," the reductionism of "survival strategy," the Latino-centrism of the "urban social movement model," and the conceptual perplex-ity of "resistance literature"—I like to assess the politics of the urban marginals in the developing world from a different angle, in terms of "the quiet en-croachment of the ordinary." I believe that this notion might be able to over-come some of those inadequacies and better capture the important aspect of urban subaltern politics in conditions of globalization.[45]

The notion of "quiet encroachment" describes the silent, protracted, but pervasive advancement of the ordinary people on the propertied, powerful, or the public, in order to survive and improve their lives. They are marked by quiet, largely atomized and prolonged mobilization with episodic collective action—open and fleeting struggles without clear leadership, ideology, or structured organization. While quiet encroachment cannot be considered a "social movement" as such, it is also distinct from survival strategies or "every-day resistance" in that, first, the struggles and gains of the agents are not at the cost of fellow poor or themselves (as is the case in survival strategies), but of the state, the rich, and the powerful. Thus, in order to illuminate their shel-ters, the urban poor tap electricity, not from their neighbors, but from the municipal power poles; to raise their living standard, they would not prevent their children from attending school in order to work, but rather squeeze the timing of their formal job, in order to carry on their secondary work in the informal sector.

In addition, these struggles are seen not necessarily as defensive merely in the realm of *resistance*, but cumulatively encroaching, meaning that the actors tend to expand their space by winning new positions to move on. This type of quiet and gradual grassroots activism tends to contest many fundamental as-pects of the state prerogatives, including the meaning of order, control of pub-lic space, of public and private goods, and the relevance of modernity.

I am referring to the lifelong struggles of the floating social clusters—the migrants, refugees, unemployed, underemployed, squatters, street vendors, street children, and other marginalized groups, whose growth has been ac-celerated by the process of economic globalization. I have in mind the pro-tracted processes in which millions of men and women embark on long mi-gratory journeys, scattering in remote and often alien environs, acquiring

work, shelter, land, and living amenities. The refugees and international migrants encroach on host states and their provisions, the rural migrants on the
cities and their collective consumption, the squatters on public and private
lands or ready-made homes, and the unemployed, as street-subsistence workers, on the pubic space and business opportunity created by shopkeepers. Thus,
millions of rural migrants, the urban poor, and the impoverished middle class
quietly claim state/public lands on the outskirts of the cities or take over cemeteries, rooftops, and other urban spaces creating vibrant spontaneous communities and informal life. Once settled, encroachments continue in many
directions. Counter to formal terms and conditions, the residents add rooms,
balconies, and extra space in and on buildings. Those who have formally been
given housing in public projects built by the state illegally redesign and rear-
range their space to suit their needs by erecting partitions, and by adding and
inventing new space.[46] Often, whole communities emerge as a result of intense
struggles and negotiations between the poor and the authorities and elites in
their daily lives.[47]

Within such communities, the encroachers tend to compel the authorities
to extend urban services to their neighborhoods by otherwise tapping them
illegally, using them free of charge. However, once utilities are installed, many
simply refuse to pay for their use. Some 40 percent of poor residents of Hayy
el-Sellom, a south Beirut informal community, for instance, refused to pay
their electric bills in the late 1990s. Similar stories are reported in urban Chile
and South Africa, where the poor have periodically refused to pay for urban
public services after struggling to acquire them, often against the authorities'
will. Millions of street vendors in the cities of the global South have occupied
the streets in the main commercial centers, infringing on favorable business
opportunities the shopkeepers have generated. Large numbers of inhabitants
in these cities subsist on tips from parking cars in streets that they control and
organize in such elaborate ways as to create maximum parking space. Finally,
as in many Third World cities, such as those in South Korea, the encroachment of the street vendors on copyrights of labels and trademarks has invariably caused protests by multinational companies.[48]

As state employees and professionals, the previously privileged segments
of the workforce, feel the crunch of neoliberal policies, they too resort to their
own repertoires of quiet encroachment. Thus, to compensate for their meager
monthly salary, the schoolteachers in Egypt, for instance, turn to private paid
tutoring of their own pupils. By doing so, they have created a massive sector of

illegal private teaching that generated in early 2000 some EL12 billion ($3 billion) a year, and at least 25 percent of the annual earning of Egyptian families."[49] Similarly, "street lawyers" or "unregistered practitioners" may encroach on the legal profession. These street lawyers do not hold law degrees but have acquired some legal knowledge by working as employees in law offices. They then share their legal experience with new law graduates (who cannot afford the high cost of establishing law offices) to offer competitive services.[50]

These actors carry out their activities not as deliberate political acts; rather, they are driven by the force of necessity—the necessity to survive and improve life. Necessity is the notion that justifies their often unlawful acts as moral and even "natural" ways to maintain a life with dignity. Yet these very simple and seemingly mundane practices tend to shift them into the realm of contentious politics. The contenders become engaged in collective action and see their actions and themselves as political chiefly when they are confronted by those who threaten their gains. Hence, a key attribute of quiet encroachment is that while advances are made quietly, individually, and gradually, the defense of their gains is often, although not always, collective and audible.

Driven by the force of necessity (effects of economic restructuring, agricultural failure, physical hardship, war, and displacement), these actors set out on their ventures rather individually, often organized around kinship and friendship ties, and without much clamor. They even deliberately avoid collective effort, large-scale operation, commotion, and publicity. At times the squatters, for instance, prevent others from joining them in specific areas; and vendors discourage their counterparts from settling in the same vicinity. Many even hesitate to share with similar groups information about their strategies of acquiring urban services. Yet as these seemingly disparate individuals and families pursue similar paths, their sheer cumulative numbers turn them into an eventual social force. This is another feature of quiet encroachment.

But why individual and quiet direct action, instead of collective demand making? Unlike the factory workers, students, or professionals, these people represent groups in flux and structurally operate largely outside institutional mechanisms through which they can express grievances and enforce demands. They lack an organizational power of disruption—the possibility of going on strike, for example. They may participate in street demonstrations or riots as part of a general expression of popular discontent, but only when these methods enjoy a reasonable currency and legitimacy (as in the immediate postrevolutionary Iran, Beirut during the civil war, or after the fall of Suharto in Indo nesia in 1998), and when they are mobilized by outside leaders. Thus, urban land takeovers may be led by left-wing activists; and the unemployed and street vendors may be invited to form unions (as in Iran after the revolution, in Lima, or in India). This, however, represents an uncommon phenomenon, since more often than not, mobilization for collective demand making is prevented by political repression in many developing countries, where these struggles often take place. Consequently, in place of protest or publicity, these groups move directly to fulfill their needs by themselves, albeit individually and discreetly. In short, theirs is *not* a politics of protest, but of redress, struggle for an immediate outcome through individual direct action.

What do these men and women aim for? They seem to pursue two major goals. The first is the *redistribution of social goods* and opportunities in the form of the (unlawful and direct) acquisition of collective consumption (land, shelter, piped water, electricity, roads), public space (street pavements, intersections, street parking places), opportunities (favorable business conditions, locations, labels, licenses), and other life-chances essential for survival and acceptable standards of living.

The other goal is *attaining autonomy*, both cultural and political, from the regulations, institutions, and discipline imposed by the state and modern institutions. In a quest for an informal life, the marginals tend to function as much as possible outside the boundaries of the state and modern bureaucratic institutions, basing their relationships on reciprocity, trust, and negotiation rather than on the modern notions of individual self-interest, fixed rules, and contracts. Thus, they may opt for jobs in self-employed activities rather than working under the discipline of the modern workplace; resort to informal dispute resolution than reporting to police; get married through local informal procedures (in the Muslim Middle East under local sheikhs) rather than by governmental offices; borrow money from informal credit associations rather than modern banks. This is so not because these people are essentially non- or antimodern, but because the conditions of their existence compel them to seek an informal mode of life. Because modernity is a costly existence, not everyone can afford to be modern. It requires the capacity to conform to the types of behavior and mode of life (adherence to strict discipline of time, space, contracts, and so on) that most vulnerable people simply cannot afford. So while the disenfranchised wish to watch color TV, enjoy clean tap water, and possess the security of tenure, they are weary of paying taxes and bills or reporting to work at specified times (see Chapter 9).

But how far can the urban subaltern exercise autonomy in the conditions of globalization, amid expanding integration? The fact is that not only do the poor seek autonomy, they also need security, that is, freedom from the state's surveillance, because an informal life in the conditions of modernity is also an insecure life. To illustrate, street vendors may feel free from the discipline of modern working institutions, but they suffer from police harassment for lacking business permits. The struggle of the poor to consolidate their communities, to have schools, clinics, or sewerage would inevitably integrate them into the prevailing systems of power (i.e., the state and modern bureaucratic institutions) that they wish to avoid. In their quest for security, the urban poor are in constant negotiation and vacillation between autonomy and integration. Yet they continue to pursue autonomy in any possible space available within the integrating structures and processes.

BECOMING POLITICAL

If encroachment begins with little political meaning attached to it, if illegal acts are often justified on moral grounds, then how does it turn into a collective/political struggle? So long as the actors carry on with their everyday advances without being confronted seriously by any authority, they are likely to treat their advances as ordinary, everyday exercises. However, once their gains are threatened, they tend to become conscious of their doings and the value of their gains, defending them in often collective and audible fashion. Examples may be found in the mobilization of the squatters in Tehran in 1976, and of the street vendors in the 1980s, and street riots by the squatters in several cities in the early 1990s. Alternatively, the actors may retain their gains through quiet noncompliance, without necessarily engaging in collective resistance. Instead of collectively standing by their businesses, the mobile street vendors in Cairo or Istanbul simply retreat into the backstreets once the municipal police arrive, and they immediately resume their work when the police are gone. At any rate, the struggles of the actors against the authorities are *not* about gaining, but primarily about defending and furthering already-won gains. But they almost invariably involve state power.

The state's position vis-à-vis this type of activism is affected, first, by the extent of their capacity to exercise surveillance and, second, by the dual nature of quiet encroachment (infringing on property, power, and privilege and, at the same time, being a self-help activity). Third World states seem to be more tolerant of quiet encroachment than are those in the industrialized countries such as the United States, where similar activities, albeit very limited, also take place. The industrial states are by far better equipped with ideological, technological, and institutional apparatuses to conduct surveillance of their populations. In other words, people have more room for autonomy under the vulnerable and "soft states" of the global South than in the advanced industrialized countries, where tax evasion, infringement of private property, and encroachment on the state domains are considered serious offenses.

On the other hand, quiet encroachment, although it is an infringement on the public, property, and power, may in many ways benefit Third World governments, for it is a mechanism through which the poor come to help themselves. It is no surprise, then, that these governments often express contradictory reactions toward these kinds of activities. The "soft" and vulnerable states, especially at times of crisis, tend in practice to allow the encroachments when the latter still appear limited. On their part, the encroachers attempt constantly to appear limited and tolerable while in fact expanding so much that resistance against them becomes formidable. They do so by resorting to tactical retreats, going invisible, bribing the officials, or concentrating on particular and less strategic spaces (for instance, squatting in remote areas or vending in less visible locations).

However, once their real expansion and impact are revealed, when the cumulative growth of the actors and their doings passes beyond a tolerable point, the state crackdown becomes expectable. Yet in most cases the crackdowns fail to yield much, since they are usually launched too late, when the encroachers have already spread, becoming visible and past the point of no return. Indeed, the description by the officials of these processes as "cancerous" brings home the dynamics of such nonmovements.

The sources of conflict between the actors and the state are not difficult to determine. First, the often "informal" and free-of-charge distribution of public goods exerts a heavy pressure on the resources that the state controls. Besides, the rich—the real estate owners, merchants, and shopkeepers—also lose properties, brands, and business opportunities. The alliance of the state and the propertied groups adds a class dimension to the conflict. On the other hand, the actors' drive for autonomy in everyday life creates a serious void in the domination of the modern state. Autonomous life renders the modern states, in particular the populist versions, rather irrelevant. Moreover, autonomy and informality (of agents, activities, and spaces) deprive the states of the knowledge necessary to exert surveillance. Unregulated jobs, unregistered peoples and places, nameless streets and alleyways, and policeless neighbor-hoods mean that these entities remain hidden from the government's books. To be able to control them, the states need to make them transparent. Indeed, programs of squatter upgrading may be seen in terms of this strategy of open-ing up the unknown in order to be able to control it. Conflict between these encroachers and the state, therefore, is inevitable.

Nowhere is this conflict more evident than in the "streets," this public space par excellence. Since the "streets" serve as the only locus of collective expression for, but by no means limited to, those who generally lack an insti-tutional setting to express discontent, including squatters, the unemployed, street-subsistence workers, street children, members of the underworld, and housewives. Whereas factory workers or college students, for instance, may cause disruption by going on strike, the unemployed or street vendors can voice grievances only in the public spaces, the streets. Indeed, for many of these disenfranchised, the streets are the main, perhaps the only, place where they can perform their daily functions—to assemble, make friends, earn a living, spend their leisure time, and express discontent. In addition, streets are also the public places where the state has the most evident presence, which is expressed in police patrol, traffic regulations, and spatial divisions—in short, in public order. The dynamics of the power relationship between the encroachers and the authorities are what I have termed "street politics." By "street politics," I mean a set of conflicts and the attendant implications between a collective populace and the authorities, which are shaped and expressed episodically in the physical and social space of the "streets," from alleyways to the more visible street sidewalks, public parks, and pub-lic sport facilities. It describes the articulation of discontent by people who operate usually outside the modern institutions (like the unemployed, or casual workers or housewives); or by those groups who may enjoy the insti-tutional settings (such as factory workers or students), but wish to gain support and solidarity beyond the confines of their institutions among the general public.[51]

Two key factors render the streets an arena of politics. First is the use of public space as a site of contestation between the actors and the authorities. In this sense, what makes the streets a political site is the active or participative (as opposed to passive) use of public space. This is so because these sites (side-walks, public parks, intersections, etc.) are increasingly becoming the domain of the state power, which regulates their use, making them "orderly." It expects the users to operate them passively. An active use challenges the authority of the state and those social groups that benefit from such order.

The second element shaping street politics is the operation of what I have called the "passive network" among the people who use and operate in the public space. By "passive network" I mean an instantaneous communication among atomized individuals that is established by a tacit recognition of their common identity, and which is mediated through real and virtual space. When a woman enters a party full of male guests, she instantaneously notices another woman at that party. Vendors on a street are most likely to recognize one another even if they never meet or talk. Now when a threat occurs to the women in the party or the vendors in the street, they are likely to get together even if they do not know each other or have not planned to do so in advance. The significance of this concept lies in the possibility of imagining mobilization of atomized individuals, such as the quiet encroachers, who are largely deprived of organizations and deliberate networking. "Passive network" implies that individuals may be mobilized to act collectively without active or deliberately constructed networks. Street as a public space has this intrinsic feature that makes it possible for people to become mobilized through establishing passive networks. Once the individual actors, the encroachers, are confronted by a threat, their passive network is likely to turn into an active communication and cooperation. That is how an eviction threat or a police raid may immediately bring together squatters or street vendors who did not even know one another. Of course, the shift from passive network to collective resistance is never a given. Actors might feel that tactical retreat would yield far better result than confrontation, a tendency common in today's Cairo's streets, but uncommon in the revolutionary Iran, where on-the-spot collective resistance prevailed.[52]

I suggested at the outset that a major consequence of the new global restructuring has been a double process of integration, on the one hand, and social exclusion and informalization, on the other. Both processes tend to generate discontent on the part of many urban grass roots in the global South. First, there are many among the urban grass roots who find it difficult to function, live, and work, within the modernizing economic and cultural systems characterized by market discipline, contract, exchange value, speed, and bureaucracy, including the state organizations. These people attempt to exit from such social and economic arrangements, seeking alternative and more familiar, or informal, institutions and relations. Second, globalization has also a tendency to informalize through programs of structural adjustment, rendering many people unemployed or pushing them to seek refuge in informal production, trade, housing, and transportation. Transnational street vendors (circulating, for instance, between the new Central Asian republics and Istanbul, or between Jamaica and Miami) are the latest product of this age. In short, the new global restructuring tends to intensify the growth of subjectivities, social space, and terrain of political struggles that are coming to characterize the cities of the developing world.

Although the prevailing perspectives (survival strategy, urban social movements, and everyday resistance) provide useful angles to view the activism of the urban subaltern, they do, however, suffer from major drawbacks, as discussed earlier. I suggested that the "quiet encroachment" perspective might offer a way out of those conceptual problems. From this vantage point, the poor not only struggle for survival, but strive in a lifelong process to improve their lot through often individualistic and quiet encroachment on the public goods and on the power and property of the elite groups. In this process, the grass roots do not directly challenge the effect of globalization. Rather, in their quest for security, they get involved in constant negotiations with globalization to maintain or seek autonomy in any space remaining unaffected. At the same time, in this process, the unintended consequences of their daily encroachments and negotiations beget significant social changes in urban structure and processes, in demography, and in public policy. We saw earlier how crucial such a strategy is in the lives of the urban grass roots. Yet the question remains as to how far this quiet encroachment can take these actors.

Given their existential constraints (poor skills and education or meager income, connection, and organization), quiet encroachment serves as a viable enabling strategy for the marginalized groups to survive and better their lot. However, this nonmovement neither is able to cause broader political transformation nor aims to. The larger national movements have the capacity for such a transformation. Yet, compared to global/national mobilization, these localized struggles are both *meaningful* and *manageable* for the actors–meaningful in that they can make sense of the purpose and have an idea of the consequences of these actions; and manageable in that *they*, rather than some remote national leaders, set the agenda, project the aims, and control the outcome. In this sense for the poor, the local is privileged over the global/national.

It is true that the disenfranchised succeed relatively in extending their life-chances, often through lifetime struggles; nevertheless, crucial social spaces remain out of their control. The poor may be able to take over a plot of land to build shelters, may tap running water or electricity illegally from the main street or neighbors; they may secure a job on the street corner by selling things and may be able to bribe or dodge the municipal police every now and then. But how can they get schools, health services, public parks, paved roads, and security—the social goods that are tied to larger structures and processes, the national states, and the global economy? In other words, the largely atomistic and localist strategies of the disenfranchised, despite their own advantages, render a search for social justice in the broader, national sense poorly served. The urban grass roots are unlikely to become a more effective player in a larger sense unless they become mobilized on a collective basis, their struggles linked to broader social movements and civil-society organizations.[53] Yet it is crucial to stress that until this is realized and its result is tested, quiet encroachment remains a most viable enabling strategy, which the urban disenfranchised pursue to cause change in their own lives, and in the domains of social policy, urban governance, and public order.

4 THE POOR AND THE PERPETUAL PURSUIT OF LIFE CHANCES

HOW DO the Middle Eastern poor manage to live in the current new-liberal times, and what does their life struggle mean to urban politics in the region? Prior to the advent of the political-economic restructuring of the 1980s, most Middle Eastern countries were largely dominated by either nationalist-populist regimes (such as Egypt, Syria, Iraq, Libya, Sudan, and Turkey) or pro-western rentier states (Iran, the Arab Gulf states). Financed by oil or remittances, these largely authoritarian states pursued state-led development strategies, attaining remarkable (21 percent average annual) growth rates.[1] Income from oil offered the rentier states the possibility of providing social services to many of their citizens, and the ideologically driven populist states dispensed significant benefits in education, health, employment, housing, and the like.[2] For these postcolonial regimes, such provision of social welfare was necessary to build popularity among the peasants, workers, and middle strata at a time that these states were struggling against both the colonial powers and old internal ruling classes. The state acted as the moving force of economic and social development on behalf of the populace.

The authoritarian nature of these states restricted meaningful political participation and the development of effective civil-society organizations. The regimes' etatist ideology and patrimonial tendencies rendered the states the main, if not the sole, provider of livelihoods for many citizens, in exchange for their loyalty. In etatist models, the state controls the bulk of the economic, political, and social domains, leaving little space for society to develop itself and for interest groups to surface, compete, and act autonomously. In the Middle East, such ideology often led to the demobilization—or, at best, controlled mobilization—of certain segments of the population, as exemplified by the corporatist unions under Gamal Abdel Nasser and currently in Syria; the state-run syndicates under the Shah of Iran; the Islamic Associations under Ayatollah Khomeini; and the People's Councils in Libya.[3]

The advent of "liberalization" and marketization through the International Monetary Fund–sponsored Economic Reform and Structural Adjustment programs (ERSA) has, since the early 1990s, provoked important socioeconomic changes. Free-market economies have made consumer commodities vastly more accessible and have enriched the upper socioeconomic strata while also increasing income disparities and causing critical changes in labor markets. Informal and marginalized groups, such as the unemployed, casual workers, and street-subsistence laborers, have expanded. A large number of public-sector workers and rural laborers, as well as educated, once well-to-do members of the middle class (government employees and college students), have been pushed into the ranks of the urban poor in labor and housing markets.

In the meantime, states have gradually been retreating from the social responsibilities that characterized their early populist development. Many social provisions have been withdrawn, and the low-income groups largely have to rely on themselves to survive. For instance, in Egypt, state subsidies on certain basic foodstuffs such as rice, sugar, and cooking oil have been removed, and subsidies on items such as fuel, power, and transportation have been reduced. Rent control is being reconsidered; a new land law has ended tenant farmers' control over land; and pubic-sector reform and privatization continue, all with significant social costs. As early as 1993, a United States Agency for International Development report warned of the "deteriorating social conditions in Egypt."[4] Although certain social indicators such as life expectancy and infant mortality have improved, unemployment, poverty, and income gaps reportedly increased in the 1990s.[5] Similar changes are taking place in Jordan, resulting from a series of events such as the second Gulf War, which deepened the crisis there.[6] In Iran, the government has been vacillating between etatism and free-market policies since 1990. Compared with that in other countries in the region, the direction of economic liberalization in Iran has been slow, due partly to labor resistance and partly to the struggle among political factions. Although the Syrian economy remains predominantly under state control, the private sector is being allowed to expand gradually.[7]

Concurrent with these political-economic developments has been the globalization of the ideas of human rights and political participation, which have placed economic rights and citizen participation on the political agenda and subsequently helped to open new spaces for social mobilization. The inability of populist states to incorporate or suppress the new social forces (such as lower-middle and middle classes) that they have helped to generate has led to the growth of civil-society institutions. When states are unable to meet the needs of these classes, they resort to (and encourage the establishment of) civil associations to fulfill them.[8] Surveys on civil society in the Middle East suggest that, despite the authoritarian nature of many states, human rights activists, artists, writers, religious figures, and professional groups have brought pressure to bear on the governments for accountability and openness.[9]

These overall economic and social changes—notably, the deteriorating social conditions of the poor, on the one hand, and the expansion of the public sphere and civil institutions, on the other—raise some crucial questions. How do the grass roots in the Middle East react to their changing social and economic realities? And if they indeed confront their changing circumstance, what is the logic behind the shift in the nature of demands, sites of protests, and patterns of struggles in the region? To what extent is "pressure from below" required for meaningful policy change and institutional reform conducive to social development for defending people's livelihoods and rights? By addressing such questions, this chapter explores the ways in which the urban disenfranchised strive to defend their livelihoods and assert their right to the city. While past mass urban protests and labor unionism have failed to improve the living conditions of a large number of people, community activism has been feeble, and social Islam and NGOs address only some of the problems. Middle Eastern societies thus seem to foster *quiet encroachment* as a prevalent strategy that gives the urban grass roots some power over their own lives and influence over state policy.

URBAN MASS PROTESTS

The urban riots of the 1980s were an early expression of discontent with some aspects of neoliberal policies in the Middle East, as various countries tried to reduce their deficits through austerity policies, such as cuts in consumer subsidies. These reductions violated the social contract between the states and the masses, triggering anger and discontent. Although it is difficult to determine the precise profile of the participants, the urban middle and lower classes were among the main actors. In August 1983, the Moroccan government reduced consumer subsidies by 20 percent. Even though public-sector salaries were raised by an equal amount, riots broke out in northern Morocco and other regions. Similar riots occurred in Tunis in 1984 (89 killed) and in Khartoum in 1982 and 1985 (number of dead unknown). In the summer of 1987, Lebanese involved in the civil war got together to stage a massive demonstration in Beirut against the drop in the value of the Lebanese pound. Algeria was struck by cost-of-living riots in the fall of 1988, and Jordan experienced similar violence in 1989.[10] This list excludes many political protests that raised issues concerning individual freedoms, regional autonomy, and professional matters (e.g., at Egypt's Military Academy in 1986 and in the Iranian cities of Tabriz and Qazvin and, later, among students in 1999).

Despite the acceleration of neoliberal policies, urban mass protests ebbed noticeably during the 1990s. Several factors played a part. Alarmed by the earlier unrest, governments imposed tighter controls while delaying or implementing unpopular policies only gradually. Aside from internationally sponsored safety nets, such as the Social Fund for Development in Egypt and Jordan, additional outlets were offered by the growth of welfare NGOs and social Islam.

The experience of the Islamic Revolution and the war with Iraq distinguished Iran from its regional counterparts. While many regimes in the Middle East were shedding their populism during the 1980s and 1990s, Iran began to experience that only after the revolution. The Islamic regime's rhetoric in favor of the "downtrodden" contributed to the mobilization of the grass roots. The war suppressed internal dissent; once it ended, a new opportunity for collective activities, such as urban mass protests, arose. Thus, unlike the relatively quiet 1980s, six major protests took place in Tehran and other Iranian cities in the early 1990s. Riots in Tehran in August 1991 and in Shiraz and Arak in 1992 were carried out by squatters because of demolition of their shelters or forced evictions. Even more dramatic unrest took place in the city of Mashad in 1992 and Tehran's Islamshahr community in 1995. In Mashad, the protests were triggered by the municipality's rejection of demands by city squatters to legalize their communities. This massive unrest, on which the army failed to clamp down, left more than one hundred buildings and stores destroyed, three hundred people arrested, and more than a dozen people dead. The three-day riots in Islamshahr, a large informal community in South Tehran, in April 1995, had to do with the postwar economic austerity—notably, increases in bus fare and the price of fuel—under President Hashemi Rafsanjani.

Urban protests in the Middle East have had mixed results. Following immediate repression, governments in many cases have had to revoke unpopular measures (as in Egypt in 1977, Tunisia and Morocco in 1984, Sudan in 1985, Algeria in 1988, Jordan in 1989, and Iran on many occasions). At times, they have made tactical concessions, such as increasing wages; this, however, affects only wage earners, at the expense of the self-employed poor and the unemployed.[11] Where the protests are local or small-scale, the governments usually have managed to end them by force. In the early 1980s, workers in Kafr al-Dawwar in Egypt managed to fulfill only part of their demands. The Egyptian farmers' protests in 1998 across isolated villages failed to modify the new policy that ended tenant farmers' long-term control over land. However, when social protests have gained national support by embracing diverse issues and actors (such as students and the middle classes making economic as well as political claims), they often provoke significant changes, including political reform (as in Algeria, Jordan, Tunisia, and Turkey in the late 1980s).

Despite their drama and, at times, their remarkable impact, urban mass protests are usually spontaneous, ad hoc, and consequently uncommon; they often involve violence and a risk of repression. Urban riots are a response to the absence of effective institutionalized mechanisms of conflict resolution. The social groups without institutionally based power to disrupt (such as the unemployed, who cannot strike) and those who enjoy such power but find it inadequate (workers, students) are likely to follow leaders in initiating mass protests. This is not to say, as some have claimed, that Middle Eastern masses essentially lack a "truly collective life," resorting instead to "mob action."[12] For in favorable conditions, they also engage in modern forms of collective action, notably, trade unionism.

TRADE UNIONISM

Trade unionism represents an older and sustained institution through which working people have defended their rights or exerted pressure on economic elites and governments to bring about social change. Trade unions have the potential to respond rapidly and systematically to unjust labor practices, distributive issues, and political matters. At the same time, they are most affected by the current neoliberal economic policies, including new labor discipline and lay-offs which in the end undermine the power of the unions.

Originally, trade unions in the Middle East emerged in the context of European colonial domination. Their struggles, therefore, involved both class and nationalist dimensions—usually a tense strategic position. At independence, most trade-union organizations were integrated into the state structure or the ruling parties, resulting in the current situation, in which unitary, compulsory unions make up the majority of labor organizations. This type of union, in which public-sector workers constitute the core members, operates in countries with populist pasts (such as Algeria, Egypt, Iraq, Libya, and Syria) as well as in Kuwait and Yemen. The Arab Gulf states, using mostly foreign workers, impose tough discipline and disallow labor organizations in exchange for relatively high pay. Surveillance, however, has not prevented occasional outbreaks of labor unrest, such as the Palestinian workers' strike in the Saudi oil industry in the 1980s and the riots of Egyptian workers in Kuwait against discrimination in October 1999.[13] Only Jordan, Lebanon, Morocco, and Turkey have pluralist unions that are relatively independent from the state or ruling parties.

Union structure affects workers' ability to maintain their gains or to advance them. Independent unions, more than corporatist ones, are likely to defend workers' rights. However, in the experience of the region, workers tend to use the existing corporatist organizations to further their own interests, as shown in the state-controlled workers syndicates before the Iranian Revolution and workers' shuras and the Union of Unemployed Workers after.[14] This applies also to the corporatist trade unions in Egypt established by Nasser following the liberal era (1928–52), when labor unions enjoyed a period of relative independence.[15]

Currently, organized public-sector workers, more than any other group, feel the immediate consequences of economic adjustment. Thus, trade unions are concerned with and often struggle against cuts in consumer subsidies, price rises, reductions in wages and allowances, layoffs, and government interference in union affairs. A human-rights organization reported seventy strikes against large companies in Egypt during 1998, most of which involved state security forces. The main cause of the industrial actions was "government reform policy."[16] The Egyptian press, citing official statements, reported in early 1999 the occurrence of more than five strikes and sit-ins per week. These actions resulted largely from reductions in allowances and perquisites and the introduction of fines.[17] In Iran, the 1990s saw a rapid increase in worker strikes. During the first half of 1991, some two thousand strikes were reported.[18] According to one account, strikes by workers trying to catch up with inflation were so common that the authorities hardly noticed them.[19] New labor laws, redrafted to accord with the neoliberal era and economic realities, have been hotly contested, because they often strip workers of several traditional rights, notably, job security. In Egypt, the labor unions compelled government and business to accept in 1994 an exchange of "the right to strike for the right to fire."[20] In Iran, labor law remained a matter of dispute between the ruling clergy and pro-labor forces for more than a decade.

Some observers tend to underestimate the capacity of organized labor in the Middle East to affect social and political developments on the grounds that strikes, the workers' major weapon, are illegal and often involve the risk of arrest and imprisonment. In addition, they argue, states usually co-opt the leaderships of these largely corporatist labor unions, thus rendering union activism practically ineffective.[21] It is true that strikes are illegal, and labor leaders may be bought off, with many of them becoming part of the ruling parties and the state bureaucracy. However, as Posusney rightly argues, "labor has been able to pursue economic demands and wring concessions from the state, in spite of corporatist controls," and its ability to do so "is contingent on the specific issue at hand and how policy around that issue is made."[22] The fact is that even the corporatist leadership must be somehow responsive to the views and concerns of its rank and file. Not only do labor leaders often express opposition to certain government policies (e.g., removal of subsidies, privatization, aspects of labor law), but the rank and file tend to wage unofficial industrial action when the leadership fails to take the initiative. In Egypt, for instance, opposition by organized labor has been the main cause of delays in the implementation or renegotiation of terms of adjustment with the International Monetary Fund both currently and under previous governments.[23]

Notwithstanding its social and political impact, organized labor in the Middle East has continued to comprise only a small portion of the total workforce. The vast majority have been self-employed, with a large fraction of wage earners working in small workshops in which paternalistic labor relations prevail. Although tension between bosses and employees is not uncommon in these establishments, laborers are more likely to remain loyal to their bosses than to ally with their colleagues in the shop next door. On the whole, between one-third and one-half of the workforce in the cities (Egypt, 43%; Iran, 35%; Turkey, 36%; Yemen Arab Republic, 70%) are active in the informal sector and thus remain unorganized and beyond the provisions of labor law.[24] The economic restructuring of the 1980s has further undermined organized labor, as the public sector, the core of trade unionism, is shrinking because of closures, downsizing, and early retirements. Numerous reports point to the declining capacity of the region's labor movements to mobilize. Organized labor in Egypt, Lebanon, Morocco, Tunisia, and Iran is described as "disjointed," "defensive," "decapitated and de-proletarianized."[25] Sporadic unrest notwithstanding, labor is becoming more informal and fragmented, with less or no protection, and dispersed across vast arrays of activities and spaces among the unemployed, casual workers, and domestic labor, in the small workshops, and on street corners.[26]

COMMUNITY ACTIVISM

For the urban grass roots, then, urban community or neighborhood may offer a sense of common identity and a ground for collective action in the stead of the workplace. For in the neighborhoods, most face the same difficulties in ensuring secure housing, paying rent, and acquiring access to urban amenities, schools, clinics, cultural centers, and the like. Community-based collective struggles for such "collective consumption" through institutional settings are what in a sense characterize the urban social movements. This kind of community activism, often contentious, should be distinguished from the notion of "community development." The latter has had a double effect of both maintaining the status quo and engendering social change. Indeed, the program of community development in the West was originally aimed at counter-insurgency against communism (in the colonies), containment of discontent among the black underclass (in the United States), and management of the poor by providing community solutions (in the United Kingdom).[27] Yet community development may also open space to cultivate resistance against the elites and foster social change. This is often the case when the grass roots initiate development on their own or are mobilized by local leaders, NGOs, religious groups, or politicians (as in Brazilian barrios or in the Self-Employed Women's Association in India). Here mobilization may not necessarily be contentious; it could express cooperative community engagement whereby people work together to improve their lives and communities with a degree of control over decisions and their outcome. How do the Middle Eastern cities fare in terms of such community activism?

In recent times, a number of community mobilizations that took place in Middle Eastern cities bore some resemblance to urban social movements. Take, for instance, the campaign of the people of Ezbet Mekawy, a low-income community in Cairo, against industrial pollution in the area, where smelters had caused major health and environmental problems.[28] They used traditional strategies of communication within the community, as well as modern tactics such as engaging the media, lobbying politicians, and resorting to the court system as a means of registering opposition. In a different example, members of the Shubra al-Khaima community in Egypt rapidly responded to a governorate's plan in August 1994 to demolish an unauthorized section of a community complex (a mosque, a clinic, and a pharmacy) that had taken inhabitants ten years to build with their own money.[29]

At certain periods—notably, when states become more vulnerable—even more enduring and large-scale mobilization develops. The collapse of the state during the Lebanese civil war caused quiet encroachment and community mobilization in the Muslim south, where its institutions continue to this day. Thousands from the south moved to the southern suburb of Beirut, building illegal settlements that currently make up 40 percent of the homes in the area. Following the Iraqi invasion of Kuwait in August 1990, networks of volunteer and associational groups played a vital role not only in supporting civil disobedience, but also in filling the vacuum created by loss of municipal services.[30] The Palestinian Popular Organizations acted as the main organs of social provisioning and development in the occupied territories, both during the intifada and after.[31] Immediately after the Iranian Revolution of 1979, many poor families took over hundreds of vacant homes and half-finished apartment blocks, refurbishing them as their own properties and establishing apartment councils to manage them collectively. In the meantime, land takeovers and illegal construction accelerated. With the help of local and outside mobilizers, squatters got together and demanded electricity and running water; when they were refused or encountered delays, they acquired them illegally. They established roads, opened clinics and stores, constructed mosques and libraries, and organized refuse collection. They further set up associations and community networks and participated in local consumer cooperatives. A new and a more autonomous way of living, functioning, and organizing community was in the making.

However, when compared with movements in some Latin American countries, these experiences, as exemplary of urban social movements, seem acutely uncommon. They tend to happen in extraordinary social and political circumstances—in revolutionary conditions or in times of crisis and war, when the state is undermined or totally absent, as in Palestine. Thus, few such activities become a pattern for sustained social mobilization and institutionalization in normal situations. Once the exceptional conditions come to an end, the experiments begin to wither away or become distorted. In Iran, community activism did not get a chance to consolidate itself. Lack of experience, rivalry of outside mobilizers and political groups, and especially the hostility of the government seriously undermined the experiment. Instead, mosque associations not only were established to offer the locals assistance in distributing basic necessities such as food during the war with Iraq, but served also to control political discontent in the neighborhoods. They resembled the three thousand Community Development Associations (CDAs) that currently operate throughout Egypt.[32] Although CDAs contribute to the poor's social well-being, their mobilizing impact is minimal. As a field researcher working in a popular quarter of Cairo stated: "Even in the highly politicized Sayyeda Zeinab, organized social action that involves the area's inhabitants seems minimal. The residents' role is usually limited to that of beneficiaries of whatever services . . . are available."[33]

Needless to say, urban communities are not blank spots devoid of social interaction. Surely, they are more than small villages subject to individualism, anonymity, and competition. Nevertheless, they contain numerous forms of networks and institutions. In the modern city of Tehran, neighborly relations still prevail; members participate in assisting one another, pay visits, consult, and take part in weddings and funerals.[34] In Egyptian cities, migrant associations have institutionalized some of these functions; funeral activities and maintaining cemeteries for the people from "home villages" are their main activity.[35] Influential individuals may take advantage of the state-controlled neighborhood councils. But the informal credit systems serve as perhaps the most important form of community network in urban centers. Social networks that extend beyond kinship and ethnicity remain largely casual, unstructured, and paternalistic. The weakness of civic or nonkinship cooperation at the community level only reinforces traditional hierarchical and paternalistic relations with people depending on local leaders (*kibar*, shaykhs, Friday prayer leaders), problem solvers, and even local bullies, rather than on broad-based social activism. In such social conditions, the modern institutions such as political party branches, local NGOs, or police are susceptible to clientelism. Thus, while the Egyptian lower classes, for instance, are aware of environmental problems, they undertake little in the way of collective action, either through communal engagement to upgrade the community itself or through protest actions to demand that officials do this for them.[36]

Why is community activism, a social action for collective consumption, relatively uncommon in the Middle East? Why is the region a "blank space" in the global map of community action, as some observers have put it?[37] One reason has to do with the legacy of populism, which continues to influence the political behavior of the ordinary people in most Middle Eastern countries. Populist regimes established a social contract between the lower and middle classes and the state, whereby the state agreed to provide the basic necessities in exchange for their support, social peace, and consequent demobilization, or just a controlled mobilization. This was not an agreement between the state and independent classes. Rather, it was an agreement between the state and a shapeless mass, an aggregate of individuals and corporate institutions in which independent collective identity and action were seriously undermined. Although distributive populism is currently waning and market forces are escalating, many people still tend to look at the states as the main source of protection as well as misfortune. In countries where authoritarian populism still predominates (such as Iran in the 1980s, Libya, and Syria), the statesman's dread of the public sphere has given a structure to the regimes that in some ways incarcerate the entire population.

This legacy has also contributed to the tendency among many ordinary people to seek individualistic solutions to their problems.[38] More often than not, families of different social strata tend to compete when resources are scarce. This occurs even more often in the new and heterogeneous communities (such as Dar el-Salam, Madinat al-Nahda, and Kafr el-Seif in Cairo, and Islamshahr and Khak Sefid in Tehran) than in the old city quarters, where the relative homogeneity of inhabitants and the longevity of residence have produced a spatial identity. The coexistence of identifiable strata in a community—such as old-timers and newcomers, those with and without security of tenure, and different ethnic groups—often sharpens the existing competition, leading to conflicts.[39] Consequently, with solidarity intangible among the people, recourse to the mighty state—this provider and punisher—becomes an alternative way to achieve their goals. Many of them know, however, that the bureau-

cracy is unable or unwilling to respond formally to the growing demands of
the urban poor, and they tend to seek informal, individualistic, and even opportunistic ways to cultivate connection or bribe the officials. "The best way
to get whatever you want done," said a resident of the Sayyeda Zeinab district
of Cairo, "is to pay a bribe to any of the assistants of any of the area's big politicians and they will do for you whatever you want."[40]

A key contributor to such social response is the lack of a structure of opportunity for mobilization. The advent of neoliberal economies in the Middle
East has not accompanied a sufficiently democratic polity.[41] Put simply, most
governments in the region are still apprehensive of and tend to restrict independent collective mobilization for fear of losing political space. In many states,
public demonstrations and gatherings are largely illegal. As a street vendor in
Cairo's Madinat al-Nahda invoking Egypt's emergency law said: "If I call my
neighboring street vendor to get together and do something collectively, this
would be called mobilization, and I could be taken in for that."[42] A human
rights agency's account of farmers' protests in twenty-five villages against
the new land law in Egypt in the course of eight months reported fifteen
deaths, 218 injuries, and 822 arrests.[43]

Alternatively, the governments may allow popular initiative in order to
control it. Where it succeeds in doing so, the popular classes tend to lose interest, with the result that their activism fails to sustain itself. Because the supporting environment is lacking, they fail to experiment and learn new ways of
doing things. Thus, most of the genuine popular institutions transform into
the extension of the states.

Political democracy is instrumental in another way. In a truly competitive
polity, political forces are compelled to bargain with and thus mobilize the
grass roots to win their electoral support. This is how the urban poor in Iran
became the subject of an intense competition between the ruling clergy and
various oppositional groups in the early 1980s. Similarly, a sustained competitive system in Turkey allowed the Islamist Rifah Party to mobilize the urban
masses in the twenty-six municipalities it controlled, thereby giving the elec-
torate strong bargaining power. Manipulative electoral practices in Egypt,
however, tend to limit the oppositional parties to restricted local campaigns,
as in Ezbet Mekawy described earlier.

Finally, collective patronage may also lead unintentionally to social and
political mobilization when patrons bargain with their poor clients' leaders in
their quest for personal and political power. Mobilization of street vendors in

Mexico City through negotiation between the vendors' union leaders and politicians is partly the result of this type of political patronage.[44] In much of the Middle East (except in Lebanon and in the case of Istanbul's street car parkers' "mafia"), however, patronage seems to work more through individual channels and rarely leads to group activities. Favors are granted more to individuals or families (in getting the security of tenure or jobs, for instance) than groups who then can bargain with their patron in exchange for his support.

In brief, community activism in the form of urban social movements seems to be largely a Latin American model rooted in sociopolitical conditions of that region (although it can be found in South Africa and, to a lesser extent, in India). The likes of local soup kitchens, neighborhood associations, church groups, and street trade unionism are hardly common features in the Middle East. The prevalence of authoritarian states and the legacy of populism, together with the strength of family and kinship ties in this region, render primary solidarities more pertinent than secondary associations and social movements.

ISLAMIST MOVEMENTS AND SOCIAL DEVELOPMENT

Some observers view the current Islamist movements in the region as the Middle Eastern model of urban social movements. In this vision, Islamism—in particular, "social Islam"—articulates the concerns and struggles of the underprivileged urban Middle Easterners. For many, the seemingly disadvantaged background of the radical Islamists is indicative of the nature of the movements. Others look at the locations of their activities, in poor areas, to arrive at similar conclusion.[45]

No doubt, Islamist movements—notably, "social Islam"—represent a significant means through which some disadvantaged groups survive hardship or better their lives. The Islamist movements contribute to social welfare first by directly providing services such as health care, education, and financial aid; at the same time, they offer involvement in community development and a social network, most of which are carried out through local, nongovernmental, mosques. Second, the Islamist movements tend to foster social competition wherein other religious and secular organizations are compelled to become involved in community work. Finally, the governments, in order to outmaneuver the Islamists and regain legitimacy, are often forced to implement social policies in favor of the poor.

Although Islamic social welfare has a long history in the Middle East, it has multiplied and taken on new forms in recent decades. During the 1980s growth of Islamism in Turkey, "mosques and their attendant religious associations represented direct channels of neighborhood organization and recruitment."[46] The Islamist Rifah Party continued in the 1990s to focus on grassroots community issues—"garbage, potholes and mud." Many Rifah Party mayoral candidates even distributed in-kind incentives to secure support. This grassroots strategy led to the party's massive victory in the 1994 elections, capturing 327 municipalities throughout Turkey, including Ankara and Istanbul. Mayors have boasted about successfully addressing the problems of congested transportation, water and fuel shortage, inadequate housing, pollution, corruption, and the like.[47] Similarly, the Islamic Salvation Front (FIS), a coalition of different Islamist parties in Algeria, prevailed in municipal elections in June 1990 in a very similar fashion. When the National Liberation Front allowed a multiparty system in 1989, FIS activists began to work within the existing Charity Associations (mosque-centered networks) that had been established in the 1980s by religious activists. Supported by the Charity Associations, the FIS took its political ideas into the neighborhoods.[48]

In a quite different context, Hizbullah filled the vacuum created by the absence of the state in southern Lebanon to construct the infrastructure for social development. During the 1980s, Hizbullah began gradually to address social problems faced by the Shi'i community. It developed plans to offer medical care, hospital treatment, electricity, and water trucking. It also paved roads, built housing, managed sewage systems, set up gas stations, and operated schools, nurseries, hospitals, and sports centers.[49] It provided 130,000 scholarships, aid for 135,000 needy families, and interest-free loans. Repairing war-damaged houses and attending to daily needs of the population in areas of Shi'i concentration were priority areas of intervention.[50]

Egypt's social Islam has become perhaps the most pervasive phenomenon in the region. The Islamic associations, often centered in nonstate mosques, grew extensively in part because the government's development programs had fallen into crisis in the past two decades. They accounted for one-third of all Egyptian private voluntary organizations (PVOs) in the late 1980s, and at least 50 percent of all welfare associations (or 6,327) in the late 1990s,[51] offering charity and health services to millions. More than four thousand zakat (religious tax) committees organized in mosques mediate between the donors and the needy. Some estimates put the number of beneficiaries of the Islamic welfare (health) services at 15 million people (in 1992), as opposed to 4.5 million in 1980.[52] Indeed, the mosques came to provide alternative support services to low-income groups to compensate for the government's withdrawal of support after adopting more liberal economic policies. One typical association, the Ansar al-Muhammadiya Association in the poor community of Imbaba, built a mosque and two schools and provided day care, medical treatment, and an elaborate welfare program.[53] Others offered video clubs, computer training centers, and similar services to cater to the needs of such groups as the high-school graduates who are the potential recruits of the radical political Islamists. Contrary to the common perception, radical Islamists such as al-Gama'a al-Islamiyya and al-Jihad were far less involved in urban community work. As rural and urban guerrillas, their strategy centered on armed attacks, targeting the state officials, police, and tourism. Nevertheless, where possible, they combined their political agitation with some welfare activities, as they did in such poor quarters of Cairo as Ain Shams and Imbaba.[54]

What makes all of these activities "Islamic" is the combination of an alternative to both the state and the private sector, the religious conviction of many of their activists, Islamic-based funding and, finally, the provision of affordable social services. It is widely agreed that such Islamic community activities often outdo their secular counterparts. The availability of funding in the form of zakat (2.5% of income) from Muslim businesses and activists, various donations (saadaqat), khums (a fifth) levied on the savings of Shi'i Muslims, and external aid (e.g., from Iran to Hizbullah and from Saudi Arabia to the FIS) renders these associations comparatively advantageous. In the early 1990s, the Nasser Bank, which supervises the zakat committees in Egypt, reported a $10 million zakat fund.[55] The additional advantages include the spirit of voluntarism, as well as legal favor. That is, unlike secular NGOs, which have to surmount many bureaucratic hurdles to raise funds, the religious PVOs tend to get around the law by obtaining donations and other contributions from Muslim believers in places of worship.[56]

The grassroots activities of the Islamists, in the meantime, compelled other social forces to enter into the competition, hoping to share this political space. The Turkish religious orders (tariqas) emulated one another in community activities through mosques and their attendant associations.[57] Al-Azhar, the pillar of establishment Islam in Egypt, began to offer similar social services to the needy in competition with the Muslim Brotherhood and al-Gama'a al-Islamiyya. Similarly, secular groups—notably, secular NGOs—seem to work hard to offer their own piecemeal alternatives. An estimated five million poor benefited from the health, educational, financial, and community services of Egyptian PVOs in 1990.[58] In addition, the governments were affected, as they feared losing the political initiative to the Islamists. The Egyptian government's measures to upgrade slums and squatter areas in the early 1990s clearly reflected the influence of Imbaba, the slum community in Cairo in which by 1992 militant Islamists had created, according to foreign media, "a state within the state."[59]

Given these activities, to what extent does Islamism represent a Middle Eastern model of urban social movements? To what degree does Islamism embody grassroots activism in communities or work collectives? How far do the Islamists encourage the grass roots to participate in their own affairs, to defend and extend their social rights? I suggest that although Islamism, notwithstanding its variations, may be considered a form of social movement, it does not express an *urban* social movement. The identity of Islamism does not derive from its particular concern for the urban disfranchised. It has never articulated a vision of an alternative urban order around which to mobilize the community members, whom the Islamists see as deserving welfare recipients to be guided by leaders. The members are rarely expected to participate actively in making their communities.

The Islamist movements have more extensive aims than simply focusing on the disfranchised, although many activists work through the poor communities to pursue broader objectives. Not all, however, operate even in this fashion. For example, in Iran before the revolution, neither the clergy nor nonclerical Islamists, such as Ali Shariati, were particularly interested in mobilizing the poor; nor did the poor take an active part in the Islamic Revolution. The mobilization of the urban grass roots by the ruling clergy in Iran began mainly after the revolution. The clergy lent its support to the poor through the rhetoric of the downtrodden (*mustaz'afin*), first, to offset the stands in favor of the lower class taken by the left and the Mujahedin-e Khalq, and second, to win over the poor as their social basis in their struggles against the Left, liberals, and the remnants of the ancien régime. The honeymoon between the poor and the ruling clergy was over when the poor were polarized. A segment was integrated into the state structure as members of the revolutionary institutions, such as the Revolutionary Guards, Construction Crusade, and the like; others remained outside, and their struggles for development brought them into confrontation with the regime.

The Lebanese Hizbullah, with its law enforcement apparatus, fell somewhere between a social movement and a quasi-state. Among other things, Hizbullah constructed an infrastructure of social development, but few of these services were free.[60] As of early 2000, the Hizbullah and Amal movements controlled the poor suburban municipalities of South Beirut. Although they use the United Nations Development Program discourse of participation and mobilization, their attitudes toward the local people remain paternalistic. They often select (not elect) people for municipality councils and cooperate with those NGOs that are closer to them.[61] However, alongside their mobilization of the grass roots, Turkey's Rifah Party and Algeria's FIS adopted exclusivist and divisive measures. The Rifah-dominated municipalities practiced nepotism and patronage, laid off secular employees in favor of religious ones, favored contractors who donated money to the party, and overlooked illegal real-estate construction in exchange for donations. The Rifah Party's policy of "cultural purification" tended to divide communities.[62] Taking a similarly exclusionary stand, Egypt's al-Gamaʿa al-Islamiyya in Imbaba forced women to veil themselves, burned video shops and hairdressing salons, and beat men who drank alcohol. The Christian residents turned fearful and insecure. While organized labor generally has remained out of the Islamists' reach, the relationship between the Islamists and the urban poor has been complex. For instance, contrary to common perception, Islamic social-welfare organizations in Egypt are not sites of Islamist political activity. They simply act as service organizations. The vast majority have no link to political Islam as such. Only a few were affiliated with the Muslim Brotherhood, and a mere handful with the radical Islamists, notably al-Gamaʿa al-Islamiyya. The rest operate on the basis of humanitarian commitment or simple business rationale in a country where the market for "Islamic" commodities (Islamic fashion, books, education, and entertainment) has been thriving. The explicit political stance emerged in the welfare associations not in the poor areas, but in the middle-class neighborhoods and among professional associations of doctors, engineers, and lawyers who were allied with the Muslim Brotherhood.[63] However, the spread of Islamic services and commodities is not restricted to the poor neighborhoods or exclusively to Muslims. It extends to middle-class and affluent districts and to the Christian community. The Islamic schools are not free of charge but are private institutions that virtually exclude the poor. In the Imbaba slum, for instance, only a fraction were admitted for free.[64] The Islamic schools are geared largely toward the well-to-do, urban middle classes.

Although it has links to diverse classes, Islamism in the Middle East is primarily a movement not of the disfranchised, but of the marginalized middle classes. Middle-class agitators in turn tend to activate the youth and the educated unemployed, as well as the socially well-to-do and politically marginalized groups. It is these groups that are considered the main agents of social change. Activities among the poor are largely limited to the provision of social services, often charity, and mobilization during elections in which free balloting takes place. In exchange, the Muslim poor in the cities approach the Islamists in pragmatic terms. Many of those who have no direct interaction with the Islamists remain confused as to their intentions. Others who benefit from their activities appear both appreciative and apprehensive. There is no evidence suggesting that the urban poor as a whole have offered an ideological allegiance to the Islamists or to the governments that have fought against the Islamists. Islamist movements, therefore, are distinct from Latin American liberation theology. The strategic objective of the liberation theology has been the "liberation of the poor"; the interpretation of gospel follows from this point of departure.[65] The Islamist movements, however, generally have broader social and political objectives (e.g., an Islamic state, law, and morality) than simply helping the downtrodden, and secular issues such as social justice for the poor follow only from the establishment of Islamic order—the most noble objective.[66] In addition, what most Islamists share is a particular moral vision of society, which is repressive in terms of gender relations and intolerant of religious minorities and modern–secular forces with a stake in building a nonreligious democratic polity. Ideological monopolies disrupt the process of pluralist democratization and frustrate the truly participatory framework that is essential for a sustained social development. But does the vision behind nonreligious NGOs offer a more viable alternative for the poor?

THE POLITICS OF THE NGOs

The remarkable expansion of the Islamic welfare associations in the 1980s and 1990s is as much a reflection of the trend toward Islamization as of the explosive growth of NGOs in the Middle East in general. The notable gathering in Cairo in May 1997 of some seven hundred NGO delegates from almost all of the Arab countries to follow up their discussions during the 1994 International Conference on Population and Development marks the growing significance attached to this sector.

Associational life is not new in the Middle East. Many countries in the region have a long history of philanthropic activities. Early-nineteenth-century associations were religious, drawing either on the Islamic notions of compassion and good deeds (as in paying zakat and *sadaqiat*) or on the Christian value of charity. They were followed in the early twentieth century by largely secular welfare and charitable associations, some of which were also used to cover anticolonial campaigns. Many of the welfare associations were run mainly by women of aristocratic families, who through work in such associations aimed to play a role in the public sphere, a domain occupied almost exclusively by men. Although the legacy of such associational culture has continued to the present, the recent NGOs are of a different breed and follow a different logic.

In the late 1990s there were some fifteen thousand registered NGOs in Egypt, double the number that existed in 1977. By comparison, Tunisia developed five thousand NGOs, of which 10 percent are charity-based. Lebanon's NGOs grew from 1,586 in 1990 to more than 3,500 by 1996, in a population of three million; Jordan's NGOs have increased from 112 in 1980 to over 800 today. The Palestinian Indigenous (Ahli) Organizations (IAOs) increased from 1,000 (including 800 in the occupied territories and some 200 in Israel) in the early 1990s to 1,800 today. (A number of them were registered with either Israeli or Jordanian authorities. But perhaps the more important ones, known as "mass-based organizations," were largely unregistered.) With regard to Iran, some accounts put the number of NGOs as high as fifteen thousand. However, this is likely to be an exaggerated figure. During the 1980s, in the course of the war with Iraq, many informal people's associations were set up. Yet because of the predominance of populism and Iran's "closed door" policy, the country's record of development NGOs is insignificant when compared with those of other Middle Eastern countries. Many relief and welfare activities in Iran are carried out by governmental or governmental–nongovernmental organizations— notably, the Imam's Relief Committee, the Foundation of Martyrs, the Construction Crusade, the Housing Foundation, and the Volunteer Women's Community Health Workers' Organization. However, since the late 1990s, a new trend has arisen toward setting up professional, women's health, and environmental NGOs. The Network of Women's NGOs included between fifty-eight and one hundred organizations, for instance. The new thinking, since the era of President Mohammad Khatami, has been that the local councils should be turned into the locus of popular participation, while the NGOs, currently numbering about 2,500, should be in charge of delivering services and charity.[67]

NGOs in the region fall into four general types in terms of their rationale or the impetus behind their activities. The religiously motivated associations are organized by mosques and Islamic figures or by churches and Christian institutions. They are inspired by religious obligations or religious–political factors. Classical welfare associations, run mostly by upper-class families, have now incorporated some developmental functions, such as income generation, training, and community upgrading. Professional NGOs are managed largely by upper-middle-class professionals and, at times, by development experts who are driven by their training and humanistic urge or simply by material self-interest. And, finally, there are a host of state-sponsored "NGOs," such as the Egyptian Community Development Associations and the Iranian Foundation of the Dispossessed. These groups remain, in effect, an extension of the state. Put together, these NGOs are active in diverse fields of human rights, women's issues, welfare, culture, business, and development. Here I will focus on welfare and development NGOs that target disadvantaged groups.

Several factors have contributed to the spectacular growth of the NGOs. First, as elsewhere, there was a need in the region's poorer countries (such as Egypt, Jordan, and Tunisia) to fill the gap left by the states' inability and unwillingness to face the challenge of social development following the implementation of neoliberal policies. Population growth and urban migration had already placed great pressure on urban social services. Where a state was absent or defunct, as in Lebanon and Palestine, organized self-help filled the vacuum. The second factor is the flow of foreign funding resulting from new donor policies that extend aid largely to NGOs rather than to individual states. External funding not only encouraged the establishment of NGOs but often influenced their activities. When there was money for human-rights activities, for example, human-rights organizations were established. Third, there seemed to be a unique consensus along the political spectrum—among neoliberals, the World Bank, governments, and liberal and leftist opposition groups—in support of the NGOs. The conservatives wanted to shift the burden of social provisions from the state to individuals. For them, NGOs acted as a safety net to offset the possibility of social unrest caused by the repercussions of neoliberal policies. In the view of Prince Talal Abdel-Aziz al-Saud of Saudi Arabia, "NGOs are the central component of development." According to a prominent Arab NGO advocate, "NGOs have replaced class struggle and socialism."[68] Middle Eastern liberals and the Left also supported the NGOs for their perceived role as agents of social change from below, contributing ultimately to development and democracy. Thus, for a Palestinian activist, "the most important role of NGOs in a future Palestinian self-authority is to accelerate the speed of change, to mobilize the rural population and to democratize the society."[69] Because of their small size, efficiency, and commitment to the cause of the poor, NGOs are seen as true vehicles for grassroots participation in development. Consequently, they serve as a bulwark against the creeping spread of Islamic fundamentalism by offering an alternative outlet to the Islamist agendas.

How effective are the development and welfare NGOs in facing the challenge of social development in the Middle East? Most studies confirm that the sector is "a vital component of the nations' social safety net and important provider of valued social services."[70] In Iraq, Lebanon, Palestine, and Sudan, where the states have been absent, defunct, or in deep crisis, NGOs played a vital role in survival, emergency aid, and relief. According to the World Bank, Palestinian NGOs in 1994 accounted for 60 percent of primary health-care services and 50 percent of all secondary and tertiary health-care services; 100 percent of the programs for the disabled and preschool children; and a sizable portion of agricultural, housing, small business credit, and welfare services.[71] In addition, given the growing privatization and high costs of health care and education, the poorest segments of society would hardly be able to afford their increasing costs without these associations. In a sense, NGOs assist the declining public sector on which millions of citizens still rely. In my research in Cairo, for example, NGO premises often served a community function and could be used free of charge or for a nominal fee as day-care centers; medical clinics; family-planning services; recreational and vocational training classes in sewing, doll making, electrical appliance repair; and the like. One association that provided microcredit loans to single mothers had made it possible for hundreds of women to set up vending enterprises in their localities and thereby become functionally self-sufficient. NGO headquarters often served a social function, as well, allowing local poor families, mostly women, to gather in public and learn social skills, such as how to talk in public or behave "properly." An estimated 5 million poor people benefit from such associations.[72] The 3,000 Egyptian CDAs alone serve some 300,000 people by implementing programs in health care, food production, women's projects, family planning, income generation, and child and youth development.[73]

Social development, however, is more than mere survival, relief, and safety net, with total dependence on charity or precarious foreign aid.[74] In addition, in the current development discourse, social development does not only mean fulfilling basic needs; it also involves achieving social and economic rights and being self-sustaining. This requires, in Anisur Rahman's words, "creating a condition where people can think, use their abilities, and act, that is, to participate."[75] Ideally, an "NGO should work so as to make itself progressively redundant to any group or set of groups with which it has been working intensively." In short, they should mobilize the grass roots. How well do the Middle Eastern development NGOs meet this goal of mobilization? Many NGO advocates have complained about the absence of a spirit of participation in the NGOs. Despite a recent tendency to establish professional and advocacy associations, Jordanian NGOs remain largely "charity-driven."[76] Activists hope that they will adopt an "enabling approach."[77] Lebanese NGOs continued to carry the legacy of war and have been active largely in the fields of relief and emergency; like their Palestinian counterparts, they depended heavily on external humanitarian assistance.[78] Only recently has there been a clear shift from relief and humanitarian assistance to the developmental and advocacy associations (human rights, women, and democracy).[79] The charitable societies in Palestine have managed to alleviate (in the areas of relief, health, education, and culture) the pressure generated by daily needs. They play a "preventive role at best, by maintaining basic social care, but they do not perform a developmental role in the full sense of the term."[80] Accordingly, NGOs' overwhelming focus on services at the cost of ignoring productive activities has pushed the Palestinians toward further dependence on the Israeli economy.

Several accounts of NGOs—notably, the likes of the traditional welfare associations in Egypt—point to their largely paternalistic attitudes and structure.[81] Paternalism is reflected both in local NGOs' top-down internal organization and in their relationship with the beneficiaries. The main decisions in NGOs are made by one or two people, with rare participation of staff, including the extension workers. In turn, staff are motivated not by altruistic incentives but by monetary motives. With the dearth of voluntarism, NGO work for status-conscious but low-paid employees appears to be no more than a dull job experience.

Paternalistic NGOs perceive their beneficiaries more as recipients of assistance than as participants in development. For their "favors" and benevolence,

NGOs often expect loyalty, support, and service. It is not the place of beneficiaries to question the adequacy and quality of services or the accountability of the NGOs, for this would be interpreted as interfering in the NGOs' affairs. It is not the target groups but the NGO leaders and donors who define the needs and priorities of a given NGO. A common problem among Middle Eastern NGOs is project duplication, which results not only from inadequate coordination, but also from ignoring the specific concerns of the beneficiaries. Competition and factionalism among NGOs, and the variations in donors' (often intermediary NGOs) policies, prevent coordination of development strategies and add up to the problem of duplication. Indeed, local associations are often subjected to clientelistic relations with the intermediary NGOs, who extend funds to the former.

The professional NGOs, which have grown exponentially since the 1990s, seem to have overcome some of the administrative and attitudinal shortcomings of the more traditional welfare associations. They attempt to practice participatory methods both internally and in relation to their clients, placing the emphasis on professionalism, education, and efficiency. A number of women's, human-rights, and advocacy NGOs reflect this trend today.[82] However, certain features of professional organizations—hierarchy of authority, fixed procedures, rigidity, and the division of labor—tend to diminish the spirit of participation. Rema Hammami has shown in the case of Palestine that local activism and mass organizations before the peace process were mostly mobilizational—that is, the activities were initiated, decided on, and carried out with the involvement of the grass roots. After the Palestinian National Authority (PNA) was set up, however, the conditions of foreign funding turned these groups into organizations of the professional elite, with particular discourses of efficiency and expertise. This new arrangement tends to create distance between NGOs and the grass roots.[83] Thus, what NGO activism means in reality is the activism of NGO leaders, not that of the millions of targeted people. These NGOs serve more their employees than the potential beneficiaries.

In addition to the internal problems (paternalism and administrative inadequacy), government surveillance poses a real obstacle to autonomous and healthy operation of NGOs. In general, as with the grassroots associations, states in the region express a contradictory position toward NGOs: they lend them support as long as the NGOs reduce the burden of social-service provision and poverty alleviation. In the late 1990s, recognition was growing among

Middle Eastern states of the contributions made by the voluntary sector in social development, as reflected in new and more favorable NGO laws and the public expression of support for the organizations (as in Egypt, Iran, and Jordan). Yet the governments also fear losing political space, because there is the possibility of NGOs turning oppositional. Professional associations (in Egypt, Jordan, Palestine, and Iran) are often drawn into politics, compensating for the absence or inadequacy of political parties. Consequently, governments, while allowing associational life, impose strict legal control by screening initiators; they also check fund-raising and unilaterally outlaw nonconformist NGOs. This contradictory position is partly related to the states' economic and political capacities. Thus, while economic weakness in a country may generate space for people's self-activity as in NGOs, the states' political weakness usually restrains it. To illustrate, the Iranian government, lacking financial resources to curb population growth in the early 1990s, mobilized more than 20,000 female volunteers, who managed educational work to achieve successful family-planning and primary health-care programs in cities, contributing to bring the growth rate down from a high of 3.4 percent in 1987 to 1.4 percent by 1996. Yet the government fiercely rejected these women's demand to set up an association, because it feared independent organization.[84] In a way, this implies that in practice the state favors certain NGOs (depending on what they do) and is leery of others. For instance, associations that belong to well-connected high officials are treated better than are critical human-rights and women's rights organizations.[85] It is therefore crucial not to approach the NGO sector as a homogeneous entity. Just as with the concept of "civil society," class and connection intervene to stratify the private voluntary sector.

These handicaps are partially cultural and attitudinal (e.g., the paternalistic approach to development and status orientation) and partly structural. Unlike those of trade unions and cooperatives, the beneficiaries of an NGO are not its members and therefore cannot hold it accountable for inadequacy. The same relationship, in turn, persists between local NGOs and donor agencies; as a result, the NGOs are accountable not to their beneficiaries but to their donors.[86] Mahmood Mamdani is perhaps correct in saying that the NGOs do undermine the existing clientelism, yet they simultaneously create a new type.[87] The question, then, is whether the present NGOs are structurally able to foster grassroots participation for meaningful development. Perhaps we simply expect too much from NGOs, as Neil Webster, writing on India, has noted. Maybe we attribute to these NGOs "development qualities and abilities that they do not in fact possess."[88] Whatever our expectations, the fact remains that self-activity—collective or individual mobilization—remains a crucial factor in poor people's elevation to a point at which they can meaningfully manage their own lives. In the Middle East, the existing forms of activism in the communities—or through labor unions, social Islam, and the NGOs—do contribute to the well-being of the underprivileged groups. However, they fall short of activating and directing a great number of people in sustained mobilization for social development. The sociopolitical characteristics of the Middle East instead tend to generate a particular form of activism—a grassroots nonmovement that, I think, has far-reaching implications for social change. I am referring to the "quiet encroachment of the ordinary."

THE QUIET ENCROACHMENT OF THE ORDINARY

In the previous chapter, I described the quiet encroachment as the silent, protracted, and pervasive advancement of ordinary people on the propertied and powerful in a quest for survival and improvement of their lives.[89] They are characterized by quiet, largely atomized, and prolonged mobilization with episodic collective action—open and fleeting struggles without clear leadership, ideology, or structured organization. Although the quiet encroachment is basically a nonmovement, it is different from survival strategies or "everyday resistance" in that, first, the struggles and gains of the grass roots are at the cost not of fellow poor people or themselves (as in survival strategies), but of the state, the rich, and the general public. In addition, these struggles should be seen not as necessarily defensive merely in the realm of resistance, but as cumulatively encroaching, meaning that the actors tend to expand their space by winning new positions to move on. This kind of quiet activism challenges many fundamental state prerogatives, including the meaning of "order," control of public space, and the meaning of "urban." But the most immediate consequence is the redistribution of social goods in the form of the (unlawful and direct) acquisition of collective consumption (land, shelter, piped water, electricity), public space (street pavements, intersections, street parking places), and opportunities (favorable business conditions, locations, and labels).

Postrevolution Iran experienced an unprecedented colonization, mostly by the poor, of public and private land, apartments, hotels, street sidewalks, and public utilities. Between 1980 and 1992, despite the government's opposition, the land area of Tehran expanded from 200 square kilometers to 600 square kilometers; well over one hundred mostly informal communities were created in and around Greater Tehran. The actors of the massive informal economy extended beyond the typical marginal poor to include the new middle classes, the educated salary earners whose public-sector positions rapidly declined during the 1980s. In a more dramatic fashion, millions of rural migrants and the urban poor in Egypt have quietly claimed cemeteries, rooftops, and state and public lands on the outskirts of the city, creating largely autonomous communities. Greater Cairo contains over 111 spontaneous settlements (*ashwaiyyat*) housing more than six million people who have subdivided agricultural lands and put up shelters unlawfully. Throughout the country, 344 square kilometers of land has come under occupation or illegal construction, mainly by low-income groups. Some 84 percent of all housing units from 1970 and 1981 were informally built. To these informal units one should add "vertical encroachments"—the addition of rooms, balconies, and extra space on top of buildings. The capital for construction comes mainly from the informal credit associations (*gama'iyyat*) located in neighborhoods. Many rent the homes unlawfully to other poor families. The prospective tenant provides the "key money," which he borrows from a credit association, to a plot holder, who then uses it to build but rents it to the provider of the key money. The plot holder becomes a homeowner, and the tenant finds a place to live. Both break the law that allows only one year's advance on rent.[90]

Once settled, the poor tend to force the authorities to extend living amenities, or collective consumption, to their neighborhoods by otherwise tapping them illegally. Many poor in Tehran, Cairo, Istanbul, Tunisia, and other cities illegally use electricity and running water by connecting their homes to electricity poles, extending water pipes to their domiciles, or sharing or manipulating utility meters. For instance, in the late 1990s, illegal use of piped water in the city of Alexandria alone cost, on average, some $3 million a year. A cursory look at Cairo-based communities such as Dar al-Salam, Ezbet Sadat, Ezbet Khairallah, Ezbet Nasr, and Basaatin shows evidence of this widespread phenomenon. In late April 1996, the municipality reported that it had cut off eight hundred illegal electricity lines in the Dar a-Salam and Basaatin communities in a single raid.

This informal and often uncharged use of collective services leaves governments little choice but selectively to integrate the informal settlements, hoping to commit the residents to pay for services they have thus far used illegally. Securing property and community tax is another consideration. Although the poor welcome the extension of provisions, they often cannot afford to pay the bills. Therefore, it is not uncommon to see reinformalization springing up from the fringes of the new formalized communities. In the domain of work, "street-subsistence workers" quietly take over public thoroughfares to conduct their business in the vast parallel economy. The streets in the commercial districts of Middle Eastern cities are colonized by street vendors who encroach on favorable business opportunities that shopkeepers have created. Cairo reportedly has 600,000 street vendors, and Tehran, until recently, had some 150,000. Informality means not only that the actors generally escape the costs of formality (tax regulation, for instance), but that they also benefit from the theft of imported goods, brands, and intellectual property. With capital of $6, a Cairene vendor could make up to $55 a month.[91]

Thousands of poor people (in Cairo, Istanbul, and Tehran, for instance) subsist on tips from parking cars in the streets that they control and organize in such a way as to create maximum parking space. They have turned many streets into virtual parking lots, which they control by creating working gangs with elaborate internal organization. Establishing alternative transportation systems is another way to make a living. Ezbet Khairallah in Cairo typifies thousands of similar neighborhoods in the region, where vans carry passengers without even registration plates. A newspaper described this community as one in which "no official has ever entered since its establishment" in the early 1980s.[92] The logic behind these types of encroachment is reflected in the words of a Cairene street vendor, who said, "When dealing with the government, you have to take the proverb, 'What you can win with, play with.'"[93]

Governments usually send mixed signals about quiet encroachment. On the one hand, they see the people helping themselves by building their own shelters, getting their own services, creating their own jobs. On the other hand, they realize that these activities are carried out largely at the cost of the state, the propertied, and the public. Equally important, the poor tend to outadminister the authorities by establishing a different public order, acting independently and often tarnishing the image of modernity the nation seeks to portray. "We are not against the vendors making a living," says the chief of Cairo's security department, "but not at the expense of Egypt's reputation. They spoil the picture of Cairo, they block the streets, they crowd the pavements."[94]

Yet encroachment is tolerated in practice as long as it appears limited. Once it goes too far, governments often react. Postrevolutionary Iran, for instance, saw many bloody confrontations between the security forces and encroachers. Daily police harassment is a common practice in many Middle Eastern cities. Nevertheless, the frequent offensives against squatters and street vendors often fail to bring a result. The actors either resort to on-the-spot resistance (as in Iran) or, more commonly, resume their activities quietly following each tactical retreat (as in Egypt). For instance, while the municipal police drive around to remove street vendors—in which case the vendors suddenly disappear—the vendors normally return to their work once the police are gone. "Everything we are doing is useless," says an Egyptian official.[95] The Iranian authorities became even more frustrated when "anti-vending squads" failed to clear public spaces. Confronting quiet encroachment is particularly difficult for vulnerable governments. The municipalities, using stick-and-carrot tactics, may indeed manage to demolish communities, drive vendors away from the main streets, or track down unregistered transportation. Nevertheless, they have to yield to the actors' demands by offering alternative solutions. Where removals or demolitions have actually been carried out, the dispossessed have been offered alternative street markets, housing, or regulated taxi service. Only thirteen of a total eighty-one squatter settlements in Cairo (excluding Guiza) were in 1998 identified for demolition (for safety reasons); the rest were planned to be upgraded.[96]

Quiet encroachment, therefore, is not a politics of collective demand making, a politics of protest. Rather, it is a mix of individual and collective direct action. It is accentuated under the sociopolitical circumstance characterized by authoritarian states, populist ideology, and strong family ties. The authoritarian bureaucratic states make collective demand making both risky (because of repression) and less than effective (owing to bureaucratic inefficiency); populism tends to obstruct the public sphere and autonomous collectivities, rendering primary loyalties the more functional mechanism of survival and struggle. Yet, in the long run, the encroachment strategy generates a reality on the ground with which states often find no option but to come to terms. In the end, the poor manage to bring about significant changes in their own lives, the urban structure, and social policy. It is precisely this centrality of the agency, of the urban grass roots, that distinguishes quiet encroachment from any incremental social change that may result from urbanization in general. Although this kind of activism represents a lifelong, sustained, and self-generating advance, it is largely unlawful and constantly involves risk of harassment, insecurity, and repression. As a fluid and unstructured form of activism, encroachment has the advantage of flexibility and versatility, but it falls short of developing legal, financial, organizational, and even moral support. The challenge is to encourage convergence of the mobilizational element of quiet encroachment, the institutional capacity of NGOs, and the consent of the authorities.

Early reaction by the urban grass roots to aspects of structural adjustment policies during the 1980s included developing coping strategies and mounting urban riots. These strategies, however, seem to have given way to more institutionalized methods of dealing with austerity. The safety nets provided by social Islam and NGOs (coupled with state repression) contributed to this shift in method. With political Islam undermined (institutionalized, co-opted, or curbed) by the end of the 1990s, social Islam, "NGOization," and quiet encroachment, despite their flaws, appear to have become the dominant forms of activism that now contribute to improving some aspects of people's lives in Middle Eastern countries. Although quiet encroachment has a longer history, the spread of Islamism and NGOs gained new momentum in the 1980s and especially in the 1990s, the period in which neoliberal economic policies began to be implemented. The growth of these types of activism (along with the new social movements associated with women and human rights) coincides with the relative decline in traditional class-based movements—peasant organizations, cooperative movements, and trade unionism. The transformation of the rural social structure, "de-peasantization," and growing urbanization are eroding the social bases of peasant and cooperative movements. The weakening of economic populism, closely linked to the new economic restructuring, has resulted in a decline of public-sector employment, which constituted the core of the corporatist trade unionism; at the same time, it has led to a growing fragmentation of the work-force, expressed in the expansion of the informal urban economy. State bureaucracy (as a segment of the public sector) continues to remain weighty; however, its employees, unlike workers in industry or services, largely have been unorganized. A large segment of low-paid state employees survive on incomes deriving from second or third jobs in the informal sector.

In the meantime, the increasing informality of economies and expanded urbanization in the Middle East tend to cause a shift in popular needs and demands. The growth of informality means that struggles for wages and conditions, the typical focus of traditional trade unionism, are losing ground in favor of broader concerns for jobs, informal work conditions, and affordable cost of living. Rapid urbanization, however, increases the demand for urban collective consumption—shelter, decent housing, electricity, piped water, transportation, health care, and education. This desire for citizenship, expressed in community membership and developmental rights, is one that traditional trade unionism is unable to address. The task instead falls on community movements that remain feeble in the Middle East. At the same time, the scope of social Islam and NGOs, despite their contributions to social welfare, is also unable to realize fully the goal of social development. Even though by the close of the 1990s, some Middle Eastern governments (in Jordan, Iran, the Palestinian Territories) were cautiously recognizing the activities of some civil-society organizations, especially the social-development NGOs, they fell short of empowering civil-society organizations from above and encouraging social development from below. It is, therefore, mainly to the strategy of quiet encroachment that the urban disenfranchised in the Middle East resort in order to fulfill their growing needs. Through quiet encroachment, the subaltern create realities on the ground with which the authorities sooner or later must come to terms.[97] Joan Nelson's contention that, because the poor are never organized well enough, they fail to exert influence on national policies is true.[98] Yet the cumulative consequence of poor people's individual direct actions may, in the end, result in some improvements from below and policy changes from above. Given the gradual retreat of states from their responsibilities in offering social welfare, the poor in the Middle East would have been in a far worse condition had grassroots actions been totally absent. Yet grassroots activities do have limitations in terms of their own internal constraints, in their capacity to win concessions adequately, and in relation to the constraints directed from the states. It is a mistake to leave the entire task of social development to initiatives from below; a bigger mistake is to give up on the states—in particular, on their crucial role in large-scale distribution. Yet imagining policy change and the concrete improvement of people's lives without their pressure or direct action seems no more than an unwarranted illusion.

5 FEMINISM OF EVERYDAY LIFE

FEMINISTS HAVE LONG argued that probably all modern states possess, albeit in different degrees, patriarchal tendencies. But patriarchy figures especially prominently in those authoritarian regimes and movements that exhibit conservative religious (Islamic, Christian, Jewish, or Hindu) dispositions. Indeed, patriarchy is entrenched in religious authoritarian polity.[1] In many authoritarian Muslim states, such as Egypt, the Sudan, Saudi Arabia, or the Islamic Republic of Iran, where conservative Islamic laws are in place, women have become second-class citizens in many domains of public life. Consequently, a central question for women's rights activists is how to achieve gender equality under such circumstances. A commonly proposed strategy consists of organizing strong women's *movements* to fight for equal rights. Movements are usually perceived in terms of collective and sustained activities of a large number of women organized under strong leaderships, with an effective network of solidarities, procedures of membership, mechanisms of framing, communication, and publicity—the types of social movements that are associated with images of marches, banners, organizations, lobbying, and the like.

It is a credit to women in most western and democratic countries for creating sustainable movements that have achieved remarkable outcomes since the 1960s. While it may be that many women in Muslim (and non-Muslim) authoritarian states do wish and indeed strive to build similar social movements,

---

Adapted from "A Women's Non-Movement: What It Means to Be a Woman Activist in an Islamic State," *Comparative Studies of South Asia, Africa, and the Middle East* 27, no. 1 (2007), pp. 160–72.

their struggles are often thwarted by the repressive measures of authoritarian/ patriarchal states as well as the unsympathetic attitudes of many ordinary men. Consequently, the type of collective actions practiced mostly in democratic settings, which have come to dominate our conceptual universe as *the* women's movements, may not deliver under nondemocratic conditions, if they are ever allowed to emerge. The conventional social movement is concerned chiefly with politics of protest, contentious politics where collective actors exert pressure (by threat, disruption, or causing uncertainty) on adversaries to meet their demands. How do we account for a women's activism that may rarely deploy organization and networking, mobilizing strategies, street marches, picketing, strikes, or disruption, and yet is able to extend their choices?

In the aftermath of a revolution in which they had participated massively, Iranian women faced an authoritarian Islamic regime that imposed forced veiling, gender segregation, and widespread surveillance, and revoked the prerevolutionary laws that favored women. Women resisted these policies, not much by deliberate organized campaigns, but largely through mundane daily practices in public domains, such as working, playing sports, studying, showing interest in art and music, or running for political offices. Imposing themselves as public players, women managed to make a significant shift in gender dynamics, empowering themselves in education, employment, and family law, while raising their self-esteem. They reinstated equal education with men, curtailed polygamy, restricted men's right to divorce, demonized religiously sanctioned temporary marriage (*mut'a*), reformed the marriage contract, improved the employment status of women, brought back women as judges, debated child custody, and to some degree changed gender attitudes in the family and in society. Women's seemingly peculiar, dispersed, and daily struggles in the public domain not only changed aspects of their lives; they also advanced a more inclusive, egalitarian, and woman-centered interpretation of Islam.

Not only the Islamic republic, but many other Muslim societies have also experienced similar dispersed activities, albeit with varying effect, depending on the degree of misogyny of the states and the mobilizational efficacy of women. Nevertheless, because of their largely mundane and everyday nature, such women's practices are hardly considered a particular type of *activism* that can lead to some far-reaching consequences. How do we characterize such activities? How do we explain the logic of their operation? Drawing on the experience of women under the Islamic Republic of Iran, my purpose in this essay is to suggest that there are perhaps different ways in which Muslim women under authoritarian regimes may, consciously or without being aware, defy, resist, negotiate, or even circumvent gender discrimination—not necessarily by resorting to extraordinary and overarching "movements" identified by deliberate collective protest and informed by mobilization theory and strategy, but by involving ordinary daily practices of life—by working, playing sports, jogging, singing, or running for public offices. This involves deploying the *power of presence*, the assertion of collective will in spite of all odds, refusing to exit, circumventing constraints, and discovering new spaces of freedom to make oneself heard, seen, felt, and realized. The effective power of these practices lies precisely in their *ordinariness*, since as irrepressible actions they encroach incrementally to capture trenches from the power base of patriarchal structure, while erecting springboards to move on. Conventional social movements with identifiable leaderships may be more readily prone to repression than such dispersed but common practices by a large number of actors whose activism is deeply intertwined with the practices of daily life. Their end result can amount to a considerable modification in gender hierarchy and discrimination. This particular strategy of Iranian women to achieve equal rights may give us an opportunity to perhaps rethink about what it means to be a woman activist, or what may constitute a woman's "nonmovement," under authoritarian regimes in contemporary Muslim societies.

WOMEN AND THE ISLAMIC STATE

The Iranian Revolution of 1979 was a nationwide popular movement where diverse groups and classes—modern and traditional, religious and secular, middle-class and poor, male and female—massively participated.[2] Apart from a few obvious cases (such as the clergy and royalist upper classes) as winners and losers, debate still continues as to which social groups, and in what respects, really benefited from it.[3] In general, women are regarded to be on the losing side. Perhaps no social group felt so immediately and pervasively the brunt of the Islamic Revolution as the middle class, especially secular women. Only months into the life of the Islamic regime, new, misogynous policies angered women who only recently had marched against the Shah. The new regime overturned the less male-biased Family Protection Laws of 1967; overnight, women lost their right to be judges, to initiate divorce, to assume child custody, and to travel abroad without permission from a male guardian.

Polygamy was reintroduced and all women, irrespective of faith, were forced to wear the veil in public.[4] In the early years, social control and discriminatory quotas against women in education and employment compelled many women to stay at home, seek early retirement, or go into informal and family business.[5]

The initial reaction to these drastic policies came from secular women. Thousands demonstrated in Tehran on March 8, 1979, vilifying Ayatollah Khomeini's imposition of the hijab, or veiling. Even though Khomeini retreated temporarily, the decree was gradually enforced. Shocked by the onslaught on their liberty, secular women organized dozens of albeit-desperate organizations mostly affiliated with sectarian leftist trends for whom the gender question was subordinated to the class emancipatory project.[6] All these groups were put down by the Islamic regime once the war with Iraq began in 1980. Then followed a decade of repression, demoralization, and flight. While secular women in exile continued with feminist education and activism, those in Iran began to emerge from their tormenting abeyance into the world of arts, literature, journalism, and scholarship only at war's end.

Although traditionalist clerics favored keeping women at home, away from "moral dangers," others, however, compelled by the remarkable presence of women in the revolution, adopted a discourse that exalted Muslim women as both guardians of the family and active public agents. This broad discursive framework guided a spectrum of "Muslim women activists." Inspired by the writings of Ali Shariati and Morteza Motahhari, they set out to offer an endogenous, though abstract, "model of Muslim women,"[7] in the image of the Prophet's daughter Fatima and his granddaughter Zeinab, who were simultaneously "true" homemakers and public persons.[8] Out of dozens of Islamic groups and organizations, the Women's Association of the Islamic Revolution (WAIR) gathered prominent Islamist women, including Azam Taleqani, Fereshte Hashemi, Shahin Tabatabaii, Zahra Rahnavard, and Gawhar Dastgheib. Most were members of prominent clerical families and held that the (socialist) East treated the woman as a mere "working machine," and the (capitalist) West as a "sex object," while only Islam regarded women as "true humans."[9] Instead of equality, these activists advocated the complementary nature of men and women. Some justified polygamy on the grounds that it protected widows and orphans. Although some objected to forced veiling and the abrogation of the Family Law, they stopped short of any concrete protest but contended that wearing the veil should be enforced through education, not by coercion. Most refused to acknowledge, let alone communicate with, secular western feminists, whom they saw as "provoking women against men" and questioning religious principles and the sanctity of shari'a.[10] Indeed, alarmed by the danger of gender debates, Shahla Habibi (President Rafsanjani's advisor on women's issues) committed herself "against overstating women's oppression" and identity politics. Instead, she placed emphasis on the "family [as] the heart of the society, and women the heart of family."[11] Thus, daycare centers became "harmful for children,"[12] even though their closure would throw many women out of work. Muslim women activists accepted "tradition" (Qur'an, hadith, *fiqh,* and *ijtihad*) as an adequate guide to ensure women's dignity and well-being.[13] "In an Islamic state led by the rule of a supreme jurist (*velayat-i faqih*) there would be no need for special organizations to defend women's rights," argued Maryam Behroozi, a woman and member of Parliament.[14] While the moderates agreed with "women's freedom to study, to choose suitable jobs, and have access to various social and administrative fields,"[15] the more conservative Islamists (such as the parliamentarians Marzieh Dabbagh, Rejaii, Dastgheib, and Behroozi) viewed gender division in occupations, tasks, and activities as a divine order.[16] In their paradigm, women, as Muslims, had more obligations than rights.

With the onset of the war with Iraq (1980–88) debate about women's status was suppressed. The authorities continued to project women as mothers and wives, who were to produce manpower for the war, for the glory of Islam and the nation. But by the late 1980s dissent simmered in women's "politics of nagging." Women complained in public daily, in taxis, buses, bakery queues, grocery shops, and in government offices, about repression, the war economy, the war itself. In so doing, they formed a court of irrepressible public opinion that could not be ignored. A certain iconic moment shattered the illusion of the "model of Muslim women," when on national radio a young woman expressed her preference for Osheen, a character in a Japanese television series, over Fatima, the Prophet's daughter. Only then did authorities realize how out of touch they had become regarding women's lives in Iranian society. Some ten years into the Islamic republic, Azam Taleqani admitted bitterly that "poverty and polygamy are the only things that poor women have obtained from the revolution."[17]

War and repression had surely muted women's voices but had not altered their conviction to assert themselves through the practices of everyday life, by resisting forced Islamization, pursuing education, seeking employment, yearning for arts and music, practicing sports, and socializing their children according to these pursuits. Mobilization for the war effort had already placed them in the public arena as "model Muslim women," making them conscious of their power. Beyond illusions imposed by men, there were also facts. In a mere twenty years, women's unprecedented interest in education had more than doubled their literacy rate: in 1997 it stood at 74 percent.[18] By 1998, more girls than boys were entering universities, a fact that worried some officials, who feared that educated women might not be able to find men with higher or equal status to marry. But for young women college offered not only education, but a place to socialize, gain status, and have a better chance for jobs and more desirable partners.

While for some the sheer financial necessity left no choice but to seek employment in the cash economy,[19] most middle-class and well-to-do women chose working outside the home in order to be present in the public realm. After an overall decline in female employment, largely in industry, of 40 percent between 1976 and 1986, the share of women at work in cities rose from 8.8 percent in 1976 to 11.3 percent in 1996. This excluded those who worked in informal occupations, family businesses, or part-time jobs.[20] By the mid-1990s, half of the positions in the government sector and over 40 percent in education were held by women. Professional women, notably writers and artists, reemerged from domestic exile; at the first Book Fair of Women Publishers in Tehran, in 1997, some forty-six publishers displayed seven hundred titles by women authors. Over a dozen female filmmakers were regularly engaged in their highly competitive field, and more women than men won awards at the 1995 Iranian Film Festival.[21] But few of their internationally acclaimed productions helped elevate the underdog image of Iranian Muslim women in the world.

The economic conditions of families made housewives more publicly visible than ever before. Growing economic hardship since the late 1980s forced middle-class men to take multiple jobs and work longer hours, so that "they were never home." Consequently, all domestic and outside chores (taking children to school, dealing with the civil service, banking, shopping, or fixing the car) that had previously been shared by husbands and wives shifted exclusively to women.[22] A study confirmed that women in Tehran, notably housewives, spent on average two hours per day in public places, at times until ten at night, traveling by taxi, bus, and metro.[23] This public presence gave women self-confidence, new social skills, and city knowledge and encouraged many to return to school or to volunteer for NGOs or charities. One impressive example of voluntarism was the Ministry of Health's mobilization of some 25,000 women in Tehran in the early 1990s to educate urban lower-class families about hygiene and birth control; mounting population growth (3.9 percent between 1980 and 1985 and 3.4 percent between 1985 and 1990) had caused the regime great political anxiety,[24] and these women contributed to decreasing the rate to a low of 1.7 percent between 1990 and 1995.[25]

Women did not give up on sports, even if a woman's body, and sports along with it, had been at the center of the regime's moral crusade. The hardship of sweating under a long dress and veil did not deter many women from jogging, cycling, or target shooting, or from playing tennis, basketball, or even climbing Mount Everest. Nor did women avoid participating in national and international—albeit exclusively female or Muslim—tournaments.[26] They also defied the state policy banning women from attending male competitions; some disguised themselves in male attire,[27] while the more assertive simply forced their way in. In 1998 hundreds of women stormed into a massive stadium full of jubilant young men celebrating a national soccer team victory. From then on women were assigned to special sections in the stadium to attend events. Their demand to play soccer in public bore fruit in 2000 when the first women's soccer team was formally recognized.[28] Faezeh Rafsanjani, the president's daughter, played a crucial role in promoting and institutionalizing women's sports. The first College of Women's Physical Education had already been established in 1994 to train school sports staff.

While the new moral order and imposition of the veil had a repressive effect on secular and non-Muslim women, it brought some degree of mobility to their socially conservative counterparts: traditional men felt at ease allowing their daughters or wives to attend schools or appear at public events.[29] Moreover, the regime's mobilization of lower classes for the war effort, street rallies, and Friday prayer sermons dramatically increased the public presence of women who would have otherwise remained in the confines of their unyielding dwellings. Meanwhile, the women who felt stifled by the coercive moralizing of the government resisted patiently and fiercely. Officials invariably complained about *bad-hijabi*, or young women neglecting to properly wear the headcover. With the jail penalty (between ten days and two months) for improper hijab, showing inches of hair sparked daily street battles between defiant women and the agents of multiple official and semi-official morals-enforcing organizations such as Sarallah, Amre beh Ma'ruf, Nahye as Monker, and

Edareh Amaken. During a four-month period of 1990 in Tehran, 607 women were arrested, 6,589 were forced to submit written affidavits, and 46,000 received warnings.[30] Nevertheless, by the late 1990s, the *bad-hijabi* became an established practice.

Women's daily routines and resistance to the Islamic government did not mean their departure from religiosity. Indeed, most displayed religious devotion, and many were willing to wear light head-covers in the absence of force.[31] Yet they insisted on exerting individual choice and entitlement, which challenged both the egalitarian claims of the Islamic state and the premises of orthodox Islam. Women wanted to play sports, work in desirable jobs, study, listen to or play music, marry whom they wished, and reject the grave gender inequality. "Why are we to be acknowledged only with reference to men?" wrote one woman in a magazine. "Why do we have to get permission from Edareh Amaken [morals police] to get a hotel room, whereas men do not need such authorization?"[32] These seemingly mundane desires and demands, however, were deemed to redefine the status of women under the Islamic republic, because each step forward would encourage demands to remove more restrictions. The effect could snowball. How could this general dilemma be resolved?

The women's magazines *Zan-e Ruz*, *Payam-e Hajar*, and *Payam-e Zan* were the first to reflect upon such dilemmas. At the state level, the Social and Cultural Council of Women and the Bureau of Women's Affairs were established in 1988 and 1992, respectively, to address such issues and to devise concrete policies. Even Islamists, such as Ms. Rejaii, wife of a former prime minister, expressed reservations about the "model of Muslim women," attacking "narrow-minded" anti-female ideas and obsession with the veil.[33] Interestingly, many of these women worked in public office, including Parliament, and had been given a taste of discrimination by their traditionalist male colleagues. The Women's Association of the Islamic Revolution was shut down and its views attacked; the Islamic Republic Party incorporated the magazines *Zan-e Ruz* and *Rah-e Zeinab*; and once her parliamentary term ended, the prominent female Islamist Azam Taleqani fell out of the government's graces. In the end, the rather abstract philosophical approach of Islamist women proved insufficient to accommodate women's desire for individual choice within an Islamist framework. Post-Islamist feminists, however, emerged to take up the challenge.

A POST-ISLAMIST FEMINISM?

In a departure from the Islamist women activists, post-Islamist feminism articulated a blend of piety and choice, religiosity and rights. It set out a strategy for change through discussion, education, and mobilization in a discursive frame that combined religious and secular idioms. With a clear feminist agenda, the post-Islamist strategy derived not from an abstract model but from the reality of women's daily lives. Activists held Islam in its totality as a system that could accommodate women's rights only if it was seen through the feminist lens. These feminists valued women's autonomy and choice, emphasizing gender equality in all domains. For them, feminism, irrespective of its origin (secular, religious, or western) dealt with women's subordination in general. The West was no longer a monolithic entity imbued with immorality and decadence (a view held by secular revolutionary and Islamist women); it was also home to democracy and science, to feminists and exiled Iranian women with whom they wished to establish dialogue. This position transcended the dichotomy of "Islamic" versus "secular" women. Post-Islamist feminists were different from such Islamist women activists as the Egyptian Heba Rauf, who were primarily Islamist but happened to be women and raised women's issues. Post-Islamist feminists were feminists first and foremost, who utilized Islamic discourse to push for gender equality within the constraints of the Islamic republic. They did not limit their intellectual sources only to Islam but also benefited from secular feminism.[34] The women's magazines *Farzaneh*, *Zan*, and *Zanan* spearheaded this trend by running articles on, for instance, how to improve one's sex life, cooking, women's arts in feminist critical discourse, deconstruction of patriarchal Persian literature, and legal religious discussions, written by Muslim, secular, Iranian and western authors, including Virginia Woolf, Charlotte Perkins Gilman, Simone de Beauvoir, and Susan Faludi.[35] *Zanan* appealed in particular to educated young urban women.[36]

The major challenge to post-Islamist feminism was to demonstrate that the claims for women's rights were not necessarily alien to Iranian culture or Islam.[37] But, as secular feminists wondered, would operating within the Islamic discourse not constrain endeavors for gender equality when "all Muslims, from the very orthodox to the most radical reformers, accept the Qur'an as the literal word of Allah, unchanging and unchangeable"?[38] Post-Islamist feminists responded by undertaking women-centered interpretations of the sacred texts in a fashion similar to that of early European feminists such as Hildegard of Bingen (1098–1179), Christine de Pizan (1365–1430), Isotta Nogarola (1418–66), or Anna Maria von Schurman (1607–78), to name only a few, who deconstructed the Bible-driven perceptions about the "sinful" and "inferior" disposition of Eve/women.[39] *Zanan* set out to deconstruct the "patriarchal readings" of the scriptures, offering gender-sensitive perceptions that would allow women to be equal with men, to take on social and political positions as judges, presidents, religious sources of emulation (*marja'*), or Islamic jurists (*faqih*). "There are no deficiencies in Islam [with regard to women]. Problems lie in political and patriarchal perceptions," they contended.[40] Within this emerging "feminist theology," interpreters questioned misogynist legislation and the literal reading of Qur'anic verse; they emphasized instead the "general spirit" of Islam, which, they argued, was in favor of women. If in his twenty-three years of struggle the Prophet of Islam changed many antiwomen practices of his time, post-Islamist feminists were to extend this tradition of emancipation to modern times. Methodologically grounded on hermeneutics, philology, and historicism, women interpreters transcended literal meanings in favor of interpretive and historical deductions. To refute the "innate superiority of men" that orthodox readings deduced from Qur'anic verses (such as Surah 4:34 Nisa, where men are favored over women), *Zanan* writers shifted the basis of hierarchy from sex to piety by invoking the gender-free verse: "The noblest among you in the sight of God is the most God-fearing of you" (S. 49:13). Accordingly, child custody was not automatically the right of men (as the shari'a seems to authorize) but was determined by the well-being of children, which Islam stresses highly.[41] Against a 1998 parliamentary bill that called for the separation of men and women in medical treatment, *Zanan* argued not only that the Qur'an ruled against any forced guidance in general (because people are responsible for their choices, good or evil), but also that in Islamic theology religion exists to serve humans rather than the other way around. Instead of obligation, it concluded, the bill should recognize the patient's choice over his medical treatment.[42]

Building on linguistic analyses, post-Islamist feminists deconstructed the verse "al-rejal qawwamoun ala-nisa" (Nisa, 4:34), on which many of the misogynist deductions are based. Feminist theologians attributed the word *qawam* not to the Arabic root "qym," meaning "guardianship over other," but to "qwm," signifying "rising up," "fulfilling needs," or "protecting."[43] Thus, rather than meaning "men exert guardianship over women," the verse could imply "men protect or fulfill the needs of women." In the same fashion, they stated the verb *darb* in the Qur'an should be understood not simply as "to beat," but also "to put an end to" or "to go along with."[44] Consequently, the Qur'an did not authorize the right to divorce to men alone or deny such a right to a woman.[45] Indeed, the gender-neutrality of the Persian language, as reflected in the constitution of the Islamic Republic, offered much discursive opportunity for women to campaign for equal rights.[46] For instance, eligibility conditions for the country's presidency, such as "rejal-e mazhabi" (religious personalities) or "faqih-e adel" (just jurist), can apply to *both* men and women. While in Arabic the word *rajol* was generally accepted as meaning "a man," in Persian, they contended, it referred to (political) "personality" in general, thus arguing women were also eligible to run for president.[47] The major novelty of these gender-sensitive theological debates was that, beyond a few enlightened clerics,[48] women themselves were waging them, and they were doing so in the pages of the popular daily press.

The new women's activism alarmed the clerical establishment, ordinary men, and conservative women. A male pathologist commented with dismay how "the freedom of women in Iran has been misconceived. . . . In the past few years some women who apparently became protagonists in the struggle for equal right have gone astray. They talked so much about men's domination that people became enemies, and this was a blow to our society."[49] Ayatollah Fazel Lankarani of the Qom Seminary warned the activists "not to question Islam's principles by your intellectualism. . . . Who says there is no difference between men and women?" he challenged. "Who are you to express opinions [. . .] before God and his prophet?"[50] The Friday prayer leader in Rasht denounced women who "questioned religious authorities on hijab and shari'a," warning them "not to cross the red line, not to dismiss the Qur'an and Islam."[51] Others, like Ayatollah Mazaheri, were outraged by the activists' demand that the Iranian government endorse the UN charter against discrimination against women, because this would entail the western domination of the nation.[52] Islamist women in Majlis (Monireh Nobakht and Marzieh Vahid Dastjerdi) proposed to curtail feminist debates in the press and public, because they "create conflict between women and men" and undermine shari'a and fundamentals of the religion.[53] Such attacks became intellectual justifications for hard-line mob and media to harass *bad-hijab* women on the streets, denounce women's sports and recreation, and fight against the return of "decadence, fashion, and individual taste."[54] *Zanan* was taken to court in 1998 on charges of inciting women against men and "spreading homosexuality."[55] The cleric Mohsen Saidzadeh, whose women-centered essays on theology and Islamic law had dismayed the conservative clerics, was jailed in June 1998.[56]

Despite all this pressure, the "nonmovement" made considerable inroads, empowering women through education, employment, and family law, and raised self-esteem. The opportunity of equal education with men made a comeback following the official restrictive quotas that favored men. Polygamy was seriously curtailed, men's right to divorce restricted, and religiously-sanctioned *mut'a*, or temporary marriage, was demonized. At its height in 2002 (1381), only 271, or one out of 1,000 marriages, were "temporary."[57] In cases where husbands initiated divorce proceedings, women won a financial reward equal to the value of their involuntary housework during marriage, even though applying such rulings proved to be difficult. New laws authorized financial rewards to widowed working women, increased maternity leave to four months, reestablished nurseries for the children of working women, and decreased women's working hours to 75 percent of the time required of men. New legislation also made bride price payable in the current value, allowed early retirement after twenty years of work, offered financial protection for women and children deprived of male support, obliged the government to provide women's sport facilities, and authorized single women over twenty-eight years old to study abroad without a male guardian.[58] In 1998, a pilot project to prevent wife abuse was launched.[59] Child custody was intensely debated, while the struggle for women to be judges led to their appointment as judicial counselors in lower courts and co-judges in high courts. In 1997, fifteen female deputies sat in the Women's Affairs Commission of Parliament.[60]

These struggles, meanwhile, led to changes in power relations between women and men within the family and society. Female suicide and the rising divorce rate (27 percent in 2002, 80 percent of which were divorces initiated by women) were seen as what an Iranian sociologist called the "painful modernization of our society."[61] Meanwhile, opinion polls on women's public role showed that 80 percent of respondents (men and women) were in favor of female government ministers, while 62 percent did not oppose a female president.[62] The prevailing perception of Iranian women as helpless subjects trapped in the solitude of domesticity and hidden under the long black chador proved to be an oversimplification.

A NONMOVEMENT?

This is not to overstate the status of Iranian women in the Islamic republic. Indeed, as late as 1998, feminist lawyer Mehrangiz Kar warned against reading too much into what women had achieved. She listed a dozen areas in Iranian law where flagrant gender inequalities persisted,[63] as they did in most political, legal, and family institutions imbued with patriarchal relations. Inequalities remained in men's right to divorce, child custody, polygamy, and sexual submission, and the amount of a man's blood money was still twice that of woman's. Yet it is also true that the daily struggles of women in the public domain not only changed aspects of their lives, but also advanced a more democratic interpretation of Islam. Women's most significant achievement was subverting the conventional gender divide of public men and private women. Against much resistance, Iranian women imposed themselves as public players.

The paradoxical status of women under the Islamic republic perplexed many observers, and activists themselves, trying to grasp the nature of women's activism. Had Iranian women forged a "social movement" of their own? Many commented in the negative, on the grounds that women activists were few, dispersed, and unclear about a strategy for change, and did not engage in theoretical work.[64] Moreover, this nonmovement lacked known leaders identified as "feminists" to mobilize the mass of ordinary women.[65] For these commentators, women's sporadic activism represented the existence of not a social movement but a "social problem."[66] In contrast, activists unequivocally characterized women's struggles in terms of a social movement,[67] even though some uttered the language of "movement" in qualified terms,[68] phrasing it as a "silent," "decentralized," or "leaderless movement."[69] They charged those denying the "movement" character of the women's activities with trying to subordinate gender issues to the larger reformist, democratic, or class politics. Even if an organized movement might seem far-fetched, they suggested, women did express a shared feeling, "hamdeli," about their inferior position in society and wished to do something about it.[70]

Clearly, the hegemony of a westo-centric model of "social movements" confined these conceptual imaginations to two opposing positions—either there was a women's movement or there was not—as if alternative forms of struggles beyond the conventional contentious politics were unthinkable. Afsaneh Najmabadi's argument that the very question (of whether there existed such a thing as a women's social movement) was irrelevant and even harmful, because it privileged one form of struggle over others, carried much weight. Yet the objection did not resolve the question of what it really was. How do we characterize such activisms; how to determine the logic of their operation? If Iranian women failed to develop a movement of their own, then how did the fragmented yet collective and nondeliberate practices lead to some tangible outcome?

Iranian women's activism readily conjures up what James Scott has famously phrased "everyday forms of resistance," by which he describes the struggles of the Javanese poor peasants to withstand the encroachment of the superordinate classes by such discreet, illicit, and individualistic actions as foot dragging, dissimulation, false compliance, slander, or sabotage.[71] Looked at from this perspective, Iranian women could be said to subvert or resist, in their everyday practices, the state policies that tend to undermine women's rights. There was certainly a strong element of "resistance" in both discourse and actions of women protagonists. Yet Iranian women's struggles were neither merely "defensive," hidden, silent, nor illegal and merely individualistic. Rather, they were also collective and progressively encroaching, in the sense that actors would capture trenches from the patriarchal legal structure, public institutions, and family to move forward, so that each gain would act as a stepping-stone for a further claim. Protagonists, in addition, were involved in some degree of ideological elaboration and discursive campaign. Indeed, women's involvement in hundreds of NGOs, solidarity networks, and discourses by the late 1990s pointed to some degree of organized activism. Women's groups held rallies, participated in international women's meetings, lobbied politicians and clerical leaders, and campaigned in the Majlis. Women's Weeks, book fairs, film festivals, and sporting events were sites of their mobilization. In 1995 independent activists, together with moderate officials such as Shahla Habibi, coordinated a Women's Week Festival during which they held sixty-two seminars, three thousand celebrations, 230 exhibits, and 161 contests.[72] Over two dozen women's magazines (such as *Zanan*, *Farzaneh*, *Hoquq-e Zan*, *Zan-e Rouz*, *Neda*, *Rayhaneh*, *Payam-e Hajar*, *Mahtab*, *Kitab-e Zan*, and *Jens-e Dovvom*[73]) and an increasing number of websites (such as *bad-jens* and *zanan-e iran*) communicated ideas, advertised events, and established solidarity networks. Between 1990 and 2002, thirty-six new women's journals were published. Feminist ideas permeated universities, with female student groups publishing newsletters on gender issues, and by the late 1990s four Iranian universities had established women's studies programs, though their operation left much to be desired.[74]

    Can this kind of activism then be characterized in terms of the "new social movements," which are suggested to focus on reclaiming individuals' identity from the colonization of the lifeworld by the state and the market in post-industrial societies? It is true, Iran's women's activities do seem to resonate with a "new social movement" in the sense of fragmented activisms devoid of structured organization, coherent ideology, and clear-cut leadership, but which galvanizes collective sentiments and identities. Yet this perspective, or what Alberto Melucci phrases as "collective action without collective actors," helps us little to account for the particular ways in which women's identities were forged, actions taken, and advances made. The new social movements, even with dispersed activities, multiclass actors, and unclear leadership, still rely on overt, deliberate, and collective mobilization—lobbying, street protests, political contention, and discursive campaigns—something that did not feature prominently among the Iranian women. The dynamics of claim making among them followed a different logic and course.

    Iran's women's activism signified largely a "nonmovement," embodying an aggregate of dispersed collective sentiments, claim making, and everyday practices involved in diverse gender issues, chiefly, assertion of women's individualities. Collective identities were formed less in women's distinct institutions than in (albeit controlled) public spaces: workplaces, universities, bus stops, rationing lines, shopping markets, neighborhoods, informal gatherings, and mosques. Beyond some conscious network building, "passive networks" served as the most important medium for the construction of collective identities. Passive networks signified instantaneous and unspoken communication between atomized individuals established through gaze in public space by tacit recognition of commonalities expressed in style, behavior, or concerns.[75] Thus, for instance, nonconformist women with similar "improper" outfits, who might not even know or meet one another, would spontaneously feel empathy and affinity; they would share a common threat from the morals police and solidarity with one another.

    Occasions of intense political tension, threat, or opportunity would often turn women's passive networks into communicative actions. For instance, the housewives or mothers of war victims, since they lacked institutional settings to express discontent, would often take their grievances into the streets while standing in long rationing lines at bakeries or butcher shops, or at bus stops, where they perfected the irrepressible practice of "public nagging." They deliberately deployed the one gender-based comparative advantage, maternal impunity, or their power as mothers and homemakers, to protest and yet remain immune from backlash. While the protests of men and the young were often suppressed, women's maternal status offered them protection. The wives of war victims compounded this "maternal impunity" with their political capital as the family of martyrs, to launch successful campaigns against the patriarchal interpretation of shari'a that granted the custody of their now-fatherless children to their grandfathers.

Yet public protestation of this kind constituted only an insignificant aspect of women's general activities. Most women, apart from activist groups, rarely articulated shared demands about women's rights and gender equality; at best, they did so individually and usually after they had encountered legal or institutional obstacles. For the most part, they went ahead on their own to claim them directly in the domains that they could: in educational institutions, workplaces, sport centers, or courts. Theirs, then, was not, at least until early 2000, a conventional social movement so often associated with solid organization, strategizing, nonroutine collective action with banners and marches. Rather, Iran's women's activism represented a *movement by consequence*, or a "nonmovement"—that is, dispersed collective endeavors embodied in the mundane practices of everyday life, but ones that would lead to progressive effects beyond their immediate intent. This nonmovement operated through an incremental and structural process of claim making—similar to "quiet encroachment," but intimately attached to the imperative of women's persistent public presence. In this structural encroachment every claim justified the next, creating a cycle of opportunities for further claims, ultimately leading to more gender equality and individual entitlements. Thus, the effective power of women's activism first lay in its being based on ordinary, everyday, and so irrepressible, practices; and second, it benefited from an incremental encroachment onto the power base of patriarchal structures.[76]

Against Islamist gender bias, the mere public presence of women was an achievement, but it also acted as a springboard for women to encroach on or negotiate with patriarchal power. Women got involved in the war effort and in voluntary work, and they sought paid jobs; they pursued education and sports, jogged and cycled, and participated in world championships; they worked as professionals, novelists, filmmakers, and bus or taxi drivers, and ran for high public office. And these very public roles beset the social and legal imperatives that had to be addressed—restrictive laws and customs needed to be altered to accommodate the requisites of public women within the prevailing patriarchal system. College education, for example, often required young women to live independent from their families, something that would otherwise be deemed inappropriate. Women's public activity raised the issue of their hijab (of its compatibility with the nature of a woman's work), association with men, sexual tensions,[77] and equality with men in society. Why should women not be elected president or supreme leader? If women could act as high officials, would they still need to obtain their husbands' permission to attend a foreign conference? Women's public presence would in addition challenge male superiority in personal status laws, entitling women to demand equal rights in divorce, inheritance, blood money, and child custody. When more women than men enter and graduate from universities, women are likely (though not necessarily) to occupy positions supervising men who would have to accept if not internalize their authority. These processes contributed to tilting gender-power relations in public and in households.[78]

In their day-to-day struggles, the fragmented actors pushed for their claims, not as deliberate acts of defiance, but as logical and natural venues to express individuality and to better their life chances. Women did not get involved in car racing or mountain climbing because they wished to defy the patriarchal attitudes or religious state; they did so because they found fulfillment in such activities even though in the context of the Islamic republic they appeared defiant. The crucial point is that despite much constraint and pressure, women did not give up but kept on pursuing those interests, which in turn led to serious normative and legal consequences. For they compelled patriarchal and political authority to acknowledge women's role in society, and thus their rights. In sum, what underlined Iran's women's activism was not collective protest, but collective presence. The women's nonmovement drew its power not from the threat of disruption and uncertainty—as in the case of contentious politics; rather, it subsisted on the *power of presence*—the ability to assert collective will in spite of all odds, by circumventing constraints, utilizing what exists, and discovering new spaces of freedom to make oneself heard, seen, felt, and realized. In this nonmovement, women did not usually take extraordinary measures to compel authorities to make concessions; in a sense, the very ordinary practices that they strived for (e.g., studying, working, jogging, initiating divorce, or running for political office) accounted for the actual gains. Not only did the element of ordinariness make the movement virtually irrepressible, it also allowed women to gain ground incrementally without seeming to constitute a threat.

Adversaries did often recognize the "danger," even though they could do little to stop the momentum. Indeed, it was the "danger" of "incremental encroachment" that alarmed the conservative clergy, who had some thirty-five years earlier expressed opposition to the Shah's granting voting rights to women in local elections. "Voting rights for women, in addition to its own troubles, would lead to their participation in the parliamentary elections; then this would lead to equality of men and women in divorce, in being judges, and the like.... No doubt these practices would stand against our religious principles."[79]

The women's nonmovement could not fully operate only at a practical level. It was bound to move into the realm of intellectual and ideological struggles. Women's incremental practices needed to be backed up by careful argumentation and discursive campaign. Women activists had to address the legal and theological contradictions that their actual encroachment had exposed. To this end activists deployed sophisticated legal, theological, and theoretical articulations to take advantage of the opportunity that their public presence offered them. Specialized publications and women lobbyists in the Majlis played a crucial role in such discursive campaigns, the ammunition for which they drew from alternative legal and theological interpretations.

How was it that women became visible despite surveillance? Women's drive for a public presence was fueled by the memory of their prerevolution status, economic necessity, and the globalization of women's struggles. But the more immediate factor was the *discursive opportunity* that women's own struggles had already generated. Their massive participation in the revolution of 1979 had compelled many religious leaders, chiefly Ayatollah Khomeini, to publicly acknowledge women's social and political agency. Khomeini's appeal to women voters during the first referendum of the Islamic republic established their public power. "Women do more for the [revolutionary] movement than men; their participation doubles that of men," he admitted.[80] He continued, "That Muslim women are to be locked up in their homes is an utterly false idea that some attribute to Islam. Even during early Islam, women were active in the armies and war fronts."[81] Later, Muslim feminists would invoke Khomeini's statements to defy conservative clerics who wished to drive them back into the private realm. In the end, women's pervasive publicness, their power of presence, was bound to challenge many of patriarchal structures of the Islamic state and gender relations, establishing for them a new autonomous identity. This in turn framed women's demands for equality and their insubordination to many "traditional" roles.[82]

Speaking of such nonmovements, the collective action of the noncollective actors, in this manner is not meant to downplay the significance of organized and sustained women's social movements; nor is it at the same time to devalue the strategy of nonmovements in comparison to the conventional social movements. My intention, rather, has been to highlight the mode of operation of a particular mobilization under social and political constraints. At any rate, nonmovements may well evolve into contentious collective challenge in opportune times; and the Iranian women activists have often tried to utilize such strategy by organizing social protests, rallies, and more impressively, the campaign of one million signatures. In fact, by the middle of the first decade of this century, Iran's women's nonmovement seemed to develop into a nascent social movement, when activists pushed for more intense self-reflection, greater networking and organization, and wider deliberate mobilization. This movement played a remarkable part in mobilizing scores of women in the presidential elections of June 2009 and in the subsequent street protests that came to galvanize Iran's Green Movement for civil and political rights. These tendencies, notably activists' attempts to articulate, think about, discuss, and conceptualize their activism, distinguished it from nonmovements of the urban poor or globalizing youth. Yet so long as such organized, sustained, and easily identifiable social movements face state repression, nonmovements—these elusive, flexible, dispersed, and yet encroaching collective endeavors—remain a critical option.

6 RECLAIMING YOUTHFULNESS

THERE SEEMS TO BE a great deal of both alarm and expectation about the political weight of Muslim youth in the Middle East. While many express anxiety over the seeming desire of the young in the Arab world to act as foot soldiers of radical Islam, others tend to expect youth (as in Iran or Saudi Arabia) to push for democratic transformation in the region.[1] Thus, youths are projected to act as political agents, social transformers, whether for or against Islamism. Indeed, the recent history of the region is witness to the political mobilization of the young, as scores of Muslim youth have been involved in radical Islamist movements, from Saudi Arabia to Egypt to Morocco, or have defied the moral and political authority of the doctrinal regimes in the region, such as in the Islamic Republic of Iran. What do these events and involvements tell us about youth politics in general and "youth movements" in particular? Do they point to the necessarily transformative role of the young? Are youth movements revolutionary or ultimately democratizing in orientation? How can the prevalent "social movement theory" help us understand the nature of youth politics broadly, and that of the Muslim Middle East specifically?

While studies on youth-related themes such as AIDS, exclusion, violence, or religious radicalism have flourished in recent years, "youth" as an analytical category appears in them for the most part incidentally. Thus, many studies on "youth religious radicalism," for example, are primarily about religious radicalism per se, where the young people (like others) only

Adapted from Asef Bayat, *Making Islam Democratic: Social Movements and the Post-Islamist Turn* (Palo Alto, Calif.: Stanford University Press, 2007), pp. 59–65, 161–64.

happen to be involved. This is different from an approach that takes "youth" as the point of departure, as the central category, to examine religious radicalism. On the other hand, youth as a social category has curiously been absent from the prevalent social movement debates. In general, scholarly attempts to conceptualize the meanings and modalities of youth movements remain rare. At best, it is assumed that such conceptual tools as ideology, organization, mobilization, framing, and the like would be adequate to assess youth as a collective body. Consequently, youth activisms, those which do not fall into the frame of classical social movements, have fallen into the realm, and are viewed largely from the prism, of "social problems" or subcultures. Whereas historical studies and journalistic accounts do talk about such collectives as youth movements (referring, for instance, to political protests of the 1960s or the subcultures of hippies or punks), they presume a priori that youth movements are those in which young people play the central role. Thus, student activism, antiwar mobilization, and counterculture trends of the 1960s in Europe and the United States, or the youth chapters of certain political parties and movements such as Communist youth, are taken to manifest different forms of youth movements.[2] My approach differs from these.

I would like to suggest that a discussion of the experience of youth in the Muslim Middle East, where moral and political authority impose a high degree of social control over the young, can offer valuable insight into conceptualizing youth and youth movements. By comparing youth activisms in the Muslim Middle East, I suggest we can productively construct "youth" as a useful analytical category, which can then open the way to understanding the meaning of a youth movement. I propose that rather than being defined in terms of the centrality of the young, youth movements are ultimately about claiming or reclaiming youthfulness. And "youthfulness" signifies particular habitus or behavioral and cognitive dispositions that are associated with the fact of being "young"—that is, a distinct social location between childhood and adulthood, where the youngster in a relative autonomy is neither totally dependent (on adults) nor independent, and is free from being responsible for others. Understood as such, the political agency of youth movements, their transformative and democratizing potential, depends on the capacity of the adversaries, the moral and political authorities, to accommodate and contain youthful claims. Otherwise, youth may remain as conservative as any other social groups. Yet, given the prevalence of the doctrinal religious regimes in the Middle East whose legitimizing ideologies are unable to accommodate the youth habitus, youth movements possess a great transformative and democratizing promise.

YOUNG PEOPLE, YOUTH, AND YOUTH MOVEMENTS

The idea of youths as a revolutionary class is not new. The widespread mobilization of young people in Europe and the United States during the capitalist boom of the 1960s convinced many observers that youths (then active in universities, in antiwar movements, and in producing alternative lifestyles) were the new revolutionary force of social transformation in western societies. For Herbert Marcuse in the United States, and Andre Gorz in France, youths and students had taken the place of the proletariat as the major agent of political change.[3] In this vein, youth movements have often been equated and used interchangeably either with student movements or with youth chapters or branches of this or that political party or movement.[4] Thus, the youth section of the Fascist Party in Germany is described as the German youth movement. Or the youth organization of the Iraqi Ba'th Party is assumed to be the youth movement in Iraq.[5]

I would suggest that a youth movement is neither the same as student activism nor an appendage of political movements; nor is it necessarily a revolutionary agent. First, movements are defined not simply by the identity of their actors (even though this factor affects very much the character of a movement), but primarily by the nature of their claims and grievances. Although in reality students are usually young, and young people are often students, they represent two different categories. "Student movements" embody the collective struggles of a student body to defend or extend "student rights"—decent education, fair exams, affordable fees, or accountable educational management.[6] On the other hand, activism of young people in political organizations does not necessarily make them agents of a youth movement. Rather, it indicates youth support for, and their mobilization by, a particular political objective (e.g., democracy, Ba'thism, or fascism). Of course, some youth concerns may be expressed in and merge into certain political movements, as in German Fascism, which represented aspects of a German youth movement, or in the current pietism of Muslims in France, which partially reflects the individuality (e.g., through putting on headscarves) of Muslim girls. However, this possibility should not be confused with the situation where young people happen to support a given political organization or movement.

But is the political ideal of the young necessarily revolutionary? By no means. Indeed, the political conservatism of many young people in the West after the 1960s, which compelled Marcuse to retreat from his earlier position, shattered the myth of youths as a revolutionary class. If anything, the political or transformative potential of youth movements is relative to the degree of social control their adversaries impose on them. For instance, a political regime, such as that in present-day Iran or Saudi Arabia, that makes it its business to scrutinize individual behavior and lifestyle is likely to face youth dissent. Otherwise, youth movements per se may pose little challenge to authoritarian states unless they think and act politically. Because a youth movement is essentially about *claiming youthfulness*, it embodies the collective challenge whose central goal consists of defending and extending the youth habitus, by which I mean a series of dispositions, ways of being, feeling, and carrying oneself (e.g., a greater tendency for experimentation, adventurism, idealism, autonomy, mobility, and change) that are associated with the sociological fact of "being young." Countering or curtailing this habitus, youthfulness, is likely to generate collective dissent.

But, as the experience of today's Saudi Arabia shows, the mere presence of the young people subject to moral and political discipline does not necessarily render them carriers of a youth movement, because young persons (as age category) are unable to forge a collective challenge to the moral and political authority without first turning into youth as a social category, that is, turning into social actors. When I was growing up in a small village in central Iran during the 1960s, I of course had my friends and peers, with whom I talked, played, cooperated, and fought. However, at that point we were not "youth," strictly speaking; we were simply young persons, just members of an age cohort. In the village, most young people actually had little opportunity to experience "youthfulness," as they rapidly moved from childhood, a period of vulnerability and dependence, to adulthood, the world of work, parenting, and responsibility. Many youngsters never went to school. There was little "relative autonomy," especially for most young girls, who were rapidly transferred from their father's authority to that of the husband and were effectively trained into their roles as housewives long before puberty (that boys were usually exempted from such responsibility indicates how gender intervenes in the formation of youth).

It is partially in this light that Bourdieu has famously contended that youth is "nothing but a word," suggesting that talking about youth as a social unit is itself a manipulation of the young.[7] How can we imagine youth as a single category, he argues, when the youngsters of different classes (rich and the poor) have little in common? Indeed, I must add, the differences in the life-worlds of male and female youngsters have been even more remarkable. Yet Bourdieu's contention pertains primarily to the pre-schooling situation, when young persons experience radically different lifeworlds. But as he himself acknowledges, in modern times mass schooling has changed all this. It has produced youthfulness on a massive national, as well as global, scale.

Youth as a social category, as collective agents, are an essentially modern, indeed urban, phenomenon. It is in modern cities that "young persons" turn into "youth," by experiencing and developing a particular consciousness about being young, about youthfulness. Schooling, prevalent in urban areas, serves as a key factor in producing and prolonging the period of youth, while it cultivates status, expectations, and, possibly, critical awareness. Cities, as loci of diversity, creativity, and anonymity, present opportunities for young people to explore alternative role models and choices, and they offer venues to express individuality. Mass media, urban spaces, public parks, youth centers, shopping malls, cultural complexes, and local street corners provide arenas for the formation and expression of collective identities. The fragmented mass of young individuals might share common attributes in expressing common anxieties, in demanding individual liberty, and in constructing and asserting subverting identities. Individuals may bond and construct identities through such deliberate associations and networks as schools, street corners, peer groups, and youth magazines. However, identities are formed mostly through "passive networks," the nondeliberate and instantaneous communications among atomized individuals that are established by the tacit recognition of their commonalities and that are mediated directly through the gaze in public space, or indirectly through the mass media.[8] As present agents in the public space, the young recognize shared identity by noticing (seeing) collective symbols inscribed, for instance, in styles (T-shirts, blue jeans, hairstyle), types of activities (attending particular concerts and music stores, and hanging around shopping malls), and places (stadiums, hiking trails, street corners). When young persons develop a particular consciousness about themselves as youth and begin to defend or extend their youth habitus, their youthfulness in a collective fashion, a youth movement can be said to have developed. Where political repression curtails organized activism, youth may form nonmovements.

Unlike student movements, which require a good degree of organization and strategy building, youth "nonmovements" may augment change by their very public presence. With their central preoccupation with "cultural production" or lifestyles, the young may fashion new social norms, religious practices, cultural codes, and values, without needing structured organization, leadership, or ideologies. This is because youth nonmovements are, I would suggest, characterized less by *what the young do* (networking, organizing, deploying resources, mobilizing) than by *how they are* (in behaviors, outfits, ways of speaking and walking, in private and public spaces). The identity of a youth nonmovement is based not as much on collective *doing* as on collective *being*; and the forms of their expression are less collective protest than *collective presence*. The power of Muslim youth in the Middle East lies precisely in the ability of their atomized agents to challenge the political and moral authorities by the persistence of their merely alternative presence. Even though youth (non)movements are by definition concerned with the claims of youthfulness, nevertheless they can and do act as a harbinger of social change and democratic transformation under those doctrinal regimes whose legitimizing ideologies are too narrow to accommodate youthful claims of the Muslim youth.

In Iran, where moral and political authority converged, draconian social control gave rise to a unique youth identity and collective defiance. Young people both became central to and were further mobilized by the post-Islamist reform movement. The assertion of youthful aspirations, the defense of their habitus, lay at the heart of their conflict with moral and political authority. With the state being the target of their struggles, Iranian youths engendered one of the most remarkable youth nonmovements in the Muslim world. The struggle to reclaim youthfulness melded with the struggle to attain democratic ideals. In contrast, Egyptian youth, operating under the constraints of "passive revolution," opted for the strategy of "accommodating innovation," attempting to adjust their youthful claims within existing political, economic, and moral norms. In the process, they redefined dominant norms and institutions, blended divine and diversion, and engendered more inclusive religious mores. Yet this subculture took shape within, and neither against nor outside, the existing regime of moral and political power. Egyptian youth remained distant from both being a movement and involvement in political activism until the late 2000s, when a new Web-based opportunity seemed to offer some venues for a collective mobilization.

IRAN'S "THIRD GENERATION"

The spectacular activism of young people in the Islamic Revolution,[9] the war with Iraq, and in the new revolutionary institutions earned them a new, exalted position, altering their image from "young troublemakers" to "heroes and martyrs." This was the image of the "spectacular male youth" drawn sociologically from lower- and middle-class families. At the same time, the young were seen as highly vulnerable to corrupting ideas and therefore needing protection and surveillance. To reproduce an ideal "Muslim man," the Islamic regime launched in 1980 the "cultural revolution" program to Islamize educational culture and curricula. Universities were shut down for two years, Islamic associations were set up in schools, and all public places came under the watchful gaze of morals police and proregime vigilantes.

What sustained this regime of surveillance for a decade were revolutionary fervor, preoccupation with war, and the repression of dissent. Young men were either on the war front or fleeing the country, preferring the humiliation of exile to "heroic martyrdom" in a "meaningless" battle. Although adolescents sought refuge in schools, often by deliberately failing exams to postpone graduation, they lived in anxiety, gloom, and depression. One out of every three high school students suffered from a behavioral disorder. Girls in particular were more susceptible to stress, fear, and depression.[10] The poetic reflections of a young girl talking to herself capture the depth of her inner gloom as she witnesses the gradual erosion of her youth:

My father never recognizes me on the street.
He says "all of you look like mourners."
Yes, we dress in black, head to toe in black.

Sometimes, I get scared by the thought of my father not recognizing me in this
    dark colorlessness . . .
I stare at the mirror,
And I see an old woman.
    Am I still sleepy?
    Oh . . . I feel aged and unhappy.
    Why should I be so different from other 20-year-olds?

They liken my joy to sin,
They close my eyes to happiness,

They stop me from taking my own steps . . .
Oh . . . I feel like an old woman. . . .
No, no, I want to be young,
Want to love,
To dress in white, be joyful, have fun,
And move to fulfill my dreams. . . .
I look at myself in the mirror.
I look so worn out and aged . . .[11]

Few officials noticed this inner despair in youngsters' lives. Blinded by their own constructed image and by their doctrinal animosity toward joy, Islamist leaders failed to read the inner minds and hearts of this rapidly growing segment of the population. The shocking truth emerged only in the postwar years when some officials noticed "strange behavior" among the young. With the war over and postwar reconstruction under way, the young began to publicly express their selfhood, both individually and collectively. The media carried stories about the "degenerate behavior" of Iranian youth. Boys were discovered disguised as women walking on the streets in a southern city. Tomboy girls wore male attire to escape harassment of morals police. College students refused to take religious studies courses,[12] and "authorities in an Iranian holy Muslim city launched a crackdown on pop music, arresting dozens of youths for playing loud music on their car stereos."[13] Other reports spoke of groups of young males dancing in the streets next to self-flagellation ceremonies on the highly charged mourning day of 'Ashura.' Young drivers had fun by crashing their cars into each other, or by playing a form of the game of "chicken": racing while handcuffed to the steering wheel and trying to escape before flying off a cliff.[14] Drug addiction soared among schoolchildren. The average age of prostitutes declined from twenty-seven to twenty, expanding the industry by 635 percent in 1998.[15]

Yet alongside individual rebellion, the young took every opportunity to assert open and clandestine subcultures, defying the moral and political authority. The severe restriction of music did not deter them. When the reformist mayor of Tehran, Gholam Hussein Karbaschi, established numerous cultural centers in South Tehran, young people comprised 75 percent of those who rushed to fill classical-music classes and concert halls. Smuggled audio and video recordings of exiled Iranian singers filled big-city main streets, while MTV-type music videos found widespread popularity. The young blared loud music from speedy cars, to the dismay of Islamists, while across the capital, underground pop and rock bands thrived at covert late-night parties. Teenagers enjoyed not only the music but its subculture and fashion—tight or baggy pants, vulgar English slang, tattoos—acquired through smuggled videos.[16] Rap and heavy metal music in particular became popular. By 1999, music subcultures had become so widespread that the reformist Ministry of Culture was compelled to recognize and even organize the first concert of "pop music" in the Islamic republic. Some teens ran away from home to join rock bands, attracted by a sense of belonging, though many were incarcerated by the morals police.

Indeed, runaway teenagers became a major social problem. In 2000, Tehran was reportedly faced with an "escalating crisis of runaway girls frequently becoming victims of prostitution rings and human trafficking." Between 1997 and 1998 the number of reported runaway teenagers tripled. In Tehran alone nine hundred girls ran away in 2000, and four thousand in 2002,[17] when the nationwide number was reportedly sixty thousand.[18] Assertion of individuality—freedom to have a male partner (42 percent) and freedom from family surveillance—seemed to be the main cause.[19] "I want to leave Iran," lamented a young female who had been arrested for leaving home. "I don't like Iran at all. I feel I am in prison here even when I am sitting in the park."

Although dating openly had become a prime casualty of Islamic moral code, the young devised ways to resist. Well-to-do young boys and girls made contacts not only at private parties and underground music concerts, but also in public parks, shopping malls, and restaurants, often discreetly arranged by cell phone. In such "distanciated dating," girls and boys stood apart but eyed each other from a distance, chatted, flirted, and expressed love through electronic waves. To seek privacy and yet appear legitimate, young couples hired taxis to drive them around the city in anonymity, while they sat back for hours to romance or take delight in their companionship. The popularity of Valentine's Day revealed an abundance of "forbidden love" and relationships in which sex, it seemed, was not excluded. In fact, scattered evidence indicated widespread premarital sex among Iran's Muslim youths, despite the high risk of harsh penalties. An academic claimed that one out of three unmarried girls, and 60 percent in North Tehran, had had sexual relations. Out of 130 cases of AIDS cases reported in hospitals, 90 were unmarried women.[20] An official of Tehran municipality reported "each month at least 10 or 12 aborted fetuses are found in the garbage."[21] Although public information did not exist, researchers and medical professionals were alarmed by the extent of unwanted pregnancies. Doctors unofficially spoke of the fact that "not one week passes by without at least two or three young girls coming in for abortion."[22] Reportedly, some 60 percent of patients requesting abortions were unmarried young girls.[23] The United Nations Population Fund officials in Tehran referred to a survey on "morality" (meaning sexuality) among young people, but the results were so "terrible" that they had to be destroyed.[24] Attention to self, physical appearance, clothing, fashion, and plastic surgery became widespread trends among young females.

Clearly, sexuality among the young posed a major challenge to the Islamic state, testing the capacity of Islamism to integrate youths, whose sensibilities were inherently subversive to it. In the early 1990s, President Rafsanjani came up with the idea of "temporary marriage" as an "Islamic" solution to the crisis. It meant controlling sexual encounters through fixed short-term (as short as a few hours) relationships called "marriage." Ayatollah Ha'eri Shirazi proposed "legitimate courtship" (without sex), an openly recognized relationship approved by parents or relatives.[25] Others called for some kind of official document confirming the legitimacy of such relationships, meaning something like temporary marriage in which the couple would not live together.[26] And in 2000, conservative Islamists put forward the idea of a Chastity House, where men seeking sex were to "temporarily marry" prostitutes to "legitimize" their encounters.

The desperate cultural politics of young people shattered Islamists' image of them as self-sacrificing individuals devoted to martyrdom and moral codes. By challenging the regime's moral and political authority, the young subverted the production of "Muslim youth." Anxiety over the increasing *bad-hijabi* (laxity in veil wearing) among school and university girls haunted officials. "We are encountering a serious cultural onslaught. What is to be done?" they lamented.[27] Over 85 percent of young people in 1995 spent their leisure time watching television, but only 6 percent of them watched religious programs; of the 58 percent who read books, less then 8 percent were interested in religious literature.[28] A staggering 80 percent of the nation's youth were indifferent or opposed to the clergy, religious obligations, and religious leadership,[29] while 86 percent of students refrained from saying their daily prayers.[30] Official surveys confirmed the deep mistrust separating the young from the state and whatever it stood for. The vast majority (80 percent) lacked confidence in politicians,[31] and most (over 70 percent) saw the government as being responsible for their problems.

Yet this distrust of the Islamist authorities did not mean that the young abandoned religion. Indeed, they expressed a "high religiosity" in terms of fundamental religious "beliefs" and "feelings,"[32] with some 90 percent believing in God and the idea of religion, according to a study.[33] But youth remained largely indifferent to religious practices; religious belief and knowledge seemed to have little impact on their daily lives. God existed but did not prevent them from drinking alcohol or dating the opposite sex. To them, religion was a more philosophical and cultural reality than it was moral and doctrinal. While most refused to attend mosque ceremonies, they flocked to public and private lectures given by the "religious intellectuals," which spread during the mid-1990s. Like their Egyptian counterparts, the globalized Iranian youth reinvented their religiosity, blending the transcendental with the secular, faith with freedom, divine with diversion.

In an ingenious *subversive accommodation*, many youngsters utilized the prevailing norms and institutions, especially religious rituals, to accommodate their youthful claims, but in doing so they creatively redefined and subverted the constraints of those codes and norms. This strategy was best expressed in the way the North Tehrani youths treated the highly charged ritual of Muharram, which commemorates the death of Imam Hussein, the grandson of Prophet Muhammad. By inventing "Hussein parties," the young turned this highly austere occasion of mourning into an evening of glamour, fun, and sociability. Boys and girls dressed in their best, strolled through the streets, joined parades of mourners, and used the occasion to stay out until dawn to socialize, flirt, exchange phone numbers, and secretly arrange dates.[34] In a similar spirit, they reinvented the "sham-e ghariban" (the eleventh night of the month of Muharram), the most dreary and sorrowful Shi'i ritual in Islamic Iran, as a blissful night of sociability and diversion. Groups of fifty to sixty girls and boys carried candles through the streets to large squares, where they sat on the ground in circles, often leaning on one another in the romantic aura of dim candlelight, and listened to the melancholic *nowhe* (sad religious songs) while chatting, meditating, romancing, or talking politics in hushed tones until dawn.[35]

These rituals of resistance did not go unpunished by violent vigilante *baseeji*es, or bands of "fundamentalist" youth who attacked the participants and disrupted their assemblies and in so doing turned their "subversive accommodation" into political defiance. The cultural became overtly political. In January 1995, a hundred thousand young spectators of a Tehran soccer match went on a rampage following a disagreement on the result of the competition. Riots destroyed part of the stadium and led to a mass protest of youths chanting: "Death to this barbaric regime"; "Death to the Pasdaran."[36] In 2004, over five thousand youths battled with violent vigilante groups in North Tehran; and much earlier, the city of Tabriz had witnessed thousands of young spectators raging against *basiji* bands for objecting to the "improper behavior" of a few individuals in the crowd. Even more than collective grief and violence, collective joy became a medium of subversion. For the mass expression of "happiness" not only defied puritan principles of grief and gloom but circumvented its aura of repression. The success of Iran's national soccer team in Australia in November 1997 and at the World Cup in Paris against the United States in June 1998 sent hordes of young boys and girls into the streets in every major city to cheer, dance, and sound their car horns. For five hours security forces lost control, stood aside, and watched the crowd in its blissful ecstasy.[37] In the city of Karadj, the crowd overwhelmed the *basijies* by chanting, "*Basiji* must dance!" But even defeat was a pretext to show collective defiance. Hours after Iran's team lost to Bahrain in 2001, hundreds of thousands took to the streets, expressing deep-felt anger at the Islamist authorities. In fifty-four different areas of Tehran, young people marched, shouted political slogans, threw rocks and handmade explosives at police, vandalized police cars, broke traffic lights, and lit candles in a sign of mourning for the defeat. Other cities, Karadj, Qom, Shiraz, Kashan, Isfahan, and Islamabad, also witnessed similar protests. Only after eight hundred arrests did protestors go home.[38] But perhaps nothing was more symbolic about the young's defiance than setting off fireworks to celebrate Nowruz, the coming of the Iranian New Year. The Islamic state had outlawed this ancient Persian tradition. But by setting off millions of firecrackers, youngsters turned urban neighborhoods into explosive battle zones, scorning the official ban on the ritual and the collective joy that went with it.[39] The "mystery of firecrackers," as one daily put it, symbolized outrage against officialdom that the young saw as having forbidden joy and jolliness.[40]

The younger generation's defiance deepened the conflict between reformists and conservatives in government. Reformists blamed the youth unrest on the conservatives' overbearing moral pressure and the "suppression of joy." Launching a public debate on the necessity of leisure, the reformists called for tolerance and understanding.[41] In so doing, the reformists supplied the young with a platform, political support, and moral courage. Backed by reformist friends at the top, the young further pushed for their claims, not only through defiance, but also by engagement in civic activism. In 2001, some fifty youth NGOs were registered in Tehran, and four hundred in the country.[42] Within two years they reached 1,100, of which 850 participated in the first national congress of youth NGOs in 2003.[43] Still thousands more flourished informally throughout the country, working in cultural, artistic, charity, developmental, and intellectual domains. They organized lectures and concerts, did charity work, and coordinated bazaars, at times with remarkable innovation. On one occasion, a group of youths presented President Khatami with a plan for alternative young cabinet members to form a "government of youths." But reclaiming public space to assert their youthful sensibilities remained the major concern of those whose globalized subcultures (expressed in sexuality, gender roles, and lifestyle) were distancing them even from post-Islamists' commitment to largely traditional moral conventions.[44] Youth's behavior infuriated conservative puritans, who clamored against what they considered a "cultural invasion," "hooliganism," and "anti-Islamic sentiments," blaming them on Khatami's "failure to ameliorate unemployment, poverty and corruption."[45] Thus, they launched new crackdowns on events, gatherings, places, and behaviors that were seen to cause "immorality," "depravity," and "indecency"; they dispatched special units with groups of uniformed men who carried machine guns and hand grenades to reassert the republic's moral order.[46]

This simultaneous condition of both suppression (of youthfulness by the politico-moral authority) and opportunity (valorization and encouragement of the young) offered these youth a spectacular sense of self and the possibility to act collectively, a status their Egyptian or Saudi counterparts largely lacked. But there was more to the emergence of a national Iranian youth movement than politics. Sweeping social change since the early 1980s had helped form "youth" as a social category. Demographically, by 1996 Iran had experienced a dramatic rise in its number of young people, with two-thirds under the age of thirty. Of these, a staggering twenty million, one-third of the population, were students (an increase of 266 percent since 1976). Most lived in cities, exposed to diverse lifestyles with spaces for relative autonomy, extrakinship identities, and social interactions on a broad scale. In the meantime, as urbanity was permeating the countryside, an "urbanized" generation of rural youth was in the making. The spread of Open University branches throughout the country, for instance, meant that on average every village had two university graduates, a very rare phenomenon in the 1970s. Rural youth began to acquire legitimacy based on competence and merit and became major decision makers, which the dominance of seniority had previously made unthinkable. With sweeping social changes in the countryside and expanding communication technologies that facilitated the flow of young people, ideas, and lifestyles, social barriers separating rural and urban youth began to crumble, giving the country's young a broader, national constituency. Meanwhile, the weakening of parental authority over the young (resulting from the state's valorization of youth) and the reinforcement of child-centeredness in the family (an outcome of rising literacy among women and mothers) contributed to the individuation of the young and their militancy.[47]

By the mid-1990s, Iran's postrevolutionary young had become "youth," a social agent. But theirs was not a conventional social movement, an organized and sustained collective challenge with articulated ideology or a recognizable leadership. Rather, theirs was a nonmovement, the "collective conscience" of the noncollective actors, whose principal expression lay in the *politics of presence*, tied closely to the young's everyday cultural struggles and normative subversion. This fragmented mass of individuals and subgroups shared common attributes in expressing common anxieties, in demanding individual liberty, and in constructing and asserting their collective identities. The individual youngsters were tied together not only within dispersed subgroups (youth magazines, NGOs, peer groups, and street-corner associations), but more commonly through "passive networks": those nondeliberate communications formed by the youngsters tacitly recognizing their commonalities through sight and sound in public spaces, by identifying shared symbols displayed in styles (T-shirts, blue jeans, hair), types of activities (attending particular concerts and music stores), and places (sport stadiums, shopping malls, hiking tracks), and by the sound of their music or firecrackers. Thus, the birth of youth as a social category of national scale, operating in uniquely simultaneous conditions of both repression and opportunity, drove the Iranian youths to reclaim their youthfulness in a battle in which the state became the target. Reclaiming youth habitus from state control and moral authority defined Iran's youth nonmovement.

POLITICS OF EGYPTIAN YOUTHS: "ACCOMMODATING INNOVATION"

"Youth" as a social category also developed in Egypt. Quite similar to Iran, in 1996 about half of Egypt's sixty million people were under twenty, and 64 percent under thirty.[48] Although the total student population in 1996 (11.6 million) was only just over half of Iran's, Egypt had the same number of college students (1.1 million).[49] Similarly, the peculiarity of the Egyptian countryside (with comparatively large villages concentrated along the Nile Valley and Delta and in close proximity to each other and large cities) contributed to their growing urbanity during the 1980s and 1990s. The abundance of electricity; new means of communication; commercialization; the flow of people, goods, and information; and increasing occupational specialization marked the shifting social structure of post-open-door rural settings.[50] The spread of mass schooling provided the raw materials to produce educated youth. And urban institutions such as college campuses, coffee shops, shopping malls, concert venues, festivals of saints, and street corners provided spaces for social interaction, active and passive networks, and the construction of youth identities. In brief, the young as social actors had emerged in both Iran and Egypt in a more or less similar pattern.

But the simultaneous processes of urbanization, Islamization, and globalization had fragmented the young generation in Egypt. Alongside actively pious and provincial adolescents had emerged new generations of globalized youths who had been increasingly exposed to the global cultural flows. Clearly, different class and gender experiences had given rise to multiple youth identities. Whereas harsher social control in the Islamic republic had pushed male and female youth to develop similar aspirations, gender distinction in Egypt remained more enunciated. For example, the difference in social aspirations between adolescent boys and girls in Egypt was so pronounced that observers spoke of "more separate male and female cultures than a single youth culture." Especially crucial were male perceptions of women, which seriously threatened their identity as youths' shared habitus. Rarely would men (in Egypt only 4 percent) marry a woman who had premarital sex.[51] "No one goes out with a girl and marries her. Ninety-nine percent of men would not marry a girl they ever touched," stated a university student in Egypt. And the girls felt this bitter truth. "This is what we hate about the boys; they rarely marry the girl they go out with."[52]

But in both Iran and Egypt, the mainstream young attempted to assert their habitus, to exert their individuality, aspired for change, and created youth subculture. They did so by recognizing the existing moral and political constraints and trying to make the best out of the existing institutions. However, compared to their Iranian counterparts, Egyptian youth remained demobilized in the political and civic domains. While they showed interest in participating politically, they lacked the means to do so. Unlike in Iran, where ageism was breaking down and youth was remarkably valorized, the elders and political elites in Egypt did not trust the young in the political arena. Egyptian politics, both governmental and oppositional, continued to remain in the grip of very old men, with an average age of seventy-seven in 2002.[53] Meanwhile, the young distrusted party politics, which happened to be the only legitimate channel for activism.[54] A survey by the Ahram Center for Political and Strategic Studies revealed that 67 percent of young people were not registered to vote.[55]

Lack of trust in electoral games pushed the young further away from politics, and restrictions on campus activism put a damper on youth political mobilization. The mobilization of middle- and lower-middle-class youth in the Islamist movement during the 1980s did not repeat itself in other political fields. In the late 1990s political activity on campuses was paltry, as state security intervened to prevent Islamist, leftist, and Nasserist candidates from running for student unions. Only Israel's reoccupation of the Palestinian Territories in early 2000 galvanized social and political mobilization.[56] The remarkable involvement of Egyptian youths in collecting food and medicine for Palestinians was indeed a watershed in youth voluntarism, but it was the result of the unique political and moral aura of the siege of Palestinians by Likud's repressive incursions. Otherwise, the young showed slight interest in public service or voluntarism. Even the youths of elite families, whose social and financial resources often make them the prime source of donations, remained indifferent. Of twenty hand-picked students of Egyptian universities, only one had engaged in any volunteer activities.[57] Genuine youth initiatives such as Fathi Kheir NGO were exceptions. The prevailing notion was that the state, not citizens, was to take charge of social provisions.

Clearly, the young were bearing the brunt of Egypt's "passive revolution," in which the "secularreligious" state had appropriated the initiative for change through a remarkable blend of concession and control. Egyptian youth were not under the same moral and political control as their counterparts in Iran or Saudi Arabia. Depending on their social and economic capacities, they were able to listen to their music, follow their fashions, pursue dating games, have affordable fun, and be part of global trends so long as they recognized their limits, beyond which their activities would collide with the moral authority and the state. Youths were to be integrated and guided by the state.

To do so, the state would provide the young with "scientific advance-ment" or technical education to catch up and compete in the world, and at the same time guide them into religious piety in order to withstand both for-eign cultural influences and home-grown political Islam.[58] Indeed, the 1999 presidential decree to rename the Supreme Council of Youths (established in 1965) the Ministry of Youths and Sports displayed official anxiety over the "youth problem."[59] Their protection from political and moral ills had be-come a matter of "national security." The Ministry of Youth with its control of four thousand Youth Centers was to help materialize these objectives. Government loans were to enable the young to settle down and marry by purchasing flats,[60] to provide access to ICT, and to acquire technical training through NGOs.[61] Meanwhile, the Youth Centers, some kind of state-controlled NGOs, would organize summer camps, debates, entertainment, training pro-grams, religious education caravans, and sporting events. But the deplorable state of most of these centers, their poor amenities, garbage-infested athletic fields, poor libraries, and the state's control rendered them inadequate to carry out this enormous task. Often, only lower-class youngsters, almost all of them male, attended the centers. Many remained "youth centers without youths," as an official weekly put.[62] If the televised annual "dialogue" of the president with "Egyptian youths" was any indication, a deep distrust sepa-rated youths from the state.[63] The young took solace in nonstate spaces that infringed only marginally on political and moral authorities. They resorted to the cultural politics of everyday life, where they could reassert their youth-ful claims.

For over a decade, young Egyptians were seen in the image of Islamist militants waging guerrilla war, penetrating college campuses, or memorizing the Qur'an in the backstreet mosques of sprawling slums. Moral authorities, parents, and foreign observers expected them to be characteristically pious, strict, and dedicated to the moral discipline of Islam. Yet in their daily lives, the mainstream young defied their constructed image, often shocking moral au-thorities by expressing defiance openly and directly. "The youth of this coun-try are rebelling against the old traditions," stated a twenty-year-old female student in Cairo. "We are breaking away from your chains; we are not willing to live the lives of the older generations. Women smoking *shisha* is the least shocking form of rebellion going on. Face the changes and embrace our gen-eration; do not treat us as if we are children. Our generation is more exposed than yours, and this is a simple fact."[64]

Reports of "satanic youth" in January 1997 demonstrated not only prevailing moral panic over the alleged vulnerability of youths to global culture, but those youths' emerging self-assertion. Every Thursday night hundreds of well-to-do youngsters gathered in an abandoned building to socialize, have fun, and, above all, dance to heavy metal music. Six weeks of sensational media coverage and the arrest of dozens accused of "satanism" (later released for lack of evidence) proved the existence of underground subcultures that few adults had noticed. The music subculture, however, did not die out after the satanist myth. It reappeared in the form of raving. Egyptian raves began with small bands and small crowds, but after 1998 professional organization and commercialization helped them grow rapidly. They encompassed music genres from around the world, including Egyptian pop, and catered to young elites of "glamour, high fashion and lifestyle."[65] For many, the rave became "a community which you have grown to know, at least recognize, centered around a common interest in the music."[66] The Egyptian rave was largely sex-free, but it did involve alcohol and (unofficially) drugs (in the form of Ecstasy). Indeed, studies indicated that experimentation with alcohol went beyond the well-to-do young. One out of every three students in the cities had drunk alcohol, mainly beer.[67] Although only somewhat more than 5 percent admitted experimenting with drugs (85 percent of whom were cannabis users), the problem became more severe in the early 1990s. Law enforcement professionals warned that the use of Ecstasy in particular was on the rise.[68]

While in general a "culture of silence" prevailed regarding sexuality,[69] premarital sex seemed to be widespread among Muslim youth, despite normative and religious prohibition. In an approximate but indicative survey of one hundred high school and college girls in various Cairo districts, 8 percent said they had had sexual intercourse, 37 percent had experienced sex without intercourse, 23 percent had kissed, and 20 percent had only held hands. In a survey of 100 school and college male students in Cairo, 73 percent said they would not mind having premarital sex as long as they would not marry their partners.[70] A more comprehensive study found "substantial rates of premarital sex among university students."[71] In AIDS education classes, students posed questions about specific sexual practices that surprised health educators.[72] Although comprehensive surveys did not exist, the use of pornography by males appeared to be quite widespread.[73] Ninety out of one hundred respondents said they masturbated regularly, and 70 percent of those ninety thought they were doing something religiously and physically wrong.[74] Beyond influences from satellite dishes, illicit videos, and later the Internet, the changing structure of households seemed to facilitate youth sexual practices. The father figure, once so important, was changing even in villages. One out of three families was fatherless, resulting from divorce, abandonment, and mostly (20 to 25 percent) fathers working abroad; children might use the home for romance when their mothers went out.[75] Otherwise, lower-class Cairo couples found romantic solace on the benches of inconspicuous metro stations, where they sat and talked or romanced while pretending to wait for trains.[76]

Most of these young people were religious. They often prayed, fasted, and expressed fear of God. A few heavy metal "satanists" whom I interviewed considered themselves devout Muslims but also enjoyed rock music, drinking alcohol, and romance. The mainstream young combined prayer, partying, and pornography, faith and fun. Notice how, for instance, a lower-class young man working in Dahab, a tourist resort where many foreign women visit, blended God, women, and police in pursuit of his mundane and spiritual needs: "I used to pray before I came to Dahab. My relationship to God was very strong and very spiritual. Now, my relationship to God is very strange. I always ask him to provide me with a woman, and when I have a partner, I ask him to protect me from the police."[77]

This might sound like a contradiction, but it expresses more a consolation and an accommodation. The young enjoyed dancing, raving, having illicit relationships, and fun but found solace and comfort in their prayers and faith. "I do both good and bad things, not just bad things. The good things erase the bad things," said a law student in Cairo.[78] A twenty-five-year-old religious man who drank alcohol and "tried everything" also smoked "pot in a group sometimes to prove [their] manhood." He prayed regularly, hoping that God forgave his ongoing misdeeds. Such a state of liminality, this "creative inbetweeness," illustrates how the young attempted to redefine and reimagine their Islam in order to accommodate their youthful desires for individuality, change, fun, and "sin" within the existing moral order. Not only did they redefine their religion, they also reinvented notions of youthfulness. "During adolescence," a nineteen-year-old student said, "all young men do the same; there is no halal or haram [right or wrong] at that age."[79] Similarly, many young girls saw themselves as committed Muslims but still uncovered their hair or wore the veil only during Ramadan or only during fasting hours. Many of those who enjoyed showing their hair found consolation in deciding to cover it after marriage, when their youthful stage was over.

To assert their habitus under the prevailing moral and political constraints, Egyptian youths resorted to *accommodating innovation*, a strategy that redefined and reinvented prevailing norms and traditional means to accommodate their youthful claims. Yet the young did not depart radically from the dominant system but made it work for their interests.[80] The relatively widespread practice of *urfi* (informal) marriage since the late 1990s exemplified this strategy. *Urfi* marriage is a religiously accepted but unofficial oral contract that requires two witnesses and is carried out in secret. The minister of social affairs spoke of 17 percent of university female students going through *urfi* marriage, causing a public uproar over this "danger" to "national security."[81] Officials cited declining social authority, absence of fathers, and the employment of mothers as the cause of this "frightening phenomenon."[82] Experts pointed to the lack of housing and especially the absence of a "religious supervision" over youth.[83] But in essence, the young utilized this traditional institution to pursue romance within, but not outside or against, the moral and economic order, to get around the moral constraints on dating and the economic constraints on formal marriage.[84] With the same logic, lower-class youth resorted to, but also modified the meaning of, such religious occasions as Ramadan (the time of fasting), Eid al-Adha (the festival of sacrifice), and the birthdays of saints as occasions of intense sociability and diversion.

Indeed the phenomenon of Amr Khaled, Egypt's most popular young lay preacher, who since the late 1990s spoke about piety and the moralities of everyday life, should be seen in a similar sense of a reinvention of a new religious style by Egypt's globalizing youth.[85] In a sense, Egyptian cosmopolitan youths fostered a new religious subculture—one that was expressed in a distinctly novel style, taste, language, and message. It resonated in the aversion of these young from patronizing pedagogy and moral authority. These globalizing youth displayed many seemingly contradictory orientations; they were religious believers but distrusted political Islam if they knew anything about it; they swung back and forth from (the pop star) Amr Diab to Amr Khaled, from partying to prayers, and yet they felt the burden of a strong social control by their elders, teachers, and neighbors. As young Egyptians were socialized in a cultural condition and educational tradition that often restrained individuality and novelty, they were compelled to assert them in a "social way," through "fashion." Thus, through the prism of youth, this religious subculture galvanized around the "phenomenon of Amr Khaled" was partly an expression of "fashion" in a Simmelian sense—in the sense of an outlet that accommodates contradictory human tendencies: change and adaptation, difference and similarity, individuality and social norms. Resorting to this type of piety permitted the elite young to assert their individuality, undertake change, and yet remain committed to collective norms and social equalization.[86]

Although innovative, these strategies conformed to the prevailing regime of power, meaning that Egyptian youth stood largely demobilized within social and political constraints. Egypt's "passive revolution" had ensured this demobilization by offering room to exercise a limited degree of innovation, but only within the political discipline of the "seculareligious" state. It was only toward the end of the first decade of the twenty-first century that Egyptian youth managed to collectively break through the rigid case of the state to mobilize—not in the streets, but on the screens of computers. With the new technological opportunities, e-mail, weblogs, and especially Facebook, some seventy thousand educated youths linked up to produce what came to be known as the April 6 Youth Movement. Utilizing such a venue to campaign against political repression, economic stagnation, and nepotism, the young activists augmented a new way of doing politics, a step further than what Kifaya movement had begun earlier on.[87] For now, we may not be able to judge the political efficacy of such postmodern nonmovements, but they attest to the fact that the subaltern utilize any opportunities to outmaneuver state surveillance and push for change. Yet the point is not to wait for opportunities, but to constantly generate them.

What, then, of youths as a political force in the Muslim Middle East? Do youth non/movements possess the capacity to cause political and democratic transformation? If indeed the youth movements, as I have suggested, are ultimately about claiming and reclaiming youthfulness, then their transformative and democratizing potential would depend on the capacity of the moral and political authorities to accommodate youthful claims. If their youthful claims are accommodated, youth movements would by definition cease to exist, and young people may remain as conservative politically as any other social groups. To act as democratizing agents, the young will need to think and act politically, as the Egyptian April 6 Youth Movement in 2008 illustrates. Yet, because the current doctrinal religious regimes in the Middle East possess limited capacity to contain the increasingly global youth habitus, youth movements retain a considerable transformative and democratizing promise. Thus,

Muslim youth, perhaps similar to their non-Muslim counterparts, remain in constant struggle to assert, claim, and reclaim their youthfulness, by taking advantage of available venues, including resorting to religion or subverting it. Negotiating between their youthfulness and Muslimness, mediated through political and economic conditions, marks a central feature of Muslim youth habitus.

7 THE POLITICS OF FUN

IN DECEMBER 2002, on a plane from Aleppo, Syria, I happened to be sitting next to a twenty-year-old Syrian cleric on his way to Cairo to spend some time in Al-Azhar, the seat of Egypt's official Islam. He asked if he could borrow my Syrian newspaper, which he quickly skimmed through until he reached the sports pages. Only after the young cleric had thoroughly observed the entire section did I start a conversation with him. He said he loved soccer and prayed that his favorite teams, Bayern Munich and Barcelona, would win their national tournaments. Music was his other interest, not only that of Um Kulthoum and Fairouz, but also that of the Egyptian pop star Amr Diab. Young mullahs also need to have fun, it occurred to me. Observing this man of religion taking such pleasure in temporal diversions, I could not help wondering why puritan Islamists express such hostility toward fun and joy.

One of the ironies of "fundamentalist" Islamism is that it has tenaciously withstood waves of political challenges but has felt powerless before simple displays of spontaneity and joy and the pursuit of everyday pleasures. It seems as though every occasion of mundane festivity, private parties, and gatherings at bustling street corners, teahouses, shopping malls, and secular celebrations becomes a matter of profound doctrinal anxiety and delegitimation. It is as if these ordinary pursuits would enfeeble the Islamist moral paradigm, just as the erotic taste of chocolate perturbed the *tranquillité* of the French village in Joanne Harris's novel *Chocolat*. So, why are Islamists so distinctly

Adapted from Asef Bayat, "Islamism and the Politics of Fun," *Public Culture*, 19, no. 3 (October 2007), pp. 433–59.

apprehensive of the expression of "fun"—a preoccupation most people in the world seem to take for granted?

By *fun*, I mean an array of ad hoc, nonroutine, and joyful pursuits—ranging from playing games, joking, dancing, and social drinking, to involvement in playful art, music, sex, and sport, to particular ways of speaking, laughing, appearing, or carrying oneself—where individuals break free temporarily from the disciplined constraints of daily life, normative obligations, and organized power. Fun is a metaphor for the expression of individuality, spontaneity, and lightness, in which joy is the central element. While joy is neither an equivalent nor a definition of fun, it remains a key component of it. Not everything joyful is fun, such as routine ways of having meals, even though one can make food fun by injecting joyful creativity in preparing or consuming it. Thus, fun often points to usually improvised, spontaneous, free-form, changeable, and thus unpredictable expressions and practices. There is a strong tendency in modern times to structure and institutionalize fun in the form of, for instance, participating in organized leisure activities: going to bars, discos, concerts, and the like. However, the inevitable drive for spontaneity and invention renders organized fun a tenuous entity.

Fun may be expressed by individuals or collectives, in private or public, and take traditional or commoditized forms. Fashion, for instance, represents a collective, commoditized, and systematic expression of fun, yet one that is constantly in flux because it responds to the carefree and shifting spirit of fun. Fun appeals to almost all social groups (the rich and poor, old and young, modern and traditional, men and women), yet youths are the prime practitioners of fun, embodying a greater tendency toward experimentation, adventurism, idealism, and a drive for autonomy, mobility, and change—and thus the main target of anti-fun politics. Perhaps that is why fun is often conflated with and identified by "youth culture." However, fun in fact constitutes only one, albeit significant, component of youth culture, in the same way that lower-class festivities, such as the activities celebrating the birthdays of saints (*mulids*) in Egypt, are but one aspect of folk culture, and the creations of avant-garde artists one element of a counterculture. But the differential habitus of these social groups tends to orient them to different fun practices and therefore to subject them to different degrees of prohibitions and regulations that can be subsumed under the rhetoric of "anti-fun." For instance, whereas the elderly poor can afford simple, traditional, and contained diversions, the globalized and affluent youth tend to embrace more spontaneous, erotically charged, and commodified pleasures. This might help explain why globalizing youngsters more than others cause fear and fury among Islamist anti-fun adversaries, especially when much of what these youths practice is informed by western technologies of fun and is framed in terms of "western cultural import."

The fear of fun is not restricted to Islamists and Islam but extends to most religions. It is not even a merely religious concern; secularists, whether revolutionary or conservative, have also expressed apprehension of and animosity toward fun. Rather than simply a doctrinal question, "anti-fun-damentalism" is a historical matter, one that has to do significantly with the preservation of power. In other words, at stake is not necessarily the disruption of the moral order, as is often claimed, but rather the undermining of the hegemony, the regime of power on which certain strands of moral and political authority rest. By "moral-political authority," I refer not only to state or governmental power, but also to the authority of individuals (for instance, shaykhs or cult leaders) and sociopolitical movements—those whose legitimacy lies in deploying a particular doctrinal paradigm. The adversaries' fear of fun revolves ultimately around the fear of exit from the paradigm that frames their mastery; it is about anxiety over loss of their "paradigm power."

ISLAMISM AND THE STRUGGLE OVER FUN

The history of Islamism has been one of a battle against fun, playfulness, and diversion, with the hostility coming from both the Islamist movements and the Islamic states. In the late 1980s, Islamist students who dominated university campuses in the south and north of Egypt disrupted concerts and plays, and harassed male and female students who were associating freely with one another or who were simply pursuing pleasures of everyday life. The Islamist student unions banned films, dancing, and popular and classical music, because they were deemed "alien to Islamic culture."[1] Later, the radical Islamist group al-Gama'a al-Islamiyya imposed strict codes of conduct, both on the young and on women in a Cairo neighborhood under its control; it forbade beauty salons and video shops and put an end to joyous music at weddings. Even the moderate Muslim Brothers held "exemplary Islamic weddings" that eliminated joyful music or allowed only the performance of *inshad*, featuring chanting and percussion. Many Islamists in Egypt wished to undo the country's happy culture of Islam, in particular its highly festive Ramadan observance, denouncing the festivals of saints' birthdays for their cheerful semblance.[2] Morality among the young became a matter of serious concern not only for

Islamists, but also for the conservative media. The state-owned weekly *Al-Ahram al-Arabi* lamented that coffee shops and youth hangouts had become "dens of drugs, booze, sexual movies and *urfi* [unofficial] marriage" and were frequented by "girls who smoke hookahs and wear clothes that are uncalled-for." The paper called for surveillance to protect "our youth."[3] The measures advanced by opposition Islamists and conservative media were quite soft when compared with the puritan policies of self-declared Islamist states such as Saudi Arabia, Afghanistan, and Iran.

Saudi Arabia's state control of leisure and diversion in the name of morality and piety has a longer history. The kingdom has banned dating, cinemas, concert halls, discos, clubs, and theaters. Even the innocent joy of flying kites is not tolerated. Yet nowhere was the dark side of puritanism probably more evident than in Taliban Afghanistan. During its draconian rule (1996–2001), the Taliban erased all signs of diversion, fun, secular aesthetics, the pursuit of individuality, and creativity. Music, television, painting, and sculpture, not to mention dancing, acting, public jubilance, the expression of beauty, and attention to the self, were harshly suppressed. Women were forced to wear the *burkha,* and men to grow long beards. Thus, when in November 2001 the Afghan capital, Kabul, fell to Northern Alliance forces, many Afghans began their human expression of joy in public. They played music in shops and turned on television sets, while some women shed their *burkha*s and men shaved their beards.

But it was in Iran where the expression of fun turned into a site of the most dramatic social polarization, pitting masses of dissenting women and the young against the Islamic state. Throughout the 1980s and 1990s, conservative Islamists battled against those who desired to demonstrate public joy. Fun, playfulness, lightness, and laughter were seen as instances of immorality, laxity, and waste, while entertainment in general was cast as a "counter-value" (*zedd-e arzesh*). "The most dangerous thing that threatens humanity," declared Mohammad Taqui Mesbah Yazdi, an Iranian conservative cleric, "is for men to forget devotion to God, to establish cultural centers instead of mosques and churches, and to be driven by film and art rather than prayer and supplication."[4] Unsolicited mixing of the sexes was perceived as one of the greatest diversions and was therefore "extremely dangerous." It "represents the hell-hole of individuals," an immoral practice that threatened the spiritual and physical health of society.[5] Gender segregation, therefore, was to act as yet another instrument of social control and discipline. A reader of the Islamist weekly *Hafteh-name-ye Sobh* echoed the profound anguish of the conservative establishment over the "dishonorable ways in which teenage girls *walk* in the streets. How will they respond to the blood of our martyrs? I am ashamed seeing girls wearing short *jackets*, of musical bands in Tehran who go as far as dancing . . . !"[6]

Although the purists had confirmed that there was no fun in Islam, this did not mean that Islamists rejected any concept of pleasure. In contrast to the general hostility of ethical religions toward sexuality, whose temptations were thought to divert man from his mystical quest and whose "essential irrationality" threatened self-control and discipline,[7] Iranian Islamists recognized (men's) carnal desires. To fulfill them, they proposed the "marriage of pleasure" (*mot'a*), which in the Shi'i Islam tradition is contracted for a specified period of time, ranging from a few hours to years.[8] They went as far as planning to establish "institutions" where men and women could meet, invoking a saying of Imam Sadeq, who had "wished to see every man among you practice a *mot'a* at least once in his life."[9] This plan, however, was a controlled, and indeed a rationalized, pursuit of worldly pleasure and was directed essentially toward male passion. Indeed, a 2002 initiative in the Islamic republic to channel some three hundred thousand prostitutes into "chastity houses," where men in pursuit of sex could temporarily "marry" prostitutes, follows similar logic of both control and legitimation of morality. Islamists were concerned, not about sex, but about the control of sexuality.

Yet for Islamists true joy lay in spiritual, mystical, and inner pursuits, in a sort of pious pleasure—of family, bravery, and sacrifice. They revered a metaphorical "drunkenness," but one that was induced "by divine love," and cherished "amusement," but only "around prayer." They treasured the "joy of pious deeds," "devotion to the path of *velayat* [clerical rule]," and good "health" to carry on with the true path.[10] In essence these marked the behavioral disposition of the Islamist "ideal man": heavy, austere, warriorlike, controlled, resolute, selfless, and highly emotional—in short, an extraordinary personality who stood against the expression of lightness, carefreeness, and spontaneity—in a word, ordinariness.[11] To the extent that such a character plays down or represses humanistic impulses and desires, the nobility of life loses significance and the propensity to celebrate "noble death" or sacrifice increases. Thus, the annihilation of self and the "other" in the name of a "higher cause" assumes grand value. Iran's puritan zealots, or "mourners of joy" as some described them, deplored with great sorrow the secular delight associated with Nowruz, Persian New Year, reminiscing with astonishing melancholy about their "unforgettable happy days" on the war fronts.[12] This admiration of sacrifice and death, directed toward both self and other, was echoed in myriad slogans that exclusively emphasized "Death to . . . ," instead of "Long live . . ."[13] The two Islamic months of Muharram and Ramadan, highly charged occasions of martyrdom after the revolution, became even more dreary and sorrowful. Ayatollah Khomeini recognized the significance of these rituals by proclaiming, "It is these grievings that have kept Islam alive." The Islamic Republic's calendar became a testimony to the official sanction of grief over joy. While the authorities commemorated fully the deaths, or "death days," of religious and political figures, their birthdays were widely ignored (the AH 1380/2001 calendar indicated only three official birthdays as opposed to ten official death days). Iranian zealots were astounded to see joyful practices of popular Islam in other Muslim societies, describing them as *jahili* (pagan, pre-Islamic) and as a manifestation of "American Islam."[14] "In many Arab countries, Ramadan evenings have turned into evenings of fun, joy, parties and jokes," lamented a commentator in Iran's weekly *Jebhe*.[15] Even the slightest expressions of societal vigor and color disturbed puritan sensibilities. "Just take a look at the town," bemoaned the weekly *Shalamche*, "Western rationalism has dominated our existence. Painlessness and pleasure seeking have assumed rational justification. From athletic fields to classrooms, it is the god of pleasure that is worshipped."[16] *Shalamche* lashed out at the reformist minister of culture for the production of anthems (*soroud*), which it claimed were "even more joyful than disco songs."[17] There was even little tolerance for expressions such as clapping, whistling, and joyful cheers. The public castigation of teenage boys for hanging around girls' schools in the "backstreets of forbidden love" became a stark reminder of a land in which the mighty moral state made it its business to interrogate love, to suppress desire, and to place the most innocent expression of youthfulness under the political microscope. "It is horrible to be in love in this country," youngsters often lamented. The moral masters made a dangerous venture, a sin, of the otherwise mundane exchange of a modest smile for which the terrified teen had made a daylong preparation. "Finding a love letter in a girl's pocket is like walking in the streets without a hijab," warned a school superintendent.[18] Morals police were dispatched to "cleanse" the public space and bring moral order into the private sphere to the extent of invading private parties. Sorrow, sadness, a somber mood, and dark, austere colors defined the

Islamist public space, media, and religious rituals. In such a state of virtue, the shape and color of clothing, the movement of the body, the sound of one's voice, the level of laughter, and the intensity of looks all became matters of intense control and discipline.[19]

Throughout the 1980s, the country's preoccupation with war (with Iraq), together with repression and revolutionary fervor, made the overpowering surveillance seem invincible. Yet before long, signs of underground and open defiance, primarily among the young, placed the quest for fun at the center of the nation's political contestation. With the war over and postwar reconstruction under way during the 1990s, the young began publicly to express their selfhood, both individually and collectively. They pursued music, frequented video clubs, and set up underground pop and rock bands. Against the warnings of the authorities, many followed the global tastes, fashion, and dating games, expressing them in shopping malls, public parks, underground private parties, and pursuits that did not exclude premarital sex.[20] The practice of such cultural politics subverted the authorities' portrayal of Muslim youth as a selfless mass devoid of individuality in the service of stern moral codes; it challenged the ideological edifice of the religious state. Yet the young refused to abandon religion as such. Instead, they reinvented their Islam to accommodate their youthful claims. Thus, in an ingenious strategy, what I have called "subversive accommodation," the young utilized the existing legitimate norms and institutions to lodge their youthful desires, but in doing so they subverted and redefined the meanings attached to such norms and institutions. In this fashion, the highly charged rituals of mourning could turn into occasions of glamour, sociability, and fun.[21]

These stories are not meant to valorize excess, irresponsibility, or socially harmful conducts in the name of fun. The fact is that fun, just like any exercise of freedom, has the potential to become a social problem if individual and social responsibilities are not recognized. Excessive individualism, nihilism, drug use, unfettered sexuality, AIDS, and violence would impair not only society at large, but also and primarily the fun-loving actors themselves. Saudi youngsters' resort to skidding (*tahfit*; holding on to a moving car), a dangerous pastime against widespread boredom, has taken a large toll on its practitioners.[22] And fomenting ethnoreligious violence in the name of fun by the young recruits of the Muhajir Quami Movement is causing no less than major damage to Pakistani society.[23] My attention, rather, centers chiefly on harmless fun, that which remains more or less within social expectations and generalized standards. Excess in controlling fun may also entail excess in practicing it. Reformists in Iran were concerned precisely about such extreme response and disruptions if the conservative puritans continued with their anti-fun policies.

Indeed, the battle over fun deepened the conflict between the reformist and conservative wings of the government. Reformists attributed ensuing unrest to the suppression of joy and the need for happiness; they unleashed a public debate over joy and fun by sponsoring studies, organizing seminars, and publishing articles supporting the idea that "joy was not a sin, but a deeply human emotion." Some called for a "definition" and even "management" of joy in order to develop a culture of fun and festivity among the people who had been denied that experience and were thus ignorant of the rules.[24] Dozens of seminars debated the meaning of "leisure" and the modalities of "fun among women," who had been suffering from depression in larger numbers.[25] Psychologists and journalists called for a "love of life," emphasizing that "living with joy is our right . . . [for] a depressed and austere society cannot have a solid civil foundation."[26] Proclaiming that "laughter is not deviance," some reformists lashed out at Islamists who had shunned fun and laughter, human pursuits that invigorate society.[27]

In response, the infuriated Islamists clamored against what they considered a "cultural invasion," "hooliganism," and "anti-Islamic sentiments."[28] In August 2001 the conservative judiciary, by means of public floggings, began a new crackdown on citizens committing or promoting immorality, depravity, and indecency in the public space. The police closed boutiques, cafés, and restaurants that exhibited signs of depravity.[29] Neckties were outlawed, girls wearing loose veils were photographed for police files, and men were stripped to the waist and flogged for drinking alcohol or being seen with non-familial women.[30] A year later Tehran residents watched new groups of uniformed men patrol the streets in four-wheel-drive vehicles. Some sixty special units included several hundred men wearing green uniforms and toting machine guns and hand grenades as they drove up and down the streets chasing young drivers listening to loud music, women wearing makeup or loose veils, partygoers, and alcohol drinkers.[31] The crackdowns did little to change the behavior and instead caused a public uproar in which the fundamentals of the Islamic penal code came under further attack, as scores of reform-minded clerics questioned its application in this modern age.[32]

FUN BEFORE FUNDAMENTALISM AND AFTER

Has anti-fun-damentalism been an invariable feature of Islamic history? If not, at what point did fun become a prominent political concern in Muslim societies? What kind of attitudes toward fun existed before the rise of Islamism? Certainly, anti-fun ethics are not just a recent occurrence. Muslim societies have been witness to both a desire for and a battle against fun. However, the dynamics of its politics have been different. Historically, anti-fun sentiments and rulings focused overwhelmingly on "wine, women, and song." They were framed essentially in terms of "forbidding wrong," an Islamic injunction rooted in a number of Qur'anic verses that call on Muslims to "command right and forbid wrong."[33] However, the questions of what is wrong, who forbids, and how to forbid remain contested.[34] It is also not certain whether the Qur'anic phrases meant what the ulema (Muslim clerics) later took them to mean.[35] In principle, wrongs included morally reprehensible practices such as dishonest commercial activity and usury, but especially singing, wine drinking, immodesty, and prostitution. The enforcers of morality were overwhelmingly puritanical and assertive ulema who led bands of devotees acting as their foot soldiers.[36] Surveillance, then, came largely from those *individual* zealots confronting wrongdoers, who in their daily lives remained overwhelmingly indifferent to such puritanical ethics and who continued pursuing their mundane pleasures. "In the first four centuries of Islam," reports Franz Rosenthal, "the representatives of ascetic piety were comparatively few, and their voices were not heeded. On the contrary, there existed a pronounced predilection for humor and gaiety which knew few restrictions."[37] Scholar Michael Cook cites evidence suggesting that in the medieval Muslim world drinking as a social practice was a "normality"—a tradition from which even women were not excluded.[38] Humor, poetry, and music seem to have been even more widespread. The legends of Ash'ab, the singer, dancer, and comedian of Medina and Mecca in the ninth century, and the more recent figure of the famous Nasreddin Hoca represent historical prototypes of humor in Muslim societies. Indeed, the genre of *adab* literature in the Middle East is replete with jokes and anecdotes (*muzah*) relating to politics, religion, and everyday life.[39] In Sufi Islam the ecstasy of divine experience was and still is tightly intertwined with poetry, dance, and music. Joyful religious practice to a large extent remains a character of folk Islam. To the dismay of religious purists, every year millions of Muslim men, women, and children join the *mulid* festivals to celebrate the birth of revered saints with food, fun, and a fair, often for several days and nights.[40] On such occasions, a fusion of piety, prayer, and rapture is embedded in religious songs (*aghani diniyya*) in the spirit similar to that of the joyous culture of the Afro-American group of the Episcopal Church in the United States. In these religious songs, the line separating secular and sacred is not easy to draw.[41]

While in premodern times conflict over everyday pleasures derived from and was restricted to sporadic intrusions by individual religious purists into people's public behavior (exceptions include the twelfth-century al-Mohad dynasty in Morocco and the eleventh-century Fatimid caliph Hakim in Egypt), with the advent of modern states, social movements, and the Westernization of Muslim societies, especially the development of new modes, means, and spaces of sociability, such as radios, televisions, cafés, concert halls, bars, restaurants, and holiday resorts, the dynamics of anti-fun politics shifted.[42] First, instead of merely individual ulema, powerful *movements* raised the banner of the battle against mundane pleasures. Second, the target of anti-fun-damentalism was no longer just fun-loving individuals, but also those secular states that allowed and accommodated ordinary joys of everyday life—music, cinema, entertainment, dating, or any sort of pastime that could be seen as morally reprehensible. Thus, Abul-Ala Mawdudi of India's Jama'at-i Islami and Sayed Qutb of Egypt's Muslim Brotherhood spearheaded later militant movements that branded modern Muslim states and societies, such as that of Egypt of the 1950s, as corrupt and *jahili*. These states, according to the militants, needed to be transformed (through revolution) into Islamic moral entities so as to guide their "corrupt societies" onto the right path. In other words, it was incumbent on the states (and not simply individuals or movements) to take on the duty of righting moral wrongs. With the establishment of full-fledged monolithic Islamic states, as in Saudi Arabia, Afghanistan, and Iran, curbing fun became a prominent political concern in society. Ironically, modernity displaced the individual zealots and gave rise to overpowering states that confronted people's private desires, interests, and expressions. In Saudi Arabia the concerted anti-fun campaign began with the emergence of the purist Wahhabi movement (led by Muhammad ibn Abd al-Wahhab [d. 1792]) in Nejd in the eighteenth century. The movement gave rise to three episodes of the Saudi state in Arabia. During the first Saudi reign (1745–1818), rulers in the Hijaz banned tobacco, scrapped musical instruments, and obliged people to attend mosques and to pray more regularly.[43] Through the years, they expanded the scope, types, and geographical coverage of anti-fun rulings and by the late 1920s established the Committee for Commanding the Right and Forbidding the Wrong. Although during the reign of Ibn Saud (1902–52) puritan ethics were undermined and people were allowed to have their fun, in the late 1950s as the tide of Nasserist republicanism swept through the Arab world, Saudi rulers revived a new and far more severe strategy of moral discipline.[44] Likewise, Afghanistan's strict anti-fun policies came to fruition with the Taliban puritan regime (1996–2001), which established a ministry to determine and enforce a pervasive moral surveillance.[45]

Unlike the Saudi and Taliban rulers, the Islamic regime in Iran faced a formidable challenge in launching its moral crusade, for it confronted a populace that had a longer and more widespread experience with secular diversions than had the populations of Saudi Arabia and Afghanistan. In Iran the secular trend had reached its peak in the same decade, the 1970s, as the Islamic revolution. In the years just prior to the 1979 Islamic revolution, there was a tremendous boost in the dissemination and consumption of both domestic and imported cultural goods. Western cinema and television programs, popular music, youth centers, bars, casinos, and Caspian Sea holidays had become significant components of Iran's urban culture. The number of movie viewers had increased by 50 percent between 1969 and 1975, nearly twice the rate of population growth in the same period. Every year during the 1970s, Iranian cinemas showed over five hundred foreign films, one-quarter of which were American. By 1975 half the urban population owned a television set, compared with less than 4 percent in 1960, and 65 percent of total households owned radios.[46] During the 1970s hundreds of thousands of middle-class Iranians regularly vacationed at Caspian Sea resorts to take pleasure in the globalized experience of sea, sun, sand, and sex. Iranian Muslims did not abandon commemorating the somber occasions of Muharram and Ramadan, yet both the rich and the poor, Muslim and non-Muslim, found great joy in celebrating the pre-Islamic Nowruz for thirteen days, by wearing new clothes, visiting relatives and friends, taking trips, partying, and picnicking—a highly secular tradition the Islamic regime has been struggling to undermine. By the late 1970s the media had molded a highly festive popular culture, embodied in the songs and performances of dozens of vastly popular singers, actors, and comedians such as Gugoush, Haydeh, Aghasi, Sousan, Arham Sadr, Vahdat, Parviz Sayyad, Fardin, and the sultry Foruzan. Comedy, humor, and jokes, even though at times cynical, had become an integral part of both artistic life

and popular idiom at large. This growing culture of fun and festivity, especially the western imports, dismayed and disappointed many puritan clerics.
They condemned cinema, radio, and television, since in Ayatollah Khomeini's view they were used to "corrupt our youth."[47] They deplored the urban
"bright light" culture and holiday resorts and bemoaned the sins of summer
vacations at the Caspian Sea. The office of *Inhafteh*, the Iranian equivalent of
Playboy magazine, was bombed. These measures, however, did little to impede the expression of everyday diversion and enjoyment. It was only by the
ascendancy of the Islamic state that fun became the site of a major political
struggle in society.

ISLAM AND FUN

Why did Islamists insist on preserving puritan values despite the political
cost? What lay behind their fear of fun? The prevailing western view is that
animosity toward fun and joy had roots in the rigid ethics of Islam. According
to this vision, Islam embodies a "world in which human life doesn't have the
same value as it does in the West, in which freedom, democracy, openness
and creativity are alien."[48] Indeed the Islamic doctrine appears to contain
rulings that disdain fun and festivity. For instance, a number of hadith, pro-
phetic sayings and practices, seem to emphasize *haya'* (modesty in character),
scorning crass and trivial manners.[49] The exegeses indicate how the Prophet
disliked those who used undignified language to make people laugh.[50] Reportedly, 'A'ishah, his wife, "never saw [the Prophet] laughing to an extent
that one could see his palate; he always used to smile only."[51] In the spirit of
minimizing distractions from devotion to God, the Prophet deplored indul-
gence in activities such as poetry when they diverted people from God's re-
membrance, religious knowledge, and the recitation of the Qur'an.[52] Thus
some Muslim jurists prohibited the performing arts, drawing, and sculpture,
for fear that they would lead to idolatry (*shirk*), since only God was the creator,
even though the performing arts were present during *eid*s and other festive
occasions. Some jurists disallowed any play, amusement, or diversion, as vain
and wasteful in conditions of prolonged war and strife that demanded a total
focus on jihad.[53] Indeed, the literature on *bid'a* (innovation in religion), notably those attributed to Ibn Taymiya, carried decrees against (among others)
joy, laughter, and hedonistic ethics.[54] Shi'i sources include similar pronounce-
ments that interpret excessive amusement, laughter, and fun as "satanic" acts,
which cause scandals (*aberurizi*) and diversion from the faith.[55] They revere

modesty, shyness, and asceticism (*zohd*) and disdain the love of material wealth.[56]

But there is more to this. Doctrine, indeed the very same sources, simultaneously endorses ethics of joy and jollity. In contrast to the severe conduct of today's Islamists, the Prophet is also championed as a messenger of tolerance and tenderness. He despises those like ʿUmar whose "harsh" and "stern" character frightened fellow Muslims. "By Him in Whose Hands my life is," the Prophet addressed a forbidding ʿUmar, "whenever Satan sees you taking a way, he follows a way other than yours."[57] These words come from a man who smiled at those who were rude to him. Numerous sources mention his gentle and merciful nature and his pleasant and mild manner in his daily interactions.[58] Some rulings in Shiʿi sources clearly reject violence and coercion, calling instead for softness, jollity, fun, and amusement.[59] Imam Sajjad is cited as saying that for the Prophet, "the noblest deed before God is to bring joy to other people."[60] According to Imam Sadeq, cheerful (*khoshrou*) persons are so revered that God reserves the heaven for them.[61] By comparison, reports on the Prophet's sayings on dancing and singing remain vague, but in them the Prophet does not appear to forbid these acts.[62] Moreover, and contrary to self-righteous puritans who in the name of morality easily charge fellow Muslims with sin and *kufr* (nonbelief in God), Prophet Mohammad is emphatic that "all the sins of my fellows will be forgiven, except those of the *Mujahirin* [who decidedly repeat their evil doings]."[63] So, you should not be extremists."[64] "Do not take upon yourselves except deeds which are within your ability."[65] Indeed, charging a believer with *kufr* is equal to murdering him or her.[66]

It appears that Islam, similar to other religions, does not offer a definite theory of fun. As scholar Khaled Masoud suggests, the conflicting narratives in the doctrine, including the hadith, reflect uncertainty and plurality of views over such issues in early Islam, thus leaving behind a tradition that remains open to contesting readings.[67] Islam's position on the issue of fun, consequently, depends largely on who interprets it. Thus, in contrast to the conservative puritans, Iran's reformists of the 1990s proclaimed that Islam had never forced asceticism on Muslims. Instead, it had asked them to recognize their limits in order to promote and harmonize human instincts and life's pleasures with reason and responsibility. The reformists reminded the puritan Islamists not to force people to do "more than what God has asked" because "they will deliver less."[68] In the view of the young cleric Hojjat al-Islam Gholami, "Islam has, in fact, called for practices that induce happiness, like traveling, festivities, marriage, diversion, games and fun."[69] If "Imam Ali was both playful (*shoukh tab'*) and very jolly (*khande-rou*)," the sheikh objected, then why should the "clerics appear so heavy and sour-faced"?[70] Many ordinary Muslims wondered why the Islamic authorities harassed men wearing short sleeves or women in colored outfits, when there was no religious or legal basis for such prohibitions.[71] Why did Islamists insist on the suppression of delight, joy, self-expression, and love of life—human qualities that most people in the world take for granted? Whatever their motives, Islamists in the end drew on certain teachings of their religion, on exegeses and opinions of some early Muslim jurists. But is this tendency peculiar to Islam and Islamists?

ANTI-FUN-DAMENTALISM BEYOND ISLAM, BEYOND RELIGION

In truth, traces of rigid piety and ascetic tendencies can be seen in most religions. Most religions, and not just Islam, have raised, in their particular readings, the banner of martyrdom or admiration for dignified death. Socrates, the "secular saint," is said to represent the genesis of martyrdom in the West, while Christianity, with its story of crucifixion, developed a distinct theology of martyrdom.[72] In addition, most religions, in their distinct interpretations, have expressed hostility toward sexuality, holding that it binds humans to the animal world and diverts them from their mystical quest by threatening self-control and discipline.[73] Arts and music have not been spared from pietistic wrath. Protestant puritans replaced the Church as the medium of salvation, resorting to pietistic practices such as hard work and "avoiding cards, dancing, theatre-going, and essentially every action which could be seen as a concession to 'the world'" in order to assure their eternal redemption.[74] Drawing on Protestant ethics, Max Weber suggests that while "orgiastic" or "ritualistic" religions were inclined toward song, music, pictorial arts, and poetry, "rational religions" (such as Judaism, ancient Christianity, and Protestantism) showed animosity toward the arts. According to this logic, art, sexuality, and by extension fun had the potential to disrupt the influence of reason on human conduct or divert humans from full attention to the transcendental.[75]

There is surely some truth about diversion from the transcendental as a major cause of religious aversion to fun, levity, art, or sexuality, even though in reality not all followers of a faith have similar puritan values, as seen so far—some oppose them, others ignore them, and still others, in particular those

in authority, often uphold and enforce them. However, anti-fun sensibilities are not restricted to religious doctrines. The most irreligious movements—French Jacobins and Russian Bolsheviks—have expressed similar sentiments. In pre-revolution Europe authorities had campaigned in the name of morality to suppress all forms of lower-class public entertainment. Football, public drunkenness, wearing masks, and dancing were prohibited, and the traditional carnivals came under strict surveillance.[76] With the French Revolution "bourgeoisie asceticism" seemed to reach its high point. During 1793–94, France witnessed the Jacobins attempting to cleanse Paris by shutting down brothels and gambling houses and eliminating drunkenness. In what Crane Brinton described as the "republic of virtue," even dancing and festivals were outlawed.[77] Citizen Jacobins' imposing such moral restrictions on people in public differed little from that of the morals police in the Islamic Republic of Iran in the 1980s. Within days after Robespierre went under the guillotine, ordinary Parisians took over the public space with their simple but subversive pleasures. They engaged in jubilation, horse racing, bear baiting, and Christmas festivities, filling dance salons while often dressed in revealing attire. Games, jokes, street dancing, and singing dominated public squares at times in a rowdy and tactless manner.[78] This subaltern culture of fun and festivity, or what E. P. Thompson called "arts of living," disturbed bourgeois sensibilities and capitalist work ethics—ethics that revered discipline, self-control, hard work, and "rationality."[79]

Not just the French bourgeois Jacobins but also Russian communists expressed revulsion against "wine, women, and song." The Bolsheviks' ban on jazz as a "decadent bourgeois art" might perhaps be justified, but their prohibition of vodka in the land of Russia is like today's Islamists' eliminating music from Egyptian weddings. Bolsheviks were just as "ascetic" in their expression of contempt for ordinary comfort as were the Calvinists, both of whom considered that it was the everyday sins that needed to be eliminated.[80] In Brinton's view, such "religious" puritanism of both Jacobins and Bolsheviks originated from the revolutionary "reign of virtue" that emerges during times of crisis.[81] But his explanation does not make clear why puritanism has to be religious in essence. Nor does he justify why it should be exclusively the consequence of revolutions—after all, the Eastern European revolutions of the 1990s did not suppress mundane pleasures. Indeed, similar puritanism characterized the behavior of some Iranian Marxist guerrilla leaders, who in their underground lives *before* the Islamic revolution would have associated fun with nonrevolutionary and bourgeois mind-sets. They imposed celibacy, forbidding romance and playfulness among members, and placed restraints on ordinary consumption such as eating and sleeping, on reading materials, and on what came from joyful individual desires and expressions.[82]

Thus far, two broad approaches to explain the battle against fun stand out. The first, religious reasoning, focuses on diversion from God or faith as the principal cause for the suppression of fun. The second revolves around modernist sensibilities, including bourgeois rationality ("time is money"), according to which modernity discards collective fun because of the latter's counterdiscipline—immoral, irrational, and disorderly dispositions. According to this view, those in pursuit of fun challenge the idea of the modern individual as an organized, disciplined, proper, and in-control being. These two approaches each offer valuable insights to understanding antagonism toward festive behavior. However, they also involve serious analytical limitations. Why are fun and amusement and not, say, preoccupation with making a living or seeking knowledge largely considered sources of diversion from God? More important, as discussed earlier, anti-fun sentiments are not confined to religion per se; nonreligious and antireligious individuals likewise espouse similar attitudes. Brinton's claim that atheist Bolsheviks and secular Jacobins behaved in essentially religious ways neither rescues the religious reasoning as such nor sheds light on the source of the revolutionaries' austere behavior. What it does is to reify religion by making puritanism its intrinsic and exclusive attribute. Moreover, the explanation around modernist sensibilities not only fails to account for religion-inspired fear of diversion (from God), but also fails to explain the position of premodern (e.g., early or medieval Islamic and Christian) moral authorities who fought against joy and the pleasures of life. The claim that such premodern puritans just like the current austere Islamists in fact exhibited a modernist mind-set conjures up the same kind of circular argument that Brinton makes with respect to atheists behaving religiously. In addition, the fact is that fun as such, in the sense of diversion, joy, and amusement, poses little threat to the modern authority—one that is characterized by an ideological open market and inclusive social order and is able to accommodate, incorporate, commoditize, and even promote public and private, hedonistic and consumerist, pleasures. The entertainment industry—concerts, music, games, films, comedy, variety shows, and sports—constitutes a significant sector in the modern capitalist economy. Consequently, it is not merely the revolutionary nature of regimes as such or exclusively religious states or particularly the modernist authority, but rather the doctrinal politics (left or right, old or new, espoused by individuals or groups) and the ideologically monolithic regimes (e.g., Jacobin, Bolshevik, or Islamic) that feel the hazard of fun ethics. But why?

WHY ANIMOSITY TOWARD FUN?

What then explains, beyond the rhetoric, the underlying reason for similar anti-fun passions that a strain of individuals, movements, and regimes from diverse worldviews—premodern and modern, religious and secular, bourgeois and communist—express? Is there a broad explanatory framework to integrate the different perspectives that try to show the cause of anti-fundamentalism? Commenting on the European carnival festivities of the late Middle Ages, Mikhail Bakhtin characterizes collective fun in terms of a ritualized rebellion against authority in all forms.[83] In their wild delirium, or "dancing mania," the poor created a utopian moment of freedom, community, and equality, which defied all normal hierarchies—men wore women's costumes and ordinary people acted as clerics, kings, or priests. For Bakhtin, the plebian laughter represented an "element of victory not only over supernatural awe, over the sacred, over death," but it also meant "the defeat of power . . . of all that suppresses and restricts."[84] Laughter, as depicted in Umberto Eco's novel *The Name of the Rose*, protects the lowly from the feelings of fear that the nobility, by behaving exceedingly stern and austere, try to impose on the poor.[85] In Bakhtin, the carnival embodied a folk consciousness, one that acted as a medium of class struggle against the power elites. And it was this subversive element in subaltern culture that caused upper-class anxiety over festive rituals. While Bakhtin offers a plausible argument with respect to the politics of lower-class pleasures in late medieval Europe, there is more to fun than can be reduced to a particular class, or to class politics. Victor Turner's notion of *communitas* seems to carry more explanatory power, for it extends the politics of joy beyond class into the struggle against structures of hierarchy at large. In Turner, *communitas* is the status of ritual participants who break away from the everyday norms and structures to operate in an ad hoc state of liminality, or in-between-ness, where they form an egalitarian community of equal individuals in which the authority of the ritual leader is temporarily recognized. *Communitas* embodies a state in human behavior where people act against or outside the prevailing structures, that is, the differentiated system of social positions.[86]

What Turner and Bakhtin seem to have in mind when they speak of "structure" is primarily the structure of hierarchy. And the festive rituals that they describe were not themselves free from possessing some structural features: they were more or less routinized collective practices performed by specific actors in fairly specific times, places, and formats, which differed from everyday, free-form, ad hoc, spontaneous, unpredictable, individualistic, or collective fun. In these latter forms, fun has the potential to defy not only hierarchy and differentiation but any kind of structure. Thus, it is partially this antistructure disposition of spontaneous, free-form, and public fun that seems to cause anxiety and antagonism among political-moral authorities. For it disturbs the sense and security of order, stability, and tranquility that characterize the conservative image of a sensible world.

It would be a mistake, however, to reduce the threat of fun to merely its potentially antistructure disposition. Nor should an understanding of the subversive element in fun be limited to considering the rowdy, unruly, and undisciplined crowd action in pursuit of simple pleasures—those that feature the carnival festivities of early modernity.[87] The fact is that even the private, harmless, and commoditized expressions of pleasure are also strictly regulated and inhibited. What possible injury is done to the ideological state by the innocent act of flying kites, by the joyous movement of the body in a private wedding festivity, or by the exchange of harmless smiles between timid teenagers in the tense moments of backstreet love? Why should a mighty state be apprehensive of colorful outfits, the showing of a few inches of hair, the intense pleasure of joking and play among intimate friends, or the expression of impulsive jubilance for the victory of one's national soccer team? My argument is that beyond its physicality, fun also presupposes a powerful paradigm, a set of presumptions about self, society, and life that might compete with and undermine the legitimizing ideology of doctrinal power when these ideologies happen to be too narrow, rigid, and exclusive to accommodate ethics of fun. It is particularly this aspect of fun that causes fury among the Islamist moral-political authority.

Anti-fun ethics, whether religious or secular, modern or premodern, bourgeois or communist—and espoused by individuals, movements, or states—are not merely doctrinal concerns; they are primarily historical-political matters. More immediately, they represent and embody a particular technique of power, a discursive shield that both legitimizes and insulates moral or political authority by binding it to "what is not to be questioned," to the sacrosanct, the untouchables—God, the Revolution, the Resistance, the Proletariat, the Nation. Fear of fun, consequently, is not necessarily about diversion from the higher powers or noble values as such, but about the fear of exit from the paradigm that frames and upholds the mastery of certain types of moral and political authorities, be they individuals, political movements, or states.

Any type of authority, including Weber's famous ideal types, may be realized only within its own discursive paradigm—a body of consistent concepts, meanings, and understandings. Billy Graham may hold authority only among a segment of American Christians to whom his message makes sense. For the rest of Americans, or Egyptian Muslims for that matter, he holds little power. Graham's authority not only derives from what and how he preaches but also is realized specifically within the paradigm or discursive frame that allows him to operate and communicate with his audience. This is the "paradigm power." It refers to the discursive space that enables those in charge within a particular paradigm to maintain their position by making them meaningful and acceptable to their subjects. Thus, any challenge from without or departure from within this discursive space amounts to a challenge to those in authority. Because when subjects exit from the shared paradigm, by way of adhering to a different value system and way of life, they effectively leave the masters' field of influence and in effect render them powerless. Note how an Iranian hard-line weekly expresses this apprehension of exit: "When the chants of Allah-Akbar [God is Great] are replaced by whistling and clapping hands, prayers will come to an end, God will be overlooked, and the doors of lustfulness will be wide open. In such conditions, you cannot hear the voice of God; you will commit anything in this state of unconsciousness. Even Imam Khomeini's cries will fall on deaf ears."[88] This anxiety is basically about how the rival paradigm (fun) may come in between the moral authority and its followers to divert the latter's devotion to the former. A powerful conservative ayatollah in Iran declares films, arts, and cultural centers "as the most dangerous thing[s] that threaten humanity," because he fears that they would push mosques, churches, prayers, supplication, and ultimately devotion to God to the sidelines.[89] His feeling of threat lies not simply in people forgetting God (after all, people themselves are assumed to be responsible before God), but in undermining the "divine-driven" (khoda-mehvar) doctrinal paradigm that ensures his moral mastery. In a different, secular setting in July 2005, armed militants from the al-Aqsa Martyrs Brigades disrupted a music concert in the Palestinian town of Nablus, because, they argued, the joy of love songs would divert the public's attention from devotion to the great sacrosanct, the "resistance." "These people [the militants] don't want us to be happy," protested the embattled singer Amar Hasan; "they want us to sit in the ruins and cry."[90] The brigade militias' apprehension of "happiness" follows the same logic of power—fear of a rival frame of mind that could ultimately undercut their authority.

The subversiveness of fun in the conduct of the young, the artists, and the musicians and their audiences evokes the notion of the "counterculture"—values and norms of behavior that challenge those of the social mainstream.[91] Certainly, these practices of fun can be said to embody some kind of contentious collective sentiments that affect the cultural field. Beyond this, however, the parallel does not hold, since the ethics and values of fun as espoused by the young, the artists, or the poor do not run counter to those of the social mainstream; rather, for the most part, they *are* the social mainstream—although suppressed—which runs counter to those of the political elite and moral minority. Nor can such joyful behaviors easily be labeled and prohibited as western "cultural imports," even though many elements and mediums of fun deployed by globalizing youths—such as films, fashion, music groups, and dating games—are inescapably informed by the western commodity and media logic. The Islamists may be opportunistic in denouncing them as part of a western "cultural invasion," but what is to be said when it comes to the inhibition of the innocent and indigenous manifestation of public joy, dancing or singing at one's wedding, wearing colorful dress, or joking, whistling, and clapping? The fact is that fun, whether foreign and commoditized or indigenous and innocent, can be subversive. And the threat is not simply a perception but a reality. Fun disturbs exclusivist doctrinal authority because, as a source of instantaneous fulfillment, it represents a powerful rival archetype, one that stands against discipline, rigid structures, single discourse, and monopoly of truth. It subsists on spontaneity and breaths in the air of flexibility, openness, and critique—the very ethics that clash with the rigid one-dimensional discourse of doctrinal authority. Jokes bring pleasure and laughter because, according to Freud, they break the taboos and speak the unspeakable. Fun builds on the joy of immediate and instant pleasures rather than on those of distant and abstract referents such as the hereafter, the sacrosanct, and the untouchable—the very referents on which the authority of the doctrinal movements and regimes rests.[92]

In the "fundamentalist" paradigm the ideal individual is an "abstract person," a selfless subject estranged from his or her individuality, particularistic faculties, and features; this individual is massed together with others who share a devotion to "divine values" defined and prescribed by the moral masters.[93] The experiences of fun and expressions of joy, lightness, and spontaneity through the arts, amusements, play, and creativity signify "human" (*insan-mehvar*) resolve for individuality, differentiation, and selfhood—the very ethics that the fundamentalist paradigm cannot accommodate. Selfhood departs from and competes with what the Islamists perceive as divine values from which all high values are believed to emanate and by which Muslims are to abide.[94] Surely, there exists an anti-fun individualism of pietistic youths, such as those active in the conservative counterculture of evangelical churches in the United States, who disdain MTV, drugs, and premarital sex and embrace the conservative ethos of marriage, family, and discipline. But this represents rather a controlled, structured, and restrictive individualism, one that is distinct from the light and carefree selfhood that informs much of subversive fun.

To maintain their authority, masters have to either modify their paradigm by enlarging it to embrace fun ethics (in which case they cease to be exclusive) or resort to curbing diversion/desertion and combating the alternative ways of thinking, being, and doing things. The extent of discipline varies depending on the forms of fun practiced (traditional or commoditized, erotically charged or not charged, private or public), the target populations (young or old, men or women, rich or poor), and the type of adversaries (individual puritan zealots or the doctrinal states). Certain forms of fun (e.g., those expressed through sexuality, drugs, or alcohol) more than others (e.g., laughter, music, or games) are subject to prohibition and regulation. And certain target groups (e.g., young women) more than others are subject to severer surveillance. In conditions where the moral authority is merged with a state whose legitimizing ideology is too exclusive to accommodate contending discourses, the battle against diversion takes the form of systematic discipline and coercion. It is no accident that the control of individual deeds and desires in Saudi Arabia, Taliban Afghanistan, and the Islamic Republic of Iran (all doctrinal regimes) has been far more extensive than in Egypt and Algeria and more generally in the premodern conditions where, instead of the state, largely individual purists and groups initiated moral discipline.

The dissenting aspect of fun should not be overstated, however. Fun can be pacified, commoditized, institutionalized, and incorporated. The subversive effect of fun, at any rate, depends ultimately on the capacity of adversaries, the ideological frame of the moral and political authority, to absorb and contain its adverse fallouts. Whereas inclusive politics, as in liberal democracies, have succeeded in normalizing and institutionalizing most fun practices, the monolithic doctrinal movements and regimes—for example, the Bolsheviks during Russia's revolutionary crisis and current Islamist regimes—are apprehensive in allowing and incapable of adapting the ethics of fun and the joy of everyday pleasures. The Bolsheviks feared, as did the Jacobins, that the frame of mind associated with nonrevolutionary joy and lightness would compete with, and instigate exit from, the ideological paradigm that sheltered their mastery. Such politicization of the everyday lay at the heart of extending and maintaining their revolutionary power.[95] Islamists have had similar anxieties. The suppression of fun and diversion in Saudi Arabia, for instance, is often attributed to the Wahhabi doctrine of the Saudi ruling family, notably its principle of *tawhid* (unity of God). Since in this doctrine, nothing like saints, convocation (*do'a*), or *nazri* (extending charity to secure God's favor) are to come between the worshipper and God, and no *bid'a*, or innovation, is to be allowed; plays, films, and harmless joy distract Muslims from God and hence must be suppressed.[96] But in fact the revival and spread of this doctrinal order since the 1960s has, to a great extent, political roots. It served the Saudi ruling family as a discursive shield against the threat of secular nationalism and republicanism that the Nasserist revolution had unleashed in the Arab world.[97] Reports of the Saudi rulers secretly indulging in what their doctrine prohibits suggest their imposition of this moral order as a means of social control. In short, the issue for Islamists is not simply people diverting from God but the fear of people exiting from them.

**STREET POLITICS AND THE
POLITICAL STREET**

Part 2

8 A STREET NAMED "REVOLUTION"

ON FEBRUARY 11, 1979, Tehran radio announced the victory of the Iranian Revolution with feverish jubilation, thus heralding the end of a 2,500-year-old monarchy.[1] A tremendous mood of ecstasy overtook the populace, who poured into the streets en masse. Young people danced, and women milled through the crowd, handing out candies and sweet drinks, *sharbat*. Vehicles sounded their horns in unison, their lights beaming as they drove up and down the main streets, which only days before had witnessed bloody battles between the revolutionaries and the imperial army. Indeed, some of these very streets became the focal point of world photojournalism, the theme of some of the most arresting snapshots of the revolution in Iran, ones that convey the common images of great political turning points around the globe—the sea of people rallying in public squares, the burning streets, comrades carrying wounded revolutionaries, the sober yet nervous expression of soldiers, and of course falling statues and the breaking of prison gates. They all represent the "street politics" of exceptional junctures, common features of many monumental insurrections that come to fruition in distinct spatial locations, in the "streets of discontent." In Tehran, such space was Enghelab Square, especially Enghelab Street; in Cairo, Tahrir Square; and in Istanbul, Taqsim Square.

Why is that particular spaces act as venues for the expression of contention and the extension of solidarity? What distinguishes them from other

---

Adapted from Asef Bayat, "Streets of Revolution," in *Unsent Dispatches from the Iranian Revolution*, ed. Akbar Nazemi (Vancouver, BC: Presentation House Gallery, 2005).

places? Much of the groundbreaking contributions on space and politics as espoused by, for instance, Foucault, Lefebvre, and others, focus on how power (politics) configures space—how, for instance, the modern prison or the spatial division of streets and alleyways was deployed to discipline the bodies (the way we move or walk in public, and the like) of modern subjects; how functional specialization in homes (such as separating kitchen, bedrooms, and sitting rooms) was aimed at the moral repair of the working class; and how modern open boulevards (as transparent spaces) targeted restricting riots by exposing insurgents to police surveillance.[2] This chapter looks at the other side of the coin, at the *spatiality of discontents*, that is—how particular spatial forms shape, galvanize, and accommodate insurgent sentiments and solidarities. To illustrate, I focus on the revolutionary mobilization during the Iranian Revolution of 1979 and its spatial dimensions, making references also to Cairo's and Istanbul's street politics and their sites during the late 1990s.

THE REVOLUTION

In Iran, the victory day was the culmination of more than eighteen months of mass demonstrations, violent confrontations, massive industrial actions, a general strike, and many political maneuverings. Yet the genesis of the revolution was far back; indeed, it was rooted in the structural changes that had been under way since the 1930s, when the country began undergoing a process of modernization. It accelerated after the CIA-engineered coup in 1953 that toppled the nationalist prime minister, Muhammad Mossadegh, and reinstated the Shah. These structural changes engendered many conflicts, chief among them the tension between socioeconomic development and political autocracy.[3] State inefficiency, corruption, and a sense of injustice among many sectors of Iranian society accelerated political conflict in the country.

The modernization policy and economic change, initiated by the state under both Reza Shah (1925–46) and his son, Shah Mohammad Reza Pahlavi, gave rise to the growth of new social forces, to the dismay of the traditional social groups. By the late 1970s, a large and well-to-do modern middle class, modern youth, public women, an industrial working class, and a new poor consisting of slums and squatters, dominated the social scene. With the exception of the latter, these represented the beneficiaries of economic development, enjoying relatively high status and comparable economic rewards. However, the persistence of the Shah's old-age autocracy prevented these thriving social layers from participating in the political process. This angered them. At the same time, the old social groups—a segment of the traditional *bazaari*s, the old urban middle strata, the clergy, and other adherents to Islamic institutions—were also frustrated by the modernization strategy, as it undermined their economic interests and social status.

With all the conventional institutional channels closed to the expression of discontent as a result of repression, the populace was increasingly alienated from the state. In the meantime, corruption, inefficiency, a sense of injustice, and a feeling of moral outrage characterized the social psychology of many Iranians. So, during the tense years of 1970s, at the height of the Shah's authoritarian rule and remarkable economic development, many people (except perhaps the upper class and the landed peasantry) seemed dissatisfied, albeit for different reasons. But all were united in blaming the Shah and his western allies for that state of affairs. It is not surprising, then, that the language of dissent and protests was largely antimonarchy, anti-imperialist, Third World-ist, and nationalist, turning in the end to religious discourse.

The opportunity for popular mobilization arrived with what we, college students, used to call the "Carterite breeze" (*Nasseem-e Carteri*). President Carter's human rights policy in the late 1970s forced the Shah to offer a political space for a limited degree of expression. This expression, in the process, cumulatively built up, and in the course of less than two years it swept aside the monarchy. It all began with a limited relaxation on censorship, allowing some literary/intellectual activities (in the Goethe Institute and in universities in Tehran) and public gatherings by political Islamists (in Quba Mosque). It continued with the distribution, by the intellectuals and liberal politicians, of critical open letters to high-level officials. In this midst, an insulting article in a daily paper, *Ettelaat*, against Ayatollah Khomeini triggered a demonstration in the shrine city of Qum, in which some demonstrators were killed. To commemorate these deaths, a large-scale demonstration took place in the Azeri city of Tabriz in the north. This marked the beginning of a chain of events that formed a nationwide, revolutionary protest movement in which diverse segments of the population, modern and traditional, religious and secular, men and women, massively participated, and in which the *'ulama'* came to exert its leadership. But why did the clergy in particular lead the revolution?

For over twenty-five years of autocratic rule, since the 1953 coup, all the effective secular political parties and nongovernmental organizations had been removed or destroyed. The United States–led coup crushed both the nationalist and Communist movements; trade unions were infiltrated by the secret police, SAVAK; publications went through strict censorship, and there remained hardly any effective NGOs.[4] The main organized political dissent came from the underground guerrilla organizations, Marxist Fedaian and radical Islamic left Mujahidin-e Khalq, whose activities were limited to isolated armed operations.[5] Student activism also remained restricted either to campus politics inside the country or to those carried out by Iranian students abroad. In short, the secular groups, while extremely dissatisfied, were organizationally decapitated.

Unlike the secular forces, however, the clergy had the comparative advantage of possessing invaluable institutional capacity, including its own hierarchical order, with over ten thousand mosques, *Husseiniehs* (informal and ad hoc religious gatherings), *Huwzehs* (theological seminaries), and associations that acted as vital means of communication among the revolutionary contenders. Young Islamists, both girls and boys, along with young clerics, linked the institution of the *'ulama'* to the people. A hierarchical order facilitated unified decision making, and a systematic flow of both order and information ensured discipline; higher-level decisions in the mosques were disseminated to both the activists and the general public. In short, the clerics' *institutional capacity*, in addition to the remarkable generality and *ambiguity* in their revolutionary message ensured their leadership. What maintained that leadership was, beyond the lack of a credible alternative, the relatively rapid conclusion of revolutionary events—there was little time for debate and dissent, for a social movement to emerge, or for a possible alternative leadership to develop. Thus, the nascent Islamic movement of the 1970s rapidly transformed into a new state. "Islamization," then, unfolded largely *after* the victory of the revolution, and was enforced primarily from above by the new Islamic state. It was manifested in the establishment of clerical rule, the Islamic legal system, new cultural practices and institutions, and the moral surveillance of the public space.

STREETS OF DISCONTENT

Clearly, revolutions are not merely the exceptional junctures of insurrections and regime change, of "moments of madness," as they have been termed. Nor are revolutionaries just the visible street actors. Millions work backstage in these highly complex dramas: workers in factories, landless peasants on farms, students in schools, employees in offices, and leaders, often behind closed doors. Yet it is ultimately in the streets, public spaces par excellence, that collective challenge against invincible power holders is galvanized, where the destiny of political movements is often decided. In other words, beyond the temporal component, revolutions in the sense of insurrections possess an inescapable spatial dimension. Thus, in addition to thinking about why revolutions take place, who participates in them, and how events unfold, we should also be thinking about *where* they actually take place. More specifically, why do certain spaces/places, such as urban streets, more than others become the sites of acts and expressions of public discontent?

The Iranian Revolution was primarily an urban movement. Massive demonstrations, protests, and clashes took place overwhelmingly in the large cities, particularly in Tehran.[6] It is true that many rural inhabitants, farmers, and landless peasants were also mobilized, yet they would go to the *cities* to communicate their collective discontent. The idea of cities as centers of discontent is perhaps as old as the cities themselves. As the seat of concentrated wealth, power, people, and needs, cities are also sites of amassed contradictions and social conflicts.[7] Thus, by the eve of the 1979 revolution, the Iranian capital, Tehran, was just such a contradictory site. With a population of some five million, Tehran exhibited a remarkable and perhaps unique class (economic, social, and cultural) hierarchy. Located on a north-to-south-sloping landscape, the geographical pyramid of the city reflected its social and economic hierarchy. To the far north, the highest district was the site of the most affluent residents and the most opulent neighborhoods, crowned by the royal palace standing at the very summit of the city. The middle areas, from east to west, housed the relatively large middle classes, the state employees, professionals, and small-business families. The poor (new rural migrants and the lower strata of working people) were pushed away to seek shelters in the lowest lands of the city, in slums and squatter settlements with few urban amenities and services.[8] (See Map 1.) Indeed, the inequality of the capital embodied the prevailing social, economic, and political order of the nation as a whole. Yet, beyond its profound socioeconomic disparity, the spatial dimension of Tehran, its strategic streets, squares and institutions, offered an additional element for the expression of contentious politics.

Among the many "revolutionary thoroughfares" such as Takht-e Jamshid Avenue, Khiaban Kargar, and Maidan Zhaleh, a long east–west street—one that was appropriately renamed "Revolution Street" (Khiaban-e Enghelab)— stood as the most contentious space in the nation. It was here that the international press recorded some of the most remarkable images of the revolutionary

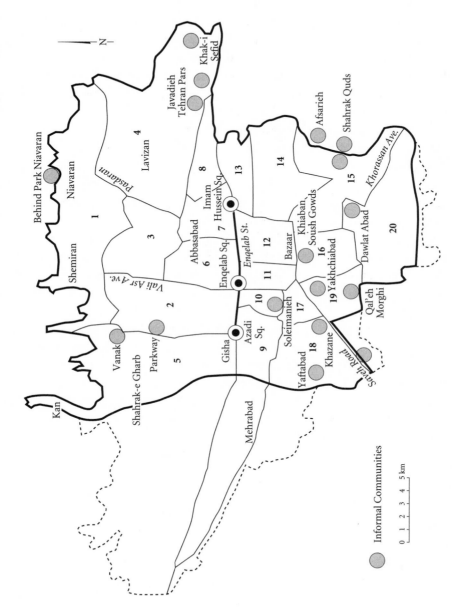

Map 1. Tehran, 1980s. Source: Asef Bayat, *Street Politics: Poor People's Movements in Iran*. New York: Columbia University Press, 1997, p. 28.

Behind Park Niavaran

Khak-i Sefid

Javadieh Tehran Pars

Lavizan

Shahrak Quds

Afsarieh

Niavaran

Pasdaran

Shemiran

1

Imam Hussein Sq.

8

13

14

Khorasan Ave.

15

Abbasabad

3

7

Enqelab Sq.

Enqelab St.

Khiaban, Soush Gowds

6

12

Bazaar

Dawlat Abad

Vali Asr Ave.

11

16

Yakhchiabad

20

Vanak

2

10

Soleimanieh

19

Qal'eh Morghi

Parkway

Azadi Sq.

17

Shahrak-e Gharb

5

Gisha

9

Khazane

18

Saveh Road

Kan

Mehrabad

Yaftabad

Informal Communities

0 1 2 3 4 5 km

struggles. I can recall how, as young intellectuals and activists, my friends and I would rush to that particular street to collect news, demonstrate, attend rallies, obtain literature, participate in discussions, or meet with comrades. It was there that most clashes also occurred, both during and after the revolution, so much so that it was imagined as the spatial core of the revolution. Why did this particular street attract so many contenders? What made it a distinct space of contention?

By their very nature, streets represent the modern urban theater of contention par excellence. We need only to remember the role "the street" has played in such monumental political turning points as the French Revolution, nineteenth-century labor movements, anticolonial struggles, the anti–Vietnam War movement in the United States, the "velvet revolutions" in Eastern Europe, and, perhaps, the current global antiwar movement. The street is the chief locus of politics for ordinary people, those who are structurally absent from the centers of institutional power. Simultaneously social and spatial, constant and current, a place of both the familiar and the stranger, and the visible and the vocal, streets represent a complex entity wherein sentiments and outlooks are formed, spread, and expressed in a remarkably unique fashion. The street is the physical place where collective dissent may be both expressed and produced. The spatial element in street politics distinguishes it from strikes or sit-ins, because streets are not only where people protest, but also where they *extend* their protest beyond their immediate circle. For this reason, in the street one finds not only marginalized elements—the poor and the unemployed—but also actors with some institutional power, such as students, workers, women, state employees, and shopkeepers, whose march in streets is intended to extend their contention. For a street march brings together the "invitees" and also the "strangers" who might espouse similar, real or imagined, grievances. It is this epidemic potential, and not simply the disruption or uncertainty caused by riots, that threatens the authorities who exert a pervasive power over public spaces—with police patrols, traffic regulation, and spatial division—as a result. The police tactic of encircling demonstrators in a corner, separating them from the normal flow of street life, as frequently happened in Cairo's 2002 spring of discontent, was devised to subvert the potential of *extension* of sentiments to the passers-by.

Beyond this generality, however, "streets of discontent" possess their distinct sociology, a blend of several socio-spatial features. First, they are spaces where a mobile crowd can easily and rapidly assemble before it is forced to disperse. Thus, the vicinities of an urban campus of a university (such as that in Tehran), or a large mosque (such as al-Azhar in Cairo), or promenades of bookstores and theaters that attract an intellectual crowd are all potential sites of contention. Thus, the proximity of Cairo's Kasr El-Nil and Tal'at Harb streets, with their bookstores and intellectual cafés, including the historic Café Riche, where, the legend goes, the Egyptian Revolution of 1952 was planned, provides the same intellectual import to Cairo's Tahrir Square as does Istiqlal Street to Istanbul's Taqsim Square, and Revolution Street to Tehran's Revolution Square. Second, the streets of discontent would usually have a historical or symbolic significance, either in some inscribed memories of insurrection and triumph, or, just like Cairo's Tahrir Square in terms of the sites and symbols of state power—palaces, parliament, courts, ministries of justice or the interior, and the like.

Third, as the locus of mass transportation networks—the bus, taxi, or metro terminals—which facilitate access to mobile participants, the streets of discontent are distinguished from the suburban slum neighborhoods, where the protests of the poor (over demolition of shantytowns, water shortages, or electricity cuts) often remain localized and contained. Thus, in the late 1970s, the intended long march of angry squatters of South Tehran toward the Shah's palace in the far north of the city was aborted by the long distance. In a similar vein, massive protests of squatters against Tehran municipality's demolition squad in the suburban community of Khak-e Safid failed to spread further, despite their intensity and violence.[9] Even the mass protests by workers in Helwan, in the outskirts of Cairo in spring 2008, remained by and large circumscribed, compared with the city center's political rallies of 2006 inspired by the Kifaya movement and other prodemocracy groups. Centrality, proximity, and accessibility, both in space and in time, are crucial features of any street of discontent.

Fourth, equally important is flexibility. Streets of discontent need to be a maneuverable space, where protestors can easily flee from the police—a space that is open yet surrounded by narrow alleyways, shops, or homes that can offer respite or sanctuary to revolutionary fugitives. No wonder Cairo's Tahrir Square, Tehran's Enghelab, and Istanbul's Taqsim Square are all encircled by a maze of side streets and alleyways, where political escapees can disappear in the event of a police chase. In Europe, modern large boulevards were designed partially to counter the political challenge of just such tangled or dense spaces of contention. In the Middle East, insurrectionists are likely to leave the open and exposed boulevards to the official marches of regime loyalists, who have no reason to fear police and prosecution.

Finally, beyond mere physicality, the streets of discontent hold a distinct sociality, whereby solidarity is communicated, discontent extended, and the news disseminated beyond the immediate surroundings. Here, I am referring to the role of the bus, taxi, or train terminals to transfer people, news, and knowledge not only beyond the city limits, but farther, into faraway provinces and beyond national borders. A location such as Tahrir Square, which holds in its orbit diverse headquarters of the press, television stations, foreign hotels, tourists, and journalists, as well as bus terminals, is likely to attract disgruntled insurgents.

"Revolution Street" in Tehran possessed many of these distinct sociospatial qualities. The magnificent presence of the Tehran University campus (established in 1934) on a stretch of several blocks housing over 20,000 students surely contributed to the militancy of the area. Across the university compound, on the opposite side of the street, were hundreds of bookshops and publishing houses that had uniquely turned these few blocks into the intellectual epicenter of the nation. This exclusive book bazaar, the hangout of Iran's intellectual window-shoppers, offered not only academic materials, but also underground revolutionary literature. Like the densely packed old bazaars, this book market assumed its own distinct identity and had a solid internal network—a place where news was spread and rumors were verified. During the revolution, many of these bookshops in Revolution Street sheltered the fugitive street protestors. The secular, leftist aura of the place and its goods stood in stark contrast to the more religious but far less spectacular districts around southern Tehran's traditional Grand Bazaar, which served as the political hub of earlier, 1950s and 1960s, political activity. Surely Tehran University contributed to the politicization of the area. But perhaps more important factors were involved.

In earlier periods, such as the early 1950s, political crowds would congregate not around Tehran University, but primarily in the grand Baharestan Plaza, which embraced the parliament located in South Tehran. By the late 1970s, the social and spatial transformation of Tehran had pushed the physical and "political center" of the city farther north, to Revolution Street. Thus, located halfway between the north and the south, this street carved the city into two distinct geographical and social universes. In a sense, it signified a virtual "green line," demarcating the "affluent north" (*bala-ye shahr*) and "poor south" (*pain-e shahr*)—a distinction that was unequivocally registered in the popular imaginary and language. Not only the intersection of the rich and poor zones, this street was also the meeting point of the urban and the rural. In the far eastern end of the street, roughly the edge of the city, stood the massive Shahyad Square (renamed Azadi [Liberation] Square, after the revolution), which, together with its neighboring Reza Shah Square (later, Revolution Square), gathered the largest insurgent crowds in pre- (and post-) revolution Iran. As hubs of intercity bus and taxi terminals, these two squares contained the crucial transportation networks linking the capital city to the nearby villages and provincial towns. A traveler to Tehran would disembark in these very grand roundabouts. Here, the plebeian visitors would rest on the pavements, eat in the cheap street food-stands or tea houses, stroll around, buy gifts from street vendors, get the news of the town, and perhaps see possible demonstrations before leaving the city. In the absence of free press and media, it was from places like this that the travelers would spread the news of the revolution. In summary, then, Revolution Street represented a unique juncture of the rich and the poor, the elite and the ordinary, the intellectual and the layperson, the urban and the rural. It was a remarkable political grid, intersecting the social, the spatial, and the intellectual, bringing together not only diverse social groups, but also institutions of mobilization (the university) and the dissemination of knowledge and news (the chain of bookstores).

Thus, the first incidents of collective protest during 1977 emerged from Revolution Street. Students' demonstration for free speech following ten autumn evenings of literary–political rally at the Goethe Institute catalyzed a chain of street mass protests, riots, and military confrontations that eventually toppled the monarchy. The monumental victory day did not mark the end of street action. After the revolution, new episodes of street politics with more complex configurations unfolded. Yet Revolution Street continues to maintain its centrality in Iran's geography of contention even to this day.

9 DOES RADICAL ISLAM HAVE AN URBAN ECOLOGY?

IN THE EARLY MORNING of January 10, 1993, some fifteen thousand Egyptian military personnel seized the squatter settlement of Munirah Gharbiyya, in Cairo's Imbaba quarter, to "cleanse" this poor community of the militant Islamists, al-Gamaʿa al-Islamiyya, who had turned it, in the words of one journalist, into an Islamic "state within the state." Over the following six weeks, police rounded up some six hundred suspects, while an extensive search followed for the remaining culprits. This incident, and the scattered reports of Islamist mobilization in the slums of Algiers and Istanbul in the late 1990s, evoked the older and more spectacular image of Iran's Islamic Revolution of 1979, in which the urban dispossessed are believed to have played a crucial part. Similarly, the takeover by Turkish Islamists of the reins of power and the victory of the Islamist Hamas movement in the dense urban quarters of the Palestinian Territories represent more recent instances that seem to resonate the view that Islamism appeals to the urban masses, especially to recent rural migrants to cities.

These events have triggered a sustained debate and discourse on the urban ecology of the poor, often reviving century-old assumptions about the social consequences of urban transition and the ideological inclination of urban marginals in contemporary Muslim societies. They have inspired narratives that tend to weave together histories of Islamism and those of the urban

Adapted from Asef Bayat, "Radical Religion and the Habitus of the Dispossessed: Does Islamic Militancy Have an Urban Ecology?" *International Journal of Urban and Regional Research* 31, no. 3 (September 2007), pp. 579–90.

disenfranchised. Thus, militant Islamism is represented as though it were the movement of the urban downtrodden, a perception that has led some scholars to draw parallels between Middle East Islamism and the Latin American liberation theology of the 1960s and 1970s.[1] Mike Davis's influential survey *Planet of Slums*, for instance, portrays Islamism (along with the Pentecostalist movement) as the "song of the dispossessed." Drawing on the slums of the Gaza Strip and Baghdad, Davis gives a new radical religious agency to slum dwellers as those with "gods of chaos on their side."[2] Not only does Islamic radicalism in some ways represent the poor people's moral, ethical, and religious sensibilities, the very existential character of the urban dispossessed, their ecological reality, renders them amenable to embracing the extremist ideas of radical Islam.

A key assumption underlying many of these narratives is that there is an urban ecological and cultural affinity between the habitus of the urban poor and militant Islamism. Urban poverty and the concentration of the poor in the sprawling slum communities infected by anomie and alienation are thought to generate a habitus of violence, lawlessness, and extremism, where Islamism emerges out of the rubble of hopelessness and moral decay to give a religious expression to that mode of life. At the same time, deep religiosity, populist desires, shared language, institutions, and finally a propensity for "traditionalism" are assumed to bring together the urban poor and militant Islamists as strategic allies. This way of thinking resonates most in the mainstream media, which often take for granted the link between urban ecology and religious extremism in the Muslim world. As an urbanist in Egypt, I have been contacted repeatedly by western media to comment on their storylines about the causal relationship between rural migration and Islamism, poverty, and violence, or the lack of housing (and its privacy) in an atmosphere of moral oppression and sexual frustration that allegedly makes poor young men resort to extremism and violence.

Does militant Islamism have an urban ecology? Is there a necessary convergence between the social existence of the urban disenfranchised and radical religious ideologies? Does the urban subaltern constitute the natural locus of Islamist politics? Neither has Islamist radicalism in general shown a genuine political or moral interest in the urban poor, nor have the urban poor expressed an ideological commitment to Islamist "distant politics," the politics that largely remain abstract from the daily anguish of plebeian life. Militant Islamism, chiefly a middle-class movement and preoccupied with moral politics and ideological struggles, fails to act as the social movement of the urban disenfranchised, who may lend support to Islamists only contingently. The urban dispossessed tend to follow their own folk religiosity, relatively autonomous informal life, and "intimate politics" of the everyday. Free from strict ideological loyalties, they are generally oriented toward strategies and associations that are direct and immediate, meaningful, and manageable—strategies whose outcomes they feel they can control. What characterizes the social life of the urban dispossessed in the Muslim Middle East is neither simply anomie, alienation, and a "culture of poverty" nor a particular penchant for embracing Islamist politics, but primarily the practice of "informal life"—a social existence characterized by autonomy, flexibility, and pragmatism, where survival and self-development occupy a central place. The urban disenfranchised tend pragmatically to lend support to diverse political trends and movements, both governmental and oppositional, including militant Islamism, so long as they contribute to those central objectives.

Islamism refers to the ideologies and movements that, notwithstanding their variations, aim in general for the establishment of an "Islamic order"—a religious state, Islamic laws, and moral codes. Concerns such as establishing social justice and improving the life of the poor would be only secondary to this strategic target.[3] Historically, Islamism has been the language of self-assertion to mobilize the largely middle-class overachievers who have felt marginalized by the dominant economic, political, or cultural processes in their societies, those for whom the failure of both capitalist modernity and socialist utopia has made the language of morality (religion) a substitute for politics. While the gradualist and reformist Islamists, such as the Muslim Brothers in Arab countries, pursue nonviolent methods of mobilizing civil society—through work in professional associations, NGOs, local mosques, and charities—the militant trends, such as al-Gama'a al-Islamiyya in Egypt, resort to armed struggle to seize state power through a strategy akin to Leninist insurrectionism. They often operate clandestinely in urban areas or neighborhoods where the state has a minimal presence. Militant Islamists such as al-Gama'a al-Islamiyya in Egypt follow strategies similar to those of the leftist guerrillas in Latin America during the 1960s and 1970s. But they differ from the current jihadist trends, such as groups associated with al-Qaeda. Whereas militant Islamism represents political movements operating within the given nation-states and targeting the secular national-states, the jihadists are transnational in ideas and operations and represent fundamentally "ethical movements."[4]

THE MUSLIM POOR: URBAN ECOLOGY
OF VIOLENCE?

While a classic perception, often expounded by the national elites, considers the urban dispossessed in the Muslim Middle East as passive plebeians who are busy struggling to make ends meet—a disposition in line with the "culture of poverty"— the more recent and more powerful view reflects profound anxiety over the active and dangerous role the urban poor seem to play in undermining modern urbanity and political civility, paving the way for Islamist extremism.[5] Thus, Egyptian elites—journalists, planners, and politicians—often describe Cairo as a giant city choked by overpopulation seemingly resulting from the influx of fellahin (peasants) who threaten its urban configuration by turning it into a "city of peasants." Cairo's ecology, they suggest, is being transformed by the spread of massive informal settlements, *ashwaiyyat*, that are "ruralizing" the Egyptian urban landscape.[6] The prevalence of poverty, joblessness, and undermined family relations fuels concerns that rural migration is laying the groundwork for a major social upheaval. Some see *ashwaiyyat* as "unnatural" communities that trigger "social disease" and "abnormal behavior," owing to lack of privacy, overcrowding, and violence; others are outraged by the erosion of respect for parents and the prevalence of immorality. Some academics tend to perceive the slums as a Hobbesian locus of crime, lawlessness, and extremism that produces a "culture of violence" and an "abnormal" way of life, a breeding ground for the growth of Islamic fundamentalism. In short, the slums serve and sustain the marriage of the poor and militant Islamism.[7] Perhaps nowhere was this apparent convergence of radical Islam and urban ecology as alarming as in secular democratic Turkey during the 1990s, when Islamic-oriented parties swept municipal and parliamentary elections. In 1994, the landslide triumph of the Islamic Rifah Party in municipal elections, which included metropolitan Istanbul, alarmed Turkish elites. Istanbul media warned middle-class citizens that the invasion of "black Turks," or migrants from Anatolia, was "threatening" the social fabric of modern Turkish urbanity.[8] Neighborhoods such as Sultanbeyli in east Istanbul and Gazi Mahallesi in the west became the hallmark of the marriage between the migrant poor and radical Sunnis and Alevites. This new urban ecology has compelled many elite families, like their Egyptian counterparts, to seek refuge in new gated communities.

In Iran, many Islamist leaders and scholars alike had already presented the dislocated migrant poor as the natural social basis of Iran's Islamic Revolution. The "revolution of the downtrodden" was crucial to the process. Rural migrants in particular were seen as the fundamental social basis of Islamist movements.[9] Some observers considered the miserable living conditions, violent behavior, and déclassé character of the "lumpenproletariat" as factors that made them support Khomeini-type revolution.[10] In particular, the "the populist ideology of Islam seems to play a crucial role in mobilizing the masses."[11] In a neo-Durkheimian paradigm, many scholars see Islam—its institutions and rituals, in general—as offering a moral community and sense of belonging to the dislocated migrants brutalized by anomie and alienation, the key effects of competitive and atomizing modern urban life.[12]

Once they are perceived as natural allies, militant Islamism and the poor need only political opportunity to realize their alliance. One such opportunity developed in Iran, owing to its remarkable economic development and social change, spearheaded by the authoritarian Shah. The urban poor, the by-product of the modernization process, benefited little from this economic growth. Indeed, they were its victims. Though relatively few (some 20 percent of the urban population), they constituted, by the late 1970s, a fairly distinct social group and became a major support base for Islamists during and after the revolution.[13] A similar narrative is applied to Egypt, where, the story goes, in spite of Nasserite populism that offered measures to assist the "popular classes," the postpopulist era, notably the period of "open door" (*infitah*) and "structural adjustment," coincided with the gradual withdrawal of the state from its traditional social contract. The space was gradually filled by the mounting activities of the reformist and militant Islamists during the 1980s and 1990s. Dislocated rural people, disenfranchised migrants, alienated by the brutality of modern competitive and individualistic urban life, yearned for a moral community and sense of belonging, which Islamic institutions such as the mosques could readily supply.[14]

Thus, in Egypt the fusion between Islamism and the urban poor was facilitated, on the one hand, by Islamist activists mobilizing the poor through opposition mosques and Islamic associations, and, on the other, by the fact that activists originated largely from the impoverished quarters of large cities. In Gilles Kepel's view, for instance, "the milieu that is the most fertile source of Islamist militants is the 20 to 25 age-group in the sprawling neighbourhoods on the outskirts of the big cities."[15] Similar arguments were made by Nazih Ayubi, Hamid Ansari, and others to stress the militants' impoverished disposition. For others, the seemingly proletarian profile of militant Islamists, their populist rhetoric, and shared urban space (notwithstanding their violent methods) render them the movement of the urban dispossessed.[16] Islamist activists in Cairo, we are often told, had infiltrated thousands of Islamic associations and mosques located in such slums as Ain Shams, Matariyya, Imbaba, Bulaq Addakrour, and Azzawaya al-Hamrah.[17] They used mosques to assemble, communicate, organize activities, recruit new members, and preach against authorities. Some of the larger and older associations, such as the Association of Shar'iyya,[18] Jama'iyya el-Shaban el-Muslemin, and Jamai'yya Insar Sunna Muhammadiyya, had already been involved in illegal political activities.[19] Such mosques and associations also provided medical care, literacy classes, and fund-raising activities to build political support.

THE MYTH OF THE ISLAMIST POOR

There is certainly some truth in some of these narratives. The urban poor are concentrated in the slums where militant Islamists have also sought shelter. The poor are inclined to seek assistance from local nonstate agents, including mosques and religious donations. Religious associations and NGOs have become centers that, in the absence of the state, provide many types of welfare support—material, cultural, and communal—helping the dispossessed to survive in the harsh urban structure. And finally, some degree of crime and violence does exist in the informal communities, especially when the state agencies, for instance police stations, are largely absent. Yet these processes do not necessarily render the urban disenfranchised anomic, alienated, extremist, or the strategic ally and the social basis of militant Islamism.

Indeed, the "convergence argument" is grounded for the most part in a structural deduction premised on underlying assumptions that are problematic empirically. To begin with, the poor in Iran remained largely aloof from the Islamic Revolution, in which the chief participants included the urban middle classes, students, government employees, bazaar merchants, shopkeepers, and industrial workers. The poor joined the revolution only at its last stage, a month or so before the Shah's regime collapsed, when opposition leader Shahpour Bakhtiar formed the last government under the Shah. At this time, the urban poor were mobilized less through mosques and *hey'ats* than through the activities of the Islamic Consumer Cooperatives and, especially, Neighborhood Councils, through which middle-class youth brought the experience of the revolution to poor neighborhoods by offering them basic goods and fuel at the time of an acute shortage brought on by an ongoing general strike that had crippled production and distribution systems.[20]

Thus, the language of *mustaz'afin* (the downtrodden), referring primarily to the urban disenfranchised, dominated the populist discourse of Islamist officials mainly after the victory of the revolution, when mobilization of the poor became the subject of intense competition between various political groups. The ruling clergy needed to win over the dispossessed as its social basis in its mounting struggles against liberals, leftists, and remnants of the former regime. In particular, Islamic leaders aimed to disarm the left of its pro-working-class campaign. In turn, the left (various Marxist organizations and the radical Islamic Mujahedin-e Khalq) appealed to the poor on ideological principles in an attempt to build popular support for themselves. It was in this period that the political orientation of the now-ruling Islamists and the urban disenfranchised converged. Pro-poor rhetoric abounded in general exhortations to improve their living conditions, build housing, and increase community development. This honeymoon did not last long, as the new state functionaries did not and could not follow through on their rhetoric to help the urban disenfranchised. Consequently, the poor were polarized. Some segments (including groups within the newly established revolutionary institutions such as the *pasdaran, basij,* and the Construction Crusade) were incorporated into the state structure, but others remained outside the system, and their struggles for self-development (expressed in the occupation of homes and hotels, squatting on land for shelter, illegal construction, and in securing collective consumption and jobs) brought them into conflict with the Islamic state. These included hybrid elements whose ideological affinity with the Islamic government did not deter them from fighting its agents in their daily struggles.[21]

In Egypt, as pointed out earlier, claims of a fusion between Islamism and the urban poor are based on two assumptions: first, that Islamist activists mobilized the poor through opposition mosques and Islamic associations, and, second, that activists originated largely from the impoverished quarters of large cities—those that are instilled with a social ecology that supposedly breeds extremist and deviant activities and ideologies. The Imbaba incident conferred new credence to this kind of thinking. It reinforced the myth of the "Islamist dispossessed" obscuring the dynamics and constituency of political Islam. What particularly added to this mythology was, first, the Egyptian state's sudden apprehension of an emerging "Islamist threat" which in turn

caused unprecedented publicity around the theme of "urban ecology of Islamist extremism"; and, second, the subsequent "scientific" intervention of
the "expert community" (sociologists, criminologists, and journalists), who
associated the rise of Islamic militancy and violence with the spread of *ashwaiyyat*. These experts, in a sense, gave authoritative backing to the fusion of
the histories of the urban poor and political Islam. But the reality was much
more complex.

Although many militants did reside in the *ashwaiyyat*, this did not necessarily indicate a strategy devoted to mobilizing the poor. Like many middle-
class Egyptians, the militants simply did not have much choice when it came
to where they lived. The lack of affordable housing had made a spatially "marginalized" middle class (educated youth, professionals, and civil service employees) an Egyptian urban phenomenon—a trend that figures into the class
and spatial dynamics of many other cities in the global South. As the new
middle classes, especially newlyweds and the young, were excluded from the
housing market in more conventional urban quarters, they were pushed into
city outskirts, creating heterogeneous informal communities where residents,
while they shared the perils and possibilities of their common space, differed
considerably in occupations, style, education, and even worldviews. In other
words, many who live and function in these poor areas do not necessarily
belong to the sociological category of the urban poor, defined as low-skilled,
low-income, low-security, and low-status working people.[22] On the other hand,
the informal nature of these neighborhoods (without street names, house
numbers, official registration, or maps) ensured a safe haven for Islamist militants, chased by the police, who were on the run from the sugar fields of Southern Egypt. Some indeed tried to integrate in the well-off districts of Mohande-
sin, Agouza, and Maadi, but strict police surveillance compelled them to
move into the opaque neighborhoods of Ain Shams and Imbaba.[23]

Islamists did infiltrate charity associations. However, the extent of their
influence is often exaggerated. Out of thousands of religious NGOs, only a few
dozen fell under the influence of political Islamists. The rest were organized
either by non-Islamist pious Muslims or expanded owing to market rationale.[24] The sale of religious commodities grew significantly during the 1980s
and 1990s. Beyond books, recorded sermons, music, and fashion, the market
for Islamic cultural and educational goods and services expanded because of
their quality, affordability, and religious clout. Many became involved in Islamic associations, not only because they served the needy or provided spiri-

tual motivation, but also because religious associations provided them with jobs and even lucrative business. A few studies of Islamic clinics in Cairo, for instance, revealed that the incentive for many of their staff, including doctors, was not so much religious obligation as professional opportunity.[25] For the low-status occupation of nursing, Islamic associations offered a more respectable and reputable place to work. Meanwhile, many schools remained Islamic only in name.

More important, like the Iranian clergy in prerevolutionary Iran, Egyptian Islamists (both reformist and militant) showed only slight strategic interest in the political mobilization of the urban subaltern. They never considered the urban disenfranchised as a special group in which to invest politically (in the way that Marxists considered the industrial proletariat; or Frantz Fanon, the "marginal poor" in colonized Africa). In the writings and statements of al-Gama'a al-Islamiyya and El-Jihad, as in the sermons of Ayatollah Khomeini before the revolution, references to the poor, let alone views of them as political agents, were rare.[26] Obviously, the secular liberal daily al-Wafd and leftist al-Ahaly paid more attention to the plight of the poor than did the Islamist al-Sha'b or the Muslim Brothers' publications; the latter focused invariably on broader political and religious matters, such as government corruption, international Zionism, or world Islamic politics. In my regular Friday visits to a number of mosques in Cairo's poor neighborhoods (Sayyeda Zeinab, Boulaq Abul Ela, Darb al-Ahmar, Mar Girgis) during the fall of 1996, Islamic activism was limited to the sale of tapes by preachers such as Omar Abdul-Kafi, Shaykh Kishk, Ahmad Al-Ajami, and Muhammad Hissamah, or of religious books and pamphlets covering such topics as life after death, marriage, women and Islam, jinn, and the devil.

This political and ideological distance would set militant Islamism apart from Latin American liberation theology, which seemed to establish a more organic relation with the poor.[27] Whereas the point of departure for liberation theology was the "liberation of the poor," where the gospel was then reread and reinterpreted to achieve this fundamental goal,[28] Islamist movements have in general aimed for the establishment of an Islamic order (a religious state with Islamic laws and moral codes); concerns such as establishing social justice and improving the life of the poor would follow from this strategic target.[29] Thus, while for liberation theology concern for the poor was an end in itself, indeed, a doctrinal matter, the Islamists' mobilization of the poor had largely the political purpose of achieving change to clear the way for the establishment of an Islamic order.[30] Instead of being an expression of cultural identity as in Islamism, liberation theology, partially inspired by humanist Marxism, was embedded in the indigenous discourse of development, under-development, and dependency that Latin America was fiercely debating at the time. Indeed, the idiom "theology of liberation" emerged in the context of clerics exploring a "theology of development," a notion in which the emanci-pation of the poor was central.[31] Islamism, however, has had a different birth and birthplace. Broadly speaking, it arose as a language of self-assertion to mobilize those (largely middle-class overachievers) who felt marginalized by the dominant economic, political, or cultural processes, those for whom the failure of both capitalist modernity and socialist utopia made the language of morality (religion) a substitute for politics. In a sense, it was the Muslim middle-class way of rejecting those whom they considered their excluders—their national elites, secular governments, and these governments' western allies. As an alternative to existing models, they imagined a utopian society and state for Muslim humanity. *Da'wa* (an invitation to Islam), not necessar-ily the liberation of the poor, became a key objective for Islamists, and elitism continued to guide their politics.[32]

Just as the Islamists treated the urban poor in pragmatic terms, the urban grass roots in turn approached the Islamists in instrumentalist fashion. In postrevolution Iran, the disenfranchised took advantage of the intense compe-tition between ruling clergy and the political left in order to mobilize the poor. The poor came to realize their power and used the opportunity to make de-mands and improve their lot, by squatting on land and in homes, upgrading their community, and acquiring consumer goods.[33] In Egypt, many among the poor had no direct interaction with Islamists and remained confused as to their intentions, while others, such as the residents of Imbaba's *ashwaiyyat*, remained apprehensive and yet appreciative of the services they provided. The Imbaba incident placed the urban dispossessed and *ashwaiyyat* at the center of Egypt's political and developmental debates. If the *ashwaiyyat* were regarded as the fundamental locus of extremism and Islamism, then undoing them, that is, either upgrading or destroying these entities, was expected to ameliorate the situation. Thus on May 1, 1993, a year after the Imbaba inci-dent, President Mubarak authorized that "an immediate implementation of a national program in upgrading the most important services and facilities in haphazardly built areas in all governorates."[34] USAID had already moved into Imbaba with a large-scale project to pave roads and develop sewer systems.

European NGOs followed suit with community development projects in the *ashwaiyyat*. In 1996, 127 zones out of 527 targeted zones "were fully upgraded" by the Egyptian government, and by 1998, it had spent EL 3.8 billion ($700M) on community upgrading. Hasan Sultan (also known as Hasan Karate), commander of the military wing of the al-Gama'a al-Islamiyya in Imbaba, was turned into a symbol of this "integration." Having turned himself over to police after managing to escape the siege, he was now allowed to go free and establish a street kiosk in the heart of Imbaba, Munira Gharbiya.[35] The government's policy of urban renewal sought in part a common objective of turning opaque communities into transparent entities (mapping, naming the streets, and numbering homes) partly in pursuit of ensuring surveillance.

Whatever the motives behind these developmental programs, the poor welcomed both government and Islamic initiatives. Yet they declined to extend ideological allegiance to either the state or the Islamists. If anything, most of them expressed profound indignation about the use of political violence by both Islamists and the state. For the most part, the poor relied on themselves to survive and improve their lives.

CULTURE OF POVERTY OR INFORMAL LIFE?

If uncertainty and utilitarianism characterized the relationship between the poor and Islamism, then why do the predominant narratives continue to insist on the fusion of militant Islamism and the dispossessed? I suggest that these narratives reflect the profound anxieties of the elite and the media concerning the urban ecology of Islamist extremism. They are also general claims premised on erroneous presuppositions about urban society and politics in the Muslim Middle East.

First, in many Middle Eastern countries, demographic changes since the 1980s have produced a complex spatial pattern. Many large cities have ceased to be centers of rural migrants. Population movement from the countryside to large urban centers has leveled off, while rural areas have begun to assume some aspects of urban life: consumption patterns, diverse occupations, more extensive division of labor, and higher rates of literacy. For instance, in 1996, over 80 percent of Cairo's population and 86 percent of Alexandria's had been born in their city. Of the remaining migrants, over 80 percent, the overwhelming majority, had come from other cities, not the countryside. Tehran followed a remarkably similar demographic pattern, with only 15 percent of residents being migrants, and most of them, too, were from other urban centers.

Second, the politicians and academic community (sociologists and criminologists) in Egypt viewed the *ashwaiyyat* through the prism of the concept of "slums" formulated in the United States. This model emerged in part from the studies of inner-city African American ghettos, where joblessness and decayed family structure are said to be responsible for crime and violence. U.S. scholarship on "slums" is heavily informed by the notion of "neighborhood effects" that are assumed to be responsible for socially isolating the poor from conventional life-chances and norms. "Neighborhood effects" embrace many spatial metaphors, such as "concentration effects," "spatial isolation," or "ghettoized poor," that overdetermine poor people's habitus.[36] Egyptian researchers invoking the American model assumed a priori that Cairo's *ashwaiyyat*, for instance, were urban ecologies that fostered isolationism, anomie, lawlessness, extremism, and Islamist violence.[37] The fact is that local cultures have undeniable impact on the subculture of the poor wherever they are. The level of crime in the *ashwaiyyat* was not conspicuously higher than that in other areas. Serious scholarly works on Cairo's poor areas invariably confirmed the prevalence of a "cultural capital of tolerance," resourcefulness, a strong sense of community, solid family relations, firm social control of children and youth, and high hopes for the future, and showed Cairo, a megacity with enormous urban problems, to be one of the world's safest cities, a quality quite distinct from its counterparts in Latin America.[38]

Indeed, the strict official definition of what constitutes an urban unit and the invention of the notions of *ashwaiyyat, hashieye-nishini, gecekondu*s, as political categories tend to produce spatial divisions that exclude many citizens from urban participation. The *ashwaiyyat, hashieye-nishini*, or *gecekondu*s are perceived as "abnormal" places where "nonmodern" people—that is, the villagers, traditionalists, nonconformists, or unintegrated—live. But this oversimplified picture obscures the fact that populations of informal settlements are involved in the complex urban economy and division of labor. In the old sociological tradition, what in social terms defines "urban" is primarily the organic ensemble in a particular space of a variety of lifestyles and economic activities, and those of the informal settlements constitute but one significant component of the diversified whole that is the city.

It is true that many of the inhabitants of informal communities pursue an "informal life." That is, they tend to function as much as possible outside the boundaries of the state and modern bureaucratic institutions. For instance, they wish to exert some degree of autonomy in their working and cultural lives, basing their relationships on reciprocity, trust, and negotiations, rather than on the modern notions of individual self-interest, fixed rules, and contracts. Thus, they might opt for self-employment or resort to informal dispute-resolution rather than report to the police; they might be married by a local shaykh rather than at government offices; or they might borrow money from informal credit associations rather than from banks. This is the case, to repeat from Chapter 3, not because these people are essentially non- or antimodern but because the conditions of their existence compel them to seek an informal way of life. That is so because modernity is a costly enterprise, in that it requires a capacity to conform to the types of behavior (adherence to strict discipline of time, space, contracts, and so on) that most poor people simply cannot afford.

The activities of Islamist militants in Cairo's Imbaba or Istanbul's Sultanbeyli reinforced the image of "informals" as a Hobbesian locus of lawlessness, violence, and religious extremism. These may indeed be present in poor squatter areas. However, this type of behavior is not the result of inhabitants' cultural essentials, since informal communities, despite their appearance, consist of heterogeneous occupational and cultural universes. Although stigmatized as "rural," they not only receive migrants from urban core areas but are also home to young people and newlyweds—the future of these nations.[39] Informal settlements in the Middle East are not simply poverty belts but are also home to many middle-class urbanites, professionals, and civil servants. What perhaps breeds lawlessness is not the cultural essentials of residents but rather the consequences of their "outsiderness," the communities' density and lack of spatial clarity. An "outsider" community, even if it is located in the heart of the city, by definition lacks street names, house numbers, paved roads, maps, police presence, and, thus, state control. Islamist violence attributed directly to informal cities' social ecology is more complex than a phenomenon of poverty and ignorance. In Cairo, militants (from al-Gama'a al-Islamiyya and al-Jihad) were mostly young, educated individuals, many of whom lived in the *ashwaiyyat* because of Cairo's high housing costs, which exclude and marginalize many, including middle-class families. Sociologically, these young, educated people were different from the cultural type portrayed by some academics, planners, and the media, and there is paltry empirical evidence to suggest that they shared the features that characterize Oscar Lewis's "culture of poverty."

The key sociocultural mode among the Muslim poor in the Middle East is not the "culture of poverty" but "informal life."

The preceding discussions indicate that the relationship between radical Islam and the habitus of the dispossessed is more complex than often presented. The claims about organic convergence between the two often reflect fear by the national and international elites (politics and media) about the social consequences of urban marginality. In reality, however, the dispossessed show no more natural propensity toward extremism or Islamism than Islamists (notwithstanding their populist rhetoric) show strategic interest in the dispossessed as a political player or moral target. More often than not, a utilitarian politics governs the relationship between the urban disenfranchised and Islamist activists. As I have discussed elsewhere, the poor cannot afford to be ideological. Their interests lie in strategies, organizations, and associations that respond directly to their immediate concerns. To be ideological requires certain capacities (time, risk taking, money) that the disenfranchised often lack.[40] In the Muslim Middle East, the political class par excellence remains the educated middle class (students, intellectuals, and professionals), which both Islamist and secular movements target. "Low-politics," or localized struggles for concrete concerns, are the stuff of the urban dispossessed. For the dispossessed, it is largely the localized struggles, unlike the abstract and distant notions of "revolution" or "reform," that are both *meaningful* and *manageable*—meaningful in that they can make sense of the purpose and have an idea of the consequences of those actions, and manageable in that *they*, rather than some remote national (Islamist or secular) leaders, set the agenda, project the aims, and control the outcome.

10 EVERYDAY COSMOPOLITANISM

IT MIGHT SOUND out of place to invoke the idea of cosmopolitanism in global conditions dominated by the language of "clash"—clash of cultures, civilizations, religions, or ethnicities. The discourse of clash is so overwhelming that it is as though it were the sole feature of today's cultural, religious, and communal life. It may be plausible for the prevailing scholarship to pay more attention to human conflict as a subject of inquiry than to cooperation or sharing, because hierarchy and relations of power (in terms of for instance class, gender, and race) constitute the key features of human societies. But what does justify portraying the relationships between different cultures, religions, or national origins (horizontal groups) predominantly in terms of conflict? This tendency is partially rooted in the "primordialist," outlook which deems ethno-religious groupings as natural, permanent, and bounded entities with clear and everlasting lines of cultural demarcation, and thus prone to division and clash.[1] However, this line of thinking has been challenged by those who see such communities as dynamic beings, subject to continuous deconstruction, shifting boundaries, and reconstruction.[2] In other words, "communities" are not simply introverted and exclusive collectives whose relation with others is defined merely in terms of mistrust. Rather, communities also attempt to overcome their differences and live together.[3]

This chapter aims to transcend overemphasis on relations of conflict, by highlighting the other, more common but unnoticed and inaudible processes

---

Adapted from a contribution that originally appeared in Shail Mayaram, ed. *The Other Global City* (London: Routledge, 2009).

of human conduct, to show how people belonging to different cultural or religious groupings can and do reach out of their immediate selves by intensely interacting in their lifeworlds with members of other cultural or religious collectives. In short, they experience a cosmopolitan coexistence. *Cosmopolitanism* refers to both a social condition and an ethical project. In the first place, it signifies certain objective processes, such as globalization, migration, and traveling that compel people of diverse communal, national, or racial affiliations to associate, work, and live together. These processes lead to diminishing cultural homogeneity in favor of diversity, variety, and plurality of cultures, religions, and lifestyles. In this sense Dubai, for instance, represents a cosmopolitan city-state, in that it juxtaposes individuals and families of diverse national, cultural, and racial ties, who live and work next to one another within a small geographical space.

Cosmopolitanism has also ethical and normative dimensions; it is a project with humanistic objectives. In this sense, cosmopolitanism is deployed to challenge the language of separation and antagonism, to confront cultural superiority and ethnocentrism. It further stands opposed to communalism, where the inward-looking and close-knit ethnic or religious collectives espouse narrow, exclusive, and selfish interests. Cosmopolitanism of this sort also overrides the "multiculturalist" paradigm. Because although multiculturalism calls for equal coexistence of different cultures within a national society, it is still preoccupied with cultural boundaries—an outlook that departs from a cosmopolitan lifeworld where intense interaction, mixing, and sharing tend to blur communal boundaries, generating hybrid and "impure" cultural practices.

But is this cosmopolitanism not the prerogative of the elites, a bourgeois lifestyle? Certainly elites are in a better material position to experience cosmopolitan lifestyle; they are the ones who can easily afford frequent travel, by which they taste different cuisines and experience alternative modes of life and cultural products. In addition, unlike the poor, the privileged groups need not rely on exclusive communalistic networks as a venue to secure social protection—something that tends to reinforce more inward-looking communalism. However, the objective possibility to experience mixing, mingling, and sharing is not the same as the desire and ability to do so. How many of those elite expatriates residing in the metropolises of the global South, Dubai for instance, share cultural life with those of the poor of the host society? In a closer look, the cosmopolitan Dubai turns out to be no more than a "city-state of relatively gated communities" marked by sharp communal and spatial boundaries, with labor camps (of south Asian migrants) and the segregated milieu of parochial jet-setters, or the "cosmopolitan" ghettos of the western elite expatriates who remain bounded within the physical safety and cultural purity of their own reclusive collectives.[4]

What is often ignored or downplayed is the cosmopolitanism of the subaltern.[5] Evidence from early twentieth-century Cairo, Baghdad, Jerusalem, and Aleppo suggests how, beyond the elites, the ordinary members of different religious communities—Muslims, Jews, Christians, Shi'is, or Sunnis—were engaged in intense intercommunal exchange and shared lives in neighborhoods or at work;[6] they were engaged in "everyday cosmopolitanism." By everyday cosmopolitanism I mean the idea and practice of transcending self—at the various levels of individual, family, tribe, religion, ethnicity, community, and nation—to associate with agonistic others in everyday life. It describes the ways in which the ordinary members of different ethno-religious and cultural groups mix, mingle, intensely interact, and share in values and practices—in the cultures of food, fashion, language, and symbols; in history and memory. In everyday life, women in particular act as protagonists in initiating cosmopolitan exchange and association. In the mixed neighborhoods, women move easily between houses, chat, exchange gossip, lend or borrow things from neighbors. They participate in weddings, funerals, or religious festivals. Children of different confessional affiliations play together in the alleyways, teens befriend, and men may make neighborly visits. This notion of cosmopolitanism signifies how such association and sharing affect the meaning of "us" and "them" and its dynamics, which in turn blurs and problematizes the meaning of group boundaries. The "everyday cosmopolitanism" may not go as far as the often abstract and philosophical notions of Stoicist "world citizenship" but engages in the modest and down-to-earth, yet highly relevant, ways in which ordinary men and women from different communal worlds manage to engage, associate, and live together at the level of the everyday.

However, cosmopolitan association of this sort does not grow in a vacuum. It takes shape under specific structures and possesses particular geographies. Modern urbanity per se potentially contributes to cosmopolitan habitus by facilitating geographies of coexistence between the members of different religious or ethnic groups. But this may be so not just because people of different religions and cultures naturally come to live and interact with one another; after all, neighbors might dislike and distrust one another; rather because proximity and interaction can open opportunities for divergent cultural groups to experience trust between them and coexistence in daily life. But the paradox of modern urbanity is that not only can it engender cosmopolitan coexistence, but it can also facilitate communal identities. A modern city like Cairo tends, on the one hand, to differentiate, fragment, and break down the traditional face-to-face ethnic or religious-based communities by facilitating the experience of sharing with other cultural-religious groupings. At the same time, however, religious-ethnic identities may persist or get reinvented not necessarily through face-to-face interactions, but through the construction of imaginary or "distanciated" communities. The modern city has a tendency to differentiate, individualize, and fragment its inhabitants, to weaken the traditional ties, break down extended family (among people who can afford to become autonomous), and increase geographical mobility. The logic of land use, cost of housing, and jobs often determine where families settle. Spatial congregations based upon ethnic or religious affiliation gives way to class segregation, so that the ethno-religious communities based on intense interpersonal interactions are undermined as their members break up into clusters of individual families dispersing across the vast expanse of the city, where they are compelled to connect to the "larger society," and where religious members may experience real interactions and sharing with city dwellers of different religious or ethnic affiliations. But deep association and sharing between members of different communities does not mean the end of religious or ethnic identities. On the contrary, the breakdown of faith-based local collectives can, in conditions of general uncertainty and threat, give rise to different— "virtual" or "distanciated"—religious communities. Here identity is based not upon real cooperative experiences, but on imagining ties with distant, faceless, and unknown "brothers" or "sisters," whose general whereabouts are shared through modern networks of daily papers, via television, or through heresy and rumor. This dialectic of both inner-communal identity, on the one hand, and the real day-to-day cooperation with people outside, on the other, generates a more complex intercommunal dynamics than simply harmony or conflict. For individuals are likely to test their imaginary and abstract view of the "other" (resulting from, for instance, prejudice or provocation) against the experience of real association they develop with them. This is how I see Muslim–Christian relations in today's Cairo.

MAPPING THE COMMUNAL DIVIDE

In 2008, Egypt represents primarily a Muslim majority nation. Yet a substantial proportion of the population, some 8 to 10 percent, or six million, are Coptic Christians.[7] Christianity came to Egypt with the Roman conquest, but it grew largely from the mid-first century AD onwards. It is suggested that the oppressive rule of the Roman Empire created a sort of nationalistic Coptic, or Egyptian, Christianity that stood in opposition to the Byzantine authorities. With the Arab conquest in 639 AD came Islamization and Arabization of Egypt, so that by the tenth century the Muslim population had ascended to the majority.[8] Conversion to Islam was not smooth. Some embraced Islam voluntarily for its promise of justice, many did so to avoid special taxation, while still others did to acquire equal social and political status with Muslims.[9] In the meantime, Arabic gradually replaced "Coptic language"; since the government bureaucracy used Arabic language, it compelled the Coptic elite (who continued to work in the administration) to learn Arabic and teach it to their children, who would then pursue occupations like their fathers'. When in the twelfth century Pope Gabriel decreed that the church use Arabic language in its sermons, lay Copts also moved to speak in this language. In the end, Arabic became the language of Egyptians, both Muslim converts and the remaining Christians, with the Coptic language dying out sometime between the fourteenth and eighteenth centuries.[10]

Under Muslim rule during Umar (717–40), Copts became a *dhimmi* (non-Muslim) "minority," denied of serving in the army, and of high political positions, and subject to a special poll tax (in exchange for their protection), *jizya,* for centuries. It was not until the reign of Said Pasha in 1856 that the *dhimmi* status was dropped, the poll tax was lifted, and Copts became full citizens. Mamluk rulers (1250–1517) had already attempted to create a balance between the Copts and the Muslims by recruiting the former into bureaucracy and trade, so that Copts became a counterpart to a growing educated Muslim "middle class," which also aspired to positions in government offices. Modern times brought formal equality between the two communities. Muhammad Ali's Hamayouni Decree in 1856 established Coptic personal status laws, allowed them into the military, and promised freedom of religion, equality in employment, and removal of all discriminatory terms and symbols, even though the construction of churches remains a contested issue even today.

The "Liberal Age" (1923–52) was the hallmark of Coptic public presence and citizenship. Elite Copts and Muslims developed almost identical liberal lifestyles and tastes, informed by French Enlightenment and English liberal trends. In the early twentieth century two Christians became prime minister (Boutros Ghali Pasha, 1908–10; and Youssef Wahba Pasha, 1919–20). Wafd, the political party of independence, was so close to Copts that Islamists and ultra-nationalist Misr- al-Fitah labeled Wafd the "Party of Copts," and the king the "protector of Islam." Although the Revolution of 1952 treated Copts and Muslims equally in welfare dispensation and educational attainment, it inflicted disproportionate economic losses on the Coptic community. Being excessively richer than Muslims, Christians lost more to Gamal Abdel Nasser's nationalization policies than did Muslims (some 75 percent of their work and property).[11] Following the dissolution of political parties, their presence in politics and parliament drastically declined. These developments led to the first wave of Coptic emigration, to Canada, the United States, and Australia in the 1960s and 1970s. The continuing outflow of educated Copts, together with the rise of Islamist militancy in Egypt since the 1970s, has cemented a strong identity politics among the vocal Coptic community in exile and to a lesser degree among Copts living in Egypt.

Since the 1980s, the status of Coptic Christians in relation to Muslims in Egyptian history has become the site of a contentious positioning. Both the reality of Christian–Muslim relations and its representation have been deeply politicized. In this contestation, "history," as usual, has become the battle-ground. One view expressed mainly by the militant Copts in exile and at home considers Christian Copts as a distinct ethnicity with distinct ancestry, religion, and way of life, but one that has been relegated by the Muslim major-ity and the Egyptian state to the status of an oppressed "minority."[12] The very meaning of the term Copt, rooted in the word Aegyptos, or Egypt, suggests Christians to be the "true original Egyptians," a distinct racial group who over time have been turned into a "second-class" population.[13] Interestingly, mili-tant Islamists in Egypt likewise attribute a distinct ethnic character to Coptic Christians, albeit not as "oppressed" minority, but as the stooge of crusaders and western interests. In contrast, most Coptic intellectuals and church lead-ers, as well as Muslim elites inside Egypt, view Muslim–Coptic relations in a unique fashion that does not resemble any other interethnic or interreligious dynamics. Such Coptic figures as Samir Morcos, Hani Labib, Ghali Shukri, Milad Hanna and the like, together with Muslim counterparts such as Tariq el-Bishri, Salim el-Awa, or Jamal Badawi view Egyptian Christian Copts not as a sociological "minority," but as players and partners in the unique Egyptian-Arab-Islamic civilization. The Coptic population is seen as an integral element in the category of "Egyptian people," on par with their Muslim counterparts, while Egypt is constituted as a "unique entity," a "land of inherent pluralism and mélange" owing to its pharaonic, Greco-Roman, Coptic, and Islamic heritage.[14] In Gamal Hamdan's words, most of today's Egyptian Muslims are yesterday's Copts [. . .]. In fact Egyptians are made partly of Muslim Copts and partly Christian Copts, considering that the word "Copt" means "Egyptian."[15] According to Christian Hani Labib, although Islamists may consider Copts to be second-class citizens, the Egyptian constitution rules for equality, and the modern state renders the concept of *dhimmi* status redundant.[16] While the former view insists on "minority" status, "discrimination," and conflict, the latter underlies "citizenship," "equality," and accommodation. Yet both seem to characterize Coptic reality in terms of certain "objective," historical, and cultural "facts," a long standing metanarrative. There is little reference to everyday life processes, to interpersonal relations and agency, to specific episodes of conflict, to the intricate marriage of both clash and coexistence, nor especially to the spatial dimension of these processes.[17]

NARRATIVES OF CONFLICTS

Notwithstanding claims about the "unique historic affinity" between Egypt's Christians and Muslims, evidence of episodic sectarian conflict, clash, and violence abounds. In modern times, three episodes of sectarian clash stand out: British colonial period, the presidency of Anwar Sadat, and the Islamist era. During its colonial rule, Britain deployed the usual divide-and-rule strategy to separate Copts from the national movement. It recognized the Copts as an "ethnic minority," stressing their anthropological "distinctiveness." Encouraged by the British support, groups of Copts, notably wealthy families, pursued a sectarian line, demanding in 1911 a special Coptic representation in councils and the legal system, proposing a "Sunday holiday" instead of Fridays. Muslims responded with dismay, rejecting the demands. Yet the majority of Copts seemed to disapprove of the British emphasis on "Coptic distinctiveness," rejecting the attempt to insert in the 1923 constitution a clause conferring a special status to "foreigners" and "minorities," including the "Coptic community." Copts in general seemed to desire not a minority status, but

citizenship. Indeed, the "liberal era" through the 1960s under Nasser somehow fulfilled that desire, as Christians and Muslims exhibited a good measure
of national unity and cooperation at societal and governmental levels up until
the 1970s.

The presidency of Anwar Sadat in 1971 marked a turning point in Muslim–
Coptic relations. Sadat wanted to take Egypt out of the Nasserist system associated with socialism, populism, and nationalism; he wished to open up to
the West, foreign capital, and market forces. To undermine Nasserists and
Communists, Sadat gave a free hand to the growing Islamist movement, both
the reformist Muslim Brothers and the new *gama'at*, Islamist student associations, which dominated most universities, and which later turned into the
violent al-Gama'a al-Islamiyya organization. In addition, Sadat himself assumed a pious posture, speaking the idiom of Islam and passing religious
laws. He changed the constitution to enshrine shari'a as the main source of
law. These measures deemed to undermine the status of the Christians. There
were even signs of provocation to undercut Coptic authority. In 1972 a report
was said to be circulated in which the Coptic pope allegedly had called for an
increase in the Coptic population in order to return Egypt fully to Christians.[18] In addition, measures were taken to restrict new church construction
by imposing many conditions. Such pressures brought on the fury of the Coptic community, forcing Sadat to back down by passing laws on national unity
and freedom of belief.

Yet the opportunity for sectarian strife remained. In 1972, Muslim youths
in Beheira clashed with Copts, burning shops and houses, on the ground that
a Christian shop owner had shot at the provocative youths. Then, in 1977, Al-
Azhar called for passing laws to implement Islamic penal codes (*hodoud*), and
to implement the execution of apostates. The measures, which would have
brought Christians under Islamic laws, infuriated the Coptic community and
the church. The ensuing protests, statements, and hunger strikes, however, were
overshadowed by the February 3, 1977 mass urban riots; the laws went ahead,
and only the exiled Coptic community followed up the campaign. Yet the new
measures were bound to lead to communal strife. A year later, in the Upper
Egyptian towns of Menya and Assiut, priests were attacked and churches set
on fire, while officials renewed their threat to implement apostasy laws in an
attempt to silence the church. With the pope retreating to the desert as a ges-
ture of protest, the Coptic Church and Sadat's regime had a head-on colli-
sion.[19] Although a compromise and relative calm were established, they failed

to end sectarian violence. In June 1981, Egypt witnessed the worst Coptic–Muslim incident of violence. Reportedly, a personal dispute between two individuals in Cairo's poor community of al-Zawya al-Hamra turned into an armed confrontation between groups of Christians and Muslim neighbors. The violence ended with the intervention of the state. In 1981, the regime arrested twenty-two priests and bishops and deposed Pope Shenouda, as part of a large-scale crackdown on internal dissent arising following Sadat's peace deal with Israel and his new "open door" economic policy.

President Sadat was, ironically, gunned down by an Islamist group to which he had given lip service. His successor, President Mubarak, mended relations with the Christian community and the church but could not stop sectarian conflict. On the contrary, the 1980s and early 1990s, the height of the Islamist movement in the country, witnessed the most frequent and spectacular sectarian violence in Egypt's history. In March 1987, the Islamist groups instigated a band of youth to burn the Church of the Virgin Mary in the southern town of Sohag, on the grounds that some Christians had set a mosque (Qutb) on fire. September saw violent clashes in Assiut between militant Islamists and police, in which Coptic shops were destroyed. In the meantime, Muslim militants in Menya attacked a private party given by a wealthy Copt, and threw explosives into a church, which was followed by violent clashes between Muslims and Christians. In the next two years, churches were assaulted in Rod al-Farag and in Cairo's Masara, a wedding party was attacked, and more skirmishes ensued in Menya and Assiut. In March 1990, Menya's Abu-Kersas became the scene of forty-eight burnt shops belonging to Copts, and bomb attacks of more churches. Violence, largely against Coptic Christians, continued in the early 1990s in Bani Sweif, Menya, and Cairo's Ain Shams, Zeitoun, and Shubra. In 1992 alone, dozens of shops were destroyed, twenty-two people were killed, homes and places of worship were attacked. For every Muslim killed, two Copts were murdered.[20] The most dramatic sectarian violence took place in the southern village of al-Kosheh in January 2000, where at least sixteen people died. A dispute between two traders spread into the surrounding villages, where scores of businesses and homes were destroyed and residents killed in the course of three days of violence. Police regained control only after the violence had already escalated.[21]

The conflicts were not confined to these isolated acts of sabotage by some professional activists. Undoubtedly, they left their imprints on communal sentiments, reviving a new identity politics in Egypt. The hegemony of Islamism had altered the political mood in the nation, had generated a more inward-looking religious nativism, manifested in a typical defensive selfhood and communalism. As Muslims became more Muslim, Copts likewise became more Christian. Muslims grew beards, put on veils, massively attended mosques, and chose more and more religious names for their children; similarly, Copts showed off their crosses, displayed Christian icons, paid much greater attention to church activities, and called their offspring by the names of Christian saints. The two communities continued to compete in what Zeidan calls the "war of stickers"—bumper stickers on cars. The more they felt threatened, the more Coptic Christians withdrew into themselves. College students found their own sectarian groupings, with some calling for the establishment of a Coptic political party.[22] Meanwhile, occasional sectarian outcries spread from the pulpits of mosques, and slanderous books, pamphlets, and cassette tapes unleashed sentiments of communal suspicion and mistrust, often disproportionately, against the Copts. These developments became evidence to support Copts' claim as "oppressed minority," whose dissenting sentiments the church leadership tended to appease. An absence of collective action had earned them the description of "passive minority." Thus, when thousands of angry middle-class Christian youths took to the streets of Cairo in June 2001 to express outrage against a slanderous report in a newspaper against the Coptic Church (about a defrocked priest allegedly having sex with a woman on the premises of a church), it shocked the political elite. Similar collective outrage was expressed only a year later on the screening of the film *Bahab al-Sinima* (I Love Movies), made by a Copt, which had allegedly "misrepresented" the Christian way of life in Cairo. Significantly, in both cases protesters refused to seek state protection but resorted to direct protests from the nucleus of their own community, the church.[23] These represented communal protests, directed not against other religious members, but against a particular newspaper and a filmmaker.

What do these forms of incidents tell us about the nature of interreligious relations in Egypt? Violent clashes seem to occur in particular political conditions, for example, the reign of President Sadat and the rise of Islamism. Accordingly, they originate less from the communities' lay members than from elites or militants. Significantly, most of the incidents took place in rural areas or provincial towns of southern Egypt, rather than in large cities, such as Cairo, where a large concentrated Coptic population lives. Finally, these narratives of conflict represent the tales of the vocal, the noise, the shouting, burning, and killing, which are often reported, recorded, and which we hear. They are real and require serious attention. But the narratives also conceal the more intricate dynamics of communal interactions; they tell us little about how "separate" communities have nevertheless so profoundly merged into a cultural fabric that drawing boundaries between them becomes an empirical challenge. The tales of the "mainstream" often obscure the ways in which Christian and Muslim families live their lives on a daily basis, interact with one another, merge and diverge identities, and share long-standing lifeworlds, and then experience moments of mistrust and suspicion. To highlight the spatial moments of coexistence, I will focus on the Cairo district of Shubra, unique for its cosmopolitan history and high concentration of Copts (currently 30 percent) located in the Muslim megacity in which Christian population is dispersed in small pockets or individually in the vast urban landscape.

CAIRO'S SHUBRA: GEOGRAPHY OF COEXISTENCE

For centuries after Cairo's construction, Shubra remained the summer residence of the notables and the elites. In fact, the word *Shubra* is a Coptic term referring to Djebro or Sapro, meaning "countryside."[24] From the nineteenth century, the area expanded, developing especially after World War I. In 1947 Shubra had 282,000 residents, increasing to 541,000 by 1960. The natural population growth and migration turned the surrounding areas into Coptic neighborhoods. So in the current administrative division, Shubra constitutes only a segment of the adjacent districts of Rod El-Farag, Ezbekiya, and Sahel, which accommodates the highest concentration of Christians in the city. In its modern expansion, Shubra developed new European-style streets and buildings, including churches, clinics, missionary schools, and cinemas. Mohammad Ali Pasha's summer palace, built in the image of Versailles, crowned Shubra Avenue, the fashionable carriage promenade, which had become known as Egypt's Champs Elysées. With the settlement of elite families originating from the Levant, Ottoman, Syria, and Lebanon, as well as Jews, Greeks, and Italians, and most famously the singer/actress Dalida, Shubra assumed an exceptionally cosmopolitan character, attracting a host of artists, singers, writers, and poets.[25]

The twentieth-century Shubra, an extension of Ezbekiya, has been the residential area of middle-class urbanites, with a 40 percent Coptic concentration. However, in its current form, Shubra looks in many ways like hundreds of other lower-class areas in the city. The district has lost its past glory, style, elitist distinction, and cosmopolitan posture. From being Egypt's Champs Elysées, Shubra Avenue has declined into a congested, crowded road, darkened and depleted by the city's traffic fumes. The run-down remains of its old-style homes, two- or three-story villas, are now surrounded by scores of tasteless, boxy, and flimsy buildings, struggling to emerge out of layers of dust and pollution. Its urban form, shops, people, and rhythms are not radically different from other neighborhoods. Yet Shubra represents a distinct urbanity, reflected in its history and memory, in its urban "footprints," in social space, in echoes and manners.[26] It is perhaps the only *baladi*, or popular area in the city, where one can see a larger number of unveiled women shopping, walking, or working in the public space. Some of them stand behind store counters as salespersons, while older ones may sit in front-door chairs on the sidewalks. More striking perhaps is Subra's skyline. Minarets of cross and crescent conjoin sometimes in juxtaposed proximity, staring at each other in resolve and rectitude. From these structures emanate the echoes of evening prayers, filling the sky of the neighborhoods.

Indeed, for Muslim passersby, Shubra's small churches are not estranged places; they look remarkably like Muslim *zaway*s—small, single-room spaces and simple structures, with the male worshippers usually sitting on the floor, reciting from the holy book, simultaneously broadcast on rooftop loudspeakers. The large churches, such as Mar Girgis in Khalafawi, where worshippers are seated on chairs, are more complex. They often act as community centers, places of prayers, recreation, education, interpersonal relations, and spaces of communal identity and association. Both male and female Copts attend large churches, but, just as in mosques, they pray or attend religious classes in segregated halls. Similarly, the informality that characterizes Coptic churches (the apparent disorder, screaming children, men and women chatting, sipping tea, and nibbling sandwiches) resembles that of mosques. Both institutions of faith share in their regard for each other. During Muslim festivals and Ramadan, for instance, Shubra churches illuminate with colorful green lights, to express solidarity with mosques.

The experience of sharing in the public space encompasses the common use of many different institutions. Coptic and Muslim children attend the same government schools, where they play, fight, form peer groups, and experience almost identical childhoods. There are plenty of stories about Muslims who attended Christian schools, or Copts who joined Islamic (*owqaf*) schools. Educated Copts from the older generations took courses in Al-Azhar; the poet

Wahbi Tadross studied Qur'an; and Francis al-Eter attended classes by Muhammad Abdu, who decried the sectarian divide and saw nationalism as the cooperation of all citizens irrespective of religion.[27] In the localities, Muslims and Christians build deliberately nonsectarian organizations such as community associations to improve the neighborhood. Coptic and Muslim businesses and shops are invariably found next to each other, with almost no way for an outsider to know which belongs to whom, except by religious names of their owners. This integration structures daily personal interactions, for instance, in cleaning up the front shop sidewalk, watching each other's business, lending and borrowing, and neighborly chatting and discussing. I did not see any indication that Christians refer only to Christian, and Muslims to Muslim, businesses.

Business personnel of Shubra are likely to live in the vicinity, in the typical three- or four-story boxy apartment buildings, where each floor is usually tailored to enclose two or three flats, within each residing a Muslim or Christian family. The proximity of buildings across the narrow streets and alleyways is such that neighbors cannot avoid overhearing or seeing one another. In such interfaith spatial arrangement, few things remain private. For residents who have shared common life, apartment doors do not remain closed. Umm Yahya may enter into Abla Mary's flat just across the hall without knocking on her door, and engage in hour-long smalltalk, a practice not to the liking of the more autonomous younger generations. If a neighbor does not hear the usual buzz in the next-door apartment, she might wonder what has gone wrong. "Where is your mother?" recalled Safa, a Christian resident of Shubra, about her neighbor, Umm Yahya from the front balcony. Umm Yahya had not heard Safa's mother's usual "good mornings," for she had fallen ill. Upon hearing the news, "she came back, before lunch, with two big chickens and lots of macaroni," a visit that was followed by frequent calls to make sure that the children were fine.[28] "It is not clear in your story if Umm Yahya was a Christian or Muslim," I commented. "She was Muslim, God bless her; she was a neighbor," she replied. "You see at the time," Safa went on, "we did not know [notice] religion. We were not just aware if this person was Christian or that one Muslim. Actually, my father kept both the Qur'an and Bible at home. We had both; we didn't know the separation." In fact, there is little that distinguishes a Christian home from a Muslim one in middle-class Shubra. Except for the religious icons, home decorations and internal designs are almost identical—small rooms packed with heavy furniture, big and bright chandeliers, and walls filled with religious calligraphies. So, a Christian entering a Muslim home would find not a strange but a familiar habitat.

Neighborly relations widely involve the customary practice of borrowing things from each other—money, tools, or more frequently a cup of oil, sugar, rice, or beans. For those who find cash in scarcity, it is essential, as part of survival strategy, to secure access to foodstuff by lending and borrowing. The practice follows the attendant rationalities in how to keep the account, the frequency of transfers, and the time of returns. The tradition also means that food culture in both communities is essentially similar. "Coptic food and Muslims' diet is exactly the same," according to Safa, only Muslims avoid pork, and Copts camel meat. Otherwise, the main Egyptian dishes, *molukhiya*, *kushari*, *ta'miya*, and the like are an integral part of food culture in both communities. Even such Muslim delicacies as *ashura* (a special sweet made of milk, rice, and sugar) are widely consumed by the Christians, often on special occasions by "important" members of the family, men. Muslim and Christian male neighbors may get together in evening pastimes to socialize, play backgammon, and talk, while women serve them tea and delicacies, which reflects how gender relations in the two communities are remarkably similar.

The Orthodox Church stipulates that it is the man's duty to house, feed, clothe, and shelter his wife, who, in return, is obliged to obey her husband and not to leave home without his permission. Women are not allowed to make major decisions in the church, or to become deacons or priests, even though they may involve themselves in charity and service work. Just as in mosques, in churches too men and women sit separately during the prayer. Early marriage is condoned and female circumcision is practiced in both communities. Christians share more or less similar piety and moral codes as Muslims in terms of family relations, respect for elders, sexuality, and marriage. "Conservatism is not just a Muslim thing," Coptic Maged commented. "Church is also saying TV or films are not allowed."[29] However, while the conservative piety of Muslim women is often judged by their public appearance in the veil (as opposed to "modern" unveiled ones), lack of veiling among Christian women often veils their conservative ethos. What in principle determines the cultural and behavioral patterns in Egypt is not religion, but class. Muslim and Coptic middle classes share by far more than what poor and middle-class Copts do. No distinct dress codes separate members of the two faiths. Gone are the nineteenth-century days when the Copts were compelled to wear colored turbans, belts, or heavy crosses around their necks, as reported by Edward Lane, even though the use of some religious symbols (such as the cross and tattoos that in the past largely peasants displayed as protection from evil spirits) seems to be back.[30] The growth of veiling among Muslim women is a very recent phenomenon, largely since the 1980s. It is mainly the use of religious names (such as Mohammad or George) that distinguishes a Christian from a Muslim. Yet with the growing use of nonreligious names (such as Shirin or Mona), this identity marker has drastically diminished.

Followers of both faiths invariably stressed deep interfaith friendships, in particular among youths of the same sex. Beyond the schools where peer groups are formed, neighborhoods and apartment buildings are places where youngsters establish deep affinity. Male youngsters spend a great deal of time on the street corners, strolling, chatting, seeing movies, sitting in coffee shops, or playing soccer, sometimes very late at night. But young females, both Muslim and Christian, are likely to join together in the privacy of homes to build close associations. Even when Fatma, a Muslim friend of her Christian neighbor Lilian, went through a new religiosity by putting on the veil, their deep affinity was not affected.[31] Muslims in Shubra attend churches for marriage and religious festivities, while Christians may partake in Muslim weddings and such festive occasions as Eid al-Fitr, or Eid al-Adha, and Ramadan *iftars*. National ancient holidays, such as Sham Nassim, are shared by both religious members.

It is true that intermarriage is rare, but cross-religious love is not. Novels and films on Shubra often contain stories about love affairs between the Christian and Muslim youths, highlighting secret romances between the neighboring teens. The proximity of homes, windows, and balconies makes eye contact, personal interactions, and emotional exchanges between neighbors—in their ordinary or "natural" states, their T-shirts or pajamas—a way of life. Yet such tales of interfaith love often end in sorrow, in the sad realization that legal union will not be in their future.

Venturing into Shubra neighborhoods on Friday midday, one cannot escape the reverberating sound of Qur'an recitation and the *adan* (call for prayers) from the bustling mosques, large or small. The mosques soon are packed with young and old men, with the prayers lined up, soon extending into the surrounding allies and streets. In the western mainstream media, the group of bending praying men represents the most eye-catching marker of Islam (just note the images in books on Islam or in daily papers), representing a clear religious pointer that separates "us" from "them." For the Christians of Shubra, however, the scene is neither novel nor an issue, except perhaps for the traffic congestion they might cause; otherwise, they are just how things are in the neighborhood. People simply "do not see them." Indeed, the lack of awareness about many identity markers that readily stand out for an outsider is remarkable. For the month or so that I lived in Shubra's neighborhood of Khalafawi, I would be wakened, often abruptly, by the thundering noise of morning *adan*s, which blast from the loudspeakers hooked onto the front doors of neighborhood mosques. Almost every night I would wonder how the Christian neighbors felt about such piercing sounds in the middle of the night. "We don't hear them," they usually responded. This discourse of "not seeing, not hearing, or not noticing," in a sense, points to a state of unconsciousness about "difference" in the daily life of Shubra, indicating the dissipation of boundaries in some domains of social and cultural life among Muslims and Christians.

DIALECTIC OF CONFLICT AND COEXISTENCE

It is naive to present a romantic picture of harmonious sectarian relations in Cairo. What good does such sharing do if it suddenly turns into episodes of violent confrontations, of killing, burning, and destroying in the name of religious difference? What if these members do not invoke their shared lives when the overarching image of communal divide haunts them? We have already seen how Egypt experienced three decades of frequent violent conflicts between members of Muslim and Christian communities, with dozens of people killed, mosques and even more churches attacked, and scores of properties destroyed. But as indicated earlier, the violent clashes occurred in particular political episodes, were instigated primarily by militant members, took place in specific geographies, and escalated not simply out of sectarian difference, but also due to the Upper Egyptian "culture of vendetta," of revenge killing" (*tha'r*), which in essence serves to strengthen the patriarchy of lineage or tribe.[32] More importantly, incidents of conflicts take place not within the large modern cities, but overwhelmingly in villages or provincial towns.

Yet, interreligious clash does arise in everyday interactions. Conflicts may occur between the Christians and Muslims for the same reasons as within each religious group. Tensions with secular roots can be given religious colorings as a way of cultivating support or opposition in an urban locality. Radical activists on both sides attempt to highlight religious differences in their quest to build popular backing. Militant Islamists often "otherized" Copts as non-religious people in order to plant a more exclusive religious identity among their potential constituencies. National politicians at times exalt one faith over the other to nurture support. Thus, Christians often feel a profound insensitivity when political leaders or soap operas project "Egypt as an Islamic nation," a posture that subtracts the Coptic population from the national membership.[33] Yet other tensions arise directly out of differences in religious traditions; for instance, churches ringing their bells simultaneously with the mosques' calls for prayers can cause disruption and tensions.

Laypeople of the faith, as in Shubra, time and again try to find solutions to their differences. Many Shubra residents remain indifferent to the divisive tactics of national politicians. Thus, during the parliamentary elections in 2000, in the mostly Muslim district of Al-Weili in Shubra, the Muslim candidate of the ruling National Democratic Party, Ahmad Fouad Abdel-Aziz, played the sectarian card against his Christian opponent, Mounir Fakhri Abdel-Nour, from the Wafd Party. He propagated the idea that a Christian member of parliament could not represent Muslims. Yet Muslims went ahead electing the Christian candidate as their deputy.[34] In general, Cairo has seen the prevalence of sectarian coexistence more than conflict. The reason cannot be attributed simply to some natural tendency of humans to cooperate, for we have also seen periods of conflicts, even though humans do possess the capacity to coexist, largely when "right conditions" are at their disposal. Nor can the general interreligious calm be reduced to Copts' minority position, their "passivity," atypical tolerance of discrimination, or their subordination to the hegemony and cultural power of the majority. For we have seen also episodes of disquiet, protests, and the expression of collective identity. Despite that Copts constitute a distinct group in terms of shared historical memory, religion, a "proper name," or a "myth of common ancestry," undoubtedly their shared traits, homeland, history, and culture with the "larger Muslim society" play a major role in Muslim–Christian coexistence.[35] Yet there is a need to transcend generalities and abstract images of commonality, by exploring the concrete ways in which people of different ethno-religious groupings experience interconnectedness in daily life. In other words, we need to highlight the geographies within which sharing is experienced (or conflict is fostered). The modern city severely undermines the traditional pattern of immediate, local, interpersonal, and territorial ethno-religious communities. It mixes people with various primordial imaginings, facilitating experiences of interpersonal interactions and sharing; it destabilizes the total and indiscriminate image of sectarian community and solidarity. Muslim–Coptic relations in Shubra are a function of the transformation of urban space in Cairo in the twentieth century.

Social change and the modernization of Cairo in the past one hundred years have led to the breakdown of the traditional Coptic community—that is, a relatively bounded religiously based group localized in particular urban territory with regular day-to-day interpersonal relations—into a mostly fragmented population loosely tied together through a "virtual" or "distanciated community." These Copts with broad Christian identity simultaneously share and experience life with different and diverse non-Coptic individuals and groups. Janet Abu-Lughod has shown how the ecological organization of the preindustrial city in medieval times has in many ways shaped the ethnic and religious distribution of the population in today's Cairo. Built in the tenth century by the Fatimids, the walled city of Cairo did not expand considerably until the French Expedition in the early nineteenth century and the ensuing modernization process; at this time its population did not exceed some 200,000 inhabitants. Until the nineteenth century, the Muslim majority largely lived inside the walls, while some 20,000 religious minorities—Greek sects, Jews, Armenians, and some 10,000 Copts—resided outside, in the northwest corner of Cairo, and were "excluded by and in turn excluded the majority."[36] Not only the religious minorities, but also the Muslim majority, were ethnically divided into distinct groupings, including Egyptian Arabs, foreign Muslims, Mamluks, Black Nubians, and Ethiopians.[37] The ethnic and religious groups irrespective of class and status lived in distinctive shared quarters, wherein workplaces stood traditionally in close proximity to homes. Only Jews typically lived in the walled city, since their major occupation, money-changing and goldsmithing, were located inside the walls, and because they lived close to and under the protection of the ruler who crowned the walled city. The Coptic quarter was located just north of the modern Azbakiya, a site for the port town of al-Maqs, and within the Qas al-Sham'a portion of old Cairo. What determined their spatial location had to do with Copts' mainstream occupations, as scribes, account keepers, and customs officials, who resided in the proximity of their work site, the port.[38] These were the urban occupations in which the early Arab conquerors (warriors) were not interested and lacked the skill to perform.[39]

The rapid modernization process transformed occupational structure and changed many spatial features of Cairo, including the walled quarters; it created new architectural styles and institutions, a class-based spatial division, distinction of workplace and living areas, land use separation, and ethnic and religious mixing. The modern industry, education, and administration generated a new class of professionals and businesses among Muslims (*effendys*) and Copts alike. Yet Copts remained disproportionately more urban, more professional, and better-off. The Coptic tradition of secular education emphasizing professionalism seems to have contributed to the higher percentage of teachers, doctors, and engineers among them. One estimate in the 1970s found that 80 percent of all pharmacists and 30–40 percent of all doctors in Egypt were Copts.[40] They have also been involved in businesses such as moneylending or wine and pork production, in which Muslims express lesser interests. As modernization swept the nation, such wealthy and professional Copts did not hesitate to move out of the traditionally Coptic neighborhoods to disperse and merge into the newly established middle-class areas across the city. What added to a further fragmentation of ethnos and dilution of ethnic communities was that many ethnic and religious minorities, especially Jews, some middle-class Copts, and foreigners (Greek and Italian entrepreneurs, British civil servants, troops, and businessmen) left Egypt after the 1952 Revolution. By the late 1960s, close to 300,000 Egyptians were living abroad.[41] Although the walled section of today's Cairo has maintained some aspects of its traditional spatial organization, it has been strangled by the encroaching modern neighborhoods and their feeble buildings devoid of any memorable character.

Thus, the Coptic population (some 10 percent of the total inhabitants[42]) dispersed individually or in pockets of families across the vast terrain of this megacity. It was largely Shubra, an extension of the Coptic quarter in Azbakiya that maintained its historic legacy of relatively higher (40 and 30 percent respectively) Christian density. Yet even here the influx of Muslim rural migrants (partly due to the location of Khazindar bus terminal in Shubra) since the Second World War expanded Shubra while diluting its Christian density. Indeed as more rural Muslim migrants have moved in, residing in such lower-class neighborhoods as al-Wayli, Zaytoun, Shubra al-Khaymah, or al-Azawa al-Hamra, the affluent and middle-class Christians (along with their Muslim counterparts) chose to move out to settle in the more desirable districts of Muhandessin, Heliopolis, and Nozha, where they created ethnically heterogeneous and more cosmopolitan urban localities. The appeal of modern autonomous individuality, mobility, and the independent nuclear family free from traditional ties and restrictions continue to push new generations of middle-class professional Copts to seek, once they can afford it, to reside outside of their historic Coptic quarters. Consequently, Shubra over the years has been left with more variation in terms of housing styles, socioeconomic status, and ethnic composition than other districts.[43] While, relative to other areas in Cairo, Shubra still accommodates more concentrated Christian Copts, the area has nonetheless lost its more cohesive ethnic grouping or closeness in a bounded spatial location. Ethno-religious dilution in a neighborhood means diminishing the real experience of intimate and durable interaction and sharing with members from one's own ethnic grouping, simultaneously increasing the possibility of more physical proximity to, social interaction, cultural sharing, and, in short, coexistence with members of other ethno-religious clusters. So, the old Coptic quarter of Azbakiya and its Shubra extension, where Christians lived together, did business, interacted, and shared in everyday life, has given way to a more heterogeneous mélange of diverse people, interests, and interactions. It is perhaps no surprise that a Coptic intellectual would argue: "Community? What community? There is not such a Coptic community in Egypt."[44]

"DISTANCIATED" COMMUNITY

I tend to think, however, that some sort of "Coptic community" does exist in Egypt. The diminishing of localized, immediate, and territorially based religious "community" has not meant the end of collective identity, communal sentiment, and imagining. A feeling of general threat, discrimination, and distinction or a desire for what Stanley Tambiah calls "leveling" can generate collective affinity among religious members who may not even have met each other. Leveling refers to efforts to equalize entitlements, eliminating the real or perceived advantages enjoyed by the opponents and the disadvantages suffered by the self.[45] While the modern city, as in Cairo, tends to erode close-knit face-to-face and localized collectives, thus bringing out modes of cosmopolitan experience and interaction, it at the same time facilitates broader, even though distanciated and imagined, communities. For the modern city is not just physical space (neighborhood relations, immediate proximities, and the everyday) but also consists of the public sphere—the sphere of virtual communities, political process, media activities, and citizenship. The urban concentration of literacy, electoral campaigns, and mass media (news, novels, daily papers, images, TV, satellite channels, and now the Internet) provide anonymous religious members the means to associate, develop collective affinity, and form a virtual community. In modern conditions, rumors, the source of so many sectarian tensions, spread faster and farther than ever before, thus potentially rendering communal relations even more volatile and precarious. Unlike in premodern times, when conflicts would remain mostly enclosed, extinguishable, and endemic, the modern media have the capacity to broaden a small and insignificant incident into epidemics of generalized violence among overstretched imagined and distanciated communities. Only in late modernity could a few cartoons of Prophet Muhammad or Pope Benedict's statement galvanize Muslim collective outrage in such a global scale and velocity.

In Egypt, the dominance of Islamic discourse in the past three decades has made the Christians more self-conscious as a "minority." Their internal affinity has been reinforced by both real and imagined acts of discrimination. Copts in general speak of how they are under-represented in academia and professional unions; are deprived of state support for Coptic studies; have no Coptic mayors, governors, college deans, school head teachers; and are absent from high-ranking military positions, the judiciary, intelligence, and presidential offices. When the Muslim Brotherhood leader, Mustafa Mashhur, stated in the 1990s that Copts as the people of *dhimmi* were not to be allowed to serve in the Egyptian army, it implied a lack of trust in Christians. Mass media have in particular been instrumental in alienating Copts as a collective by spreading anti-Christian smears and rumors or by projecting them as second-class citizens. Popular television serials often depict Egypt as an Islamic nation, thus excluding Christians from its membership.[46] Many ordinary Christians may not experience or not be aware of these facts, but these are usually communicated through publications, via websites, and, more fiercely, by Coptic activists in exile. On the other hand, the retreat of the state from social welfare provisions tends to reinforce the sectarian divide, in that people are compelled to rely on their own communal support instead of the state, upon which all citizens equally rest. Thus, following President Sadat's open door policy, the Coptic Church took on the task of establishing a network of community development centers in rural and urban areas to provide religious education, literary classes, women's empowerment, and income generation schemes of various kinds—ones that cater largely to Christian clientele. The 1980s and 1990s saw an even more expansive "welfare pluralism," one that was deemed to buttress a new "communal identity" and loyalty.[47] Thus, Maged's uncle in Shubra established a welfare association that supports forty poor Coptic families, who are introduced by the local church or the related associations, serving only the Christian families.[48] Thus, while Shubra stands as a distinctive Christian–Muslim cosmopolitan locale in the city's imagination, the discourse of exclusivist identities does contribute to lines of tension within Shubra.

What we have, then, is a coincidence of both a daily experience of inter-religious coexistence and a sense of inner-communal belonging among Copts and Muslims. This simultaneity of exclusive communal identity and inclusive inter-communal connectedness gives rise to a different kind of ethno-religious reality, one quite distinct from those projected by both primordialist and in-strumentalist schools. One might call this "critical communalism" or "post-communalism," referring to a critical identity that unites a collective sense of ethno-religious self with cosmopolitan experience of lifeworld, and in which the sense of the "other" is complicated by the live experience of interpersonal association, sharing, and trust. In day-to-day life, judgment about "us" and "them" tends to be concrete, selective, and differential, rather than general-ized and sweeping. Selective rational judgments moderate generalized praise of self and prejudice against others, diminishing the ground for inward-looking sectarianism and collective conflict in everyday life.

Does this mean that the modern city is free from communal strife? Not quite. The extraordinary tales of sectarian violence in Beirut, Sarajevo, Mum-bai, and Delhi attest to the fact that "critical communalism" does not elimi-nate the possibility of episodic sectarian violence in cosmopolitan conditions. Civil war, destruction of property, killing, and rape are common features of what Horowitz calls the "deadly ethnic riot" in urban places. It is not uncom-mon to hear astonishing tales of carnage between long-standing neighbors and associates.[49] Of course, the experience of the sectarian divide in Egypt, even in its villages, is in no way comparable to the kind of "routinization," "ritualization," and seemingly disproportionate scale of collective violence that seem to characterize South Asian or African ethnic relations.[50] Neverthe-less, Egypt's urban landscape has not remained immune to occasional com-munal confrontations. October 2005 saw ten-day sectarian tension and vio-lence between Muslims and Christians in the historically cosmopolitan port city of Alexandria. The incident began with the media reporting news of a video recording, a DVD, of a play called *I Was Blind, but Now I Can See*. The play told the story of a young Copt who was persuaded by fundamentalist

Muslims to convert to Islam, only to return to Christianity soon after realizing the moral shortcomings of Muslims. The tabloid press seemed to exploit the DVD to undermine a Christian candidate for the parliamentary elections in favor of his Muslim rivals. The newspapers pressed the Coptic Church to issue an apology for the DVD. Upon its refusal, some five thousand Muslim protesters assembled at the gate of the church of Mar Girgis, which had been accused of distributing the DVD. The ensuing fights left three people dead, 150 injured and over 100 arrested. The incident became a prelude to yet another episode of violence some six months later, when on April 14, 2006, a Muslim man stabbed Coptic worshippers in three separate Alexandria churches, causing further sectarian dissension.[51]

How, then, can one explain the episodic feuds between individuals and families of different denominations who have been living together through communal divide? This is an extremely challenging task, and a satisfactory response is yet to emerge. Suffice here to suggest that the very coincidence of cosmopolitan interaction, on the one hand, and communal belonging, on the other, carries within itself the seeds of an exaggerated emphasis on demarcation, which can potentially grow into mass violence of extraordinary scale. Georg Simmel observed that "the degeneration of difference in convictions into hatred and fight occurs only when there are essential similarities between the parties."[52] In other words, when conflict erupts between ethno-religious groups that had a history of similarity and coexistence, rival parties make an exaggerated attempt to highlight the differences and wipe out blurring and confusion. Thus, in the words of Tambiah, speaking on South Asia, "the greater the blessings of and ambiguities between the socially-constructed categories of difference, the greater the venom of the imposed boundaries, when conflict erupts between the self and the other, 'us' and 'them.'"[53] Notwithstanding their significance, these observations reflect only an aspect of the complex whole, in that they relate to the indiscriminate intercommunal atrocities in which assailants construct an abstract and generalized picture of the target groups, lumping everyone together as the object of hatred. The fact, however, is that the times of acute tension are also times when individual opponents selectively spare, protect, and rescue neighboring "enemies" from the wrath of indiscriminate assault. They invoke their life experience of sharing and trust with people who happen to belong to a rival sect. In other words, the experience of cosmopolitan exchange renders a Muslim to project a more concrete and differentiated "Christian people," rather than massing them together as an abstract and totalized other, and vice versa. Thus, a Coptic resident referring to the sectarian confrontation in Alexandria in October 2006 would say, "This [the clash] is not going to keep me from associating with my Muslim friends." And a Muslim shopkeeper would echo, "In this neighborhood, we Copts and Muslims live together, work together, share the same hardships. It is inconceivable that a problem like this should tear us apart."[54] This process of individual differentiation in judging the "other" by lived experience of interpersonal association, sharing, and trust, that is, everyday cosmopolitanism, is likely to contain indiscriminate sectarian divide and dissension.[55] After all, in Egypt's worst urban religious "strife" in Alexandria in October 2006, only three people were killed—and they were killed not by rival sect members, but by the rubber bullets of the police.

11 THE "ARAB STREET"

IN THE TENSE WEEKS between the September 11 attacks and the first U.S. bombing raids over Afghanistan, and continuing until the fall of the Taliban, commentators raised serious concerns about what the *Wall Street Journal* later called the "irrational Arab street."[1] If the United States attacked a Muslim country, the pundits worried, would the "Arab street" rally behind Osama bin Laden and other radical Islamists, endangering other U.S. interests in the region and rendering George W. Bush's "war on terrorism" a troublesome, if not doomed, venture from the outset? As U.S. troops prepared to deploy in Afghanistan, some officials in Washington implored Israeli prime minister Ariel Sharon to exercise restraint in his campaign to crush the Palestinian uprising by force. Should Israeli incursions into Palestinian territory continue during the U.S. assault on the Taliban, they feared, the simmering rage of the Arab masses might "boil over," leaving the local gendarmes powerless to prevent the furious crowds from harming Americans, trashing U.S. property, and threatening the stability of friendly Arab regimes. Senator Joseph Biden broached the possibility that "every US embassy in the Middle East [would be] burned to the ground."[2]

Since the war in Afghanistan, and continuing through the major Israeli offensives in the West Bank and the buildup to Bush's war on Iraq, the "Arab street" became a minor household phrase in the West, bandied about in the media as both a subject of profound anxiety and an object of withering

---

Adapted from Asef Bayat, "The 'Street' and the Politics of Dissent in the Arab World," *Middle East Report*, no. 226 (spring 2003), pp. 10–17.

condescension. The "Arab street" and, by extension, the "Muslim street" became code words that immediately invoke a reified and essentially "abnormal" mind-set, as well as a strange place filled with angry people who, whether because they "hate us" or just "don't understand us," must shout imprecations "against us." "Arab or other Muslim actions" were described almost exclusively in terms of "mobs, riots, revolts,"[3] leading to the logical conclusion that "Western standards for measuring public opinion simply don't apply" in the Arab world. At any time, American readers were reminded, protesting Arab masses might shed their unassuming appearance and "suddenly turn into a mob, powerful enough to sweep away governments—"notably the "moderate" Arab governments who remain loyal allies of the United States.[4]

Worries about the "Arab street" notwithstanding, U.S. forces did move into Afghanistan, U.S. bombs did kill Afghan civilians in the thousands, the Israeli–Palestinian conflict only briefly "cooled off," and Bush moved full speed ahead with plans to attack Iraq. But, though numerous protests in the Muslim and Arab worlds did occur, no U.S. embassy was burned to the ground. Nor did the Arab and Muslim masses rally behind Bin Laden. Only when Israel invaded the West Bank in the spring of 2002 did ordinary people in the Arab world collectively explode with outrage. The millions of Arab citizens who poured into the streets of Cairo, Amman, Rabat, and many other cities to express sympathy with the Palestinians evoked memories of how Arab anticolonial movements in the postwar period were driven from below. But because the "Arab street" had not erupted at the possible U.S. bombing in Afghanistan during Ramadan, this very real example of latent popular anger in the Arab world was airily dismissed. Abruptly, the image of the "Arab street" shifted from an unpredictable powder keg to a "myth" and a "bluff," somehow kept alive despite the fact that Arab countries were filled with "brainwashed" people trapped in "apathy."[5] The implication for U.S. policymaking was clear: Arabs do not have the guts to stop an attack on Iraq or any other unpopular U.S. initiative, and therefore the United States should express "not sensitivity, but resolution," in the face of remonstrations from Arab allies.[6] Neither the slogans of the actual demonstrators nor the insistence of Arab governments that they face unbearable pressure from their populations needed to be taken at face value. The *Economist* declared the "death" of the Arab street, once and for all. It was not long before national security adviser Condoleezza Rice concluded that because the Arab peoples were too weak to demand democracy, the United States should intervene to liberate the Arab world from its tyrants.[7]

STREET POLITICS AND POLITICAL STREET

In the narratives of the western media, the "Arab street" is damned if it does and damned if it doesn't—either it is "irrational" and "aggressive," or it is "apathetic" and "dead." There is little chance of its salvation as something western societies might recognize as familiar. The "Arab street" thus became an extension of another infamous concept, the "Arab mind," which also reified the culture and collective conduct of an entire people in a violent abstraction.[8] It was another subject of Orientalist imagination, reminiscent of colonial representation of the "other," which sadly was internalized by some Arab selves. By no simple oversight the "Arab street" was seldom regarded as an expression of *public opinion* and collective sentiment, like its western counterpart still was, but was perceived primarily as a physical entity, a brute force expressed in riots and mob violence. The "Arab street" mattered only in its violent imaginary, when it was poised to imperil interests or disrupt grand strategies. The street that conveyed the collective sentiment was a nonissue, because the United States could and often does safely ignore it. Such perceptions of the "Arab street" have informed Washington's approach in the Middle East—flouting Arab public opinion with increasingly unequivocal support for Ariel Sharon while he proceeded to dismantle the Palestinian Authority, and simultaneously, with determination to wage war on Iraq.

But street politics in general and the Arab street in particular are more complex. Neither street is a physicality, nor the Arab street a mere brute force or simply dead. The "Arab street" is an expression of not simply street politics in general, but primarily of what I like to call "political street"; one whose modes and means of articulation have gone through significant changes. "Street politics" represent the modern urban theater of contention par excellence (see Chapter 8). We need only remember the role the "street" has played in such monumental political changes as the French Revolution, nineteenth-century labor movements, anticolonial struggles, the anti–Vietnam War movement in the United States, the "velvet revolutions" in Eastern Europe, and, perhaps, the current global antiwar movement. The street, in this sense, is the chief locus of politics for ordinary people, those who are structurally absent from the institutional positions of power—the unemployed, casual workers, migrants, people of the underworld, and housewives. It serves as a key medium wherein sentiments and outlooks are formed, spread, and expressed in a remarkably unique fashion. But "street politics" enjoys another dimension, that is, it is more than just about conflict between the authorities and the deinstitutionalized or "informal" people over the active use of public space and the control of public order. Streets as spaces of flow and movement are not only where people protest, but also where they *extend* their protest beyond their immediate circles to include also the unknown, the "strangers" who might espouse similar, real or imagined, grievances. That is why not only the deinstitutionalized groups such as the unemployed, but also actors with some institutional power, like workers or students, find streets arenas for the extension of collective sentiments. It is this pandemic potential that threatens the authorities, who exert a pervasive power over public spaces—with police patrols, traffic regulation, and spatial division—as a result. Students at Cairo University, for example, often stage protest marches inside the campus. However, the moment they decide to come out into the street, riot police are immediately and massively deployed to encircle the demonstrators, push them into a corner away from public view, and keep the protest a local event. Indeed this heavily guarded actual street points to the fact that the metaphorical street is not deserted so much as it is controlled.

Beyond serving as the physical place for "street politics," urban streets also signify a different but crucial symbolic utterance, one that transcends the physicality of street, to convey collective sentiments of a nation or community. This I call *political street*—a notion that is distinct from "street politics." *Political street* signifies the collective sensibilities, shared feelings, and public judgment of ordinary people in their day-to-day utterances and practices, which are expressed broadly in the public squares—in taxis, buses, shops, sidewalks, or more audibly in mass street demonstrations. The Arab street (and by extension, the "Muslim street") should be seen in terms of such expression of collective sentiments in the Arab public sphere.

THE SHIFTING ARAB STREET

How does the Arab world fare in terms of its "political street"? Arab anticolonial struggles attest to the active history of the Arab street. Popular movements arose in Syria, Iraq, Jordan, and Lebanon during the late 1950s after Nasser nationalized the Suez Canal. The unsuccessful tripartite aggression by Britain, France, and Israel in October 1956 to reclaim control of the canal caused an outpouring of popular protests in Arab countries in support of Egypt. Although 1956 was probably the last major Pan-Arab solidarity movement until the pro-Palestinian wave of 2002, social protests by workers, artisans, women, and students for domestic social development, citizens' rights, and political participation have been documented.[9] Labor movements in Lebanon, Syria, Egypt, Yemen, and Morocco have carried out strikes or street protests over both bread-and-butter and political issues. Since the 1980s, during the era of IMF-recommended structural adjustment programs, Arab labor unions have tried to resist cancellations of consumer commodity subsidies, price rises, pay cuts, and layoffs. Despite no-strike deals and repression of activists, wildcat stoppages have occurred. Fear of popular resistance has often forced governments, such as in Egypt, Jordan, and Morocco, to delay structural adjustment programs or retain certain social policies.[10]

When traditional social contracts are violated, Arab populations have reacted swiftly. The 1980s saw numerous urban protests over the spiraling cost of living. In August 1983, the Moroccan government reduced consumer subsidies by 20 percent, triggering urban unrest in the north and elsewhere. Similar protests took place in Tunis in 1984, and in Khartoum in 1982 and 1985. In summer 1987, the rival factions in the Lebanese civil war joined hands to stage an extensive street protest against a drop in the value of the Lebanese currency (see Chapter 4). Algeria was struck by cost-of-living riots in the fall of 1988, and Jordanians staged nationwide protests in 1989, over the plight of Palestinians and economic hardship, forcing King Hussein to introduce cautious measures of political liberalization. Lifting subsidies in 1996 provoked a new wave of street protests, leading the king to restrict freedom of expression and assembly.[11] In Egypt in 1986, low-ranking army officers took to the streets to protest the Mubarak regime's decision to extend military service. The unrest quickly spread to other sectors of society.

While the lower and middle classes formed the core of urban protests, college students often joined in. But student movements have had their own contentious agendas. In Egypt, the 1970s marked the heyday of a student activism dominated by leftist trends. Outraged opposition to the Camp David peace treaty and economic austerity brought thousands of students out into urban streets. Earlier years had seen students organizing conferences, strikes, sit-ins, and street marches and producing newspapers for the walls, the "freest of publications."[12] In 1991, students in Egypt, Algeria, Morocco, Jordan, Yemen, and Sudan demonstrated to express anger against both the Iraqi invasion of Kuwait and the U.S.-led war to drive Iraq out of Kuwait. Since 1986, Palestinian students have been among the most frequent participants in actions of the intifada, often undeterred by the Israeli army's policies of shooting and arresting students or closing down Palestinian universities.

Yet many things have changed drastically for the Arab street since the 1980s. The pace of cost-of-living protests has slowed down, as governments enact structural adjustment programs more slowly and cautiously, deploy safety nets such as Social Funds (Egypt and Jordan), and allow Islamic NGOs and charities to help out the poor. Indeed, the Arab world enjoys the lowest incidence of extreme poverty in the world's developing regions.[13] Meanwhile, the discontent of the impoverished middle classes was channeled into the Islamist movements in general, and the politicization of professional syndicates in particular.

On the other hand, the more traditional class-based movements—notably, peasant organizations, cooperative movements, and trade unions—have been in relative decline. As peasants have moved to the city from the countryside, or lost their land to become rural day laborers, the social basis of peasant and cooperative movements has eroded. The weakening of economic populism, closely linked to structural adjustment, has led to the decline of public-sector employment, which constituted the core of trade unionism. Through reform, downsizing, privatization, and relocation, structural adjustment has undermined the unionized public sector, while new private enterprises linked to international capital remain largely union-free. Although the state bureaucracy remains weighty, its underpaid employees are unorganized, and a large proportion of them survive by taking second or third jobs in the informal sector. Currently, much of the Arab workforce is self-employed. Many wage earners work in small, paternalistic businesses. On average, between one-third and one-half of the urban workforce are involved in the unregulated, unorganized informal sector. While relations between employers and employees are not always happy, workers tend to be more loyal to their bosses than to fellow workers.

Although the explosive growth of NGOs since the 1980s heralded autonomous civic activism, NGOs are premised on the politics of fragmentation. NGOs divide the potential beneficiaries of their activism into small groups, substitute charity for principles of rights and accountability, and foster insider lobbying rather than street politics. It is largely the advocacy NGOs, involved in human rights, women's rights, and democratization, not wealth and income gaps, that offer different and new spaces for social mobilization.

As people rely more on informal activities and their loyalties become fragmented, struggles for wages and conditions tend to lose ground to concerns over jobs, informal work conditions, and an affordable cost of living; and rapid urbanization increases demands for urban services, shelter, decent housing, health, and education. Under such conditions, the Arab grass roots resort not to politics of collective protest but to the individualistic strategy of "quiet encroachment." Individuals and families strive to acquire basic necessities (land for shelter, urban collective consumption, informal jobs and business opportunities) in a prolonged and unassuming, though illegal, fashion. Instead of organizing a street march to demand electricity, for example, the disenfranchised simply tap into the municipal power grid without authorization (see Chapter 4).

Thus, in the Arab world, the political class par excellence remains the educated middle class—state employees, students, professionals, and the intelligentsia—who mobilized the "street" in the 1950s and 1960s with overarching ideologies of nationalism, Ba'athism, socialism, and social justice. Islamism has been the latest of these grand worldviews. With the core support coming from the worse-off middle layers, the Islamist movements succeeded for two decades in activating large numbers of the disenchanted population with cheap Islamization—moral and cultural purity, affordable charity work, and identity politics. However, by the mid-1990s, it became clear that the Islamists could not go very far with more costly Islamization—establishing an Islamic polity and economy and conducting international relations compatible with the modern national and global citizenry. Islamist rule faced crisis where it was put into practice (as in Iran and Sudan). Elsewhere, violent strategies failed (as in Egypt and Algeria), and thus new visions about the Islamic project developed. The Islamist movements either were repressed or became resigned to revision of their earlier outlooks.

Anti-Islamic sentiments in the West following the September 11 events, and the subsequent "war on terrorism," have undoubtedly reinforced a feeling that Islam is under global attack, reinforcing the languages of religiosity and nativism. Several Islamist parties that, among other things, expressed opposition to U.S. policies scored considerable successes in several national elections. The Justice and Development Party in Morocco doubled its share to forty-two seats in the September 2002 elections. In October 2002, the Islamist movement came in third in Algerian local elections, and the alliance of religious parties in Pakistan won 53 out of 150 parliamentary seats. In November, Islamists won nineteen out of the total forty parliamentary seats in Bahrain, and the Turkish Justice and Development Party captured 66 percent of the legislature. However, these electoral victories point less to a "revival of Islamism"[14] than to a shift of Islamism from a political project with national concerns into more fragmented languages concerned with personal piety and global, anti-Islamic menace. If anything, we are on the threshold of a post-Islamist turn.[15] (See Chapter 13.)

Whatever its merit, a major legacy of Islamism has been to change the Arab states. It rendered the Arab states more religious (as states moved to rob Islamism of its moral authority), more nativist or nationalist (as states moved to assert their Arab authenticity and to disown democracy as a western construct), and more repressive, since the liquidation of radical Islamists offered states the opportunity to control other forms of dissent. This legacy of the Islamist movements has further complicated the politics of dissent in today's Arab world.

A RENEWAL

The revival of the "Arab street" in 2002 in solidarity with the Palestinians was truly spectacular. For a short while, states lost their tight control, and publicly vocal opposition groups proliferated, even among the "westernized" and "apolitical" students of the American University in Cairo. The Palestinian solidarity movement showed that there is more to Arab street politics than Islamism and spurred the renewal of a political tradition. In January, as the United States moved closer to attacking Iraq, one million Yemenis marched in Sanaa, chanting, "Declaration of War Is Terrorism." Over ten thousand protested in Khartoum, thousands in Damascus and Rabat, and hundreds in the Bahraini capital of Manama.[16] Twenty thousand Christians in Jordan staged a prayer for the people of Iraq, condemning Bush's war.[17] One thousand Yemeni women demonstrated in the streets to protest the arrest of a Yemeni citizen mistaken for an al-Qaeda member in Germany.[18] Large and small protest actions against the war on Iraq continued in Egypt and other Arab countries amid massive deployments of police. And with the U.S. and U.K. invasion of Iraq, street protests throughout the Arab world assumed a new momentum.

At least with regard to Palestine, however, the tremendous rise of the Arab street occurred with the tacit approval of the Arab states. The extremity of Israel's violence during the 2002 invasions, and later invasion of U.S. forces into Iraq, brought the politicians and people together in a common nationalist sentiment. In addition, street dissent was directed largely against an *outside* adversary, and protesters' slogans against their own governments were voiced primarily by the ideological leaders rather than the ordinary participants.[19]

Only in the later Cairo rallies of 2005 and 2006 did crowds demand the removal of the twenty-year-old emergency laws, which continue to hamper free public assembly, and an end to the Mubarak presidency. These rallies then evolved into an explicitly prodemocracy movement.

Why did the Arab street fail to rise against its own suppression, to demand democracy and justice? While the disenfranchised have resorted to "quiet encroachment," the Arab states have considerably neutralized the political class by promulgating a common discourse based on nationalism, religiosity, and anti-Zionism. Entrenched in the "old-fashioned Pan-Arab nationalism," and seduced by the language of religiosity and moral politics, the Arab intelligentsia failed to seize the moment to win political concessions from their own authoritarian states. Israel's occupation of Palestinian lands, with material and diplomatic U.S. support, has trapped generations of Arab intelligentsia in a narrow-minded nativism and cultural nationalism from which the authoritarian Arab states largely benefit. The nativist often dismisses ideas and practices, however noble, that can be described as rooted in alien, usually "western," cultures and romanticizes ideas and practices of the "self" even if they are oppressive. Human rights, for example, may simply be discarded as a western import or a manipulative U.S. ploy.

On the other hand, the Arab governments allow little room for independent dissent. Since 2000, demands for collective protests against the United States and Israel were ignored by the authorities, while unofficial street actions faced intimidation and assault, with activists being harassed or detained.[20] On February 15, 2003, the day that over ten million people throughout the world demonstrated against the U.S. war on Iraq, thousands of Egyptian riot police squeezed some five hundred demonstrators into a corner, separating them from the public.

Faced with formidable challenges to expression in the street, Arab activists developed new means of articulating dissent, mostly in the form of civic campaign—boycott campaigns, cyberactivism, and protest art among them. As the Arab states exercised surveillance over the streets, activism was pushed inside the confines of civil institutions—college campuses, schools, mosques, professional associations, and NGOs. Given the lack of a free political climate, professional associations offered venues for political campaigns, to the extent that they often assumed the role of political parties, where intense competition for leadership prevailed. Their headquarters served as sites for political rallies, meetings, charity work, and international solidarity campaigns. Other civil associations, chiefly the new advocacy NGOs, began to promote public debates on human rights, democratization, women, children, and labor rights. In early 2000, some ninety to one hundred human rights organizations operated in the Arab world, along with hundreds of social service centers, and many more social service organizations that began to employ the language of rights in their work.[21]

Innovations in mobilization, styles of communication, and organizational flexibility are bringing a breath of fresh air to stagnant nationalist politics. The Egyptian Popular Committee for Solidarity with the Palestinian Intifada represented one such trend. Set up in October 2000, the committee brought together representatives from Egypt's various political trends—leftists, nationalists, Islamists, and womens' rights groups. It set up a website, developed a mailing list, initiated charity collections, organized boycotts of American and Israeli products, revived street actions, and collected two hundred thousand signatures on petitions to close down the Israeli embassy in Cairo. The Egyptian Anti-Globalization Group and the National Campaign Against the War on Iraq, as well as the Committee for the Defense of Workers' Rights and some human rights NGOs, adopted similar styles of activism.[22] It was these organizations and styles that served as the precursor for the emergence of a new kind of politics in Egyptian political tradition. It was galvanized in Kifaya and other prodemocracy movements.[23]

Grassroots charity and boycotts, or product campaigns, became new mediums of political mobilization. Collecting food and medicine for Palestinians has involved thousands of young volunteers and hundreds of companies and organizations. In April 2002, students at the American University in Cairo gathered thirty 250-ton truckloads of charitable products from factories, companies, and homes in the space of four days and nights, bringing them to Palestinians in Gaza. Millions of Arabs and Muslims joined in boycotting American and Israeli products, including McDonald's, KFC, Starbucks, Nike, and Coca-Cola. The remarkable success of local products caused Coca-Cola to lose some 20 to 40 percent of its market share in some countries, while fast-food companies also lost sales.[24] The Iranian ZamZam Cola captured a sizable Middle Eastern market, extending to Pakistan, Malaysia, Indonesia, and several African countries. Within four months, the company exported ten million cans to Saudi Arabia and Persian Gulf states. Some European countries, Denmark and Belgium, began to import ZamZam. Alongside ZamZam, Mecca Cola appeared in Paris to cater to European Arabs and

Muslims who boycotted the U.S. beverages. It sold 2.2 million bottles in France within two months. Mecca Cola allocated 10 percent of the revenue to Palestinian children.

Information technology was also increasingly employed to direct political campaigns. "Small media" have a longer history in the Middle East. The sermons of Islamic preachers like Shaykh Kishk, Yusuf al-Qaradawi, Shaykh Fadlallah, and the popular Egyptian televangelist Amr Khaled have been disseminated on a massive scale through audio and videocassettes. Followers of Amr Khaled, who was banned from preaching in late 2002, could gather over ten thousand signatures in his support via websites. Later, activists began to use e-mails to publicize claims or mobilize for rallies and demonstrations. These media proved instrumental in disseminating news, calling for rallies, and street mobilization. In February 2003, Egyptian Coalitions in Solidarity with Palestine and Iraq planned to send one million petitions to the UN and to the U.S. and British embassies via the Internet. Alternative news websites have become probably the most important sites through which networks of critical and informed constituencies are formed. The increasing use of Facebook, the social networking site, allowed Egyptian youth in 2008 to build what came to be known as the April 6 Youth Movement. The "movement" mobilized some seventy thousand, mostly educated, youths who called for free speech and economic welfare and decried corruption. Activists succeeded in organizing street protests and rallies and, more spectacularly, in initiating a general strike on April 6, 2008, in support of the striking textile workers. The venue for networking has gained a considerable ground in most Arab countries, where Facebook is among the ten most-visited sites on the web.[25] In addition, satellite TV has been rapidly spreading in the Arab world, bringing alternative information to break the hold of the barren domestic news channels. The skyline of Damascus, bristling with satellite dishes, helps to explain the soullessness of the street newsstands where the ruling party's dailies are displayed. While cybercampaigns remain limited to the elite (despite increased Internet use), the politics of the arts reaches a mass audience. The Israeli reoccupation of the West Bank in 2002 revived the political legacy of Umm Kulthoum, Fairuz, and Morocco's Ahmed Snoussi. Arab artists, movie stars, painters, and especially singers became oracles of public outrage. In Egypt, major pop stars such as Amr Diab, Muhammad Munir, and Mustafa Qamar produced best-selling albums that featured exclusively religious and nationalist lyrics. Munir's high-priced *Land and Peace, O Prophet of God* sold 100,000 copies in a short period. Other singers, including Ali al-Hajjar, Muhammad Tharwat, and Hani Shakir, joined together to produce the religio-nationalistic album *Al-Aqsa, O God,* which cornered Arab marketplaces.

Of course, the extent and efficacy of these new spaces of contention remain modest. Yet the growing tendency of most Arab governments to try to control them—closing NGOs, banning publications or songs, and arresting Web designers, and the protagonists of "Facebook Revolution"—offers a hint of their potential to compensate for the impediments facing the Arab street. The street remains the most vital locus for the audible expression of collective sentiments, so long as the local regimes or the global powers ignore popularly held views. The Arab street has been neither "irrational" nor "dead," but it is undergoing a major transformation caused by both old constraints and new opportunities brought about by global restructuring. As a means and mode of expression, the Arab street may be shifting, but the collective grievance that it conveys remains. Will Islamism occupy the center stage as the ideological articulation of these grievances?

12 IS THERE A FUTURE FOR ISLAMIC REVOLUTIONS?

THE FORWARD MARCH of Muslim militancy—from Iran to Lebanon, from Algeria to Palestine, from North Africa to South Asia, extending to the immigrant communities in Europe, not to mention the transnational al-Qaeda—seems to confirm the view that the world is on the verge of Islamist revolutions. It is as though the late twentieth century has impregnated history to give birth to Islamic revolutions with the same intensity and vigor that the early twentieth century produced socialist rebellions. Is globalization pushing religion, Islam, onto the center stage of world radical politics?

This chapter attempts to show that ours may be an age of widespread socioreligious movements and of remarkable social changes, but these may not necessarily translate into the classical (rapid, violent, class-based, and overarching) revolutions. What most accounts of Islamism refer to do not signify Islamic revolutions; rather, they point to heightened but diffused sentiments and movements associated, in one way or another, with the language of religiosity. Perhaps we need to rethink our understanding of "revolutions" in general and the Islamic version in particular. In the Muslim Middle East, the future is likely to belong to a kind of sociopolitical change that might be termed "post-Islamist refolution."

Adapted from Asef Bayat, "Is There a Future for Islamic Revolutions? Religion, Revolt, and Middle Eastern Modernity," in *Revolution in the Making of the Modern World*, ed. John Foran, David Lane, and Andreja Zivkovic (London: Routledge, 2008), pp. 96–111.

MODERNITY AND REVOLUTIONS

Revolutions and revolutionary movements are integral features of modernity, and the Middle Eastern experience is no exception. In this context, modernity implies the solidification of the nation-states that forge material infrastructure, such as a modern army and conscription, education and media, through which people can "imagine" and develop a sense of nationhood.[1] Nationalist movements are the likely outcome if the nation is under colonial domination.[2] Second, modernity is also characterized by the formation of modern centralized states, with the sole power of constituting laws and the monopoly of coercive powers over people whose rights (as citizens) within the framework of the nation-state are recognized. In short, it involves rule over people who hold rights. Modern states, in turn, not only enact laws to regulate dissent (establishing organizations, unions, procedures, and protection) but also tend to become targets of contention by political forces. Third, it is indeed under modern conditions that broader modular contentions become possible, when the localized struggles for parochial concerns of premodern times give way to generalized and epidemic movements.[3] Finally, (capitalist) modernity involves an overarching contradictory tendency, which is followed by deep-rooted contentions fostered by both the remaining old social classes and groups as well as the historically novel ones (such as the new middle class, women, youth, etc.). Here I am not referring to the Marxian labor–capital contradiction, even though it remains a fundamental one. I am, rather, pointing to a more general anomaly. Simply put, modernity offers unparalleled opportunities for many people to thrive, forge identities, and get ahead in life, and yet it excludes and ravages the fortunes of many others. Modern capitalist economy and science, urbanization, education, and the idea of citizenship are closely tied to the flourishing of new social groups such as the bourgeois, professional classes, youth, and public women who foster new social existence and habitus, and engender particular demands. At the same time, on the margins of the modern political economy, ways of life, and institutions, lies a great humanity that is excluded from the modern offerings, in terms of life-chances, respect, equality, and meaningful political participation. Revolutions are the outcome of the collective contention of such social beings whose often "partial interests," moral and material, converge and become the basis of collective identity and action. Revolutionary struggles target the state and are waged only within the confines of a particular nation-state.

As such, none of the above on its own may explain the actual making of revolutions. Revolutions are more intricate phenomena than mere structural contradictions and agency. The making of revolutions involves, in addition, a complex set of material, moral, and cognitive conditions as well as political (internal or international) opportunities. One needs to determine how the potential revolutionaries perceive and interpret their real or imagined misfortunes and marginalization. And, if they do so at all, whom do they blame as being responsible: themselves, God, the state, their immediate superior at work, or fate? Do they find possible ways to get out of their hardship, such as reliance on family, kin, or traditional institutions of support? But if they opt for change, what kinds of resources have they to deploy, as Tilly and others have wondered?[4] Finally, to what extent does a "structure of opportunity" allow for action, how far are states able to withstand the demand of their citizens for change, and what (coercive or reformist) strategies do they deploy to undermine revolutionary movements?[5]

MIDDLE EASTERN MODERNITY AND REVOLUTIONS

These propositions find resonance also with respect to the modern Middle East, notably those countries with oil and other kinds of rentier economies. Despite claims to be otherwise,[6] Middle Eastern modernity has had its own particularities, even though it is by no means "peculiar or exceptional," as the Orientalists would suggest. In the Middle East, the modernization process (characterized by capitalist relations, national markets, human mobility, urbanization, and new education systems, and of modern national states) has by and large been a synthesis of both internal dynamics and colonial encounters.[7] For Hisham Sharabi, this "hybrid" formation reflects "neo-Patriarchy," defined as a mixture of "pseudo-modernism" and "Patriarchy." And patriarchy is seen as a sociocultural reality characterized by myth (rather than reason), religious (rather than scientific) truth, rhetorical (as opposed to analytical) language, authoritarian (instead of democratic) polity, communal (rather than citizenry) social relations, and kin-based rather than class-centered social relations.[8] Although Sharabi's neopatriarchy focuses on the cultural dimension of modernity (ideas, behavior, and relations) in the Arab world, its structural dimension in terms of the emergence of new social structures, social forces, economic classes, and social relations has also been far-reaching.

Thus, the gradual process of modernization inaugurated in the late nineteenth century and earlier has involved two contradictory processes. On the one hand, it has fostered opportunities for city dwelling, modern education, social mobility, and new classes and groups (such as new working and middle classes, women, and youths, who together came to coexist with the already existing merchants, artisans, and religious elite, or the *'ulama'*). On the other hand, modernization has also triggered formidable challenges for the population. Restricted political participation (by both colonial regimes and postcolonial populist states), inequality, and exclusion from economic development (the poor and marginalized groups), political structures, and conditions of reproduction (of power of the "traditional" groups, the Islamic institutions, the *'ulama'* and their legitimacy) account for the major challenges. At the same time, modernity fostered strong centralized states that commanded power over the populace and major economic resources. An overarching feature of Middle Eastern modernity has been a contradiction between social and economic development and political underdevelopment,[9] a condition ripe for democratic revolutions. Modern economy, institutions, bureaucracy, work relations, education, social classes, city dwelling, and generally the modern public sphere have been accompanied by the states that have remained, by and large, authoritarian, autocratic, and even despotic (embodied in kings, monarchs, shaykhs, or lifelong presidents). Thus, the modern middle classes often have played the leading role in all major social movements and revolutions in the region. The authoritarian character of the regimes has partly to do with the ruling elites' forging of a "traditional solidarity" (*asabiyya*), notably in the Arab states of the Persian Gulf;[10] but for most part it has to do with their control over oil revenue, an asset that has given them not only monopoly over economic resources, but also political support of foreign powers who look for a share in oil. The overwhelming power of these rentier states has been such that it has generated dissent from almost all segments of the population, including the affluent groups. No wonder Homa Katouzian views the people–state (*mellat–dawlat*) divide as the principal line of demarcation in societies like Iran, even though social conflicts within the category of "people" cannot be denied.[11] Such centralized states often evoke analogies with Marx's "Asiatic mode of production" or Wittfogel's "oriental despotism."

No doubt, many of these authoritarian regimes are the products as well as promoters of modernization, even though not in the domain of the polity. Many of these states were either installed by the colonial powers (as in Jordan, Saudi Arabia, and other sheikhdoms in the Persian Gulf, as well as both Pahlavi Shahs of Iran) or pushed to power by the rising classes. In their quest for modernization of their countries, the postcolonial regimes often encountered formidable conflicts with the power of land-owning classes, who resisted to transform themselves into the new bourgeoisie. In such circumstances, the modernizing regimes began a significant process of "revolutionary reform," often from above, on behalf of the middle classes as well as the peasantry, who then were to turn into smallholders or farm workers. In Egypt, Syria, Iraq, and Iran, the earlier political conflicts assumed the form of military coups representing the ascending classes, followed by massive social and economic transformation, nationalization, land reform, and populist dispensation in employment, education, and health.[12] Yet none of these revolutionary reforms entailed an inclusive polity and democratic governance. What they did was produce and empower social forces that in later years were to target the very same states, this time in the name of Islam.

WHAT SORTS OF MUSLIMS REBEL?

So what kinds of Muslims rebel in the age of modernity? Many accounts of Islamist movements see the basis of Muslim rebellion as reaction against modernity.[13] Beyond the perspectives of the Islamist ideologues, in general, two types of interpretations have attempted to explain the spread of religious politics in modern times. The "modernist" interpretations portray Islamism as reactive movements carried out by "traditional people," whether intellectuals or the urban poor, against western-type modernization. The movements are said to be antidemocratic and regressive in character. On the right, the "clash of civilizations," proposed by Bernard Lewis and shared by Samuel Huntington, manifests the framework within which the "antimodern" character of such movements in their encounter with western modernity is assessed.[14] On the left, one can point to Alberto Melucci and Alain Touraine, among others, who express concerns about religious revivalism. "Regressive utopianism" and "anti-movement" are how they refer to religious movements, including Islamism.[15] The second type of interpretation views Islamism as the manifestation of, and a reaction to, postmodernity. In this framework, the movements represent a quest for difference, cultural autonomy, alternative polity, and morality versus the universalizing secular modernity. Foucault described the Iranian Revolution as the "first post-modern revolution of our time," as the "spirit of a world without spirit." For Giddens it signals "the crisis of modernity."[16]

There seems to be some plausibility in such observations. The global conditions in which most of these movements emerged, and the discourses of such

Islamist leaders as Sayyid Abul Ala Maududi, Ayatollah Khomeini, Ali Shariati, Musa Sadr, Sayed Qutb, Rachid Ghannoushi, and others, attest to this tendency. Mawdudi's concept of *jahiliya*, a society characterized by the worship of
man by man and the sovereignty of man over man, had been taken up by Sayed
Qutb in Egypt, Abdul Salaam Yassin in Morocco, and Ali Shariati in Iran,
among others, to lash out on western liberalism, secular nationalism, and
imperialism, which come, in Yassin's views, in the name of enlightenment, reform, nationalism, and rationality.[17] Shariati's notion of "return to self" reflected Islamists' choice of Islam as an indigenous and all-embracing human
alternative. While Maududi proposed some kind of "Islamic cosmopolitanism" to be governed by a "theo-democracy" or a "divine democratic government," Shariati offered a "divine classless society"; and Sayed Qutb, an Islamic
state and economy. Ayatollah Khomeini called for "Islamic government" but
went along with an Islamic republic.[18]

What is not entirely clear about these observations is how their authors
have come to their conclusions. It seems that many of the assumptions rest
on texts, on the discourses of the articulated leaders of the Islamist movements. If we understand movements not in a Bourdieuian sense of solid groups
to be represented by leaders, but as heterogeneous entities with diverse layers
of activism, interests, and perspectives, then we will have to consider the variety of discourses embedded in a social movement, digging into what the
constituencies really aspire to. Living in and observing the Middle East during the past twenty years, I would argue that most of the Islamist rebels
would probably be in favor of modern conditions, would wish to be part of
them, and would desire to enjoy their offerings only if they could afford their
multifaceted costs. But they simply cannot. The central problem, therefore, is
not primordial animosity against what is modern; neither is it related to opponents' historical origin, in that premodern classes, for instance, may oppose the modern order; after all, the working class is a product of modern
capitalist economy and yet has major conflicts with this economic and social
formation. The question, rather, pertains to whether and to what extent individuals and groups have the capacity to handle modernity, so to speak, to
function within and benefit from it. The truth is that, as we have already discussed in this book, not everyone can afford to be modern, because it is a
costly arrangement. It requires the capacity to conform to the kind of material, institutional-cultural, and intellectual imperatives that many simply
cannot afford. In other words, things would likely be less volatile had the

majority of the population been enabled to cope with the various costs of modern life. Let me elaborate.

In many Middle Eastern countries, a large segment of the educated middle class (college graduates, professionals, state employees, or unemployed intelligentsia) lack the material abilities to enjoy what modernity would otherwise offer them, such as decent shelter and a possibility of forming a nuclear family with a good degree of autonomy from elders.[19] So, many are compelled to stay under the protection of extended family, fathers and elders, with all its constraining implications limiting their autonomy and the individuality that they often aspire to. Many of them wish to possess, but cannot afford, the usual consumer commodities or travel to the places about which they often have great knowledge. Consequently, they are often pushed into the ranks of the poor, marginalized in life-chances and consumption realms, while struggling hard to maintain a lifestyle and taste that match their education and status.[20] Their acute *awareness* of what is available and of their inability to acquire it gives them a constant feeling of exclusion and what Barrington Moore called "moral outrage."[21] They are likely to be revolutionaries.[22]

The urban poor often experience the same or an even higher degree of material deprivation as the educated but marginalized middle classes. Yet this state of deprivation does not engender in them the same kind of political and moral outrage as occurs among the middle classes. For unlike the middle class, the poor often live on the margin of modern offerings, be they rights at their jobs, goods, entertainment, power, opportunities, or, above all, information. As discussed in Chapter 9, the poor are immediately affected and frustrated by the complex modalities of modern working, living, and being. They often lack the capacities and the skills, both materially and culturally-behaviorally, to function within the prevailing modern regimented institutions. This does not mean that the poor are antimodern traditionalists; rather, it tells us how the conditions of their lives compel them to resort to informal ways of doing things.

Nor are the Muslim poor necessarily antimodern revolutionaries. Indeed, instead of confronting the states, the poor often seek recourse in "quiet encroachment." Yet when the opportunity arises, they tend to make tactical alliances with revolutionaries, until their expected benefits dwindle, in which case they return to the strategy of "quiet encroachment."[23] At any rate, the poor have remained largely divorced from Islamism as a political project. They surely generate their own often kin-based ties and collectives, but these do not necessarily induce revolutionary communities, as some tend to suggest.[24]

Then, there are the rich—segments from the well-off classes, mostly the new rich (notably women)—who do enjoy material well-being and economic status; they often adhere to globalized consumer behavior, in terms of consumer goods, education, and entertainment. Yet they lack the intellectual abilities to tackle the epistemological premises of late modernity, its multiple truths, to which they are widely exposed precisely because of their privileged positions (traveling, global communication, access to global cultural and intellectual products, and living in global cities). They are disturbed by modernity's philosophical and existential uncertainties, its risks. They are troubled, for instance, by the normalization of the idea that there may not be a God, that homosexual marriage may be legitimate. They are distressed by being bombarded by many "truths" from the satellite TV channels, by new "discoveries" that overturn established ethical paradigms—all these in conditions where the "gender division of sin" renders well-off women more than men or poor women susceptible to religious moral "wrongdoings" (such as appearing half-naked on beaches, showing their hair, or mingling with men), and thus to feeling remorse and regret. Such groups are likely to form their own moral communities, as spaces for existential security and certainty. Religion, Islam, can offer a core institutional and conceptual setting for such communities. In Egypt, for instance, thousands of *halaqat*, or weekly informal gatherings of women to discuss religious rituals and injunctions, serve as moral communities where participants feel empowered to face the challenges of modern ethics. These groups may not be revolutionaries but are likely to support some kind of religious transformation of society.[25]

To these modern critical classes may join the traditional merchants, artisans, and religious elites, members of the traditional religious establishments, the guardians of mosques and seminaries, who together may form a loose coalition of contentious classes in the modern Muslim Middle East. They tend to wage their collective struggle against secularist, often repressive and inefficient, postcolonial regimes that have tended to rest on the support of the secular western powers.

In the postwar period, popular classes in the Muslim Middle East were mobilized overwhelmingly around the secular ideologies of nationalism, socialism, and Ba'thism, which by the 1970s were superseded by illiberal capitalism. The Nasserist revolution of 1952 in Egypt mobilized the lower and middle classes to fight the remnants of colonial rule and to ensure social justice; it spearheaded a model of "Arab socialism" that swept the Arab world in subsequent decades. In 1961, a military coup overthrew a medieval system led by an imam that had ruled Yemen for centuries. Two years later, a revolt in Iraq brought the Ba'th Party to power. A secular nationalist movement ensured Algerian independence from the French rule in 1962; and the Libyan modern elites dismantled the Senussi monarchical dynasty, establishing a revolutionary regime in 1969.[26] A precursor to these events was the nationalist movement led by the secular prime minister Mohammad Mossadegh, who nationalized the Iranian oil industry and inaugurated a secular democracy in Iran, before he was overthrown by a CIA-engineered coup in 1953.[27] But by the 1970s, these secular ideologies seemed to fail to deliver. Arab socialism (despite some important social outcomes) soon encountered insurmountable economic pressure, as in Egypt and Algeria. Secular nationalism fell with Nasser's defeat by Israel in the 1967 war. Ba'thism lost to the despotism of Saddam Hussein and Hafez al-Assad. And the capitalist experiment led to growing social inequality and exclusion and was identified with Sadat's perceived "sell-out" in foreign policy and his heavy-handed internal polity. Then emerged political Islam with an enormous boost from the Islamic Revolution of 1979 in Iran.

THE PLACE OF ISLAM

Why political Islam? What is the place of Islam in these contentious conditions? Is Islam an inherently revolutionary religion, a religion of politics? Certainly, the religious outcome of the Iranian Revolution reinforced among many observers the image of a highly politicist Islam in the age of modernity. Projecting the outcome of the revolution to the process, even such careful scholars as Nazih Ayubi would not hesitate to state that "Islam is a political religion for it promises to control public morality."[28]

Initially, much of the attention focused on the Shi'i branch of Islam (the Iranian version) as more prone to revolution and protest than Sunni Islam. This was so supposedly because Shi'i Islam represented a minority group, a "creed of the oppressed," and thus a "religion of protest." The story of Imam Hussein's (the Prophet's grandson's) struggles against the powerful and "oppressive" Mu'awiyah was to provide the doctrinal and historical basis for the imagined radicalism of Shi'i. The writings of the Sorbonne graduate Iranian Ali Shariati gave a particularly "scientific" legitimacy to the conceptualization of what he termed as "red" or revolutionary Shi'i.[29] In fact, he brought the modern concepts of "class," "class struggle," and "revolution" into the Shi'i Islamic discourse, popularizing the battle of Karbala (where Imam Hussein fought against Mu'awiyah) as the historical stage of a premodern revolution. He was instrumental in turning Islam into a political ideology. Following Shariati, Iran's Mujahedin-e Khalq organization, with an ideological blend of Islam and Marxism-Leninism, put revolutionism into practice by establishing a Latin American–type guerrilla organization in the 1960s.[30] Hamid Dabashi's massive volume *Theology of Dissent* represents an exploration of this revolutionary character of Shi'i Islam in retrospect. Beyond Iran, the rise of Hizbullah in Lebanon in the late 1980s onto the center stage of world radical politics, and its relentless struggle to oust Israeli occupation forces from Lebanon, further reinforced the revolutionary image of Shi'i Islam in the world, until September 11, 2001, when attention was shifted to Sunni Islam as the religion of violence and revolution.

In truth, Sunni Islam has also had some revolutionary elements. The Egyptian Hasan al-Banna, a leader of the oldest and largest Islamist movement in the Arab world, brought the concept of *jahili* state and society from the Indian Abul Ala Maududi, who himself was influenced by Lenin's perspective on organization and the state. Maududi's notion of Islamic "theo-democracy" was not very dissimilar to a model of the communist state. Al-Banna, however, was remarkably Gramscian in strategy (in "war of maneuver" and hegemony), even though there is no evidence that he actually read Gramsci. More recently, in the 1980s, many Sunni Marxists (such as Tariq al-Bishri, Mohammad Emarah, Mustafa Mahmoud, Adel Hussein, Abdulwahab el-Massiri, and others) were turning to Islamism, thus bringing many Marxian visions and vocabularies into political Islam, projecting the latter as an endogenous Third World-ist ideology to fight imperialism, Zionism, and secularism.[31] However, it was the events post-9/11 that mostly exonerated the revolutionism of Shi'i Islam, shifting attention to Sunni radicalism, notably its Wahhabi version. Not only were all culprits in the 9/11 attacks Sunni Islamists, the rise of post-Islamist reformists in Iran in the late 1990s had already undermined essentializing assumptions about Shi'i revolutionism. And then the violent insurgency of the "Sunni triangle" in Iraq against the U.S. occupation was often contrasted with the "reasonable" and "moderate" Shi'i clerical leader, Ayatollah Al-Sistani.

I have argued elsewhere that the revolutionary/reactionary, democratic/undemocratic character of religions, say Islam, should be seen not by reference to some "intrinsic" dispositions of the faith, but by the historically conditioned faculties of the faithful. In other words, we should focus not on Islam as such, but on the historical Muslims, who come to define and redefine their religion, both in ideas and practice, in diverse fashions. In short, it is the Muslim humanity with diverse moral and material interests, loyalties, and orientations that come to construct different types of Islams—revolutionary, conservative, democratic, or repressive.[32]

Through this prism, the role of Islam in radical politics is important in at least two main respects. First, Islam can act, and has done so, as the ideological and moral structure within which contentious politics and revolutions are given meaning. Any act of contention first goes through the filter of the prevailing moral and communal values through which "injustice" is perceived, defined, and resisted, and where struggle assumes its meaning. Islam can provide that structure. Islamic codes and concepts can also be deployed, deliberately, to frame a revolutionary movement, that is, to justify, legitimize, dignify, and extend the appeal of movements. Muslim revolutionaries attempt to present Islam as an alternative social, political, moral, and even economic order. Having an alternative on the horizon constitutes a leap for contenders to further their struggles. The ideologues' representation of Islam as an alternative social order often remains at the level of generality. This might sound like a drawback, but it is in fact projecting a broad and ambiguous prospect that may cover differences in opinions and expectations and thus ensure unity. In the chaos of revolutionary hope, the generality of objectives ensures uniformity and guides action, leaving the potentially divisive details to the free imagination of each contender to construct their own ideal outcome.[33]

Islam may intervene in revolutionary struggles not merely as an ideology, frame, and model, but also as a harbinger of vested interests. In the Middle East, the "Islamic sector" (consisting of religious institutions, mosques, shrines, madrasa, rules, rituals, tastes, and the associated personnel, property, and power) has historically been pervasive. Within it, the *'ulama'* (the clerical class), as the articulated gatekeepers, have served as the main legitimizing factor for Middle East rulers.[34] The sector continues to reinvent itself in the face of modernity's challenges. Yet the advent of the modern state, citizenship, education, finance, and taxation has seriously undermined the legitimacy and power as well as the material gains and control of many functionaries, notably the "spiritual elites" involved in the religious sector. The *'ulama'*, as a status group controlling the "spiritual property," could see their status, legitimacy, material gains, and especially their "paradigm power" (that is, the discursive frame that allows them to communicate and exert their hegemony) being eroded. The new education system deprived them of being the sole transmitter of knowledge and literacy; the modern justice system pushed them aside from the helm of religious arbitration; the new taxation and financial institutions undercut their ability to raise religious tax (zakat, *khom*s, and *sadaqat*), while the modern states brought many of the religious endowments (*awqaf*) under the control of the bureaucrats, consequently seriously undercutting the financial independence of the religious authorities. Associated with these changes, religious sensibilities and the power that they bring to the religious elites are challenged. In short, Islam, in this sense, may move into the center of a revolutionary struggle because of religious elites' vested interests. In the experience of Iran, the Shi'i clerics who had managed to maintain their autonomy (financially and politically) succeeded in retaining a good part of the religious sector independent from the diktat of the Shah's regime by relying on various religious taxes and donations (zakat, *khom*s) from the faithful and the revenue from the remaining endowments. But Egyptian *'ulama'* and with them much of the Islamic sector were incorporated into the state structure, first by Muhammad Ali in the nineteenth century, and later and more fiercely by Nasser in the 1960s. In Iran, the *'ulama'* became a major revolutionary force, while in Egypt, it was not the *'ulama'*, but the lay Muslim activists, who in the form of the Muslim Brothers raised the banner of re-Islamization of Egyptian society and polity.

This is not to fixate on Islam and the Islamic *'ulama'* as essential subjects of revolutionary transformation. Indeed, "modernizing" *'ulama'* may well cohabit and cooperate with Middle Eastern secular states. The top segment of Egypt's religious establishment and its elites have for decades pursued a policy of coexistence and cooperation with the government. Indeed, today most regimes in the region enjoy the general blessing of "establishment Islam," for example, Al-Azhar's top clerics. In Iran, the clerical class is deeply divided, along political as well as doctrinal lines. The "traditional" and "fundamentalist" *'ulama'* (as they are labeled in Iran) support a religious state, while the younger generation, and those adherents of "critical rationality," who place "reason" at the center of the management of public life, oppose the very idea of an "Islamic state." While the unity of political and religious authorities tends to alienate at least a segment of the clerical class, lay Muslims have expressed far greater distrust of an Islam that is enticed by mundane political power. As the outcome of several elections in the late 1990s showed, many women and the young in Iran feel more than any other group the debilitating effect of the religious state, in their daily lives, at work, before the law, and in the public space. They have been in the forefront of the opposition against an Islam that they see as having degenerated into an office of power. Thus, Islam may be both a factor of revolution and its target. It can be not only the subject of revolution, but also its object.

THE FUTURE OF ISLAMIC REVOLUTIONS

What is the future of Islamist revolutions in the age of globalization? Is globalization conducive to the making of revolutions in general, and Islamist revolutions in particular? I think that globalization may induce dissent, social movements, and even revolts but is antithetical to classical revolutions, including the Islamic versions. Perhaps we need to revisit our understanding of "revolutions," looking at them in terms of more diffuse and nonviolent mobilization with gradual process and long-term change. Their ultimate aim may not be to challenge the global system, but to negotiate with it.

Critiques of globalization seem to generally agree that it leads to considerable instability and insurgency, in particular in the periphery of the world capitalist system.[35] National states become undermined by the normalized involvement of supranational economic and political entities and structures in the national affairs of the sovereign states. The neoliberal economic policies, often directed by the creditor nations, the International Monetary Fund (IMF), and the World Bank, oblige the postcolonial populist states to retreat from their traditional social contract in offering subsistence provisions to their needy citizens. Not only do such retreats generate popular resentment against these regimes, they also open new space (left by the withdrawal of the state from the social sector) that then is filled by oppositional forces, such as the Islamist militants in the Middle East.[36] Many view the growth of "social Islam" as a front for political Islam resulting from such an absence by the states. In the meantime, the globalization of means of communication facilitates the internationalization of national conflicts, the easy flow of information, and forging solidarities that extend beyond national boundaries. In addition, international political pressure, by the governments, civil society, and suprastate institutions (e.g., the international criminal court, the UN Charter and Security Council, human rights organizations, and the like) are likely to reinvigorate movements for political change within the individual countries of the global South. Thus, with the decline of "legitimating identities," such as nationalism and socialism, according to Castells, contenders express their resistance against the global "network society" by forming autonomous "communities" around ethnic, cultural, and religious identities ("resistance identities"). These formations may not even remain defensive but may develop into a new identity "that defines their position in society and by so doing seeks the transformation of over-all social structure," what Castells calls "project identities."[37]

The 1989 chain of revolutions in Eastern Europe, the Zapatista revolutionary movement connecting a local peasant rebellion to the international anti-globalization movement (Castells), and, most recently, the "color revolution" in the former Soviet Union between 2003 and 2005 (which, unlike the Zapatista movement, was supported by western established classes and elites) all point to the power of the transnational linkage of dissent and solidarities, of models and lifestyles that seem to penetrate the national iron curtains.[38] It is as though such momentous events of the turn of the twentieth century stand as testimony to yet another "age of revolution," reinforcing the high hopes of such postwar social theorists and activists as Hanna Arendt, who saw "almost as a matter of course that the end of the war is revolution, and that the only cause of which possibly could justify it is the revolutionary cause of freedom." Eric Hobsbawm retained such a high hope until the "halt" of the "forward march of labour" in 1978. And as late as 2000, David Harvey suggested, against the prevailing mood, that Marxism and notably the *Communist Manifesto* had never been as relevant to the global conditions as they are today. At the outset of the twenty-first century, Harvey implied, the world is ripe to free itself from the shackles of capital.[39]

However, it seemed that these theorists' "optimism of will" overshadowed their "pessimism of intellect." Arendt did not survive to observe the wave of the late-1990s revolutions against communism. Hobsbawm, in reviewing his own history, was to acknowledge, though "without apology," the "over-optimism" of those early years. And Harvey became dismayed by the absence of interest in Marxism and the politics of revolution.[40] If the idea of revolution for these observers was to free humanity from the diktat of capitalism, then the age of globalization seems to have made such a freedom ever more formidable. With the hegemony of capital and neoliberal logic in every society and major sector, space for alternative social order becomes restricted primarily and ironically to the margins, those on the exclusion zones of global capital and political order: the informal sectors, the barrios, cityscapes, and household economies, and in terms of the reviving cultural identities and ethnicities, within which some degree of autonomy is still maintained.[41] Indeed some (postdevelopment advo-cates) consider these "premodern communes" as the major alternative to the western-imposed development model.[42]

The point, then, is that a world *needing* a revolution is not necessarily the one that has the requisite forces to carry it out if the agents are figured by frag-mentation, despair, individualism, and alienation. Even in 2009, in the midst of the worst financial crisis since the Great Depression of the 1930s, no serious movement to challenge capitalism has emerged. Harvey's merit lies not so much in spelling out revolutionary conditions as it does in his attempt to offer "spaces of hope," the possibility of alternative ways of organizing society, econ-omy, work, and ecology, to undercut the debilitating pessimism of will, or the prevailing idea that "there is no alternative." What Harvey and Castells explore are not, nor do they aim for, agency and conditions for Marxian revolutions, but the constitution of dissent, social movements, and alternative ways of ar-ranging work and life.

I am inclined to think that the logic of globalization (because it tends to fragment the popular classes through informalization, NGOization, and indi-vidualization, and because it transnationalizes both the objectives and actors of revolutionary movements) may be antithetical to the making of classical revolutions. It is true that globalization does engender radical changes, but not in the form of the rapid, violent, and nationally based revolts to transform the state and society, that is, classical revolutions. For classical revolutions are ac-tualized only within the confines of the nation-state; they come to fruition by mass revolts in which the national states become the ultimate target. Because it is only within the limits of a nation-state that "rights" assume their concrete meaning, and around which dissent, mobilization, and action make sense. In addition, it is only within the confines of the nation-states that dissent finds a concrete focus, a recognizable target, and a manageable course of action. In other words, the question of revolution is ultimately tied to the question of the state— the way in which the states change (or do not change) determines whether a revolution has occurred, and what kind. If nation-based revolts lie at the core of classical revolutions, then the transnationalization of revolts, both in their agents and aims (e.g., struggles against the "West" or "global injustice"), would deprive them of broad mobilization against a concrete national objective. In short, the idea of world revolution is ironically nonrevolutionary.

Now, what of the future of "Islamic revolutions"? I think that the possibility of Islamic revolutions in the current age follows a more or less similar logic.

Iran's earlier idea of "global Islamic revolution," beginning with Iraq, clearly failed during the war with Saddam Hussein, because opposition against the Ba'thist regime did not come from within the country but had a foreign element (Iran), which in turn instigated Iraqi nationalism. Since then, the revisionist idea of "Islamism in one country" has become the accepted strategy of the Islamic republic. But there is more to the story of revolutions. Revolutions signify extraordinary change par excellence, rare moments of utopian visions and extreme measures, followed by compromise and conflicts to merge utopia and hard realities, thus leading to a surging dissent both from within the revolutionary ranks and from without. The Islamic Revolution involves particular incongruities by its distinctly religious ideology and moralist regime, which paradoxically rules over a modern citizenry through a modern state. Although, the Islamic Revolution in Iran caused dissent at home, it inspired and found friends among the Islamic movements in the Muslim world. But Islamic revolutions do not only inspire movements to emulate but also subvert similar happenings, because they make incumbent secular regimes (e.g., in Egypt or Algeria) more vigilant in suppressing potential revolts, and because their subsequent anomalies and retreat demonstrate that revolutions may not, after all, be desirable options. This pushes the nation-based Islamist movements into a state of perplexity and confusion, where they vacillate between revolutionary utopia and realpolitik, between aspirations and limitations.

Yet more significant trends seem to be under way in the dispositions of Islamism that lead it to deviate from a revolutionary path. These trends are influenced by both the internal workings of the Islamist movements and global politics, in particular the post-9/11 events. One trend is what I have called "post-Islamization." It refers to the project and movements that want to transcend Islamism as an exclusivist and totalizing ideology, seeking instead inclusion, pluralism, and ambiguity. It is nationalist in scope (as opposed to being Pan-Islamist), and consciously postrevolutionary—post-idea-of-revolution, that is. It represents primarily a political project. In Iran, it took the form of the "reform movement" of the late 1990s, which partly evolved into the "reform government" (1997–2004). A number of Islamic movements also exhibit some aspects of "post-Islamism": the new pluralist strategy of the Lebanese Hizbullah in the early 1990s, leading to a split in the movement; the emergence in the mid-1990s of the Al-Wasat Party in Egypt as an alternative to both militant Islamists and the Muslim Brothers; the Justice and Development Parties in both Turkey and Morocco; the discursive shift in the Indian Jamaat-i Islami toward

more inclusive, pluralistic, and ambiguous ideological dispositions; and finally, the emergence in Saudi Arabia of an "Islamo-liberal" trend in the late
1990s, seeking a compromise between Islam and democracy—each displaying
some diverse versions of post-Islamist trends in Muslim societies today. Most
of these movements seek a secular state but wish to promote religious societies
(see Chapter 13).

Many movements in the Muslim world still aspire to establish an Islamic
state but wish to do so within the existing constitutional frameworks; they
reject violent strategies and hope to operate within the prevailing political
norms, invoking many democratic principles. Their Islamic state and economy find an overall complementarity to capitalism. The Muslim Brothers in
Egypt and its offshoots in Algeria, Syria, Sudan, Kuwait, Palestine, and Jordan represent this trend. So did Necmettin Erbakan's locally based Rifah
Party in Turkey. Even though in classical terms they are reformist, not revolutionary, movements, they tend to engender significant social and political
change in the long run.

Global events since the late 1990s (the Balkan ethnic war, Russian domination of Chechnya, the Israeli incursions into the West Bank and Gaza, not to
mention the post-9/11 anti-Islamic sentiments in the West) created among
Muslims an acute sense of insecurity and a feeling of siege. This in turn has
heightened religious identity and communal bonds, generating a new trend of
"active piety," a sort of missionary tendency quite distinct from the highly organized and powerful "apolitical Islam" of the transnational Tablighi movement. Inclined toward individualism, diffusion, and Wahhabi-type conservatism, the adherents aim not to establish an Islamic state, but to reclaim and
enhance their own individual ethical selves, even though they strive to im-
plant such an undertaking among others. Even though the mobilization of
millions of Muslims against the Danish cartoons of the Prophet Muhammad
in 2006 demonstrated forging a new type of ethical-political practice and
protest, it also pointed to the globally disparate, reformist, and nonrevolutionary character of the dissent.

It is largely the so-called jihadi trend that pursues armed struggle and terrorism. But even here, only a segment follows the project of overthrowing the
Muslim regimes within a particular nation-state, and in this sense it is revolutionary. For the most part, these groups are consumed by the idea of jihad as
an end, perceiving the very process of struggle as an ethical journey, offering
little in the way of projecting a future state, society, and economy. Many jihadi

groups are involved in "civilizational" struggles, with the aim of combating an abstract "west," "infidel" and "corrupt'." A reading of Bin Laden's messages reveals how his priority goes little beyond "uniting opinions under the word of monotheism and defending Islam."[43] Transnational and notoriously male in aim and organization (defending the global *umma* against an "unholy West"), al-Qaeda intrinsically lacks any sort of social and political program, and thus is unlikely to succeed in mobilizing a concerted national dissent against a concrete national state.

In the current status of widespread religious sentiments and movements in the Muslim world, the growth of democratic sensibilities and movements (secular or religiously oriented) is likely to push Islamism into the post-Islamist course, paving the way, through "reformist" struggles, for a democratic change in which an inclusive Islam may play a significant role. The outcome might be termed "post-Islamist refolutions." In the end, the Iranian experience of 1979 may well remain the first and the last Islamic revolution of our time. The final chapter describes the details of this trend in the Muslim Middle East, highlighting the part that "nonmovements" and the "art of presence" may play in such a transformation.

PROSPECTS

Part 3

13 NO SILENCE, NO VIOLENCE

Post-Islamist Trajectory

DEBATE ABOUT a "democratic deficit" in the Middle East is not new. What is novel is the excessive attention given to Islam as a factor said to hinder democratic reform. With its emphasis on God's sovereignty and patriarchal disposition, Islam is argued to be essentially incompatible with democracy. Lacking concepts of citizenship, freedom, and tolerance, it encourages believers to embrace coercion, violence, and the path of jihad.[1] Thus, Islam is viewed as a "world in which human life doesn't have the same value as it does in the West, in which freedom, democracy, openness and creativity are alien."[2] Such views have been energized by many home-grown Islamists who, in the name of their religion, suspect democracy as a "foreign construct," suspend popular will in favor of God's sovereignty, and commit violence in the name of jihad. Even though many Muslims refute these charges by suggesting that God has granted sovereignty to humans to govern themselves, and that Islamic justice values life ("killing one person equals killing the whole of humanity") and disallows discrimination based on class, race, or gender,[3] the debate has in general been bogged down in entirely textual and philosophical terrains, with little effort to understand the politics of religious affiliation, and how in practice Muslims perceive their religion in relation to democratic ideals.

Adapted from Asef Bayat, *Making Islam Democratic: Social Movements and the Post-Islamist Turn* (Stanford, Calif.: Stanford University Press, 2007). For a full elaboration of the arguments raised here, and for extensive historical/empirical narratives, please refer to the book.

I would like to suggest that the question, raised so persistently, is not whether Islam is or is not compatible with democracy (itself a convoluted concept), but rather how and under what conditions Muslims can *make* Islam embrace democratic ethos. Nothing intrinsic to Islam—or any other religion—makes it inherently democratic or undemocratic, peaceful or violent. It depends on the intricate ways in which the living faithful perceive, articulate, and live through their faiths: some deploy their religions in exclusive, authoritarian, and violent terms, while others read in them justice, peace, equality, representation, and pluralism. Irrespective of whether religious beliefs and experiences relate to supernatural reality, in the end, "religion is expressed by means of human ideas, symbols, feelings, practices, and organizations."[4] In a sense, religious injunctions are nothing but our understanding of them; they are what we make them to be. Some fifty years ago many social scientists believed that Christianity and democracy were incompatible.[5] But today the most deep-rooted democracies are in the Christian heartland, even though fascism also emerged, and was associated with the church, in the heartland of Christianity. Clearly then, there are no such things as religions out there. Rather, a religion is understood, imagined, and constructed by different groups of the faithful in diverse forms. As to why individuals and groups perceive and present the same scriptures differently is a most intriguing sociological question and cannot be elaborated here. Suffice to state here that it depends largely on individual believers' different biographies, social positions, and interests.

While so much is currently discussed about the "fundamentalist Islamist" and jihadi trends that draw often on puritanical, exclusivist, and hostile interpretations of the doctrine, little is known about the ethics and experiences of those nonviolent social movements—what I have called "post-Islamism"—that aim to bridge the gap between Islam and democracy in Muslim societies today. This chapter elaborates on the workings of these movements and discusses the obstacles as well as opportunities to envisage a post-Islamist democracy in the Middle East through peaceful means.

POST-ISLAMISM

What is post-Islamism? Is it a discursive break from Islamism—the ideologies and movements that aim to establish an Islamic order (i.e., religious state, Islamic laws and moral codes), emphasizing disproportionately people's obligations over their rights? Or does it rather represent only a particular version of

Islamist politics? Does the term indicate we have reached the historical end of Islamism altogether? In 1995, I happened to write an essay entitled the "Coming of a Post-Islamist Society"[6] in which I discussed the articulation of the remarkable social trends, political perspectives, and religious thought which post-Khomeini Iran had begun to witness—a trend which eventually came to embody the reform movement of the late 1990s. Since then, a number of observers and students of Islam have deployed the term, even though descriptively, to refer primarily to what they consider a general shift in attitudes and strategies of Islamist militants in the Muslim world. In fact, partly due to its poor conceptualization and party for its misperception, the term has invited critical appraisal.[7]

In my formulation, post-Islamism represents both a condition and a project. In the first instance, post-Islamism refers to a political and social condition, in which after a phase of experimentation, the appeal, energy, and sources of legitimacy of Islamism get exhausted even among its once-ardent supporters. Islamists become aware of their system's anomalies and inadequacies as they attempt to normalize and institutionalize their rule. The continuous trial and error makes the system susceptible to questions; and the pragmatic attempts to maintain the system reinforce abandoning certain of its underlying principles. Islamism becomes compelled to reinvent itself, but does so at the cost of a qualitative shift. Not only a condition, post-Islamism is also a project, a conscious attempt to conceptualize and strategize the rationale and modalities of transcending Islamism in social, political, and intellectual domains. Yet, it is neither anti-Islamic nor un-Islamic or secular. Growing out of the anomalies of Islamist politics since the early 1990s, post-Islamism represents an endeavor to fuse religiosity and rights, faith and freedom, Islam and liberty. It wants to turn the underlying principles of Islamism on their heads by emphasizing rights instead of duties, plurality in place of a singular authoritative voice, historicity rather than fixed scripture, and the future instead of the past. It strives to marry Islam with individual choice and freedom, with democracy and modernity (something post-Islamists stress), to achieve what some have termed an "alternative modernity." It wishes to undo the discourse of violence that is so much ingrained in the ideologies and practices of some, but not all, Islamist trends today, to discard the current association of Islam with violence. Post-Islamism is expressed in acknowledging secular exigencies, in freedom from rigidity, in breaking down the monopoly of religious truth. In short, whereas Islamism is marked by the fusion of religion and responsibility, post-Islamism emphasizes religiosity and rights, even though the latter's relationship with liberalism remains tense. I should stress that, first, Islamism and post-Islamism serve primarily as conceptual categories to signify change, difference, and the root of change. In the real world, however, many Muslims may adhere eclectically and simultaneously to aspects of both discourses. On the other hand, the advent of post-Islamism as a real trend, should not be seen necessarily as the historical end of Islamism. What it should be seen as is the birth, out of Islamist experience, of a quantitatively different discourse and politics. In reality we may witness simultaneous processes of both Islamization and post-Islamization.

Whether or not Islam corresponds to democratic ideas depends primarily on whether advocates of these perspectives—Islamism and post-Islamism— are able to establish their hegemony in society and the state. The history of socioreligious movements in Iran and Egypt since the 1970s offers a fertile ground to examine the logic, conditions, and forces behind rendering Islam democratic or undemocratic. In Iran, the 1979 revolution and establishment of an Islamic state set conditions for the rise of post-Islamist ideas and movements that aimed to transcend Islamism in society and governance. The end of the war with Iraq (1988), the death of Ayatollah Khomeini (1989), and the program of postwar reconstruction under President Rafsanjani marked a turning point toward post-Islamism. It expressed itself in various social practices and ideas, including urban management, feminist practice, theological perspective, and social and intellectual trends and movements. Youths, students, women, religious intellectuals, and many state employees, among others, called for democracy, individual rights, tolerance, and gender equality, but they refused to throw away religious sensibilities altogether. Thus, daily resistance and struggle by ordinary people compelled religious thinkers, spiritual elites, and political actors to undertake a crucial paradigmatic shift. Scores of old Islamist revolutionaries renounced their earlier ideas of exclusivism, revolutionary violence, and religion as ideology and politics, and lamented the danger of religious state to both religion and the state. Numerous opponents from both without and within the Islamic state called for its secularization but stressed maintaining religious ethics in society. In fact, the reformist government of President Muhammad Khatami (1997–2004) represented only one, the political, aspect of this pervasive societal trend.

In Egypt, on the other hand, instead of an Islamic revolution, there developed a pervasive Islamist movement that held a conservative moral vision, populist language, a patriarchal disposition, and adherence to scripture. By the early 1990s, through *da'wa* (invitation to faith) and associational work, the movement had captured some large tracts within the civil society, moving on to claim space in state institutions. Although it failed to dislocate Egypt's secular regime, the movement left an enduring mark on both society and state. It succeeded in hegemonizing an "Islamic mode" in society. Engulfed by the pervasive "Islamic mode," major actors in Egyptian society, including the intelligentsia, the new rich, Al-Azhar (the institution of establishment Islam), and ruling elites, all converged around the language of nativism and conservative moral ethos, thus severely marginalizing critical voices, innovative religious thought, and demands for genuine democratic reform. In the end, threatened by expanding Islamism, the authoritarian state appropriated aspects of conservative religiosity and nationalist sentiments (which had been cultivated by the continuing Arab–Israeli conflict) to configure Egypt's "passive revolution." This Gramscian passive revolution represented a managed Islamic restoration in which the state, in reality the original target of change, succeeded in remaining fully in charge. Even though a nascent democracy movement in 2005 (Kifaya) pointed to some hopeful change in the political climate, the power structure remained authoritarian, religious thought stagnant and exclusive, and the political class nativist. Little in Egypt resembled Iran's post-Islamist trajectory.

Since the 1990s, both of these trends, Islamism and post-Islamism, have been unfolding simultaneously in other parts of the Muslim world. On the one hand, the global and domestic social and political conditions have continued to generate appeals for religious and moral politics, especially in those nations that had not experienced Islamism. Anti-Islamic sentiment in the West following the September 11 terrorist attacks, and the subsequent "war on terrorism," reinforced a profound feeling of insecurity and outrage among Muslims who sense that Islam and Muslims are under an intense onslaught. This increased the appeal of religiosity and nativism, so that Islamic parties (such as those in Morocco, Algeria, Pakistan, Bahrain, and Turkey) that among other issues expressed opposition to U.S. policy in Afghanistan have scored considerable successes in several national elections since 2002.

At the very same time, however, and against the backdrop of intensifying religious sentiments in the Muslim world, a new post-Islamist trend has begun to emerge, attempting to accommodate aspects of democratization, pluralism, women's rights, youth concerns, and social development with adherence to religion. In Lebanon, Hizbullah transcended its exclusivist Islamist platform (i.e., calling for an Islamic state in Lebanon) by adapting to the pluralistic political reality of Lebanese society, acting more or less like a confessional political party as its Lebanese counterparts. In Egypt, Hizb al-Wasat, a breakaway faction of the Muslim Brothers, disassociated itself from both the violent strategy of the al-Gama'a al-Islamiyya (which later, in 1997, renounced violence unilaterally and opted for peaceful activities) and the authoritarian disposition of its Muslim Brothers predecessors. Hizb al-Wasat privileged modern democracy over Islamic *shura* (the principle of consultation), embraced pluralism in religion, and welcomed gender mixing and ideological tendencies. In fact, the main ideologue of the party has been a Coptic Christian. In Central Asia, while the Islamist Hizb al-Tahrir has held its ground in Tajikistan, the Islamic Renaissance Party has integrated into that country's secular political process, attempting to contest political power through peaceful electoral fashion.[8] The Jamaat-e-Islami of India has experienced a qualitative shift from a movement resting on an organic, complete, and exclusivist Islam—one that rejected democracy and was intolerant of other faith lines—into a movement that embraces ambiguity and interpretation in its foundational thoughts, values democracy and pluralism, and cooperates with its ideological "others."[9] Leaders of the current Moroccan religious movement al-Adl wal-Ihsan (Justice and Benevolence) discard an exclusive understanding of Islam, rely on interpretation and historicizing, and acknowledge flexibility and ambiguity; they reject imposing shari'a laws and hijab on Muslims, and endorse human rights, pluralism, democracy, and separation of powers.[10] But more than al-Adl wal-Ihsan, it is Morocco's Justice and Development Party that has spearheaded a post-Islamist disposition by practically participating in the current multiparty electoral competition. And finally, notwithstanding an initial unease in the West about growing religious revivalism, Turkey has smoothly and rapidly transcended the Islamism of Virtue and Welfare Parties by embracing a self-conscious post-Islamist trend expressed in the Justice and Development Party (AKP)—one that advocates a pious society in a secular democratic state. Even in the highly conservative Saudi Arabia, a post-Wahhabi trend has been attempting to incorporate notions of "liberal Islam," seeking a compromise with democracy.[11] Yet, except for Turkey, which already had a multiparty democracy, none of these movements has assumed governmental power to consider how and to what extent they would be willing or able to forge democratic governance. If there is a lesson in the Iranian experience, it is that its post-Islamism was pushed back by the conservative Islamists, who control major domains of the state power.

Thus, neither did Egypt's Islamist movement succeed in fully "Islamizing" the Egyptian state, nor did Iran's post-Islamism succeed in democratizing the Islamic Republic. Both movements encountered stiff opposition from their respective power elites. In other words, the political impasse in these countries has been less a function of religion per se than of structural impediments and the longtime vested interests of ruling elites. To what extent can social movement mobilization enforce intended political and structural change? How far can states accommodate the radical projects of their social movement adversaries? And how far can social movements alter, without resorting to violent revolutions, the political status quo in the Middle East—a region entrapped by the authoritarian regimes of both secular and religious dispositions, exclusivist Islamist opposition, and blatant (threat of) foreign domination?

SOCIAL MOVEMENTS AND POLITICAL CHANGE

Multifaceted social movements are not single-episode expressions that melt away under an act of repression. Rather, they are prolonged, many-sided processes of agency and change, with ebbs and flows, whose enduring "forward linkages" can revitalize popular mobilization when the opportunity arises. Clearly, the most common work of social movements is to pressure opponents or authorities to fulfill social demands. This is carried out through mobilization and threatening disruption or uncertainty against adversaries.[12] For instance, the Islamist campaign in Egypt compelled the government to restrict many liberal publications, persecute authors, or prohibit films. Second, even if social movements are not engaged in a political campaign, they may still be involved in what Melucci calls "cultural production."[13] The very operation of a social movement is in itself a change, since it involves creating new social formations, groups, networks, and relationships. Its "animating effects," by enforcing and unfolding such alternative relations and institutions, enhances cultural production of different value systems, norms, behavior, symbols, and discourse. This process of building "hegemony" is expressed by producing alternative ways of being and doing things. Post-Islamist movements display a vivid example of such a moral and intellectual influence in civil society, through the press, publications, associations, discourse, education, and lifestyles.

Third, social movements may also induce change by discreetly operating on the fault line between the state and civil society—in educational, judiciary, media, and other institutions. In the early 1990s, Egyptian Islamists succeeded in penetrating the state education system, influencing policymakers, teachers, and, above all, a generation of students through their activities at teacher training colleges. Islamist judges enforced Islamic law, punishing seculars while supporting Islamic-oriented legal suits. Even police and the military were not immune. Finally, social movements, if they are tolerated by the incumbent regimes, may be able to capture segments of governmental power through routine electoral means. The cases of Turkey's ruling AKP and Iran's reform government under President Khatami represent only two recent examples. Both movements managed to form legitimate governments.

A great challenge of a social movement is how to retain its movement character and at the same time exert governmental power. While sharing state power may enable social movements to turn some of their ideas into public policy, failure to do so, even though due to opponents' sabotage, would undermine their support base in society, thus rendering them powerless. Clearly, then, social movements need to go beyond discursive struggles for democratic polity by consolidating their institutional foundations within the fabric of society, to link up intimately with the subaltern constituencies. For not only can a solid institutional social base compel the opponents/states to undertake political reform, as in the Mexican experience, and may even enforce a "political pact" between democracy movements and the states (as in Chile and Spain), it can also protect movements from repression and annihilation and ensure continuity and revival even after a period of downturn. Egypt's Muslim Brothers exemplify a pertinent case, where the movement has managed to survive since its inception in the late 1920s by enduring decades of ebbs and flows, thanks primarily to its deep-seated associational work in civil society and to its kinship networks.

THE ART OF PRESENCE

No doubt, reform of authoritarian states would require distinctly laborious struggles, the significance and difficulties of which one cannot discount. However, democratic societal change remains indispensable to meaningful and sustained democratic reform of the state. Change in society's sensibilities is a precondition for far-reaching democratic transformation. Social change might occur partly as the unintended outcome of structural processes, such as migration, urbanization, demographic shifts, or a rise in literacy; it may also result from global factors and the exchange of ideas, information, and models. But the most crucial element for democratic reform is an active citizenry: a sustained presence of individuals, groups, and movements in every available social space, whether institutional or informal, collective or individual, where they assert their rights and fulfill their responsibilities. For it is precisely in such spaces that alternative ideas, norms, practices, and politics are produced. The aptitude and audacity associated with active citizenry is what I have phrased the "art of presence." Muslim citizens cannot spearhead a democratic shift unless they master the art of presence—the skill and stamina to assert collective will in spite of all odds by circumventing constraints, utilizing what is possible, and discovering new spaces within which to make themselves heard, seen, felt, and realized. Authoritarian regimes may be able to suppress organized movements or silence collective resistance. But they are limited when it comes to stifling an entire society, the mass of ordinary citizens in their daily lives.

Beyond acting as a precondition to *sustain* a democratic reform, the change in society's sensibilities through the active citizenry can also *induce* and impel change onto (authoritarian) states. In this respect, I envision a strategy whereby every social group generates change in society through active citizenship in their immediate domains: children at home and at schools, students in colleges, teachers in classrooms, workers in factories, the poor in their neighborhoods, athletes in stadiums, artists through their art, intellectuals through media, women at home and as public actors. Not only are they to voice their claims, broadcast violations done unto them, and make themselves heard, but also to take responsibility for excelling at what they do. An authoritarian regime should not be a reason for not producing excellent novels, brilliant handicrafts, math champions, world-class athletes, dedicated teachers, or a global film industry. Excellence is power; it is identity. By "art of presence," I imagine a way in which a society, through the practices of daily life, may regenerate itself by affirming the values that deject the authoritarian personality, get ahead of its elites, and become capable of enforcing its collective sensibilities on the state and its henchmen. Citizens equipped with the art of presence would subvert authoritarian rule, because the state usually rules not as an externality to society; rather, it does so by weaving its logic of power— through norms, rules, and institutions—into the fabric of society. Challenging those norms, institutions, and logics of power is likely to subvert a state's "governmentality," its ability to govern.[14] And in this, women's struggle to challenge patriarchy in their day-to-day interactions becomes enormously critical, precisely because patriarchy is deeply embedded in the perception and practice of religious authoritarian polity. Even though patriarchy may evade or incorporate women's public presence, the latter still leads to undeniable effect. When girls overtake boys in colleges, women are likely (though not necessarily) to be future directors and managers whose authority men are compelled to accept, if not internalize. This alone would point to a notable shift in society's norms and balance of power.

Under authoritarian rule, such efforts to challenge patriarchy are likely to be the expression of women's nonmovements. Indeed, nonmovements, or the collective endeavors of noncollective actors, would in general constitute the key vehicle through which active citizenry may be realized. This is so because of the actors' constant mobilization against, and negotiation or engagement with, the dominant powers— the state, property holders, patriarchy, or moral authorities. Not only would the nonmovements, on their own, cause significant change in the actors' life-chances; they may in the meantime evolve into sustained social movements and contentious politics when the opportunity arises.

My focus on the "art of presence," or active citizenry, is not intended to downplay the significance of organization and concerted collective endeavors for change. Nor do I mean to substitute contentious movements with individual active citizenry; in fact, such a citizenry, as noted just above, is likely to embrace and facilitate organized collective action. After all, Iran's spectacular Green Movement (to protest electoral fraud and demand democratic reform) did not emerge out of the blue, but had roots in the various nonmovements, which then burst collectively into the open once they found a political opportunity in July 2009. Yet it is crucial to recognize that not only does authoritarian rule routinely impede contentious collective actions and organized movements, it is also unrealistic to expect a civil society to be in a constant state of vigor, vitality, and collective struggle. Society, after all, is made up of ordinary people, who get tired, demoralized, and disheartened. Activism, the *extraordinary* practices to produce social change, is the stuff of *activists*, who may energize collective sentiments when the opportunity allows. The point is not to reiterate the political significance of contentious movements to cause political change, or to ignore the necessity of undercutting the coercive power of the states. The point, rather, is to discover and recognize societal spaces in which lay citizens, with their ordinary practices of everyday life, through the art of presence, may recondition the established political elites and refashion state institutions into their sensibilities.

Such refashioning of the state may result not only from active citizenry, individuals' own initiative and education, but more pervasively from the long-term impact of nonmovements or, especially, social movement activism. Through their cultural production—establishing new social facts on the ground, new lifestyles, modes of thinking, behaving, being, and doing—movements can acclimatize states to new societal trends, compelling the authorities to take account of society's prevailing sensibilities. For instance, the Islamic regime in Iran was compelled to recognize and minimally act upon the popular desire for secularization, democratic polity, and civil liberties, which Iran's social movements had since the late 1990s helped to articulate. Similarly, the fact that the Islamic AKP has bowed to Turkey's secular democracy is neither simply a sign of deception nor merely the fear of backlash from the Turkish army. Rather, it is a position that has been nurtured and shaped by the secular democratic sensibilities of Turkish citizens, both religious and secular. I have called this laborious process of society influencing the state—through establishing new lifestyles and new modes of thinking, being, and doing things—*socialization of the state*. It means conditioning the state and its henchmen to societal sensibilities, ideals, and expectations. Socialization of the state is, in effect, "governmentality" in reverse. It can serve as a crucial venue through which citizens may cultivate and compel democratic reform onto the authoritarian states.

It would be naive to read too much into society at the expense of demonizing the state. Just as states may be oppressive and authoritarian, societies can be divided, individualized, conservative, and exploitative. Clearly, then, socializing the polity, the state, into democratic sensibilities may not succeed without politicizing society into a democratic direction. Otherwise, active citizenry can easily recede into co-optation, communalism, authoritarian ethos, or selfish individualism that can turn it into a citizenry devoid of collective sensibility, inclusive responsibility, and aspiration. It is thus crucial for an active citizenry to think and act politically, even within its own immediate sphere, even though its aim might not be revolution or regime change; it must be concerned with solidarity, social justice, and an inclusive social order.

In the Muslim Middle East, initiatives for a sustained democratic reform need to come from the region's indigenous movements, who would then determine if and how international assistance should be deployed. The painstaking reform efforts in the region will yield little if democracy is preached and pushed by foreign forces, and even far less through coercion and conquest.

NOTES

Chapter 1

1. See United Nations Development Program, *Arab Human Development Report,* vol. 1, *Creating opportunities for Future Generations* (New York: UNDP, 2002). See also Chapter 2 of the present work.

2. Adapted from Asaf Bayat, *Making Islam Democratic: Social Movements and the Post-Islamist Turn* (Stanford, Calif.: Stanford University Press, 2007), pp. 200–201.

3. For a useful discussion of how we should focus on the analysis of "revolutionary situations" instead of projecting revolutions in retrospect, see Rod Aya, "Theories of Revolution Reconsidered: Contrasting Models of Collective Violence," *Theory and Society* 8, no. 1 (July 1979), pp. 39–99.

4. See United Nations Development Program, *Arab Human Development Report,* vol. 3, *Towards Freedom in the Arab World* (New York: UNDP, 2005), p. 164.

5. For a fine discussion of "Middle Eastern exceptionalism" and the U.S. policy of "war on terror," see Mark LeVine, *Why They Don't Hate Us* (Oxford: Oneworld Publications, 2005).

6. See Alexander L. Macfie, ed. *Orientalism: A Reader* (Cairo: American University in Cairo Press, 2000); Maxine Rodinson, *Europe and the Mystique of Islam* (London: I. B. Tauris, 2002).

7. A useful recent publication is Quintan Wiktorowicz, *Islamic Activism: A Social Movement Theory Approach* (Bloomington: Indiana University Press, 2004). See also Roel Meijer, "Taking the Islamist Social Movement Seriously: Social Movement Theory and the Islamist Movement," *International Journal of Social History* 50, no. 2 (August 2005), pp. 279–92.

8. Charles Tilly, *Social Movements, 1768–2004* (Boulder, Colo.: Paradigm, 2004), p. 7.

9. For elaboration, see Asef Bayat, "Islamism and Social Movement Theory," *Third World Quarterly* 26, no. 6 (July 2000), pp. 891–908.

10. Olivier Roy, *The Failure of Political Islam* (Cambridge: Harvard University Press, 1994), pp. 8–9.

11. Joost Hiltermann, *Behind the Intifada: Labor and Women's Movements in the Occupied Territories* (Princeton, N.J.: Princeton University Press, 1991); Zachary Lockman and Joel Beinin, eds., *Intifada: The Palestinian Uprising Against Israeli Occupation* (London: South End Press, 1989).

12. See Nikki Keddie, *Women in the Middle East: Past and Present* (Princeton, N.J.: Princeton University Press, 2007), pp. 215–16.

13. United Nations Development Program, *Arab Human Development Report*, vol. 4, *Toward the Rise of Women in the Arab World* (New York: UNDP, 2006), pp. 123–39.

14. Ibid.

15. There are now some useful studies on the collective struggles of the subaltern in the Middle East—such as those of casual workers, the unemployed, and the marginals—as well as various ways of survival and individual resistance strategies. See, for instance, Stephanie Cronin, ed., *Subaltern and Social Protest* (London: Routledge, 2008); Edmund Burke III and David Yaghoubian, eds. *Struggle and Survival in the Modern Middle East* (Berkeley: University of California Press, 1993).

16. See Joel Beinin and Hossam el-Hamalawy, "Strikes in Egypt Spread from Center of Gravity," *Middle East Report Online*, May 9, 2007. See also Joel Beinin, "Underbelly of Egypt's Neoliberal Agenda," *Middle East Report Online*, April 5, 2008, www.merip.org/mero/mero040508.html.

17. See Freedom House, *Freedom in the Middle East and North Africa* (New York: Rowman & Littlefield, 2005), p. 4.

18. See Human Rights Situation in Iran (see reports by the International Campaign for Human Rights in Iran, www.iranhumanrights.org).

19. See Amnesty International, Report 2007: The State of the World's Human Rights, http://thereport.amnesty.org/eng/Regions/Middle-East-and-North-Africa/Egypt.

20. David Wolman, "Cairo Activists Use Facebook to Rattle the Regime," *Wired Magazine* 16 (October 20, 2008), p. 11; www.wired.com/print/techbiz/startups/magazine/16-11/ff_facebookegypt.

21. Asef Bayat, *Street Politics: Poor People's Movements in Iran* (New York: Columbia University Press, 1997), p. 15.

22. Asef Bayat, "Neoliberal City and Its Discontent," *Berkeley Journal of Sociology*, forthcoming.

23. See Charles Tilly, "Social Movements and National Politics," in *State-Making and Social Movements: Essays in History and Theory*, ed. C. Bright and S. Harding (Ann Arbor: University of Michigan Press), p. 304.

24. Tilly, *Social Movements, 1768–2004*.

25. Michael Hardt and Antonio Negri, *Multitude: War and Democracy in the Age of Empire* (London: Penguin, 2004), p. 223.

26. See Bayat, *Street Politics*, p. 16.

27. For the concept of "imagined solidarities," see Bayat, "Islamism and Social Movement Theory."

28. See Samantha Shapiro, "Revolution, Facebook-Style," *New York Times*, January 25, 2009, New York ed., MM34.

29. Clearly, the nature of the Middle East "soft" states—their constraints and opportunities—is different from that of the liberal democratic capitalist states in the West, where, according to Slavoj Zizek, the strategy of "infinitely demanding" proposed by Simon Critchley, that is, bombarding the state with infinite demands (because it is no more possible to "fight" the state power than it is to seize it), cannot change things; rather, such reformist demands can actually legitimize them (Slavoj Zizek, *In Defense of Lost Causes* [London: Verso, 2008]). In nonmovements, subjects do not limit themselves merely to making demands; they are often involved in action/practice.

Chapter 2

1. United Nations Development Program, *Arab Human Development Report*, vol. 1, *Creating Opportunities for Future Generations* (New York: UNDP, 2002).

2. Dudley Seers, "The Meaning of Development," in *The Political Economy of Development*, ed. N. Uphoff and W. Ilchman (Berkeley: University of California Press), pp. 123–28; Amartya Sen, *Development as Freedom* (Oxford: Oxford University Press, 1999).

3. United Nations Development Program, *Arab Human Development Report*, vol. 2, *Building a Knowledge Society* (New York: UNDP, 2003), p. 3.

4. According to Nader Fergany, the lead author of the *Report*, Florence, March 19, 2005.

5. *Middle East Quarterly* 9, no. 4 (fall 2002), p. 59.

6. According to Nader Fergany, Florence, March 19, 2005.

7. U.S. Department of State, Office of International Information Programs, October 20, 2003.

8. Galal Amin, "An Da'f wa al-Taba'iyya Fi Taqrir al-Tanmiyya al-Insaniyya al-Arabiyya," *Al-Hayat*, December 19, 2003, p. 10. For further comments, see Galal Amin, "Colonial Echoes," *Al-Ahram Weekly*, April 7, 2004.

9. Edward Said, "The Arab Condition," *Al-Ahram Weekly*, May 22–28, 2003.

10. UNDP, *Arab Human Development Report*, vol. 3, pp. 6–7.

11. United Nations Development Program, *Arab Human Development Report*, vol. 3, *Towards Freedom in the Arab World* (New York: UNDP, 2005) p. 153.

12. See Daniel Bell, *The Coming of Post-Industrial Society* (New York: Harper Colophon, 1976); Alvin Gouldner, *The Coming Crisis of Western Sociology* (New York: Basic Books, 1970); Jean-François Lyotard, *The Postmodern Condition* (Minneapolis: University of Minnesota Press, 1983); Francis Fukuyama, *The End of History and the Last Man* (New York: Free Press, 1992); Manuel Castells, *The Rise of Network Society* (Oxford: Blackwell, 1996).

13. See, for instance, Steve Fuller, "Universities and the Future of Knowledge Governance from the Standpoint of Social Epistemology," unpublished paper presented in UNICEF, 2004, p. 2. Also in: http://portal.unesco.org/education/en/ev.php-URL_ID= 35262&URL_DO=DO_TOPIC&URL_SECTION=201.html.

14. See, for instance, Steve Fuller, "Can Universities Solve the Problem of Knowledge in Society Without Succumbing to the Knowledge Society?" *Policy Futures in Education* 1, no. 1 (2003), pp. 106–24.

15. See Ibrahim El-Issawy, "Assessing the Index," *Al-Ahram Weekly*, January 9–15, 2003.

16. See Galal Amin, "Colonial Echoes."

17. UNDP, *Arab Human Development Report*, vol. 3, p. 50.

18. Ibid., p. 8.

19. Volume 3 of the *Report* also acknowledges this identity: "In this comprehensive sense, freedom is considered both the ultimate goal of human development and its foundation," p. 62.

20. Sylvia Chan, *Liberalism, Democracy and Development* (Cambridge: Cambridge University Press, 2002), especially chapter 2, "Decomposing Liberal Democracy."

21. See Massoud Karshenas and Valentine Moghadam, eds., *Social Policy in the Middle East* (London: Palgrave, 2006).

22. UNDP, *Arab Human Development Report*, vol. 3, p. 164.

23. Ibid., pp. 164, 165.

24. For "democratization by pact," see Jorge Cadena-Roa, "State Pacts, Elites, and Social Movement in Mexico's Transition to Democracy," in *States, Parties, and Social Movements*, ed. Jack Goldstone (Cambridge: Cambridge University Press, 2003).

25. The *Report* makes almost no reference to, let alone engages with, the sizeable scholarly work already devoted to the discussion of democratic transformation within the authoritarian states, for instance, various issues of the *Journal of Democracy;* Ghassan Salamé, *Democracy without Democrats* (London: Palgrave/Macmillan, 1994); Rex Brynen, Bahgat Korany, and Paul Noble, eds., *Political Liberalization and Democratization in the Arab World* (Boulder, Colo.: Lynne Rienner, 1995); Khaled Abou El Fadl, *Islam and the Challenge of Democracy* (Princeton, N.J.: Princeton University Press, 2004); Samuel P. Huntington, *The Third Wave: Democratization in the Late Twentieth Century* (Norman: University of Oklahoma Press, 1991).

Chapter 3

1. For critiques of the exaggerated globalization thesis, see Chris Harman, "Globalisation: A Critique of a New Orthodoxy" *International Socialism*, no. 73 (1997), pp. 3–33; *Marxism Today*, special issue, November/December 1998; David Gordon, "The Global Economy," *New Left Review*, no. 168 (March/April 1988), pp. 24–64.

2. See Ankie Hoogvelt, *Globalization and the Postcolonial World* (Baltimore: Johns Hopkins University Press, 1997), pp. 121–31.

3. World Bank, *World Development Report 1995* (Oxford: Oxford University Press, 1995), p. 108.

4. Vandemoortele, "The African Employment Crisis of the 1990s," in *The Economic Crisis in Africa*, ed. C. Grey-Johnson (Harare: African Association for Public Administration and Management, 1990), pp. 34–36.

5. See Central Intelligence Agency, *The 1992 CIA World Factbook* (1992).

6. For the figures, see International Labour Office, *World Employment Report, 1998–99* (Geneva: ILO, 1999); David McNally, "Globalization on Trial: Crisis and Class Struggle in East Asia," *Monthly Review* 50, no. 4 (September 1998), p. 7.

7. Neil Webster, "The Role of NGDOs in Indian Rural Development: Some Lessons from West Bengal and Karnataka," *European Journal of Development Research* 7, no. 2 (December 1995), pp. 407–33.

8. Hal Draper, *Karl Marx's Theory of Revolution* (New York: Monthly Review Press, 1978), vol. 2, p. 453.

9. Ibid., chapter 15.

10. Peter Worsley, *The Three Worlds* (London: Weidenfeld and Nicholson, 1984).

11. Frantz Fanon, *The Wretched of the Earth* (London: Penguin, 1967).

12. Samuel P. Huntington, *Political Order in Changing Societies* (New Haven, Conn.: Yale University Press, 1968); Joan Nelson, "The Urban Poor: Disruption or Political Integration in Third World Cities," *World Politics* 22 (April 1970), pp. 393–414; Samuel P. Huntington and J. Nelson, *No Easy Choice: Political Participation in Developing Countries* (Cambridge: Harvard University Press, 1976).

13. Nelson, "Urban Poor."

14. See Oscar Lewis, *Five Families: Mexican Case Studies in the Culture of Poverty* (New York: Basic Books, 1959); *The Children of Sanchez: Autobiography of a Mexican Family* (New York: Random House, 1961); *La Vida: A Puerto Rican Family in the Culture of Poverty* (New York: Random House, 1966).

15. Worsley, *Three Worlds*, pp. 190–94.

16. See Anthony Leeds, "The Concept of the 'Culture of Poverty': Conceptual, Logical and Empirical Problems with Perspectives from Brazil and Peru," in *The Culture of Poverty: A Critique*, ed. E. B. Leacock (New York: Simon and Schuster, 1971);

Charles Valentine, *Culture and Poverty: Critique and Counter Proposals* (Chicago: University of Chicago Press, 1968).

17. Janice Perlman, *Myth of Marginality* (Berkeley: University of California Press, 1976); Manuel Castells, *The City and Grassroots* (Berkeley: University of California Press, 1983).

18. My understanding of the notion of survival strategy is based upon James Scott, "Everyday Form of Peasant Resistance," *Journal of Peasant Studies* 13, no. 2 (1986).

19. Ernesto Escobar, *Encountering Development* (Princeton, N.J.: Princeton University Press, 1995).

20. See John Friedmann, *Empowerment: The Politics of Alternative Development* (London: Blackwell, 1992); John Friedmann, "Rethinking Poverty: Empowerment and Citizen Rights," *International Social Science Journal* 48, no. 2 (June 1996), pp. 161–72.

21. Perlman, *Myth of Marginality*; Castells, *City and the Grassroots*.

22. Castells, *City and the Grassroots*; Frans Schuurman and Ton van Naerssen, eds., *Urban Social Movements in the Third World* (London: Croom Helm, 1989); John Friedmann, "The Dialectic of Reason," *International Journal of Urban and Regional Research* 13, no. 2 (1989), pp. 217–36.

23. The term is Bernard Hourcade's, in his "Conseillisme, classe sociale et space urbain: les squatteurs du sud de Tehran, 1978–1981," in *Urban Crises and Social Movements in the Middle East,* ed. Kenneth Brown et al. (Paris: Editions L'Harmattan, 1989).

24. See, for instance, Matthias Stiefel and Marshall Wolfe, *A Voice for the Excluded: Popular Participation in Development* (London: Zed Books, 1994). The book, which was commissioned by the United Nations Research Institute for Social Development, has a section on urban social movements that covers exclusively the Latin American countries.

25. Asef Bayat, "Islamism and Empire: The Incongruous Nature of Islamist Anti-Imperialism," in *Socialist Register 2008,* ed. Colin Leys and Leo Panitch (London: Merlin Press, 2008).

26. Anthony Leeds and Elizabeth Leeds, "Accounting for Behavioral Differences: Three Political Systems and the Responses of Squatters in Brazil, Peru, and Chile," in *The City in Comparative Perspective,* ed. J. Walton and L. Magotti (London: John Wiley, 1976), p. 211.

27. James Scott, *Weapons of the Weak: Everyday Forms of Peasant Resistance* (New Haven, Conn.: Yale University Press, 1985).

28. See Steve Pile, "Opposition, Political Identities and Spaces of Resistance," in *Geographies of Resistance,* ed. S. Pile and M. Keith (London: Routledge, 1997), p. 2.

29. See Reeves, "Power, Resistance and the Cult of Muslim Saints in a Northern Egyptian Town," *American Ethnologist* 22, no. 2 (1995), pp. 306–22.

30. See Lila Abu-Lughod, "The Romance of Resistance: Tracing Transformations of Power Through Bedouin Women," *American Ethnologist* 17, no. 1 (February 1990), pp. 41–55.

31. Diane Singerman, *Avenues of Participation: Family, Politics, and Networks in Urban Quarters of Cairo* (Princeton, N.J.: Princeton University Press, 1995).

32. Pile, "Opposition, Political Identities, and Spaces of Resistance."

33. See Arlene Macleod, *Accommodating Protest: Working Women, the New Veiling, and Change in Cairo* (New York: Columbia University Press, 1991).

34. Something that Piven and Cloward wished the American poor people's movements had. See Frances Piven and Richard Cloward, *Poor People's Movements: Why They Succeed, How They Fail* (New York: Vintage, 1979).

35. See, for instance, Mike Cole and Dave Hill, "Games of Despair and Rhetorics of Resistance: Postmodernism, Education and Reaction," *British Journal of Sociology of Education* 16, no. 2 (1995), pp. 165–82.

36. Scott, *Weapons of the Weak*, p. 290.

37. Ibid., p. 292.

38. Nathan Brown, *Peasant Politics in Modern Egypt: The Struggle Against the State* (New Haven, Conn.: Yale University Press, 1990).

39. See Anthony Giddens, *Sociology* (Oxford: Polity Press, 2000).

40. Scott, *Weapons of the Weak*, p. 350.

41. Michel Foucault, *Power/Knowledge* (New York: Pantheon, 1980).

42. In the words of Doug McAdam, Sidney Tarrow, and Charles Tilly: "Towards an Integrated Perspective on Social Movements and Revolution," in *Comparative Politics: Rationality, Culture, and Structure*, ed. M. I. Lichbach and A. Zuckerman (Cambridge: Cambridge University Press: 1997), pp. 150–51.

43. See Diane Singerman, *Avenues of Participation* (Princeton, N.J.: Princeton University Press, 1985); Homa Hoodfar, *From Marriage to the Market* (Berkeley: University of California Press, 1986). In an interesting study of the political behavior of lower-class families in Cairo, Singerman aims to show the particular ways in which the ordinary people in Egypt participate in the political processes and even change the outcome of national policies. To this end, she shows how Cairean poor families strive to extend their familial relations through intermarriage within the communities where they can cultivate support. They set up networks of mutual help and credit associations, and diverse strategies to go around government requirements for subsidies, pensions, and so on. The result, Singerman suggests, is not passivity and fatalism, but active participation in public life and a challenge to the state.

44. Michael Brown, "On Resisting Resistance," *American Anthropologist* 98, no. 4 (1996), p. 730.

45. I have elaborated on this perspective in more detail elsewhere (see Asef Bayat, *Street Politics: Poor People's Movements in Iran* [New York: Columbia University Press, 1997]). Here, I only briefly outline some of the major points.

46. See, Asef Bayat, "Cairo's Poor: Dilemmas of Survival and Solidarity," in *Middle East Report*, no. 202 (winter 1996), special issue on "Cairo: Power, Poverty and

Urban Survival." On internal encroachments, see Farha Ghannam, "Relocation and the Use of Urban Space," *Middle East Report*, no. 202, (winter 1996), pp. 17–20.

47. See particularly Petra Kuppinger, "Giza Spaces," in *Middle East Report*, no. 202 (winter 1996), pp. 14–16.

48. See Bayat, *Street Politics*.

49. Reported by Education Committee of the Majlis al-Sha'b, cited in *Al-Wafd*, January 21, 2002, p. 6.

50. See the report in *Egyptian Gazette*, January 29, 2002, p. 7.

51. For more details on the concept of "street politics," see my *Street Politics*, chap. 1.

52. For many examples, see Bayat, *Street Politics*.

53. For an example of such a broader alliance in Peru, see Pedro Arévalo, "Huaycan Self-Managing Urban Community: May Hope Be Realized," in *Environment and Urbanization* 9, no. 1 (April 1997), pp. 59–80.

Chapter 4

1. The average gross national product growth rates for selected Middle Eastern countries during the 1970–79 period were as follows: Egypt, 7.6 percent; Iran, 22.2 percent; Saudi Arabia, 37.2 percent; Turkey, 15.1 percent; Kuwait, 22.6 percent; Syria, 15.4 percent; Iraq, 28.8 percent; Jordan, 19.6 percent ("World Tables 1991," *IMF International Financial Statistics Yearbook*, 1994, 1996 [Washington, D.C.: IMF Publications, 1996]).

2. See Hazem Beblawi, "Rentier State in the Arab World," in *The Arab State*, ed. G. Luciani (London: Routledge, 1990).

3. For a typology of the states in the Middle East, see Alan Richards and John Waterbury, *A Political Economy of the Middle East* (Boulder, Colo.: Westview Press, 1990).

4. USAID/Cairo/EAS, *Report on Economic Conditions in Egypt, 1991–1992* (Cairo: USAID, 1993), p. 2.

5. See John Westley, "Change in Egyptian Economy, 1977–1997," and Galal Amin, "Major Determinants of Economic Development in Egypt: 1977–1997," both in *Cairo Papers in Social Science* 21 (1998), pp. 18–49. See also Ragui Assaad and Malak Rouchdy, *Poverty and Poverty Alleviation Strategies in Egypt* (Cairo: Ford Foundation, 1998). For a more recent evaluation of Egypt's development process, see Richard Adams, "Evaluating the Process of Development in Egypt, 1980–97," *International Journal of Middle East Studies* 32 (2000), pp. 255–75.

6. See Roula Majdalani, "Bridging the Gap between the Development Agendas and the Needs of the Grassroots: The Experience of Jordanian NGOs," unpublished ms., Beirut, 1999.

7. See Raymond Hinnebusch, "Democratization in the Middle East: The Evidence from the Syrian Case," in *Political and Economic Liberalization*, ed. Gred Honneman (Boulder, Colo.: Lynne Rienner, 1996).

8. Saad Eddin Ibrahim, "The Troubled Triangle: Populism, Islam, and Civil Society in the Arab World," *International Political Science Review* 19 (1998), pp. 373–85.

9. See Augustus R. Norton, ed., *Civil Society in the Middle East* (Leiden, N.Y.: E. J. Brill, 1995).

10. Richards and Waterbury, *Political Economy*, p. 268. For a more thorough analysis, see John Walton and David Seddon, *Free Markets and Food Riots* (London: Blackwell, 1994).

11. See Walton and Seddon, *Free Markets*, pp. 205–14.

12. See, for instance, Ira Lapidus, *Muslim Cities in the Later Middle Ages* (Cambridge: Cambridge University Press, 1967), p. 107.

13. See *Al-Ahali*, November 3, 1999, p. 3.

14. For details, see Asef Bayat, *Workers and Revolution in Iran* (London: Zed Books, 1987). On the unemployed movement in Iran, see my "Workless Revolutionaries: The Unemployed Movement in Revolutionary Iran," *International Review of Social History* 42, no. 2 (1997), pp. 159–85.

15. See Joel Beinin and Zachary Lockman, *Workers on the Nile: Nationalism, Communism, Islam and the Egyptian Working Class, 1882–1954* (Princeton, N.J.: Princeton University Press, 1988).

16. Land Center for Human Rights, "Egypt's Labor Conditions During 1998: The Year of Strikes and Protests" (Cairo, 1998).

17. See *Al-Wafd*, February 5, 1999, p. 1.

18. See Walton and Seddon, *Free Markets*, p. 210.

19. *Middle East Economic Digest*, February 21, 1991, special report on Iran.

20. Posusney, *Labor and the State*, p. 5.

21. See, for instance, Richards and Waterbury, *Political Economy*, p. 267.

22. Posusney, *Labor and the State*, p. 10.

23. Cited in Walton and Seddon, *Free Markets*, p. 185.

24. For more detailed figures, see Richards and Waterbury, *Political Economy*, p. 140.

25. For these, I have relied on papers presented at the Workshop on Changing Labour and Restructuring Unionism, First Mediterranean Social and Political Meeting, Florence, March 22–26, 2000. See the papers by Myriam Catusse, "Les métamorphoses de la question syndicale au Maroc"; Dara Kawthar, "Labor Market in Lebanon: Evolution, Constraints, and the Role of Unionism"; Fathi Rekik, "Mobilité sociale et flexibilité de l'emploi [Tunisia]"; and Françoise Clement, "Changing Labour and Restructuring in Egypt." On Egypt, see also Fatemah Farag, "Labour on the Fence," *Al-Ahram Weekly*, May 11–17, 2000, p. 7. Deena A. Gamile, "The Working Class of Shubra al-Khaima," master's thesis, American University in Cairo, 2000.

26. For Egypt, see various reports, including Farag, "Labour on the Fence," p. 7. In Iran, the conservative parliament ratified a law in early 2000 that excludes workshops

with fewer than five workers from the provisions of the labor law in order to increase productivity and investment.

27. See *Community Development Journal*, special issue no. 32 (1997), esp. pp. 101–98 (Keith Popple and Mae Shaw, "Social Movements: Re-Assessing 'Community'").

28. See Inaz Tawfiq, "Community Participation and Environmental Change: Mobilization in a Cairo Neighborhood," master's thesis, American University in Cairo, 1995.

29. Jailan Halawi, "Mosque Stairs Spark Shubra Riots," *Al-Ahram Weekly*, August 18–24, 1994.

30. See Shafeeq Ghabra, "Voluntary Associations in Kuwait," *Middle East Journal* 45 (1991), 199–215.

31. See Joost Hiltermann, *Behind the Intifada* (Princeton, N.J.: Princeton University Press, 1991).

32. For a good analysis of the CDAs, see Maha Mahfouz, "Community Development in Egypt: The Case of CDAs," master's thesis, American University in Cairo, 1992.

33. Samer El-Karanshawy, "Governance, Local Communities and International Development in Urban Egypt," unpublished report, Cairo, 1998.

34. See Rahmatollah Sedigh Sarvestani, *Barrasi-ye Jame-shenakhti-ye Ravabet-e Hamsayegui dar Tehran* (Tehran: Tehran University, Institute of Social Studies and Research, 1997).

35. In 1990, there were 823 such associations, 80 percent of them concentrated in the greater Cairo area: see Hirofumi Tanada, "Survey of Migrant Associations in Cairo Metropolitan Society (Egypt), 1955–1990: Quantitative and Qualitative Data," in *Social Science Review* 42, no. 1 (1996).

36. See Nicholas Hopkins et al., *Social Response to Environmental Change and Pollution in Egypt* (Cairo: American University in Cairo, Social Research Center, 1998).

37. Alan Durning, "People Power and Development," *Foreign Policy* 76 (1989), p. 71.

38. This segment draws heavily on my previous article on Egypt: Asef Bayat, "Cairo's Poor: Dilemmas of Survival and Solidarity," *Middle East Report* 202 (winter 1996), 2–6.

39. For a report on Kafr Seif, see Nadia Abdel Taher, "Social Identity and Class in a Cairo Neighborhood," *Cairo Papers in Social Science* 9 (1986); and for Khak Sefid, see F. Khosrowkhavar, "Nouvelle banlieue et marginalité: La cité Taleghani a Khak-e Sefid," in *Téhéran: capitale bicentennaire*, ed. C. Adle and B. Hourcade (Tehran: Institut français de recherche en Iran, 1992).

40. See El-Karanshawy, "Governance, Local Communities," p. 11.

41. On this, see a perceptive article by Mustapha El-Sayyid, "Is There a Civil Society in the Arab World?" in Norton, *Civil Society in the Middle East*.

42. Reported in Manal M. Eid, "Informal Economy in Madinat al-Nahda: Resistance and Accommodation among the Urban Poor," master's thesis, American University in Cairo, 1998, p. 88.

43. Abdel Moula Ismail, *The Liberalization of Egypt's Agriculture Sector and Peasants Movement* (Cairo: Land Center for Human Rights, 1998), p. 136, app. 7.

44. See John Cross, *Informal Politics: Street Vendors and the State in Mexico City* (Palo Alto, Calif.: Stanford University Press, 1998).

45. See, for instance, Gilles Kepel, *Muslim Extremism in Egypt* (Berkeley: University of California Press, 1986); Nazih Ayubi, *Political Islam* (London: Routledge, 1991); Salwa Ismail, "The Popular Movement Dimensions of Contemporary Militant Islamism," *Comparative Studies in Society and History* 42 (2000): 363–93; Paul Lubeck and Bryana Britts, "Muslim Civil Society in Urban Public Spaces," in *Urban Studies: Contemporary and Future Perspectives*, ed. J. Eade and C. Mele (Oxford: Blackwell, 2001).

46. See R. Margulies and E. Yildizoglu, "The Resurgence of Islam and Welfare Party in Turkey," in *Political Islam*, ed. J. Beinin and J. Stork (Berkeley: University of California Press, 1997), p. 149.

47. Ugur Akinci, "The Welfare Party's Municipal Track Record: Evaluating Islamist Municipal Activism in Turkey," *Middle East Journal* 53 (1999), pp. 77–79.

48. Meriem Verges, "Genesis of a Mobilization: The Young Activists of Algeria's Islamic Salvation Front," in Beinin and Stork, *Political Islam*, pp. 292–305.

49. Assaf Kfoury, "Hizb Allah and the Lebanese State," in Beinin and Stork, *Political Islam*, pp. 136–43.

50. Roula Majdalani, "Governance and NGOs in Lebanon," unpublished paper, Beirut, 1999, p. 13. The literature on Hizbullah welfare activities has grown considerably in recent years. See, for instance, Lara Deeb, *Enchanted Modern: Gender and Public Piety in Shi'i Lebanon* (Princeton, N.J.: Princeton University Press, 2006); Augustus Richard Norton, *Hizbullah: A Short History* (Princeton, N.J.: Princeton University Press, 2007); Joseph Alagha, *The Shifts in Hizbullah's Ideology* (Amsterdam: Amsterdam University Press, 2006).

51. The latter figure as given by the current minister of social affairs, Mervat Tallawi, in *Aqidati* (October 28, 1997), p. 17.

52. See Amani Qandil, "The Nonprofit Sector in Egypt," in *The Nonprofit Sector in the Developing World*, ed. H. K. Anheier and L. M. Salamon (Manchester: Manchester University Press, 1998), pp. 145–46.

53. Manal Badawy, *Islamic Associations in Cairo* (master's thesis, American University in Cairo, 1999), p. 110. See also Denis Sullivan, *Private Voluntary Organizations in Egypt* (Gainesville: University Press of Florida, 1994), pp. 65–68.

54. See Hisham Mubarak, *Al-Irhabiiyuun Qademuoun!* (Cairo: Dal Al-Mahrusah, 1995).

55. Cited in Qandil, "Nonprofit Sector in Egypt," p. 146.

56. See Saad Eddin Ibrahim, *Egyptian Law 32 on Egypt's Private Sector Organizations* (Cairo: Ibn Khaldoun Center for Developmental Studies, 1996), Working Paper no. 3; Amani Qandil, "The Role of Islamic PVOs in Social Welfare Policy: The Case of Egypt," paper presented at the conference on The Role of NGOs in National Development Strategy, Cairo, March 28–31, 1993.

57. Margulies and Yildizoglu, "Resurgence of Islam," p. 149.

58. See Ibrahim, *Egyptian Law 32*, p. 34.

59. Not surprisingly, Western Munira of Imbaba, the stronghold of the Islamists, has been allocated more funding for its development than any other district in north Guiza, to the east of Cairo. Between 1992–93 and 1995–96, some 372.5 million Egyptian pounds were spent on constructing, upgrading, and burnishing this area: *Al-Ahram Weekly* (October 24–30, 1996), p. 12.

60. Kfoury, "Hizb Allah," p. 142.

61. See Mona Harb el-Kak, "Participation Practices in Beirut's Suburb Municipalities: A Comparison Between Islamic and 'Developmentalist' Approaches," paper presented at the 4th International Other Connections Conference, Sites of Recovery, Beirut, October 25–28, 1999. For more recent developments, see Deeb, *Enchanted Modern*.

62. Akinci, "Welfare Party's Municipal Track Record."

63. See Amani Qandil, "Taqdim Adaa al-Islamiyya fi-Niqabat al-Mihniyya" (Cairo: CEDEJ/Cairo University, 1993); and Carrie Rosefsky Wickham, "Islamic Mobilization and Political Change: The Islamist Trend in Egypt's Professional Associations," in Beinin and Stork, *Political Islam*, pp. 120–35.

64. See Badawy, *Islamic Associations in Cairo*.

65. See Gustavo Gutierrez, *A Theology of Liberation: History, Politics, and Liberation* (New York: Orbis Books, 1988).

66. This is expressed in many ways by the Islamists. See Youssef al-Qaradawi, *The Problem of Poverty, and How Can Islam Resolve It* (in Arabic) (Beirut: Al-Risalaa, 1985).

67. See interview with Saiid Hajjarian, a leader of Tehran City Council and an adviser to President Khatami, in *Middle East Report* 212 (1999). For the data on NGOs, see Qandil, "The Nonprofit Sector in Egypt," p. 139; Roula Majdalani, "NGOs as Power-Brokers in the Rebuilding of a Fragmented State: The Case of Lebanon," unpublished paper, Beirut, August 1999, p. 14; Majdalani, "Bridging the Gap," p. 2; Khalil Nakhleh, *Indigenous Organizations in Palestine* (Jerusalem: Arab Thought Forum, 1991); "A Little Neighborly Advice," *Cairo Times* (September 2–15, 1999), p. 21; Massoumeh Ebtekar, "Women's NGOs and Poverty Alleviation: The Iranian Experience" [in English], *Farzaneh* 4 (1998), p. 10. A report by Baquer Namazi, "Iranian NGOs: Situational Analysis" (Tehran, January 2000), provides useful early data. See also *Nowrouz*, 4 Tir 1380/2001, p. 9.

68. Both statements were made in the Regional Follow-Up Conference of Arab NGOs, held in Cairo, May 17–19, 1997.

69. See Daoud Istanbuli, "The Future Role of Palestinian NGOs in an Emerging Palestinian Self-Government," Middle East Working Group Seminar, Jerusalem, June 21–22, 1993, p. 12.

70. Among many reports expressing such views, see, for instance, Robert LaTowsky, "Financial Profile of Egypt's PVO Sector," report, World Bank, June 1994.

71. Special report, *Cairo Times* (September 2–15, 1999), p. 21.

72. Cited in Ibrahim, *Egyptian Law 32.*

73. Federation of Community Development Associations, "Fact Sheet," Cairo, March 14, 1990.

74. Egyptian NGOs, for instance, made only three million Egyptian pounds (less than $1 million) in local income in 1991, and the Ministry of Social Affairs could support no more than 35 percent of all PVOs, often unevenly. According to a different study, total state aid to PVOs provided less than 10 percent of sector revenues, and foreign aid only 5 percent. In other words, these PVOs must depend on themselves to survive. Where internal sources are scarce, as in Iraq, Palestine, and Lebanon during the war, dependence on outside funding becomes vital; see Ibrahim, *Egyptian Law 32.*

75. Anisur Rahman, *People's Self-Development* (London: Zed Books, 1993), pp. 67–73.

76. Majdalani, "Bridging the Gap."

77. See interview with Curtis Rhodes of Near East Foundation, Jordan, in *Economic Perspectives* 11 (1993), p. 7.

78. See Ghassan Sayyah, "Potential Constraints upon NGOs in Lebanon," paper presented at the workshop Reconstruction, Rehabilitation, and Reconciliation in the Middle East: A View from Civil Society, Ottawa, June 21, 1993.

79. Majdalani, "NGOs as Power-Brokers," p. 14.

80. Nakhleh, *Indigenous Organizations,* p. 50.

81. See Saad Eddin Ibrahim, "Grassroots Participation in Egyptian Development," *Cairo Papers in Social Science* 19, no. 3 (1996); Delta Business Service International: Khattab and Associates, "Analysis of Registered Private Voluntary Associations in Cairo and Alexandria," report, Agency for International Development, Cairo, June 21, 1981; El-Karanshawy, "Governance, Local Communities"; Fatma Khafagy, "Needs Assessment Survey of NGOs in Egypt," report, African Women's Development and Communications Networks, Cairo, August 1992; Bertrand Laurent and Salma Galal, "PVO Development Project Evaluation Report," report, USAID/Egypt, Cairo, December 1995. On Jordan and Lebanon, see Majdalani, "Governance and NGOs in Lebanon" and "Bridging the Gap," respectively.

82. See Susan Schaefer Davis, "Advocacy-Oriented Non-Governmental Organizations in Egypt: Structure, Activities, Constraints, and Needs," report, USAID/Egypt, Cairo, May 1995.

83. Rema Hammami, "NGOs: The Professionalization of Politics," *Race and Class* 37 (1995), pp. 51–63.

84. Homa Hoodfar, *Volunteer Health Workers in Iran as Social Activists: Can Governmental "Non-Govenental Organisations Be Agents of Democratisation?* Women Living under Muslim Laws occasional paper no. 10 (Paris: WLUML, 1998).

85. Interview with Hassan el-Banna, an official specializing on NGOs in the Ministry of Social Affairs, 1996.

86. For more detail, see Staffan Lindberg and A. Sverisson, eds., *Globalisation, Democratisation, and Social Movements in the Third World*, research report no. 35 (Lund, Sweden: University of Lund, 1995), pp. 57–58.

87. See Mahmood Mamdani's comments in ibid., p. 61.

88. Neil Webster, "The Role of NGDOs in Indian Rural Development: Some Lessons from West Bengal and Karnataka," *European Journal of Development Research* 7 (1995), pp. 407–33.

89. For these theoretical segments, I draw on my *Street Politics* (New York: Columbia University Press, 1997), chap. 1.

90. For a more detailed description, see Wikan, *Tomorrow, God Willing*.

91. See *Ru'ya* (Cairo), no. 8, p. 20.

92. *Al-Wafd* (October 18, 1997), p. 3.

93. Reported in Eid, *Informal Economy*, p. 105.

94. Cited in *Al-Ahram Weekly* (November 27–December 3, 1997), p. 12.

95. Chief of Cairo's security department referring to the spread of street vendors in Cairo, cited in ibid.

96. Reported in *Al-Wafd* (March 3, 1998), p. 3. On Iran, see Bayat, *Street Politics*. The information on Egypt is based on my research reported in an unpublished paper, "Grassroots Participation in Iran: NGOs or Social Movements" (Cairo: American University in Cairo, 1998).

97. Thus, on May 1, 1993, a year after the Imbaba incident in Egypt, President Mubarak authorized "an immediate implementation of a national program in upgrading the most important services and facilities in haphazardly built areas in all governorates." A national five-year-plan campaign was announced covering the period from 1993 to 1998, costing 3.8 billion Egyptian pounds. By 1996, 127 of 527 targeted zones had been "fully upgraded" (*Al-Ahram Weekly* 17–23 [1996], p. 12).

98. See Joan Nelson, "The Politics of Pro-Poor Adjustment Policies," report, World Bank, Country Economics Department, 1988.

Chapter 5

1. See, for instance, Paula M. Cooley, William R. Eakin, and Jay B. McDaniel, eds., *After Patriarchy: Feminist Transformations of the World Religions* (Maryknoll, N.Y.: Orbis Books, 1991), especially the chapter by Riffat Hassan, "Muslim Women and Post-Patriarchal Islam," pp. 39–64.

2. This section draws heavily on a section from chapter 3 of Asef Bayat, *Making Islam Democratic: Social Movements and the Post-Islamist Turn* (Palo Alto, Calif.: Stanford University Press, 2007).

3. See a very interesting discussion on this by Kaveh Ehsani, see "The Nation and Its Periphery: Revolution, War and Provincial Urban Change in Iran," unpublished paper, presented at the conference Iran on the Move: Social Transformation in the Islamic Republic, Leiden, April 27–28, 2005; see also Sohrab Behdad, "Winners and Losers of the Iranian Revolution: A Study in Income Distribution," *International Journal of Middle East Studies* 21 (1989), pp. 327–58.

4. See Parvin Paydar, *Women and Political Process in Iran* (Cambridge: Cambridge University Press, 1997).

5. See Zahara Karimi, "Sahm-e Zanan dar Bazaar-e Kaar-e Iran" (Women's Share in Iran's Labor Market), *Ettelaat-e Siyassi-Eqtisadi*, nos. 179–80 (Mordad-Shahrivar 1381/2002), pp. 208–19.

6. For the position of leftist groups on women's issues, see Hamed Shahidian, "The Iranian Left and the 'Woman Question' in the Revolution of 1978–79," *International Journal of Middle Eastern Studies* 26 (1994), pp. 223–47. See also Nayereh Tohidi, "Mas'aleye Zanan va Rowshanfekran Teyy-e Tahavvolaat-e Dahe-ye Akhir (Women's Issues and the Intellectuals over the Recent Decade), *Nime-ye Digar*, no. 10 (1368 /1989), pp. 51–95.

7. See, for instance, Golnar Dastgheib, "An Islamist Female Parliamentarian's Speech at the Havana Inter-Parliamentary Union," in *Under the Shadow of Islam*, ed. A. Tabari and N. Yeganeh (London: Zed Books, 1982). See also Azar Tabari, "Islam and the Struggle for the Emancipation of Iranian Women," in *Under the Shadow of Islam*, ed. Tabari and Yeganeh, p. 17.

8. See *Payam Hajar* no. 1 (Shahrivar 19, 1359/1980), p. 2. Lara Deeb's *Enchanted Modern: Gender and Public Piety in Shi'i Lebanon* (Princeton, N.J.: Princeton University Press, 2006) contains a fine a discussion about how Zeinab is deployed as a symbol of female activism in Lebanon.

9. See the statement by the Iranian Women's Delegation to the UN Decade of Women Conference, held in July 1980.

10. See, for instance, statements by two conservative Islamist women members of the Fifth Majlis, Monireh Nobakht and Marziyeh Vahid Dastjerdi, cited in *Zanan*, no. 42 (Farvardin-Ordibehesht 1377/1998), p. 3.

11. Cited in *Zanan*, no. 26, p. 3.

12. Maryam Behroozi, cited in *Ettelaat*, 3 Esfand 1361/1982, p. 6.

13. Shahin Tabatabaii, "Understanding Islam in Its Totality Is the Only Way to Understand Women's Role," in *Under the Shadow of Islam*, ed. Tabari and Yeganeh, p. 174.

14. Cited in *Resalat*, 26 Farvardin 1375/1996.

15. President Rafsanjani, cited in *Zanan* no. 26, p. 5.

16. According to Maryam Behroozi, a parliamentary deputy in the 4th Majlis, cited in Kian, "Women and Politics in Post-Islamist Iran," *Women Living under Muslim Laws*, dossier 21 (September 1998), p. 44.

17. Cited in ibid., p. 39.

18. See *Iran-e Farda*, no. 36 (Shahrivar 1376/19997), p. 12; *Zanan*, no. 27 (Azar-Dey 1374/1995), p. 6.

19. Val Moghadam, "Women's Employment Issues in Contemporary Iran: Problems and Prospects in the 1990s," *Iranian Studies* 28 (1995), pp. 175–200.

20. See Azam Khatam, "Sakhtar-e Eshtighal-e Zanan-e Shahri: Qabl va Ba'd az Enqilab" (Urban Employment Structure of Iranian Women), *Goft-o-gu*, no. 28 (summer 2000), pp. 129–39. See also Zahra Karimi, "Sahm-e Zanan dar bazaar-e Kar-e Iran" (The Share of Women in Iran's Labor Market), *Ettelaat-e Siyassi-Eqtisadi*, nos. 179–80 (Mordad-Shahrivar 1381/2002), pp. 208–19.

21. *Zanan*, no. 27, p. 42.

22. Observation by Masserat Amir Ebrahimi; see her interviews in *Bad-Jens*, 6th ed., December 2002, online.

23. Study conducted by Mina Saidi-Shahrouz, "Women's Mobility in Tehran," a presentation in the seminar "Women and the City," Tehran, College of Social Sciences, University of Tehran, December 30, 2003.

24. For an excellent report, see Homa Hoodfar, *Volunteer Health Workers in Iran as Social Activists: Can Governmental NGOs Be Agents of Democratization?* Women Living under Muslim Laws occasional paper no. 10 (Paris: WLUML, 1998).

25. Between 1990 and 1995, the population growth rate had dropped to an annual average of 2 percent. For all the population growth rate figures, see the yearbooks of the United Nations, Population Division.

26. These countries included Pakistan, Syria, Libya, and Cameroon. For women's sports activities, see a special issue of *Zanan*, no. 30; see also *Zanan*, no. 9, Bahman 1371/1991.

27. See womeniniran.com (access date June 6, 2003).

28. For the reports, see *Zanan*, no. 42, Ordibehesht 1998, p. 61; see also womeniniran.com, June 2003, for reports on women soccer teams.

29. For an excellent discussion of how the new cultural centers in South Tehran have become "safe" places for public activities of lower-class women, see Maserrat Amir-Ibrahimi, "Ta'sir Farhangsara-ye Bahman bar Zendegui-ye Ijtemaii va Farhangui-ye Zanan va Javanan-e Tehran" (The Impact of Bahman Cultural Centers on the Social and Cultural Life of Women and Youths in Tehran), *Goft-o-gou*, no. 9 (fall 1995), pp. 17–25.

30. *Ettelaat*, 15 Aban 1369/November 6, 1990.

31. In a 1994 survey, Iranian women were asked if and what type of veil they would wear if they were not obliged to do so. About 20 percent preferred no veil, 10 percent a light head-cover, 40 percent a scarf and a long coat, and 25 percent a full chador; see

Abbas Abdi and Mohsen Goudarzi, *Tahavvolat-e Farhangui dar Iran* (Cultural Developments in Iran) (Tehran: Entesharat-e Ravesh, 1999), p. 148.

32. A woman's letter to *Zanan*, no. 35 (Tir 1376), p. 26.

33. MP, Rejaii, cited in *Ettelaat*, 15 Bahman 1367/1988.

34. Post-Islamist women activists were especially encouraged by the collaborative approach of some secular feminists. For a discussion and attempts to build an alliance of post-Islamist and secular feminists, see Nayereh Tohidi, *Feminism, Demokrasy, va Islamgarayi dar Iran* (Feminism, Democract, and Islamism in Iran) (Los Angeles: Ketabsara, 1996); also see her "Islamic Feminism: Women Negotiating Modernity and Patriarchy in Iran," in *The Blackwell Companion of Contemporary Islamic Thought*, ed. Ibrahim Abu-Rabi (Oxford: Blackwell, 2006), pp. 624–43.

35. For a fine exposition of *Zanan*'s views and visions, see Afsaneh Najmabadi, "Feminism in an Islamic Republic: Years of Hardship, Years of Growth," in *Islam, Gender and Social Change*, ed. Yvonne Haddad and John Esposito (Oxford: Oxford University Press, 1998), pp. 59–84.

36. See *Zanan*'s own survey about its readers in *Zanan*, no. 52 (Mordad-Shahrivar 1374/1995), pp. 54–58.

37. Nayereh Tohidi, "The International Connections of the Women's Movement in Iran: 1979–2000," in *Iran and the Surrounding World*, ed. Nikki Keddie and Rudi Matthee (Seattle: University of Washington Press, 2002), pp. 205–31.

38. Azar Tabari, "Islam and the Struggle for Emancipation of Iranian Women," in *Under the Shadow of Islam*, ed. Tabari and Yeganeh, p. 17.

39. If Eve was "weaker," the feminists argued, then she was less guilty than Adam in causing his fall. They went on to suggest that woman (Eve) was more noble than man, because man was created from earth, while woman was from man. Indeed, woman is superior, since only she, not man, gives birth to other humans, or "increases the world." See Gerda Lerner, *The Creation of Feminist Consciousness* (Oxford: Oxford University Press, 1993), pp. 138–66. For some instances of feminist theology in Christianity and Judaism, see Jane Bayes and Nayereh Tohidi, eds., *Globalization, Gender and Religion: The Politics of Women's Rights in Catholic and Muslim Contexts* (New York: Palgrave, 2001), especially, chapter 2, "Women Redefining Modernity and Religion in the Globalized Context."

40. *Zanan*, no. 9, p. 34.

41. Attention to children is emphasized in such verses as "wealth and sons are the allurements of the life of this world" (Kahf: 45), and the ahadith "Children are the butterflies of heaven" and "no sin is greater than that of ignoring the children" exemplify the centrality of care for children. See *Zanan*, no. 38 (Aban 1376), pp. 2–5.

42. See Sayyid Mohsen Saidzadeh, "Kalbod-shekafi-e Tarh-e Entibaq-e Omour-e Edari" (An Analysis of the Project concerning the Adaptation of Administrative Affairs), *Zanan*, no. 43, p. 15.

43. See interview with Mostafa Malekian, in *Zanan*, no. 64, pp. 32–35.

44. Shokufeh Shokri and Sahireh Labriz, "Mard: Sharik ya Ra'is?" (Men: Partners or Bosses?) *Zanan*, no. 2 (March 1992), pp. 26–32.

45. *Zanan*, no. 23 (Farvardin-Ordibehesht 1374/1995), pp. 46–57.

46. See, for instance, Mehrangiz Kar, "Mosharekat-e Siyassi-e Zanan: Vaqeiyyat ya Khial" (Political Participation of Women: Reality or Dream?), *Zanan*, no. 47, pp. 12–13.

47. *Zanan*, no. 35 (Tir 1376/1997), p. 6.

48. Clerics such as Ayatollah Bojnordi of Qom Seminary would state: "Fiqh [which contains some discriminatory rulings] is nothing but the particular perceptions of fuqaha; and it can be changed," as cited in *Farzaneh*, no. 8.

49. Cited in *Mahname-ye Gozaresh*, no. 148 (Tir 1382/2003).

50. *Jomhuri-ye Islami*, 12 Mehr 1376/1997.

51. *Zanan*, no. 43 (Khordad 1377/1998).

52. Cited in *Zanan*, no. 38 (Abab 1379/2000), p. 59.

53. Reported in *Zanan*, no. 42 (Farvardin-Ordibehesht 1377/1998), p. 3.

54. *Sobh Weekly*, no. 32 (Aban 1375 /1995), and 28 (Farvardin 1375/1996).

55. See the report of the magazine's trial in *Zanan*, no. 43 (Khordad 1377/1998), p. 4.

56. For a fine analysis of the gender debates among the Iranian Shi'i clerics, see Ziba Mir-Hosseini, *Islam and Gender: The Religious Debate in Contemporary Iran* (Princeton, N.J.: Princeton University Press, 1999).

57. This is compared to 283,253 permanent or normal marriages during the same period. See *Hayat-e Nou*, 11 Aban 1381/2002, p. 11. It has to be noted that *mut'a* marriage is not always registered. Therefore, its real frequency might be higher.

58. For the list, see *Zanan*, no. 28 (Farvardin 1375/1996), p. 3.

59. *Zanan*, no. 38 (Aban 1376/1997). p. 38.

60. This 6 percent women's share in the parliament was still far short of world average (11.6 percent), but higher than that in the Arab countries (4.3 percent); see *Zanan*, no. 33, p. 76.

61. Cited in Ramin Mostaghimi, "Tights-Iran: Women Carve out Spaces within Islamic Society," *Interpress News Agency*, June 25, 2003. For the report on divorce rates, see Shadi Sadr's discussion in *Yas-e Nou*; cited at womeniniran.com (accessed May 4, 2003).

62. Cited in *Zanan*, no. 34 (Ordibehesht 1376/1997), p. 4, and no. 37 (Shahrivar-Mehr 1376/1997), p. 8. A study by Uzra Shalbaf confirmed that women (wives) with higher education had attained a more extensive decision-making power in families, even though their domestic responsibilities had changed modestly. Discussed in a master's thesis, Faculty of Social Sciences, Sociology, University of Tehran, 2001; cited at womeniniran.com (accessed May 21, 2003).

63. See *Zanan*, no. 41.

64. See Mohammad Rafi'e Mahmoudian, "Jonbesh-e Zanan-e Iran: Za'f-e Feminism va Feghdan-e Armangeraii" (Iran's Women Movement: The Weakness of Feminism and the Absence of Utopian Visions), *Zanan*, January 2003.

65. See, for instance, Hamid-Reza Jalaii-pour, "Hamelan-e Bi-Neshan" (Carriers without Identification), *Zanan*, January 2004.

66. Hamid-Reza Jalaii-pour, "Mas'ale-ye Ejtemaii, Na Jonbesh-e Ejtemaii" (Social Problem, Not Social Movement), *Yass-e Nou*, 10 (Aban 2003); see also his "Tahlili az Pouyesh-e Zanan-e Iran" (An Analysis of Iran's Women Activism), iran-emrooz.com, 12 Aban 1382/2003.

67. See Nasrin Azadeh, "Jonbesh-e Ejtemaii-ye Zananeh" (Women's Social Movement), zananeiran.com, December 11, 2003.

68. Ali Akbar Mahdi, on iran-emrooz.com, July 2002; Valentine Moghadam, "Feminism in Iran and Algeria: Two Models of Collective Action for Women's Rights," *Journal of Iranian Research and Analysis* 19 (April 2003), pp. 18–31; Homa Hoodfar, "The Women's Movement in Iran: Women at the Crossroads of Secularization and Islamization," Women Living under Muslim Laws no. 1, winter 1999; Nasrin Azadeh, "Jonbesh-e Ejtemai-ye Zananeh" (Feminine Social Movement), at www.womeninIran.org.

69. Janet Afary, "Jonbesh-e Zanan-e Iran: Gheir-e Motamarkez va Gostardeh" (Iranian Women's Movement: Decentred and Vast), *Zanan*, April 2003; Mahboubeh Abbasgholizadeh, "Dar Iran Jonbesh-e Zanan bi Sar Ast" (The Iranian Movement's Movement is Leader-less), *Zanan*, September 2003.

70. See Farideh Farhi, "Jonbesh-e Zanan va Mardan-e Eslah-talab" (The Women's Movement and the Reformist Men), *Zanan*, May 2003.

71. James Scott, *Weapons of the Weak: Everyday Forms of Peasant Resistance* (New Haven, Conn.: Yale University Press, 1985).

72. Reported in *Zanan*, no. 26, p. 5.

73. Between 1990 and 1997, some thirteen new women's magazines were published (*Neda, Rahrovan'e Somaaya, Boresh, Pegah, Me'raj, Jelveh, Payam-e Zan, Zanan, Takapu, Farzaneh, Reyhaneh, Touba,* and *Banu*). From Khatami's election in 1997 until 2002, there emerged twenty-three new women's publications: *Zan va Pazhouhesh, Zan* (newspaper), *Ershad-e Neswan, Hamsar, Mahtab, Kitab-e Zanan, Poushesh, Qarn-e 21, Zana-e Jonoub, Zan-e Emrooz, Al-Zahra, Banu, Nour-e Braran, Shamim-e Narjes, Soroush-e Banuvan, Tarh-va-Mode, Yaas, Irandokht, Motale'at-e Zanan, Melina, Arous, Zanan-e Farda, Zan-e Sharghi, Kawkab*. As of the 2000, some five of such journals had been shut down by the authorities. See *Yaas-e Nou*, May 23, 1382/2003.

74. For a critical survey of these women's studies programs, see Ziba Jalali-Naini, "Ta'sis-e Reshte-ye Motaleat-e Zanan dar Iran?" (The Establishment of Women's

Studies Programs: Expropriating a Declining Movement?) *Goft-o-gu*, no. 38 (Azar 1382/2003), pp. 7–23.

75. For an elaboration of the concept of "passive network," see Asef Bayat, *Street Politics: Poor People's Movements in Iran* (New York: Columbia University Press, 1997), chapter 1.

76. In some sense this process resonates with the strategy of "quiet encroachment" (see Chapter 3). As with the urban poor, the women's (non)movement in Iran also represents a discreet, protracted, and incremental movement of capturing gains, a process closely tied to the practices of everyday life. However, whereas quiet encroachment of the poor represents a nonmovement, where actors hardly engage in discursive struggles or collective strategy, Muslim women were involved in some kind of social movement, a "movement by consequence," which involved some degree of ideological struggles about gender relations, patriarchy, and women's daily activities. A limited degree of lobbying and political and legal campaigns was also carried out. Secondly, while quiet encroachment is fundamentally an informal and largely illegal strategy, movement by implications is inevitably entrenched in legal battles. For whereas the urban poor operate on the periphery of, and therefore can get around, both normative and (modern) legal structures, Muslim women actors need to function *within* and thus challenge the constraining codes of such structures. It is true that in both types of activism actions and gains are fundamentally identical, as in squatters taking over land, or women pursuing mechanical engineering in colleges. But while audible collective action would be inimical for poor people's quiet encroachment, it would benefit women's struggles.

77. A point to which Ayatollah Jawadi Amoli referred, to argue that women could not be qadi or faqih; see *Zanan*, no. 9, p. 30.

78. As Zahra Shojaii, President Khatami's advisor on women's issues, suggested, "Now that women have become breadwinners, is it not time to read the 'al-rijaal qawamoun al-annisaa' with new eyes?" Cited in *Zanan*, no. 37 (Shahrivar-Mehr 1376/1997).

79. Cited in Ali Dawani, *Nehzat-e Ruhanion-e Iran*, vol. 3 (Tehran: Imam Reza Cultural Foundation), p. 67.

80. *Gozideh-haaii az Maqalat-e Payam-e Hajar*, no. 1 (Tehran: Women's Association of the Islamic Revolution, July 12, 1980).

81. Cited in *Zanan*, no. 9, p. 30.

82. A study on "Jensiyyat va Negaresh-e Ejtemaii" (Sexuality and Social Outlook), sponsored by the Ministry of Culture, revealed a high discrepancy between the views of men and women on "being content in life" (*rezayat az zendegui*), with women having many more expectations than men; reported by IRNA News agency, 11 Khordad 1383/2004, cited atiran-emrooz.com.

Chapter 6

1. See, for instance, Timothy Gorton Ash, "Soldiers of Hidden Imam," *New York Review of Books* 52, no. 17 (November 3, 2005). See also Bill Samii, "Iran Youth Movement Has Untapped Potential," in RadioFreeEurope, April 13, 2005, in www.rferl.org/features/features_Article.aspx?m=04&y=2005&id=3D5DCD40-3EBC-4343-A1C9 -5BF29FFE7BB. See also Samantha Shapiro, "Revolution, Facebook-Style," *New York Times*, January 25, 2009.

2. For a listing of such youth organizations and movements, see "A Snapshot of the Global Youth Movement," www.youthmovements.org/guide/globalguide.htm. For Mao Tese-tung, "youth movement" meant the political participation of students in the anticolonial (Japan) struggle. See Mao Tse-tung, "The Orientation of the Youth Movement," in *Selected Works of Mao Tse-tung* (Peking: Foreign Languages Press, 1967), vol. 2, pp. 241–49.

3. See Herbert Marcuse, "On Revolution," in *Student Power: Problems, Diagnoses, Action*, ed. Alexander Cockburn and Robin Blackburn (London: Penguin Books, 1969), 367–72.

4. See, for instance, Colin Bundy, "Street Sociology and Pavement Politics: Aspects of Youth and Student Resistance in Cape Town, 1985," *Journal of Southern African Studies* 13, no. 3 (April 1987), pp. 303–30.

5. For the German case, see Walter Laqueur, *Young Germany: A History of the German Youth Movement* (New York: Transaction, 1962/1984).

6. For a discussion of student movements, see Alexander Cockburn and Robin Blackburn, eds., *Student Power: Problem, Diagnosis, Action* (London: Penguin Books, 1969).

7. Pierre Bourdieu, "'Youth' Is Just a Word," in Bourdieu, *Sociology in Question* (London: SAGE, 1993).

8. For an elaborate exposition of "passive networks," see Bayat, *Street Politics: Poor Peoples Movements in Iran* (New York: Columbia University Press, 1997), chapter 1. See also chapter 3 in this book.

9. See Ahmad Ashraf and Ali Banuazizi, "The State, Classes, and Modes of Mobilization in the Iranian Revolution," *State, Culture and Society*, vol. 1, no. 3 (spring 1985). Out of a sample of 646 people killed in Tehran in the street clashes during the revolution (from August 23, 1977, to February 19, 1978), the largest group after artisans and shopkeepers (189) was students (149). See Bayat, *Street Politics*, p. 39.

10. This is according to a national survey reported in *Aftab*, July 30, 2001, p. 9.

11. Cited in *Nowrooz*, 24 Shavrivar 1380 (2001).

12. Zahra Rahnavard, *in Bahar*, 29 Khordad 1379 (2000), p. 2. A one-day symposium was organized to discuss why the youth showed such a disinterest in religious lessons.

13. Cited on http://dailynews.yahoo.com, July 25, 2000.

14. See Mansour Qotbi, "Causeless Rebellion in the Land of Iran," *Iran Javan*, no. 166, Mehr 1379 (2000).

15. According to a July 2000 report authored by Muhammad Ali Zam, the director of cultural and artistic affairs for Tehran. This became a highly controversial survey, as the conservatives disputed its authenticity and negative impact on their image.

16. Drawn on official interviews with youngsters cited in Behzad Yaghmaiyan, *Social Change in Iran*, pp. 65–71.

17. See *Aftab*, January 16, 2003, p. 9; see a report by IRNA, August 5, 2001.

18. Reported by *Sina News Agency*, June 17, 2004, cited on http://iran-emrooz.net.

19. Conducted by psychologist Dawood Jeshan with 120 runaway girls in Tehran, reported in Sina News agency, cited on http://iran-emrooz.net (accessed on June 17, 2004).

20. Reported in Professor Mahmoud Golzari's paper in the workshop "Young Girls and the Challenges of Life," May 2004, cited in *ISNA News Agency*, 22 Ordibehest 1383 (2004), at www.womeniniran.com. On the practice of premarital sex in Iran, see Pardis Mahdavi, *Passionate Uprising: Sexual Revolution in Iran* (Palo Alto, Calif.: Stanford University Press, 2008).

21. In an interview with Siasat-e Rouz, cited in Mozhgan Farahi, "You Cannot Resolve Sexual Misconduct by Exhortation," in *Gozaresh*, no. 148, Tir 1382 (2003).

22. Interview with an anonymous medical anthropologist working on the subject, spring 2001.

23. Ibid.

24. Ibid.

25. See *Salaam*, 27 Shahrivar 1375 (1996).

26. See Jalil Erfan-Manesh, *Iran*, 19 Aban 1375 (1996).

27. The contribution of Muhammad Hadi Taskhiri, of the Organization of Islamic Culture and Communication in the Second International Seminar on Hijab, 28 Aban 1376, reported in *Zanan*, no. 26, Meh/Aban 1376, pp. 8–9.

28. A survey of Supreme Council of Youth, cited by Golzari in ibid., p. 9.

29. This finding was reported by the National Radio and TV, Organization of Islamic Propaganda, and the Organization of the Friday Prayers (Detad-e Namaz), cited by Emad Eddin Baaqui, *Payam-e Emrouz*, no. 39, Ordibehesht 1379, p. 14.

30. From report by the head of Tehran's cultural and artistic affairs July 5, 2000, 5:46 pm, EDT (accessed at www.nandotimes.com; site no longer exists, page was not archived).

31. Ministry of Culture and Islamic Guidance, "An Introduction to Behaviorology of the Youth," Tehran, 1994, cited in *Tahavvolat-e Farhangui dar Iran* (Cultural Developments in Iran), by Abbas Abdi and Mohsen Goudarzi (Tehran: Entisharat-e Ravesh, 1999), pp. 138–39.

32. Seyed Hossein Serajzadeh, "Non-attending Believers: Religiosity of Iranian Youth and Its Implications for Secularization Theory," a paper presented at the World Congress of Sociology, Montreal, 1999.

33. Survey conducted by National Organization of the Youth, reported in *Aftab*, 8 Ordibehesht 1380 (2001).

34. See Behzad Yaghmaian, *Social Change in Iran* (Stony Brook: State University of New York Press, 2002) for the best account of such events (pp. 61–65).

35. Interview with Azam, an anonymous participant, June 2002.

36. *Al-Hayat*, January 22, 1995.

37. Scott Peterson, "Ecstasy in Iran, Agony for Its Clerics," in *Christian Science Monitor*, December 5, 1997.

38. See *Nowrooz*, 1 Aban 1380, p. 3.

39. For some of these reports on confrontation between the youth and the Pasdaran, see *Dowran-e Emrooz*, 25 Esfand 1379 (2001), p. 4.

40. This is well illustrated in an editorial of a reformist daily; see "The Mystery of Firecrackers," *Aftab*, 25 Esfand 1379 (March 15, 2001), p. 2.

41. *Nowrooz*, 29 Mehr 1380 (2001); see also "Leisure Time and Amusement," *Aftab-e Yazd*, April 3, 2001, p. 9; "Shad Zistan-e Zanan," *Dowran-e Emrooz*, 20 Bahman 1379 (2000), p. 2; Report on seminar on the "Approaches to the Concept of Living," cited in *Aftab-e Yazd*, January 9, 2001, p. 7, and January 11, 2001, p. 7.

42. See *Hayat-e Nou*, 10 Ordibehesht 1380 (2001), p. 11, and *Nourooz*, 15 Mordad 1380 (2001), p. 9.

43. *Iran Emrooz*, August 11, 2003.

44. See *Hayat-e Nou*, 10 Ordibehesht 1380 (2001), p. 11; *Nourouz*, 15 Mordad, 1380 (2001), p. 9.

45. See Morteza Nabawi in *Resalat*, October 27, 2001, p. 2.

46. See Jean-Michel Cadiot, *AP Report*, August 20, 2001 at IranMania.com, August 20, 2001; Michael Theodoulou, "Iran's Culture War Intensifies," *Christian Science Monitor*, August 21, 2001; *Nourooz*, 20 and 21 Mordad 1380 (2001).

47. This seemed to be confirmed by large-scale survey research. See Azadeh Kian-Thiebaut, "Political Impacts of Iranian Youth's Individuation: How Family Matters," paper presented at MESA, Washington, D.C., November 24, 2002.

48. Central Agency for Public Mobilization and Statistics, *The Statistical Year Book* (Cairo: CAPMAS, 1996).

49. Central Agency for Public Mobilization and Statistics, *The Statistical Year Book, 1992–1998* (Cairo CAPMAS, 1999).

50. Eric Denis and Asef Bayat, "Egypt: Twenty Years of Urban Transformation, 1980–2000," report for the International Institute of Development and Urbanization, London, 2001.

51. Ayman Khalifa, "The Withering Youths of Egypt," *Ru'ya*, no. 7 (spring 1995), pp. 6–10.

52. Cited in Rime Naguib, "Egyptian Youth: A Tentative Study," term paper, American University in Cairo, spring 2002.

53. The ages of Egypt's political leaders by their birthdate: President Mubarak, born in 1928; Dia Eddin Dawoud (Nasser Party), 1926; Khalid Mohyeddin (leader of Tajammo' Party) 1922; Mustafa Mashur (Leader of Muslim Brothers), 1921; Ibrahim Shukri (leader of Labor Party), 1916; Noman Gom'a, the youngest opposition leader of the Wafd Party, 1934.

54. In a survey, only 16 percent of Cairo University students expressed interest in party politics. In addition some 87 percent of elders did not trust the youth to do politics; see Ahmed Tahami Abdel-Hay, "Al-Tawajjohat al-Siyasiyya Lil-Ajyal al-Jadida," *Al-Demokratiya*, no. 6 (spring 2002), pp. 117–18.

55. Shapiro, "Revolution, Facebook-Style."

56. See Andrew Hammond, "Campuses Stay Clear of Politics," *Cairo Times*, October 15–28, 1998, p. 7.

57. Reported in Khalifa, "Withering Youth of Egypt."

58. Drawn on the conclusion of a debate in Majlis el-Shura, reported in *Al-Ahram*, July 14, 2000, p. 7.

59. This information is based upon my interview with the Minister of Youths and Sports, Dr. Ali Eddin Hilal, November 3, 2001, Cairo.

60. The Ministry of Social Affairs reported having extended some EL 30 million between 1997 and 2000. See *Al-Ahram*, July 14, 2000.

61. The Ministry of Local Development was to extend some of these loans. See *Al-Ahram*, July 14, 2000, p. 7.

62. See Midhat Fuad, "Youth Centers without Youths," *Sawt ul-Azhar*, September 14, 2001, p. 2. I have especially relied on Muhammad Shalabi, "Egypt's Youth Centers: Between Ideals and Reality," paper for urbanization class, American University in Cairo, spring 2003.

63. They often presented unsubtle, pre-staged shows where the young attendees were carefully picked, the questions were rehearsed, and the oratory and flattery by which students addressed the president left little genuine interaction.

64. Hoda's statement in response to my question as to "what is it like to be young in today's Egyptian society?" spring 2003, Cairo, Egypt.

65. The ticket costs range from LE75 to LE150, with alcoholic drinks, LE20; and water, LE10. See Nadia Matar, "Glowsticks and Grooves," *Cairo Times*, March 14–20, 2002, p. 16.

66. Ibid., p. 19.

67. The figure for the country was 22 percent. Based on a survey of 14,656 male high school students in 1990; see M. I. Soueif et al., "Use of Psychoactive Substances among Male Secondary School Pupils in Egypt: A Study of a Nationwide Representative Sample," *Drug and Alcohol Dependence* 26 (1990), pp. 71–72.

68. Reportedly, the quantity seized by the police jumped from 2,276 in 2000 to 7,008 in 2001; see *Cairo Times*, March 14–20, 2002, p. 16.

69. See Population Council, *Transitions to Adulthood: A National Survey of Egyptian Adolescents* (Cairo, 1999).

70. See Khalifa, "Withering Youth of Egypt."

71. See Fatma El-Zanaty, "Behavioral Research among Egyptian University Students," MEDTEC, FHI, Behavioral Research Unit, Cairo, 1996; reported in Barbara Ibrahim and Hind Wassef, "Caught Between Two Worlds: Youth in the Egyptian Hinterland," in *Alienation or Integration of Arab Youth*, ed. Roel Meijer (London: Curzon Press, 2000), p. 163.

72. See *Cairo Times*, May 15–28, 1997, p. 12. Active sexuality of youth is also confirmed by Mona al-Dabbaqh, "Addiction among Egyptian Upper Class," master's thesis, American University in Cairo, 1996, for which she interviewed a number of "deviant" adolescents in a hospital in Cairo.

73. Interviews with youngsters by Rime Naguib, sociology student, American University in Cairo, spring 2002.

74. See Khalifa, "Withering Youth of Egypt."

75. Shahida El-Baz, cited in *Cairo Times*, May 15–28, 1997, p. 12.

76. Ironically, the partially segregated trains made the traditional young women more mobile. Parents would not mind if their daughters took trains (after which they took taxis or public buses), since segregated trains were thought to protect their daughters from male harassment. Seif Nasrawi, "An Ethnography of Cairo's Metro," term paper for Urban Sociology class, fall 2002, American University in Cairo.

77. Cited in Mustafa Abdul-Rahman, "Sex, Urfi Marriage as Survival Strategy in Dahab," term paper, fall 2001, p. 18.

78. Cited in Rime Naguib, "Egyptian Youth: A Tentative Study," term paper, spring 2002.

79. Cited in ibid.

80. Yousef Boutrous Ghali extends this "technique of adaptability" to the Egyptian psyche in general. "The Egyptian is ingeneious and he will manage a problem, weave his way around a crisis and absorb without causing a conflictual situation," cited in *Cairo Times*, May 15–28, 1997, p. 13.

81. *Al-Wafd*, May 4, 2000.

82. Ibid.

83. Ibid; and *Al-Ahram*, May 6, 2000, p. 13.

84. CAPMAS report of over 5 million bachelor boys and 3.4 million girls caused uproar in the media about the moral consequences of the state of these unmarried adults. Indeed, the age of marriage reached thirty to forty for men and twenty to thirty for women; see *Al-Wafd*, January 1, 2002, p. 3.

85. For an analysis of Amr Khaled "phenomenon," see Asef Bayat, "Piety, Privilege and Egyptian Youth," *ISIM Newsletter*, no. 10 (July 2002), p. 23, from which this paragraph has been extracted.

86. For detailed discussion of Amr Khaled, see Bayat, *Making Islam Democratic*, pp. 151–55.

87. Shapiro, "Revolution, Facebook-Style."

Chapter 7

1. Linda Herrera, "A Song for Humanistic Education: Pedagogy and Politics in the Middle East," *Teachers College Record* 10, no. 2 (2008), pp. 352–76.

2. See Mohamed Abdul-Quddus, "Mowajehe sakhina ma'a qiyadat al-television wa al-iza'a" (Severe Confrontation with the Directors of Television and Radio), *Liwa al-Islami* 43 (1988), pp. 43–44. For a more detailed discussion of how saints' festivals in Egypt are contested, see Samuli Schielke, "Habitus of the Authentic, Order of the Rational: Contesting Saints' Festivals in Contemporary Egypt," *Critique: Critical Middle Eastern Studies* 12 (2003), pp. 155–72.

3. Cited in *Cairo Times*, August 30–September 5, 2001.

4. Cited in *Iran Emrooz*, April 1, 2002.

5. Discussed in the conservative Islamist monthly *Partow-e Sokhan*, cited in *Nowrooz*, 6 Aban AH 1380/October 28, 2001.

6. *Hafteh-nameh-ye Sobh*, 22 Bahman AH 1379/February 10, 2001; my emphasis.

7. Max Weber, *The Sociology of Religion* (Boston: Beacon, 1963), pp. 236–39.

8. See the Islamist conservative weekly *Partow-e Sokhan*, 10 and 17 Esfand AH 1379/February 28 and March 7, 2000.

9. On these institutions, see *Partow-e Sokhan*, 24 Esfand AH 1379/March 14, 2000. Imam Sadeq quoted in *Partow-e Sokhan*, cited in *Nowrooz*, 6 Aban AH 1380/October 28, 2001, 11.

10. See *Jebhe*, 22 Esfand AH 1377/March 13, 1999, 8.

11. The Persian word *sangin* (heavy) signifies precisely that moral and morphological solemnity, as opposed to *sabok* (light), which connotes triviality and shallowness. Interestingly, the word *heavy* (*thaqil*) in Egyptian Arabic has a negative connotation.

12. On "mourners of joy," see *Nowrooz*, July 29, 2001. The statement on war-front days was issued by the Cultural Institute of *Jenat-e Fakkeh*, an extremist Islamist organization, on the occasion of *Nowrooz* 1998, printed in the weekly *Jebhe*, 22 Esfand AH 1377/March 13, 1999, p. 8.

13. Thus, for example, "Death to those who are against Velayat-i Faqih," instead of "Long live Velayat-i Faqih."

14. *Jebhe*, 22 Esfand AH 1377/March 13, 1999, p. 3.

15. Ibid.

16. *Shalamche*, no. 40, Mehr AH 1377/September–October 1998, p. 6.

17. Ibid.

18. For a sympathetic treatment, see Fariba Khani, "Backstreets of Forbidden Love," *Zanan*, Khordad AH 1377/May–June 1998, p. 6.

19. Such tyranny over the everyday could not escape the attention of the nation's greatest poet, Ahmad Shamloo, in his well-known piece "In This Dead End":

> They smell your breath; you better not have said, "I love you."
> They smell your heart.
> Strange times are these, my darling . . .
> And they excise smiles from lips
> and songs from mouths.
> We had better hide joy in the closet . . .

This extract is a modified version of a translation available at: poems.lesdoigtsbleus .free.fr/id187.htm (accessed July 2, 2007).

20. See Pardis Mahdavi, *Passionate Uprising: Iran's Sexual Revolution* (Palo Alto, Calif.: Stanford University Press, 2009).

21. For details, see Chapter 6 of this book.

22. Awad al-Otaibi and Pascal Menoret, "Rebels Without a Cause? Politics of Deviance in Saudi Society" in *Being Young and Muslim: Cultural Politics in the Global South and North*, ed. Linda Herrera and Asef Bayat (New York and Oxford: Oxford University Press, 2010).

23. See Oskar Verkaik, *Migrants and Militants: Fun and Urban Violence in Pakistan* (Princeton, N.J.: Princeton University Press, 2005).

24. *Nowrooz*, 29 Mehr AH 1380/October 21, 2001.

25. See "Zaman faraghat va tafrih" [Leisure Time and Amusement], *Aftab-e Yazd*, April 3, 2001; "Shad Zistan-e Zanan?" [How Can Women Live with Joy?] *Dowran-e Emrooz*, 20 Bahman AH 1379/February 8, 2001.

26. Report on the seminar "Approaches to the Concept of Living," cited in *Aftab-e Yazd*, January 9, 2001; and *Aftab-e Yazd*, January 11, 2001.

27. See "Khandidan aslan zesht neest" [Laughing Is Not Dreadful], *Iran*, March 18, 2001.

28. See Morteza Nabawi, *Resalat*, October 27, 2001.

29. See Jean-Michel Cadiot, Associated Press, IranMania.com (accessed August 20, 2001).

30. See Michael Theodoulou, "Iran's Culture War Intensifies," *Christian Science Monitor*, August 21, 2001.

31. Charles Recknagel and Azam Gorgin, "Iran: New Morality Police," *Radio Free Europe*, July 26, 2000.

32. See *Nowrooz*, 20 and 21 Mordad AH 1380/August 11–12, 2001.

33. See the Qur'an 3:104, 3:110, 9:71.

34. For an excellent survey of discussions and debates about the subject, see Michael Cook, *Forbidding Wrong in Islam* (Cambridge: Cambridge University Press, 2003).

35. Ibid., p. 3.

36. Ibid., pp. 98, 102. Hafez of Shiraz, one of the greatest Persian poets, critically takes note of the puritanical suppression of joy in his days:

> Do you know what the harp and the lute are saying?
> "Drink wine on the quiet: allegations of apostasy are being made."
> They're saying, "Do not hear or divulge hints of love";
> It is a hard saying which they are expressing.
> Love's dignity and lovers' grace are being pillaged:
> The young are prohibited and the old rebuked.

From *The Collected Lyrics of Háfiz Shíráz*, trans. Peter Avery (Cambridge: Archetype, 2007), p. 255.

37. See Franz Rosenthal, *Humor in Early Islam* (Leiden, N.Y.: E. J. Brill, 1956), p. 4.

38. Cook, *Forbidding Wrong in Islam*, p. 100.

39. According to Rosenthal, a large number of humorous tales from Arabic literature are collected by René Basset in the voluminous work *Mille et un contes, récits et légendes arabes* [A Thousand and One Arab Tales, Stories, and Legends] (Paris, 1924); see Rosenthal, *Humor in Early Islam*.

40. Samuli Schielke, "Snacks and Saints: Mawlid Festivals and the Politics of Festivity, Piety, and Modernity in Contemporary Egypt," PhD diss., University of Amsterdam, 2006.

41. *Inshad* (religious singing) focuses on "glorification of God, praise and love for his Prophet, expressions of spiritual experience, and religious exhortations." *Aghani diniyya* are sung by an ordinary *mutrib* (performer) but have religious lyrics. They may be sung by secular singers or by a shaykh or shaykha. *Aghani diniyya* are different from *inshad* in "vocal timbres, melodic styles, improvisations, contexts and religious intentions." *Inshad* is sung by *munshidin* (religious singers), not secular singers. See Michael Frishkopf, "Inshad Dini and Aghani Diniyya in Twentieth Century Egypt: A Review of Styles, Genres, and Available Recordings," *Middle East Studies Association Bulletin* 34 (2000), pp. 167, 179.

42. On premodern times, see Cook, *Forbidding Wrong in Islam*, p. 101.

43. Ibid., p. 125. See also Hamid Algar, *Wahhabism: A Critical Essay* (New York: Islamic Publications International, 2002).

44. Cook, *Forbidding Wrong in Islam*, pp. 126–27; Algar, *Wahhabism*.

45. Ahmad Rashid, *Taliban: Militant Islam, Oil, and Fundamentalism in Central Asia* (New Haven, Conn.: Yale University Press, 2001), pp. 105–7, 217–19. See also Amy

Waldman, "No T.V., No Chess, No Kites: Taliban Codes from A to Z," *New York Times*, November 22, 2001.

46. United Nations Educational, Scientific, and Cultural Organization (UNESCO), *Statistical Yearbook* (Paris: UNESCO), pp. 1960–75.

47. Cited in Hamid Nafici, "The Iranian Cinema under the Islamic Republic," *American Anthropologist* 97 (1995), p. 548.

48. Expressed by Israel's foremost "revisionist historian," Benny Morris; cited in Joel Beinin, "No More Tears: Benny Morris and the Road from Liberal Zionism," *Middle East Report*, no. 230 (2004), p. 40.

49. See M. Muhsin Khan, ed., *Al-Bukhari (Sahih)* (Beirut: Dar al-Arabia, 1985), vol. 8, hadith no. 138.

50. Ibid., hadith no. 56.

51. Ibid., hadith no. 114.

52. Ibid., hadith nos. 175 and 176.

53. *Al-Bukhari*, Kitab al-Salat, no. 435; Kitab al-Jumu'a, no. 897; Kitab al-Johad, no. 2686, cited in Muhammad Khalid Masud, "Arts and Religion in Islamic Jurisprudence," unpublished manuscript, Leiden, 2003.

54. See Maribel Fierro, "The Treatises Against Innovations (*kub al bid'a*)," *Islam* 69 (1992), pp. 204–46. See also Muhammad Umar Memon, *Ibn Taimiya's Struggles Against Popular Religion* (The Hague: Mouton, 1976).

55. See Abi Ja'far Kolaini, *Usoul-e Kafi*, 4 vols. (Tehran: Wafa, AH 1382/2003), vol. 3, pp. 485–87.

56. Ibid., pp. 175–78, 193.

57. Khan, *Al-Bukhari*, vol. 8, hadith no. 108.

58. Ibid., hadith nos. 52, 53, 64.

59. Kolaini, *Usoul-e Kafi*, vol. 3, pp. 485–87.

60. Ibid., pp. 271–76.

61. Ibid., pp. 161–62.

62. Masud, "Arts and Religion in Islamic Jurisprudence."

63. Khan, *Al-Bukhari*, vol. 8, hadith no. 95.

64. Ibid., vol. 1, hadith no. 38.

65. Ibid., vol. 8, hadith no. 472.

66. Ibid., hadith no. 73.

67. Muhammad Khalid Masud, personal communication with author, Leiden, 2003.

68. See Sayyid Hojjat Mahdavi, "Youths and the Crisis of Leisure," *Nowrooz*, 9 Tir AH 1380/June 30, 2001.

69. Cited in *Nowrooz*, 23 Tir AH 1380/July 14, 2001.

70. *Nowrooz*, 16 Tir AH 1380/July 7, 2001.

71. See Guiv Namazi, "Jeans, Short-Sleeves, Bright Color: Never!" *Nowrooz*, 17 Tir AH 1380/July 8, 2001, 8.

72. See Lacey B. Smith, *Fools, Martyrs, Traitors: The Story of Martyrdom in the Western World* (New York: Knopf, 1997).

73. See Weber, *Sociology of Religion*, pp. 236–40.

74. See John Kent, "Christianity: Protestantism," in *The Concise Encyclopedia of Living Faiths*, ed. R. C. Zaehner (Boston: Beacon, 1959), p. 121.

75. On the influence of reason on human conduct, see Weber, *Sociology of Religion*, p. 242.

76. See Barbara Ehrenreich, *Dancing in the Streets: A History of Collective Joy* (New York: Metropolitan Books/Henry Holt, 2006), pp. 97–102.

77. Ehrenreich, *Dancing in the Streets*, pp. 190–91; Crane Brinton, *Anatomy of Revolution* (New York: Vintage Books, 1965), p. 180. See also Lynn Hunt, *Politics, Culture, and Class in the French Revolution* (Berkeley: University of California Press, 1984), pp. 66–67.

78. Brinton, *Anatomy of Revolution*, pp. 218–23.

79. E. P. Thompson, "Time, Work-Discipline, and Industrial Capitalism," in his *Customs in Common* (London: Penguin, 1991), p. 401. See also Christopher Hill, *Society and Puritanism in Pre-Revolutionary England* (New York: St. Martin's Press, 1997).

80. Brinton, *Anatomy of Revolution*, pp. 188–89. For a more elaborate study of cultural politics under the Bolsheviks, see Sheila Fitzpatrick, *The Cultural Front: Power and Culture in Revolutionary Russia* (Ithaca, N.Y.: Cornell University Press, 1992).

81. Brinton, *Anatomy of Revolution*, pp. 180, 220.

82. See Vida Hajebi Tabrizi, *Dad-e bidad: Nakhostin zendan-e zanan-e siyassi* (Memoir of Iranian Women Fedaii Guerrillas) (Tehran: Enteshrat-e Baztab-Negar, AH 1383/2004), pp. 38, 39, 67, 75, 127–28.

83. Mikhail Bakhtin, *Rabelais and His World* (Bloomington: Indiana University Press, 1993).

84. Bakhtin, *Rabelais and His World*, p. 92.

85. Umberto Eco, *The Name of the Rose*, trans. William Weaver (New York: Harcourt Brace Jovanovich, 1983).

86. Victor Turner, *The Ritual Process: Structure and Anti-structure* (Chicago: Aldine, 1969).

87. Historically, carnivals in the fourteenth and fifteenth centuries represented an institutionalized form of dancing mania, whereby the poor classes would circle hand in hand and continue dancing together for hours in a wild delirium until they fell to the ground in exhaustion. Participants engaged for days in feasting, drinking, performing, and dancing, as well as animal sacrifice. In the sixteenth century French peasants would spend a total of three months of the year in carnival festivities; see Ehrenreich, *Dancing in the Streets*, p. 92.

88. Cited in *Jebhe*, 22 Esfand AH 1377/March 13, 1999, p. 8.

89. "The most dangerous thing that threatens humanity is for men to forget devotion to God, to establish cultural centers instead of mosques and churches, and to be driven by film and art rather than prayer and supplication," according to Muhammad Taqui Mesbah Yazdi, a prominent conservative cleric; cited in *Iran Emrooz*, April 1, 2002, www.iran-emrooz.net.

90. "We will wage a creative war against them, with more poems, more art, more singing," according to the singer. Reported by Mohammed Daraghmeh, "Militants Trying to Restrict Arts, as Battle over Character of Future Palestinian State Starts," *Arabic Media Internet Network*, July 12, 2005.

91. See Theodore Roszak, *The Making of a Counter Culture: Reflections on the Technocratic Society and Its Youthful Opposition* (London: Faber and Faber, 1969).

92. Some have spoken of "pious fun" by referring to the "Islamic musicians" who use a musical genre like rap or hip-hop to convey religious lyrics as a means for *da'wa*. The central purpose in these performances is not simply fun, but religious mission. Since spontaneity is either missing or suppressed (e.g., to ensure "normative conduct" women singers wear particularly conservative dress and refrain from moving their bodies), the result becomes a kind of "controlled fun." For such Islamic musicians, see www.muslimhiphop.com, www.pearlsofislam.com, and www.dawamedia.com.

93. See for instance Ayatollah Khamenei's lectures on youths, *Javan az Manzar-e Rahbari* (Youth from the Perspective of the Leadership) (Tehran: Daftar-e Nashr-e Farhang-e Eslami, AH 1380/2001).

94. According to Ayatollah Mesbah Yazdi, cited in *Shalamche*, Mehr AH 1377/ September–October 1998, 11.

95. See Hunt, *Politics, Culture, and Class in the French Revolution*, p. 56. For Bolshevik Russia, see Fitzpatrick, *Cultural Front*; see also Sheila Fitzpatrick, Alexander Rabinowitch, and Richard Stites, eds., *Russia in the Era of NEP: Explorations in Soviet Society and Culture* (Bloomington: Indiana University Press, 1991).

96. See Algar, *Wahhabism*.

97. Ibid, pp. 48–49.

Chapter 8

1. These sections draw heavily on my "Revolution Without Movement, Movement Without Revolution: Comparing Islamic Activism in Iran and Egypt," *Comparative Studies in Society and History* 42, no. 1 (January 1998), pp. 136–69.

2. See Michel Foucault, *Discipline and Punish: The Birth of Prison* (New York: Vintage, 1995); Henri Lefebvre, *The Production of Space* (Oxford: Basil Blackwell, 1991); Charles Tilly, "Spaces of Contention," *Mobilization: An International Quarterly* 5, no. 2 (fall 2000), pp. 135–59; Eric Hobsbawm, "Cities and Insurrections," in his *Revolutionaries* (London: Quartet Books, 1977), pp. 220–33.

3. See Ervand Abrahamian, *Iran Between Two Revolutions* (Princeton, N.J.: Princeton University Press, 1983); Nikki Keddie, *Roots of Revolution: An Interpretive History of Modern Iran* (New Haven, Conn.: Yale University Press, 1981); Mohsen Milani, *The Making of the Islamic Revolution in Iran* (Boulder, Colo.: Westview Press, 1986); Fred Halliday, *Iran: Dictatorship and Development* (London: Penguin Books, 1979).

4. On the antidemocratic nature of the Shah's regime and its political implications, see Fred Halliday, *Iran: Dictatorship and Development* (London: Penguin, 1977); Habib Lajevardi, *Labor Unions and Autocracy in Iran* (Syracuse, N.Y.: Syracuse University Press, 1985); Homa Katouzian, *The Political Economy of Modern Iran* (London: Macmillan, 1982).

5. On guerrilla activities in Iran, see Halliday, *Iran;* Abrahamian, *Iran Between Two Revolutions.*

6. See Asef Bayat, *Street Politics: Poor People's Movements in Iran* (New York: Columbia University Press, 1997).

7. For an excellent discussion, see Manuel Castells, *The City and the Grassroots* (Berkeley: University of California Press, 1983).

8. See Bayat, *Street Politics*, pp. 25–26.

9. For a description, see ibid., pp. 105–6.

Chapter 9

1. See, for instance, Phil Marfleet, "Globalisation and Religious Activism," in *Globalisation and the Third World*, ed. R. Kiely and P. Marfleet (London: Routledge, 1998); Jeffrey Haynes, *Religion in Third World Politics* (Buckingham: Open University Press, 1993); and John Esposito, "Religion and Global Affairs: Political Challenges," *SAIS Review: Journal of International Affairs* 18, no. 2 (1998), pp. 19–24.

2. Mike Davis, *Planet of Slums* (London: Verso, 2006), p. 54; Mike Davis, "Planet of Slums," *New Left Review* 26 (MarchApril 2004), pp. 5–34.

3. Asef Bayat, *Street Politics: Poor People's Movements in Iran* (New York: Columbia University Press, 2007), chapter 1.

4. Faisal Devji, *Landscapes of the Jihad: Militancy, Morality, Modernity* (Ithaca, N.Y.: Cornell University Press, 2005); see also Chapter 12 of this volume. Here I use the terms *urban dispossessed, disenfranchised,* and *urban poor* interchangeably, referring broadly to those laboring people who take on low-income, low-skilled, low-status, and low-security jobs, and who are pushed to live in the marginal locales of slums and squatter settlements; see Peter Worsley, *The Three Worlds* (London: Weidenfeld and Nicholson, 1984), p. 195.

5. On the theoretical shortcomings of the "culture of poverty" thesis, see Eleanor B. Leacock, ed. *The Culture of Poverty: A Critique* (New York: Simon and Schuster, 1971).

6. M. El-Wali, *Sukkan Al-ashash Wal-ashwaiyyat* [Shacks and Squatter Housing] (Cairo: Rawz al-Yusef Publications, 1992); Cairo Institute of National Plan-

ning, *Egypt Human Development Report* (Cairo: Cairo Institute of National Planning, 1996); Ministry of Planning, *Towards Modernizing Urban Upgrading Policies: Executive Report* (Cairo: Ministry of Planning and German Technical Cooperation, 1999); A. M. Umar, *Al-Ashwaiyyat al-Sukkaniya fi al-Modon al-Misriya* [Informal Housing in Egyptian Cities] (Cairo: Ministry of Religious Endowments, 2000). *Ashwaiyyat*, the plural for *ashwaiyya* (implying "haphazard") is the term used in public to refer to the informal communities in Egypt, some one hundred of which exist in the greater Cairo area (as of early 2000). Official estimates put the total number of these settlements at about 1,034, accounting for about twelve million, or 45 percent, of Egypt's urban population. Land invasion accounts for a very small proportion of these settlements, and the vast majority comprise privately owned homes that are built on purchased agricultural land but lack planning, construction permits, and most conventional urban services. See Asef Bayat and Eric Denis, "Who Is Afraid of *Ashwaiyyat*? Urban Change and Politics in Egypt," *Environment and Urbanization* 12, no. 2 (2000), pp. 185–99, on which this section of the chapter draws heavily.

7. Saad Eddin Ibrahim, *Egypt, Islam and Democracy* (Cairo: American University in Cairo Press, 1996); Adel El-Kirdassi, "Cahira el-Ashwaiyyat wa Thiqafat al-Unf" [Informal Cairo and Cultures of Violence], paper presented at the conference on Political and Religious Violence in Egypt, Cairo, May 19–20, 1998.

8. Based on a paper given by Ayfer Bartu at the International conference on Global Flows/Local Fissures: Urban Antagonisms Revisited, Istanbul, May 27–29, 1999.

9. See Ashgar Engineer, *Islam and Liberation Theology* (New Delhi: Sterling, 1990) p. 17; Eric Hooglund, *Land and Revolution in Iran* (Austin: Texas University Press, 1982); Mohammad Amjad, "Rural Migrants, Islam, and Revolution in Iran," *Social Movements, Conflicts, and Change* 16 (1993), pp. 35–51.

10. Ali Rahnema and Farhad Nomani, *Secular Miracle: Religion, Politics, and Economic Policy in Iran* (London: Zed Books, 1990).

11. Amjad, "Rural Migrants," p. 35; Rahnema and Nomani, *Secular Miracle*.

12. Farhad Kazemi, *Poverty and Revolution in Iran* (New York: New York University Press, 1980); Gilles Kepel, *Muslim Extremism in Egypt* (Berkeley: University of California Press, 1986); S. A. Arjomand, *The Turban for the Crown* (Oxford: Oxford University Press, 1988); Rahnema and Nomani, *Secular Miracle*; G. Denoeux, *Urban Unrest in the Middle East* (Albany: State University of New York Press, 1993); El-Kirdassi, "Cahira el-Ashwaiyyat wa Thiqafat al-Unf"; A. Abdulhadi, "Qiyam al-Ashwaiyyat fi Misr" [The Values of the People in Informal Communities in Egypt], *Ahwal Misriya* 7, no. 21 (2003).

13. Kazemi, *Poverty and Revolution in Iran*; Hooglund, *Land and Revolution in Iran*; Rahnema and Nomani, *Secular Miracle*; Amjad, "Rural Migrants."

14. Kepel, *Muslim Extremism in Egypt*; Ibrahim, *Egypt, Islam and Democracy*; Paul Lubeck and Bryana Britts, "Muslim Civil Society in Urban Public Spaces," in *Urban Studies: Contemporary and Future Perspectives*, ed. J. Eade and C. Mele (Oxford: Blackwell, 2001).

15. Kepel, *Muslim Extremism in Egypt*, p. 217.

16. Nazih Ayubi, *Political Islam* (London: Routledge, 1993); Hamid Ansari, "The Islamic Militants in Egyptian Politics," *International Journal of Middle East Studies* 16, no. 3 (1984), pp. 123–44; Salwa Ismail, "The Popular Movement Dimensions of Contemporary Militant Islamism: Socio-Spatial Determinants in the Cairo Urban Setting," *Comparative Studies in Society and History* 42 (2000), pp. 63–93.

17. Hala Mustafa, *Al-Dawla Waal-harakat al-Islamiya al-Mo'arida* [The State and the Islamic Opposition Movement] (Cairo: Al-Mahrousa, 1995), p. 362.

18. That is, Jamaiyya El-Shari'yaa Li-ta'avon al-Amelin Bil-Kitab wal-Sunna al-Muhammadiyya.

19. Al-Ahram Center for Political and Strategic Studies, *Taqrir Halat Eddiniyya fi Misr* [The Status of Religion in Egypt] (Cairo: Al-Ahram Center, 1996).

20. Bayat, *Street Politics*; ibid.

21. I have examined these struggles in detail in Bayat, *Street Politics*, chapter 3.

22. I adopt Peter Worsley's conceptualization of the "poor" in Worsley, *Three Worlds*.

23. Hisham Mubarak, *Al Erhabiyun Qadimoun* (Cairo: Kitab al-Mahrusa, 1995).

24. Al-Ahram Center, *Taqrir Halat Eddiniyya*.

25. I. R. Hammady, "Religious Medical Centers in Cairo," master's thesis, American University in Cairo, Department of Sociology and Anthropology, 1990.

26. For a collection of statements by al-Gama'a al-Islamiyya of Egypt, see Rif'at al-Saiid, *Nabih al-Musallah*.

27. I realize that the liberation theology movement was much more complex and fragmented than presented here. But I think that a note of comparison with militant Islamism is both important and necessary.

28. Leonardo Boff and Clodovis Boff, *Salvation and Liberation* (New York: Orbis Books, 1988).

29. Asef Bayat, "Islamism and Empire: The Incongruous Nature of Islamist Anti-imperialism," *Socialist Register 2008* (London: Merlin Press, 2008).

30. See Gustavo Gutiérrez, *A Theology of Liberation* (New York: Orbis Books, 1988); Christian Smith, ed., *Disruptive Religion: The Force of Faith in Social Movement Activism* (London: Routledge, 1996); Sharon Erickson Nepstad, "Popular Religion, Protest, and Revolt: The Emergence of Political Insurgency in the Nicaraguan and Salvadoran Churches of the 1960s–1980s," in *Disruptive Religion*, ed. Smith; Michael Lowy, *The War of Gods: Religion and Politics in Latin America* (London: Verso Press, 1996).

31. Christian Smith, *The Emergence of Liberation Theology* (Chicago: University of Chicago Press, 1991).

32. Asef Bayat, *Making Islam Democratic: Social Movements and the Post-Islamist Turn* (Stanford, Calif.: Stanford University Press, 2007).

33. Bayat, *Street Politics*.

34. *Al Ahram Weekly*, October 17–23, 1996, p. 12.

35. The Ibn Khaldoun Center for Developmental Studies in Cairo developed a program for the rehabilitation of Islamists in Egypt.

36. Paul A. Jargowsky, *Poverty and Place: Ghettos, Barrios, and the American City* (New York: Russell Sage, 1997); Kevin Fox Gotham, "Toward an Understanding of the Spatiality of Urban Poverty: The Urban Poor as Spatial Actors," *International Journal of Urban and Regional Research* 27, no. 3 (2003), pp. 723–37.

37. See Cairo Institute of National Planning, p. 56; El-Kirdassi, 1998; *Al-Wafd*, "Al-Ashwaiyyat Aana'a Hokumiya," March 5, 1999; A. F. Nasir, "Al-Ashwaiyya fi Hayatna" [Haphazardness in Our Lives], *Al-Wafd*, March 9, 1999.

38. Evelyn Early, *Baladi Women of Cairo* (Boulder, Colo.: Lynne Rienner,1993); Diane Singerman, *Avenues of Participation: Family, Politics, and Networks in Urban Quarters of Cairo* (Princeton, N.J.: Princeton University Press, 1995); Unni Wikan, *Tomorrow, God Willing* (Chicago: University of Chicago Press, 1996); Teresa P. R. Caldeira, *The City of Walls: Crime, Segregation and Citizenship in São Paulo* (Berkeley: University of California Press, 1997); Homa Hoodfar, *Between Marriage and the Market* (Berkeley: University of California Press, 1997); Farha Ghannam, *Remaking the Modern: Space, Relocation, and the Politics of Identity in a Global Cairo* (Berkeley: University of California Press, 2002).

39. See Bayat and Denis, "Who Is Afraid of the *Ashwaiyyat*?" maps 5 and 6. A random sample of the residents of Dar al-Salam, an informal community in Cairo, reveals the high degree of diversity in occupational structure. After "housewives," at 37 percent, "white collar workers" constituted the largest group, accounting for 14 percent. See Nicholas S. Hopkins, *Social Response to Environmental Change and Pollution in Egypt* (Cairo: IDRC Report, 1998).

40. Bayat, *Street Politics*.

Chapter 10

1. See Clifford Geertz, "Primordial Ties," in *Ethnicity*, ed. John Hutchinson and Anthony Smith (Oxford: Oxford University Press, 1996).

2. For a fine overview of approaches, see Hutchinson and Smith, eds., *Ethnicity*, especially pp. 3–16.

3. For a comprehensive overview of the concept of community, see Gerard Delanty, *Community* (London: Routledge, 2003).

4. For a useful take on Dubai, see Muhammad Masad, "Dubai: What Cosmopolitan City?" *ISIM Review*, no. 22 (autumn 2008), 10–11. For a more critical appraisal, see

Mike Davis, "Fear and Money in Dubai," *New Left Review*, no. 41 (September–October 2006), pp. 47–68.

5. An exception is Shail Mayaram, ed., *The Other Global City* (London: Routledge, 2009).

6. See Sami Zubaida, "Jews and Others in Iraq," *ISIM Review*, no. 22 (autumn 2008), pp. 6–7; for a historical treatment of cosmopolitanism in the Ottoman world, see Bruce Masters, *Christians and Jews in the Ottoman World: The Roots of Sectarianism* (Cambridge: Cambridge University Press, 2001); Salim Tamari, "Wasif Jawhariyyeh, Popular Music and Early Modernity in Jerusalem," in *Palestine, Israel, and the Politics of Popular Culture*, ed. Rebecca Stein and Ted Swedenburg (Durham, N.C.: Duke University Press, 2005).

7. The precise number of Coptic Christians is a matter of contention. According to government sources, Copts constitute 6 percent of the population, while Coptic sources claim it to be around 18 percent; see Ibn-Khaldoun Center, *The Copts of Egypt* (London: Minority Group International, 1996), p. 6; see also S. Ibrahim, *Al-Milal wal-Nahal wal-I'raq* (Cairo: Ibn-Khaldoun Center, 1994), p. 381.

8. Susan J. Staffa, *Conquest and Fusion: The Social Evolution of Cairo, AD 642–1850* (Leiden, N.Y.: E. J. Brill, 1977), p. 37.

9. Afaf L. A. Marsot, *A Short History of Modern Egypt* (Cambridge: Cambridge University Press, 1985), pp. 1–3.

10. E. J. Chitham, *The Coptic Community in Egypt: Spatial and Social Change*, Occasional Paper series no. 32 (Durham, N.C.: University of Durham, Center for Middle Eastern and Islamic Studies, 1988), p. 18.

11. Ibn-Khaldoun Center, *Copts of Egypt*, p. 16.

12. See Hani Labib, *Al-Muwatanah wa-al-Awlamah: Al-Aqbat fi Mujtama'a Mutaghayyir* (Cairo: Dar al-Shuruq, 2004), pp. 140–41.

13. See Aziz S. Atiya, *A History of Eastern Christianity* (London: Methuen, 1968); see also most publications of militant Copts in the United States and Canada.

14. Quote by Milad Hanna, a prominent Coptic intellectual and politician, cited in Mark Purcell, "A Place for the Copts: Imagined Territory and Spatial Conflict in Egypt," *Ecumene* 5, no. 4 (1998), pp. 432–51. For the position of other writers, see Jamal Badawi, *Muslimun wa Aqbat: Min al-Mahd Ila al-Majd* (Cairo: Dar Al-Shuruq, 2000); Labib, *Al-Muwatanah wa-al-Awlamah*; Tariq al-Bishri, *Al-Muslimun wa al-Aqbat* (Cairo: Dar al-Shuruq, 2004).

15. Gamal Hamdan cited in Badawi, *Muslimun wa Aqbat*, p. 15.

16. Labib, *Al-Muwatanah wa-al-Awlamah*, pp. 121–22.

17. The fact is that *interpretations* of Muslim–Christian relations cannot be divorced from their reality. They are part of it. For if "ethnicity" is based largely on a myth of kinship origin imagined on common ancestry, then the current debate in Egypt about the "reality" of Coptic–Muslim relations is likely to shape that reality.

In other words, advancing an argument about how Copts are not a 'minority' but 'citizens' may indeed galvanize consensus leading to an actual change in their status.

18. See Jamal Badawi, *Al-Fitna al-Taefiya fi Misr* (Cairo: Arab Press Center, 1977), pp. 13–15.

19. The reports of the conflicts here are cited from Ibn-Khaldoun Center, *Copts of Egypt*.

20. I have drawn on Ibn-Khaldoun Center, *Copts of Egypt*, p. 21.

21. See Labib, *Al-Muwatinah wal-Awlimah*, pp. 178–80; also *African Research Bulletin* 37, no. 1 (January 2000), p. 13839.

22. See D. Zeidan, "The Copts: Equal, Protected or Persecuted? The Impact of Islamization on Muslim–Christian Relations in Modern Egypt," *Islam and Christian–Muslim Relations* 10, no. 1 (1999), pp. 53–67.

23. Daily papers.

24. Gerard Viand, "Short History of Shubra," unpublished paper, submitted by the author, Cairo, August 2004.

25. Based on ibid.

26. The notion of "urban footprints" is discussed in Ash Amin and Nigel Thrift, *Cities: Reimagining the Urban* (Oxford: Polity, 2002).

27. Cited in Badawi, *Muslimun wa Aqbat*, p. 166.

28. Interview, July 2004, Cairo.

29. Interview with Maged, in Shubra, July 10, 2004.

30. Edward Lane, *Manners and Customs*, 1836, pp. 554–57.

31. Interview with both in August 2004, in Shubra, Cairo.

32. Nicholas Hopkins and Reem Saad, eds., *Upper Egypt: Identity and Change* (Cairo: American University in Cairo Press, 2005), pp. 13–15.

33. Interview with Moheb Zaki, Cairo, January 31, 2005.

34. Reported in *Cairo Times*, November 23–29, 2000, vol. 4, no. 37.

35. Here, I draw on the definition of ethnic developed by John Hutchinson and Anthony Smith as "a named human population with myths of common ancestry, shared historical memories, one or more elements of common culture, a link with homeland, and a sense of solidarity among at least some of its members." See Hutchinson and Smith, *Ethnicity* (Oxford: Oxford University Press, 1996), p. 6.

36. See Janet Abu-Lughod, *Cairo: One Thousand Years of a City Victorious* (Princeton, N.J.: Princeton University Press, 1971), p. 60.

37. Ibid., p. 59.

38. Ibid., pp. 59–60.

39. Chitham, *Coptic Community in Egypt*, pp. 78–79.

40. Ibid., pp. 82–86.

41. Ibid., p. 30.

42. Abu-Lughod, *Cairo,* p. 211.

43. Ibid., p. 210.

44. Moheb Zaki, interview, January 31, 2005, Cairo.

45. Stanley Tambiah, *Leveling Crowds: Ethnonationalist Conflicts and Collective Violence in South Asia* (Berkeley: University of California Press, 1996), p. 275.

46. Lila Abu-Lughod, "Local Contexts of Islamism in Popular Media," ISIM Papers Series, no. 6 (Leiden: ISIM). See also Lila Abu-Lughod, *Dramas of Nationhood: The Politics of Television in Egypt* (Chicago: University of Chicago Press, 2005).

47. This sectarian effect of "welfare pluralism" has been confirmed by a number of studies. See, for example, Mariz Tadros's PhD thesis; Paul Sadra, "Class Cleavage and Ethnic Conflict: Coptic Christian Communities in Modern Egyptian Politics," *Islam and Christian–Muslim Relations* 10, no. 2 (1999), pp. 219–35.

48. Interview with Maged, Shubra, July 10, 2004.

49. See, for instance, a tale of riots in Bombay, India, in Suketu Mehta, *Maximum City: Bombay Lost and Found* (New York: Knopf, 2004).

50. For a South Asian experience, see Tambiah, *Leveling Crowds*; and for a general picture, see Donald Horowitz, *The Deadly Ethnic Riot* (Berkeley: University of California Press, 2001).

51. For a full story, see Essandr El-Amrani, "The Emergence of the 'Coptic Question' in Egypt," *Middle East Report Online*, April 28, 2006.

52. Georg Simmel, *Conflict and the Web of Group Affiliations* (New York: Free Press, 1955), pp. 43–45.

53. Tambiah, *Leveling Crowds,* p. 276.

54. Reported in Robin Moger and Ho Ehab, "All Over a Play," *Cairo Magazine*, October 27, 2006.

55. Donald Horowitz's general survey of ethnic riots confirms this conclusion. ". . . when such [indiscriminate and abstract] beliefs change, the deadly riot declines"; see Horowitz, *Deadly Ethnic Riot*, p. 544.

Chapter 11

1. Robert Bartley, "Resolution, Not Compromise, Builds Coalition," *Wall Street Journal*, November 12, 2001.

2. Cited in Robert Satloff, "The Arab 'Street' Poses No Real Threat to US," *Newsday*, September 27, 2002.

3. Ibid.

4. John Kifner, "Street Brawl," *New York Times*, November 11, 2001.

5. See, for example, Reuel Marc Gerecht, "Better to Be Feared than Loved," *Weekly Standard*, April 29, 2002; and "The Myth of the Arab Street," *Jerusalem Post*, April 11, 2002. Authors sympathetic to Arab protest can have similar takes. See, for example,

Ashraf Khalil, "The Arab Couch," *Cairo Times*, December 26, 2002; and Robert Fisk, "A Million March in London, But Faced with Disaster, the Arabs Are Like Mice," *Independent*, February 18, 2003.

6. *Wall Street Journal*, November 12, 2001.

7. *Al-Hayat*, November 6, 2002.

8. Raphael Patai, *The Arab Mind* (London: Macmillan, 1983).

9. See Edmund Burke and Ira Lapidus, eds., *Islam, Politics, and Social Movements* (Berkeley: University of California Press, 1990); and Zachary Lockman, ed., *Workers and Working Classes in the Middle East: Struggles, Histories, Historiographies* (Albany: State University of New York Press, 1994).

10. On labor struggles, see Alan Richards and John Waterbury, *A Political Economy of the Middle East* (Boulder, Colo.: Westview Press, 1990); and Marsha Pripstein Posusney, *Labor and the State in Egypt* (New York: Columbia University Press, 1997).

11. Lamis Andoni and Jillian Schwedler, "Bread Riots in Jordan," *Middle East Report*, no. 201 (fall 1996), pp. 40–42.

12. Ahmed Abdalla, *The Student Movement and National Politics in Egypt* (London: Saqi Books, 1985).

13. United Nations Development Program, *Arab Human Development Report*; vol. 1; *Changing Opportunities for Future Generations* (New York: UNDP, 2002), p. 90.

14. See Reda Hilal, "Blowback: Islamization from Below," *al-Ahram Weekly*, November 21–27, 2002. See also 'Ali Abu al-Khayr, "al-Islam al-Siyasi wa al-Dimuqratiyya," *al-Wafd*, February 15, 2003.

15. See Asef Bayat, *Making Islam Democratic: Social Movements and the Post-Islamist Turn* (Palo Alto, Calif.: Stanford University Press, 2007).

16. *Al-Hayat*, January 28, 2003.

17. *Al-Hayat*, February 15, 2003.

18. *Al-Hayat*, January 20, 2002.

19. In Arab countries other than Egypt, there was little evidence pointing to demonstrators targeting their own governments' policies.

20. As reported by Human Rights Watch, in Egypt some eleven activists had been detained by security agents in February 2003 (*Cairo Times*, February 6–19, 2003).

21. Interview with Fateh Azzam, coordinator of human rights program, Ford Foundation, Cairo, February 2003.

22. Hossam el-Hamalawy, "Closer to the Street," *Cairo Times*, February 6–19, 2003.

23. For an analysis of Kifaya and new democracy movements in Egypt, see Bayat, *Making Islam Democratic*, pp. 181–86.

24. *Payvan Iran News*, October 14, 2002; *Asia Times*, January 24, 2003; *al-Qahira*, January 7, 2003.

25. See Samantha Shapiro, "Revolution, Facebook-Style," *New York Times*, January 29, 2009.

Chapter 12

1. See Benedict Anderson, *Imagined Communities* (London: Verso, 1991).

2. Stuart Hall, David Held, Don Hubert, and Kenneth Thompson, eds., *Modernity: An Introduction to Modern Societies* (Cambridge: Polity Press, 1995).

3. Sidney Tarrow, *Power in Movement: Social Movements and Contentious Politics* (Cambridge: Cambridge University Press, 1998); Eric Hobsbawm, *Primitive Rebels* (New York: Norton, 1959).

4. Charles Tilly, *From Mobilization to Revolution* (Reading, Mass.: Addison-Wesley, 1978).

5. Theda Skocpol, *States and Social Revolutions* (Cambridge: Cambridge University Press, 1979).

6. See, for instance, Simon Bromley, *Rethinking Middle East Politics* (Austin: University of Texas Press, 1994); and Isam al-Khafaji, *Tormented Births: Passages to Modernity in Europe and the Middle East* (London: I. B. Tauris, 2005), which suggest that there is little difference between the social formations in the Middle East and Europe.

7. Albert Hourani, "Introduction," in *The Modern Middle East*, ed. Albert Hourani, Philip Khoury, and Mary Wilson (Berkeley: University of California Press, 1993).

8. Hisham Sharabi, *Neopatriarchy: A Theory of Distorted Change in Arab Society* (New York: Oxford University Press, 1988).

9. Ervand Abrahamian, *Iran Between Two Revolutions* (Princeton, N.J.: Princeton University Press, 1982).

10. Ghassan Salamé, "'Strong' and 'Weak' States: A Qualified Return to the *Muqaddimah*," in *The Arab State*, ed. Giacomo Luciani (Berkeley: University of California Press, 1990).

11. See Homa Katouzian, *The Political Economy of Modern Iran* (London: Macmillan, 1981). For a discussion of this, see Asef Bayat, "Class, Historiography, and Iranian Workers," in *Workers and Working Classes in the Middle East: Struggles, Histories, Historiographies*, ed. Z. Lockman (Albany: State University of New York Press, 1994).

12. Khafaji, *Tormented Births*.

13. The next three paragraphs draw heavily on my article "Islamism and Social Movement Theory," *Third World Quarterly* 26, no. 6 (2005), pp. 891–908.

14. Samuel Huntington, *The Clash of Civilizations and the Remaking of the World Order* (New York: Basic Books, 1996); Bernard Lewis, *What Went Wrong* (London: Phoenix, 2002).

15. Alberto Melucci, *Challenging Codes* (Cambridge: Cambridge University Press, 1996), p. 104; Alain Touraine, *The Return of the Actor* (Minneapolis: University of Minnesota Press, 1988), p. 64; Alain Touraine, "Do Social Movements Exist?" paper presented at the 14th World Congress of Sociology, Montreal, July 26–August 1, 1998.

16. Michel Foucault, "An Interview with Michel Foucault," *Akhtar*, no. 4 (spring 1987), p. 43; Anthony Giddens, *Social Theory and Modern Society* (Palo Alto, Calif.: Stanford University Press, 1987).

17. Emad Eldin Shahin, "Secularism and Nationalism: The Political Discourse of 'Abd al-Salam Yassin," in John Ruedy, *Islamism and Secularism in North Africa* (New York: St. Martin's Press, 1994), p. 173.

18. Here I have cited only sources that are in English and accessible to non-native readers; see Ali Shariati, "Return to Self," in *Islam in Transition: Muslim Perspectives*, ed. John Donohue and John Esposito (Oxford: Oxford University Press, 1982), pp. 305–7; Abu-Ala Mawdudi, "Nationalism and Islam," in *Islam in Transition: Muslim Perspectives*, ed. John Donohue and John Esposito (Oxford: Oxford University Press, 1982), pp. 94–97; Abdulaziz Sachedina, "Ali Shariati: Ideologue of the Iranian Revolution," in *Voices of Resurgent Islam*, ed. John Esposito (Oxford: Oxford University Press, 1983), pp. 191–214; and Y. Haddad, "Sayyid Qutb: Ideologue of Islamic Revival," in *Voices of Resurgent Islam*, ed. John Esposito (Oxford: Oxford University Press, 1983).

19. United Nations Development Program, *Arab Human Development Report* (Washington, D.C.: UNDP, 2002).

20. Evidence for this argument is scattered. To begin with, I have utilized my unpublished survey of some 199 middle-class, largely religious, professionals in Cairo, 1990–94, including an in-depth interview with a focus group of fifteen professionals conducted by Dana Sajdi. Published studies relevant to Egypt include: Anouk de Koning, "Global Dreams: Space, Class and Gender in Middle Class Cairo," PhD thesis, Amsterdam University, 2005; Asef Bayat, "Cairo's Poor: Dilemmas of Survival and Solidarity," *Middle East Report*, no. 202 (January–February 1997), pp. 2–6, 12; Mona Abaza, "Shopping Malls, Consumer Culture and Reshaping of Public Space in Egypt," *Theory, Culture and Society* 18, no. 5 (2001), pp. 97–122; Galal Amin, *Whatever Happened to the Egyptians?* (Cairo: American University in Cairo Press, 2000). On Jordan, see E. Anne Beal, "Real Jordanians Don't Decorate Like That! The Politics of Taste among Amman's Elites," *City and Society* 12, no. 2 (2000), pp. 65–94. On Iran, Sohrab Behdad and Farhad Nomani, "Workers, Peasants and Peddlers: A Study of Labor Stratification in the Post-Revolutionary Iran," *International Journal of Middle East Studies* 34, no. 4 (2002), pp. 667–90; Asef Bayat, *Street Politics: Poor People's Movements in Iran* (New York: Columbia University Press, 1997).

21. Barrington Moore, *Injustice: The Social Bases of Obedience & Revolt* (New York: Random House, 1978).

22. Asef Bayat, "Revolution Without Movement, Movement Without Revolution: Comparing Islamic Activism in Iran and Egypt," *Comparative Studies in Society and History* 44, no. 1 (1998), 136–69.

23. Bayat, "Cairo's Poor."

24. See, for example, Guilain Denoeux, *Urban Unrest in the Middle East* (Albany: State University of New York Press, 1993).

25. See also Asef Bayat, *Making Islam Democratic: Social Movements and the Post-Islamist Turn* (Stanford, Calif.: Stanford University Press, 2007), pp. 155–61.

26. Khafaji, *Tormented Births*, p. 184.

27. Fred E. Halliday, *Iran: Dictatorship and Development* (London: Penguin, 1978).

28. Nazih Ayubi, "Rethinking the Public/Private Dichotomy: Radical Islamism and Civil Society in the Middle East," *Contention* 4, no. 3 (1995), pp. 79–105.

29. Ali Shariati, *Jahat-guiri-ye Tabaqati-ye Islam* (Tehran: n.p., 1980); Ali Shariati, *Shi'eh-ye Alavi and Shi'e-ye Safavi* (Tehran: n.p., n.d.).

30. Ervand Abrahamian, *Radical Islam: Iran's Mudjahedin* (London: I. B. Tauris, 1989).

31. Indeed, as early as 1954, Bernard Lewis implied in an essay how the ethics of Islam were compatible with the spirit of communism. See Bernard Lewis, "Communism and Islam," *International Affairs* 30, no. 1 (1954), pp. 1–12.

32. Bayat, *Making Islam Democratic*.

33. For the concept of "imagined solidarities," see Bayat, "Islamism and Social Movement Theory."

34. Hourani, *Modern Middle East*.

35. Ankie Hoogvelt, *Globalization and the Postcolonial World* (Baltimore: Johns Hopkins University Press, 1987); Manuel Castells, *Power of Identity* (London: Blackwell, 1997).

36. Paul Lubeck and Bryana Britts, "Muslim Civil Society in Urban Public Spaces: Globalization, Discursive Shifts and Social Movements," in *Understanding the City: Contemporary and Future Perspectives*, ed. J. Eade and C. Mele (Oxford: Blackwell, 2002).

37. Castells, *Power of Identity*.

38. Tarrow, *Power of Movements*; Margaret Keck and Kathryn Sikkink, *Activists Beyond Borders* (Ithaca, N.Y.: Cornell University Press, 1998).

39. Hannah Arendt, *On Revolution* (London: Penguin, 1990), pp. 17–18; Eric Hobsbawm, *Forward March of Labour Halted?* (London: Verso Press, 1981); Eric Hobsbawm, *Interesting Times: A Twentieth Century Life* (London: Allen Lane, 2002); David Harvey, *Spaces of Hope* (Berkeley: University of California Press, 2000).

40. Hobsbawm, *Interesting Times*; Harvey, *Spaces of Hope*.

41. For a discussion of these spaces in the advanced capitalist countries, see Ash Amin and Nigel Thrift, *Cities: Reimagining the Urban* (Oxford: Polity Press, 2002).

42. Arturo Escobar, *Encountering Development* (Princeton, N.J.: Princeton University Press, 2001).

43. Bruce Lawrence, ed., *Messages to the World: The Statements of Osama Bin Laden* (London: Verso, 2006); Faisal Devji, *Landscapes of the Jihad* (London: Hurst Books, 2006).

Chapter 13

1. See, for instance, Robert Spencer, *Religion of Peace? Why Christianity Is and Islam Isn't* (Washington, D.C.: Regency 2007). A number of influential individuals in the United States, such as Eliot Cohen of Johns Hopkins University and Kenneth Adelman of the Defense Department advisory policy board, suggest Islam is essentially intolerant, expansionist, and violent. Some evangelical Protestants have declared Islam an "evil" religion (quoted by William Pfaff, *International Herald Tribune,* December 5, 2002). In some ways such projections are a self-defeating teleology, because if this is so, then what can one do about it? The solution to democratization (defined by Daniel Pipes and Bernard Lewis as free elections, independent judiciary, freedom of speech, rule of law, and minority rights) seems to be to either secularize Muslims or convert them into a different, "democratic" religion. Who is able to perform such a task?

2. Expressed by Israel's foremost "revisionist historian," Benny Morris, cited in Joel Beinin, "No More Tears: Benny Morris and the Road from Liberal Zionism," *Middle East Report* 230 (spring 2004), p. 40.

3. For extensive evidence, see Bayat, *Making Islam Democratic*, pp. 71–97.

4. James Beckford, *Social Theory and Religion* (Cambridge: Cambridge University Press, 2003), p. 2.

5. In addition, influential thinkers remembering the world wars concluded for some time that Catholicism and democracy were hardly compatible; see Seymour Martin Lipset, Kyoung-Ryung Seong, and John Charles Torres, "Social Requisites of Democracy," *International Social Science Journal* 13, no. 6 (May 1993), p. 29.

6. Asef Bayat, "The Coming of Post-Islamist Society," *Critique: Critical Middle East Studies,* no. 9 (fall 1996).

7. For a detailed discussion of the debates on the concept see Asef Bayat, *Making Islam Democratic*, p. 10.

8. See Saodat Olimova, "Social Protests and Islamic Movement in Central Eurasia"; Pinar Akcali, "Secularism under Threat: Radical Islam in Central Asia," papers presented in workshop "Towards Social Stability and Democratic Governance in Central Eurasia: Challenges to Regional Security," Leiden, The Netherlands, September 8–11, 2004.

9. See Irfan Ahmad, "From Islamism to Post-Islamism: The Transformation of the Jama'at-e-Islami in North India" (PhD thesis, University of Amsterdam, November 2005).

10. Based on discussions with two young leaders of the movement; Rabat, Morocco, January 30, 2006.

11. See Stéphane Lacroix, "Between Islamists and Liberals: Saudi Arabia's New 'Islamo-Liberal' Reformists," *Middle East Journal* 58, no. 3 (summer 2004), pp. 345–65.

12. Sidney Tarrow, *Power in Movement: Collective Action, Social Movements and Politics* (Cambridge: Cambridge University Press, 1994).

13. Alberto Melucci, *Nomads of the Present* (Cambridge: Cambridge University Press, 1989), p. 60. Melucci's "cultural production" is roughly what Sztompka terms "latent change"; see Piotr Sztompka, *The Sociology of Social Change* (Oxford: Blackwell, 1999).

14. Foucault describes "governmentality" in terms of the state devising mechanisms, methods, and ideas through which citizens govern themselves in accordance with the interests of those who govern. See Michel Foucault, *Power* (New York: New Press, 1994).

INDEX

Abdel Nasser, Gamal, 67
Abu-Lughod, Janet, 202
Accommodating innovation, 120, 134
Accommodating protest, 52
Active citizenry, 249
Active piety, 237
Activism, 250
Adab literature, 145
Affluent women and religion, 228
Afghanistan, 37
Al-Adlwal-Ihsan, Morocco, 246
Al-Aqsa Martyrs Brigades, 155
Al-Azhar, 137
Al-Banna, Hasan, 230
Alexandria (Egypt), sectarian violence,
    206–207
Al-Gama'a al-Islamiyya, Egypt, 11, 139, 171,
    172, 181, 192; civilities in Cairo, 80; and
    the poor, 82
Algeria, 9
Algerian resistance, 11
Algiers, 171
Al-Kosheh, sectarian violence, 193
Al-Qaeda, 173, 238
Alternative Human Development Index,
    31
Amal movement, Lebanon, 82
American University in Cairo, 218
Amin, Galal, 35
Amnesty International, 10
Anglo-American invasion of Iraq, 32
Anomie, 46
Ansari, Hamid, 175

Anti-fun sensibilities, 139; Saudi Arabia,
    140; Taliban, 140; in Iran, 140, 142–144;
    history, 145–146; in Saudi Arabia,
    146–147; in Afghanistan, 147;
    in secular ideologies, 151; reasons of,
    152, 154–158
Antiglobalization, 45
April 6 Youth Movement, Egypt, 10, 22,
    135, 219
Arab Human Development Report, 3, 28;
    reception in West, 30; reception in
    Arab world, 31; postnationalist
    approach, 33
Arab intelligentsia, 217
Arab mind, 211
Arab socialism, 229
Arab states, 224
Arab street, 14, 210–220
Arab world, strategy for change, 34–39
Arendt, Hanna, 234
Art of presence, 26, 248–251; women's role,
    249–250
Arts of living, 151
Asceticism, 149
Ash'ab (singer), 145
Ashwaiyyat, 4, 178, 180, 182; Middle East,
    heterogeneity, 183
Asiatic mode of production, 224
Assiut, Egypt, 193
Authority, 155
Ayubi, Nazih, 175, 229
Azadi (Liberation) Square, Tehran, 170
Azbakiya (Cairo), 204